IMPERIAL CULTS AND THE APOCALYPSE OF JOHN

IMPERIAL CULTS AND THE APOCALYPSE OF JOHN

Reading Revelation in the Ruins

Steven J. Friesen

OXFORD

UNIVERSITY PRESS

2001

OXFORD

UNIVERSITY PRESS

Oxford   New York

Athens   Auckland   Bangkok   Bogotá   Buenos Aires   Calcutta   Cape Town
Chennai   Dar es Salaam   Delhi   Florence   Hong Kong   Istanbul   Karachi
Kolkata   Kuala Lumpur   Madrid   Melbourne   Mexico City   Mumbai
Nairobi   Paris   Shanghai   Singapore   Taipei   Tokyo   Toronto   Warsaw

and associated companies in
Berlin   Ibadan

Copyright © 2001 by Steven J. Friesen

Published by Oxford University Press, Inc.,
198 Madison Avenue, New York, New York 10016

Oxford is a registered trademark of Oxford University Press

Library of Congress Cataloging-in-Publication Data
Friesen, Steven J.
Imperial cults and the Apocalypse of John : reading Revelation in the ruins /
Steven J. Friesen.
p.   cm.
Includes bibliographical references and index.
ISBN 0-19-513153-3
1. Bible. N.T. Revelation—Criticism, interpretation, etc.   2. Emperor worship—Rome.
3. Christianity and other religions—Roman.   I. Title.
BS2825.6.E46 2000
228'.067—dc21   00-026806

1 3 5 7 9 8 6 4 2

Printed in the United States of America
on acid-free paper

To John and Anne Friesen

in honor of their lives of service
on their 56th anniversary

ACKNOWLEDGMENTS

This book is beginning to seem like a group project, for I have relied on many friends at every stage of the process. My thanks go out to those who helped me formulate my ideas early on: David Barr, Jill Raitt, Leonard Thompson, Mike White, and my colleagues in the Society of Biblical Literature Seminar "Reading the Apocalypse: The Intersection of Literary and Social Methods." Their input enriched my thinking and enhanced this study. Several people helped me better understand the archaeological materials relevant to this study, especially Dieter Knibbe, Ulrike Outschar, Peter Scherrer, and Hilke Thür from the Austrian Archaeological Institute; Çengiz Itçen from the Efes Müzezi, Selçuk; Wolfgang Radt of the German Archaeological Institute; Bert Smith and Chris Rattee of Aphrodisias; and Crawford H. Greenewalt, Jr., and Marcus Rautman from the joint excavations at Sardis. Their hospitality is exceeded only by their knowledge of the sites and by their patience with inquisitive visitors. Long before this project ever started, Helmut Koester and David Mitten piqued my interest in the interpretation of archaeological materials. Even now, several years later, I see their influence in my research.

Some friends read parts or all of the manuscript, and thereby saved me from many problems: Paul Johnson, Leonard Thompson, Sharon Welch, Chris Wilson, and the anonymous readers from Oxford University Press. Theirs was not an enviable task, and I appreciate their gracious methods of correction. Thanks also go to Theo Calderera, Peter Ohlin, and Cynthia Read for editorial assistance.

Funding for the research came from several sources: the Research Board of the University of Missouri, the Office of the Provost of the University of Missouri-Columbia, the Research Council of the University of Missouri-Columbia, and the Society of Biblical Literature Research and Publications Committee. Their generosity made it possible for me to set aside the time necessary to complete this project. Thanks are also due to my fellow faculty members in the Department of Religious Studies at the University of Missouri-Columbia for their commitment to research and teaching and for their collegial advice and support.

My wife, Janice, and our sons, David and Dan, endured a great deal with this project, especially in absences (physical and otherwise). Thanks for your faithfulness.

Finally, it is an honor for me to dedicate this book to my parents, John and Anne Friesen, for there is no one I admire more.

Columbia, Missouri   S. J. F.
December 31, 1999

CONTENTS

ABBREVIATIONS

EPRO	*Études préliminaire sur les religions orientales dans l'empire romain*
FiE	*Forschungen in Ephesos*
GRBS	*Greek, Roman, and Byzantine Studies*
HR	*History of Religion*
HTR	*Harvard Theological Review*
IG	*Inscriptiones Graecae*
IGR	*Inscriptiones Graecae ad Res Romanas Pertinentes*
IGS	*Inschriften griechischer Städte aus Kleinasien*
ILS	*Inscriptiones Latinae Selectae*
IstMitt	*Istanbuler Mitteilungen*
IvE	*Die Inschriften von Ephesos* = IGS 11.1–17.4
IvI	*Die Inschriften von Iasos* = IGS 28.1–2
IvMag	*Die Inschriften von Magnesia am Maeander*
IvPr	*Die Inschriften von Priene*
IvPrusa	*Die Inschriften von Prusa*
IvSm	*Die Inschriften von Smyrna* = IGS 23–24
IvSt	*Die Inschriften von Stratonikeia* = IGS 21–22
JBL	*Journal of Biblical Literature*
JDAI	*Jahresheft des Deutschen Archäologischen Instituts*
JHS	*Journal of Hellenic Studies*
JÖAI	*Jahresheft des Österreichischen Archäologischen Instituts*
JRA	*Journal of Roman Archaeology*
JR	*Journal of Religion*
JRS	*Journal of Roman Studies*
JSNT	*Journal for the Study of the New Testament*
JSSR	*Journal for the Scientific Study of Religion*
Kl.P.	*Der Kleine Pauly*
Milet	*Milet: Ergebnisse der Ausgrabungen und Untersuchungen seit dem Jahre 1899*
Mionnet	*Description de médailles antiques, grecques et romaines*
Mionnet Sup	*Description de médailles antiques, grecques et romaines; Supplément*
NTS	*New Testament Studies*
OCD	*Oxford Classical Dictionary, 3rd ed.*
OGIS	*Orientis Graeci Inscriptiones Selectae*
PCPS	*Proceedings of the Cambridge Philological Society*
P.Lond.	*Greek Papyri in the British Museum*
P.Oxy.	*The Oxyrhynchus Papyri*
PW	*Paulys Realencyclopädie der classischen Altertumswissenschaft*
PWSup	*Paulys Realencyclopädie der classischen Altertumswissenschaft; Supplement*
REA	*Revue des études anciennes*
RPC	*Roman Provincial Coins*
RPh	*Revue de philologie de littérature et d'histoire anciennes*
RSR	*Religious Studies Review*
Sardis	*Archaeological Exploration of Sardis*

SBL   *Society of Biblical Literature*
SIG   *Sylloge Inscriptionum Graecarum*
StCl   *Studii clasice*
Thasos   *Guide de Thasos,* Ecole Fançaise d'Athènes
ZNTW   *Zeitschrift für die Neutestamentliche Wissenschaft*
ZPE   *Zeitschrift für Papyrologie und Epigraphik*

IMPERIAL CULTS AND THE APOCALYPSE OF JOHN

INTRODUCTION

Throughout the last century, nearly all commentators on the Revelation of John have acknowledged that imperial cults—that is, institutions for the worship of the Roman emperors—played a crucial role in the production of John's text. This, however, is the first book-length examination of the topic, mainly because a comparison of imperial cults and the Apocalypse requires an examination of literature, inscriptions, coins, sculpture, and architecture—a daunting task.

The diversity of the materials creates two kinds of challenges: disciplinary and theoretical. Scholars in the discipline of New Testament studies are not usually trained to work with the archaeological artifacts, and scholars in Roman studies do not usually analyze early Christian literature. As a result secondary literature has been produced for specialists in one discipline or the other, without much conversation between them. One challenge in the topic, then, is to foster discussions across disciplinary boundaries. The theoretical challenge is just as great. How do we compare the remaining imperial cult monuments with a text from a marginal religious group? How shall we relate literature to material culture? What social theory will enable us to draw connections? Furthermore, we have only fragmentary evidence for either side of the comparison. The second challenge, then, is to develop, from limited data, a coherent method for the analysis of artifacts (e.g., literary, epigraphic, numismatic, sculptural) from differing societal levels.

A third challenge arises from the categories of modern interpreters, who have often wondered whether imperial cults constituted a religious or political phenomenon. To modern eyes, imperial cults often appear to be insincere religion, or mystified politics, or both. Such interpretations of imperial cults, however, represent a failure of the disciplined imagination. The third challenge is to examine the ancient evidence without inscribing inappropriate notions of "religious" and "political" on it.

The first chapter lays out the method I employed to meet these challenges. Using a phenomenological history of religions framework, I focus on four thematic categories: cosmogony, cosmology, human maturation, and eschatology. This framework provides categories broad enough for my comparative interests, but has liabilities as well. A phenomenological method tends to be static and abstract, often emphasizing the normative while ignoring dissent. So I supplement the framework with the concept of discourse to move beyond the static abstractions, and I adopt a postcolonial strategy—contrapuntal interpretation of dominant and resistant histories—to keep from ignoring marginal voices. Together, these components comprise an amended phenomenological method, one that aids analysis of texts in their socioreligious settings.

With this amended phenomenological framework, chapters 2–7 examine the roles played by imperial cults in the urban polytheism of the province of Asia during the early empire. I contend that imperial cults have been misunderstood because they have not been situated properly as an imperialist elaboration within Greco-Roman polytheism. The phenomenological categories allow us to pinpoint the specific roles played by imperial cults within the larger religious system: imperial cults had some relevance for cosmogony and human maturation, but they were primarily concerned with a heightened imperial cosmology. Space was centered on Rome and time was organized around Augustus and the accomplishments of empire. These cosmological interests were so strong that they produced an eschatological absurdity: the best one could hope for was the eternal continuation of Roman rule.

The second section of the book examines the Revelation of John through the same prism. This approach demonstrates the character of John's opposition to Roman imperialism. The overwhelming eschatology of Revelation left its cosmology severely weakened. Space was centered neither on the imperial capital of Rome nor on the sacred center of Jerusalem, and time was not organized around the actions of the emperors. In Revelation space and time centered on the absent throne of God, which was accessible only through worship. To those who were not deceived by the claims of empire and who were faithful until death, Revelation promised unending worship in the eternal presence of the Lamb and the One seated on the throne. John was on a collision course with the imperial way of life.

John's vision of the world has implications beyond his first century setting, for John was not simply anti-Roman; he was anti-empire. His understanding of his world produced a religious critique of hegemony that transcended his particular historical location. The visionary argument built a broader case, one that questions *every* imperialist project. John's apocalyptic imagery depicted Rome in ruins and would lay waste to the structures of modern hegemony as well. John's religious criticism elevates Revelation as a crucial voice in the contrapuntal Christian canon. His criticism also makes the Apocalypse an important witness to humanity's struggles for the establishment of a just community in the context of humanity's record of ubiquitous oppression.

1

RELIGIOUS CRITICISM

The worship of political leaders is not an unusual phenomenon in human history. It has been practiced at many times in many regions of the world.[1] However, scholars have treated the worship of the Roman emperors mostly with bewilderment or disdain.[2] Modern western scholars have tended to operate with a parochial definition of religion based on the recent history of Europe and North America, where politics and religion are thought to be distinct spheres of activity.

This chapter draws on the discipline of religious studies to place modern western theory in perspective and then proposes an amended phenomenological method for the comparison of Revelation and Roman imperial cults. The method draws on work in the history of religions and on aspects of postcolonial theory to develop a broader framework for a socially situated analysis of the ancient materials. This framework illuminates two forms of religious criticism: a practitioner's variety exemplified by John's Revelation and an academic variety found in the writings of several historians of religion.

Aberrant Modernity

Several religionists from diverse orientations have argued that European and American definitions of "religion" during the last few centuries have not described what most groups and individuals have experienced as religious. Three theorists provide the main lines of the argument and reveal a common problematic—the development of a comparative understanding of religion despite the hegemonic claims of western rationality.

Wilfred Cantwell Smith contextualized western rationality by constructing an intellectual history of "religion" in the west. The term has been reified over the last 2,000 years, according to Smith, and this reification reveals "a long-range development, accumulating until today, of diversion of interest from man's[3] personal sense of the holy to what we might call the observable product or historical deposit of its outworking."[4]

During the Renaissance a process began to intellectualize the concept of religion that "was part of the emerging claim of the mind to understand the universe and assert its domination; but it was part, also, of a response to the strident claims of many religious groups to refute each other."[5] Smith concluded that the academic developments were related to Europe's internal religious problems and to its imperialism.

> If we sum up this period, then, we may say that some Renascence humanists and then some Protestant Reformers adopted a concept of religion to represent an inner piety; but that in the seventeenth and early eighteenth centuries this was largely superseded by a concept of schematic externalization that reflected, and served, the clash of conflicting religious parties, the emergence of a triumphant intellectualism, and the emerging new information from beyond the seas about the patterns of other men's religious life. These provided the foundations of the concept for the modern world.[6]

The nineteenth century brought other developments. On one hand, common people in Europe were attached to the older notion of religion as piety, nourished by liturgies and catechisms and relatively detached from the intellectual arguments of the European elite. The elite arguments, on the other hand, increasingly represented religion as an abstraction with its own existence. Schleiermacher was the first to write a book on religion as a generic entity, but Hegel and Feuerbach went further. Hegel asserted that religion was "a great entity with which man has to reckon, a something that precedes all its historical manifestations."[7] Feuerbach then focused on the nature of that essence. Innumerable subsequent studies have sought the essence of a particular religion or the essence of religion itself.[8]

In this way Smith explained how modern western ideas of religion tend to mean personal piety (to discriminate religion from indifference or rebellion), an ideal system (to discriminate one religion from another), an empirically manifest system (also to discriminate between "religions"), or a generic summation (to discriminate religion from other domains of society). All four of these usages, he insisted, are misleading and unnecessary.[9] They are the result of a long process of reification that first made religion into an independent phenomenon, then came to conceive of it as an objective entity, and finally posited a series of such entities—the religions of the world.[10]

Mircea Eliade also questioned the conceptualization of religion in the modern west. Rather than building an intellectual history, Eliade explicated religion as a mythic worldview that shields humanity from "the terror of history." By this phrase he meant that the actual course of human life is brutal. Individual or communal pain is endurable if it is explicable within some larger framework. Without such a framework, suffering is insufferable.[11] Religion, then, is best understood as part hermeneutics and part theodicy. Western rationality, according to Eliade, is too limited to answer the question of whether human life has meaning in the face of human suffering.

Eliade argued that most humans have lived within a mythic view of reality. He described this orientation as archaic, premodern, or traditional, but he used none of these terms in an overtly pejorative manner. In fact, Eliade seemed to admire such an orientation, at times to the point of idealization.[12] An archaic worldview escapes the terror of history by ignoring the anomalous. It posits a transcendent, primordial reality and recognizes only those actions that imitate the archetypes of that mythic reality: "[T]he desire felt by the man of traditional societies to refuse history, and to confine himself to an indefinite repetition of archetypes, testifies to his thirst for the real and his terror of 'losing' himself by letting himself be overwhelmed by the meaninglessness of profane existence."[13]

The persuasive power of a mythic world is maintained in part through sacred sites that define geography. The world is transformed through the construction of centers that imitate celestial reality. These territories, temples, and cities link the archetypal realm and this world and channel reality to other institutions, actions, and persons.[14] Ritual plays a crucial role in this, for the sacred center provides space where divine archetypes can be imitated through drama, dance, and ceremony. According to an archaic ontology, rituals are the truest of actions, for they repeat those of the gods or of the cosmogony.[15]

Rituals also redefine the character of time for they unfold not only in sacred space but also in sacred time.[16] As rituals reenact the original divine actions, they abolish time as the sequence of events and create time anew.[17] The ritual cycle establishes a continuous renewal of time that cleanses and restores the world. History cannot terrify those who inhabit an archaic world. Through periodic, creative acts of imitation, a genuinely new era can arise.[18]

In contrast to the archaic worlds of most communities, a relatively new orientation has developed in the west, which Eliade called "historical man" or "modern man." In this condition, archetypes and repetition are rejected in favor of human autonomy.[19] Time and space are not justified by their relation to the mythic structures of the world; history is its own justification. "From Hegel on, every effort is directed toward saving and conferring value on the historical event as such, the event in itself and for itself."[20] Whereas Hegel posited the will of the Universal Spirit in history, Marx completely separated history from the transcendent. According to Eliade, "[history] was no longer anything more than the epiphany of the class struggle."[21]

From that point on, historicisms of the west made the terror of history more unbearable. Although Eliade admitted that these offer some consolation in their own ways, especially to elite groups, the end result of secularism was for him unacceptable:

> For our purpose, only one question concerns us: How can the "terror of history"
> be tolerated from the viewpoint of historicism? Justification of a historical event
> . . . by the simple fact that it "happened that way," will not go far toward freeing

humanity from the terror that the event inspires. . . . We should wish to know, for example, how it would be possible to tolerate, and to justify, the sufferings and annihilation of so many peoples who suffer and are annihilated for the simple reason . . . that they are neighbors of empires in a state of permanent expansion. . . . And in our day, when historical pressure no longer allows any escape, how can man tolerate the catastrophes and horrors of history—from collective deportations and massacres to atomic bombings—if beyond them he can glimpse no sign, no transhistorical meaning; if they are only the blind play of economic, social, or political forces, or, even worse, only the result of the "liberties" that a minority takes and exercises directly on the stage of universal history?[22]

According to Eliade, historicism cannot establish sustainable community life free from despair in the face of human suffering. Those few optimists who have tried to argue the case for historicism, Eliade suggested, have relied on their privileged positions. A more accurate reading of history comes from the Baltics, the Balkans, and the colonized world.[23]

Smith and Eliade both raised fundamental questions about the structure of modernity, but did so from different perspectives. Smith's approach was historical and personalist, Eliade's was phenomenological and concerned with questions of the construction of ontology. Smith wrote as an Islamicist and comparativist, who experienced firsthand the ethno-religious tragedies of decolonization in India, and as a Canadian in the Congregationalist Protestant tradition. Eliade, on the other hand, wrote as a comparativist and as an exile from the socialist reorganization of his native Romania. The most influential religious traditions in his life were those of Romanian Orthodox Christianity and of south Asia. Both men questioned the viability of standard secular analysis, Smith because of its peculiar view of rationality and Eliade because of its presuppositions about reality. For a better explanation of the connection between western rationality and western imperialism, however, we turn to another religionist.

Charles Long's definition of religion is similar to that of Eliade; both understood religion in terms of "the continual quest for the meaning of human existence,"[24] not to be understood in an individualistic sense.[25] Religious studies seeks to find "the existential structures of the life of human communities,"[26] and to explore "religion—or, more precisely, the holy, the sacred—as the basic element in the constitution of human consciousness and human community."[27]

Rather than charting a development in specific thinkers (Smith) or exploring the maintenance of a mythic worldview (Eliade), Long raised fundamental questions about the nature of knowledge in the west.[28] Current Euro-American epistemology evolved, Long argued, as a facet of European global conquest. The encounter with radically different peoples during European expansion into Africa, Asia, the Americas, and the Pacific created a crisis. The number and varieties of human communities were much greater than westerners had imagined. How was this diversity to be explained?

Scholars from the west drew on the western philosophical tradition to understand this strange "new world," in reality just as old as their own "world." Data from the new world were gathered and brought back to the academic centers to be organized and interpreted. The presupposition that undergirded the organization of knowledge was this: in all human knowing, there is a common mode of knowledge which is characterized by rationality and logic. This way of knowing characterized the development of the modern academic disciplines.[29]

Such an epistemology created a peculiar imaginary geography, the western world at its center and data gathered at the margins. Knowledge was generated in the peripheral areas, but the center was not subject to interrogation:

> The problem of knowledge thus constituted a structure of distance and relationships. Objectivity as a scientific procedure allied itself with the neutrality of distancing in time and space. The issue of relationship was a bit more difficult to negotiate. At what level of the knowing subject did one find a correspondence between what was known and the epistemological center?[30]

The relationships between the center and the margins have usually been described in two ways. Cultural evolution described the relation between periphery and center as distance in time, so that the exotic others represented an earlier stage of history through which western civilization had passed centuries earlier. A second alternative was to describe cultures that did not fit the epistemic norm through pathology: they were chronically irrational, hysterical, or insane.

Long called this process of defining another in terms of one's own categories signification. It was based on Saussure's theories of language, but Long meant it to indicate a social process by which the powerful determine how others will be known. As a social process, signification is arbitrary because there is normally little necessary connection between the sign and that which is signified. Signification is not, however, neutral:

> In other words, what leads one to locate the differences within what is the common [i.e., within humanity]? More often than not, the differences that bring a culture or a people to the attention of the investigator are not simply formed from the point of view of the intellectual problematic; they are more often than not the nuances and latencies of that power which is part of the structure of the cultural contact itself manifesting itself as intellectual curiosity. In this manner the cultures of non-Western peoples were created as products of a complex signification.[31]

Thus, Long brought out the imperialist origins of modern western epistemology, joining Smith and Eliade with a different objection to the claim that western rationality should be the sole arbiter of human experience. For these reasons, a study on imperial cults, the Revelation of John, or any facet of ancient religion cannot be confined by narrow definitions of "religion." The modern western intellectual tradition has fostered a secular reification of mythic consciousness that is imperialistic in intent and in historical origins. The very notion that politics can be severed from the sacred is a misconstrual that would lead this study astray and would allow one to dismiss imperial cults as "bad" religion or politics. Human experience is too broad to be confined to such narrow categories.

Critical Mythic Consciousness

Working out of very different paradigms within the study of religion, Smith, Eliade, and Long engaged in an academic practice that I call religious criticism.[32] In different ways, each used the religious experience of humanity to point out that current western intellectual trends are embedded within a complex matrix of social, economic, and political hegemony. Religious theory provides one of the best resources for analyzing imperialism, representation, and contingency, because it develops a broad historical and cultural framework within which to discuss questions of the experience of reality. Because people often confuse religion with gullibility, we need to explore the practitioner's variety of religious criticism, i.e., the phenomenon of a critical perspective based in a person's or community's religious experience.[33] I draw again on Long for an explication of the critical character of religious experience and then turn to the work of Lawrence Sullivan for a model of critical mythic consciousness within a communal setting.

Long argued that the bankruptcy of western signification leads to a much broader issue: "What is the meaning of the human now that the West must realize that those who were formerly considered lesser or second-class human beings have in fact always been fully human?"[34] They can no longer be labeled primitive to provide a foil for the "civilized" west, nor can they be labeled irrational to define western modes of rationality as universal.[35]

Long did not propose an accumulative strategy, as though harmonious, multicultural diversity would emerge from the mere collection of examples of human cultures:

> The intellectual challenge has to do with a critical language that recognizes the
> situation and is able to undercut the very structures of cultural language that
> undergird the problematical situation itself. . . . As an Afro-American, the
> situation to which I have alluded is an issue of experience and the locus of an
> intellectual critique. The religion of those who have had to bear the weight of
> this confrontation in the modern world should generate forms of critical
> languages capable of creating the proper disjunctions for a restatement of the
> reality of the human in worlds to come.[36]

Here, Long effectively used Otto's notion of the encounter with the wholly other, especially the concept of *mysterium tremendum*. According to Long, the encounter with the transcendent—that which is wholly other—is the experience of reality unmediated by signification, symbolization, or discursive practices.[37] This experience of reality as a priori elicits *mysterium tremendum*: a sense of the radical contingency of human existence. All human projects, plans, and hopes are revealed as arbitrary and insignificant, just as humans themselves are revealed in their creatureliness. Long calls this overpowering sense of reality the oppressive element in religion because it is ambiguously negative: "It is the oppressive sense evoked by the power and majesty of the divine, the belittling of the creature and the human project itself."[38]

The experience of the wholly other also relativizes the arbitrary signification that characterizes the social structures of oppression. The *mysterium tremendum* produces a sense of identity and of creaturehood that is independent of the relationships of oppression. That crucial dissonance provides not only the possibility of social criticism but also an experience that might be the basis for a new mode of human community.[39] Thus, Long's work argues that religion—specifically the religious experience of the oppressed—provides the most likely resource for a new critical language from within the relationships of oppression that undercuts those relationships and moves toward a new type of human community.

Does Long allow oppressors to be religious?[40] His writing suggests that people with a privileged position in an oppressive social system have only limited access to religious experience. In his discussion of religion in America, Long observed that mainstream American religion is characterized more by *mysterium fascinans*, that is, the entrancing, dizzying, alluring aspect of the religious experience. There is a shallowness in American culture, a disconnection from the depths of the people's heritage:

> American culture through its concealment of the blacks and the destruction of Indians has at the same time concealed from itself its inner primordial experience and a definition of the human mode of being which includes richness and variety.

> American culture has yet to come to terms with its "native sons"—and this is just another way of saying that America has yet to come to terms with itself. Religiously speaking, America must be afforded the religious possibility for the experience of the *mysterium tremendum*, that experience which establishes the *otherness* and mystery of the holy.[41]

Thus, in Long's system religious experience seems to be available to all, but one's ability to interpret it is directly related to one's location in society: those who signify are perhaps less likely to react to the experience of ultimate signification in this way. This limits his work's usefulness for analyzing dominant religion because the mainstream is defined as pathological. On a historically distant topic such as Roman imperial cults or early Christian texts, the problems are magnified because we have so much less data with which to challenge or confirm the theory. For the purposes of this study, then, I accept Long's broader definition of religion as orientation toward ultimate meaning that is both personal and communal. When working on the Roman imperial period, however, I do not grant the religions of the oppressed a privileged theoretical position.

By bracketing Long's conclusions about the religions of the oppressed, I move back toward Eliade's axiom that religious experience is fundamentally related to human suffering, but the relationship is understood as Long outlined: the experience of suffering and the encounter with death has the potential to call all human projects into question. I interpret oppression as a secondary category within the broader concept of suffering; religious experience is theoretically open to all who suffer, i.e., to everyone. The types and qualities of suffering to which one is vulnerable are distributed with great inequity in society (and in nature), and this plays a dramatic role in the evolution of religious life. In this approach, we can recognize that religion can be used in the service of hegemony as well as in support of resistance.

Lawrence Sullivan showed how a critical mythic consciousness functions in a particular social context. He also proposed an explicitly comparative model for analysis that deals with the issues raised by Smith, Eliade, and Long and provides categories applicable also to the examination of ancient Mediterranean religion.[42] Sullivan's work has several strengths to commend it. It provides a model directly related intellectually to that of Eliade and Long and more distantly to that of Smith.[43] Moreover, his model is grounded in comparative work beyond the narrow confines of Euro-American Christianity. Finally, Sullivan's choice of South America was motivated in part because the continent has been a site of conquest. South America entered "civilized" western imagination as a part of the "primitive" world.[44] By working out from an imperial geography, he hoped to develop the critical language Long called for, a language that acknowledges western conquest and critiques the knowledge generated by contact.

According to Sullivan, the critical potential of the mythic consciousness grows out of the foundational character of myth as the reflective and evolving action of the imagination:

> Myth is the imagination beholding its own reality and plumbing the sources of its own creativity as it relates to creativity in every form (plant and planetary life, animal fertility, intelligence, art). . . . Mythic symbols signify the possibility, variety, and meaning of cultural imagery. Myths are paradigmatic expressions of human culture; as significations that reveal the nature of significance, they make effective metastatements about imaginal existence.[45]

In this way myth weaves an ordered world into a wholeness expressed at many levels, but this wholeness is never total. Signification through myth is dynamic rather than static. It repeatedly pushes the limits of its own mode of knowing.

The four important foci of the critical mythic consciousness that emerged from Sullivan's study of South American religions are cosmogony,[46] cosmology, human maturation,[47] and eschatology. Sullivan proposed these categories as "the cornerstones of religious life,"[48] and they shape the comparison of imperial cults and Revelation throughout this book. None of them functions here primarily as they are used in western Christian theology, though there are generic similarities. These four categories allow us to elaborate the mythic consciousness and its critical potential.

Cosmogony may involve chaos, creation ex nihilo, and multiple ages. These eras define realms inhabited by absolute beings who are what they appear to be; there is no signification, no pointing to a greater reality, for each primordial symbol is "an exhaustive expression of its own mode of being."[49] Thus, cosmogony provides a way of imagining pure existence. Because imagining the world without signification is accomplished only through signification, the imagination is pushed to explore its own nature and significance and the primordial age provides the starting point from which the mythic imagination begins. Without this starting point, reality could not be known, but unless the primordium is left behind, there can be no real habitation of this world. So the primordial age often ends with cataclysm, disaster, and destruction. The age of absolute being must be closed so that the mythic imagination can explain why the contemporary world has appeared and the meaning of its appearance.[50]

Cosmology, Sullivan's second category, is the structure of meaning of the current symbolized universe. This world is characterized by many kinds of existence, so a mythic cosmology must both maintain and arrange multiple perspectives on reality. Diverse manifestations of the world are known primarily through space and through time. Space itself is differentiated in many ways. Each mode of being has its appropriate space. Vestigial beings of the primordium inhabit the heavens, but the underworld and the earth have a variety of beings as well. Mediating structures—such as spirits, ancestors, objects, colors—facilitate communication between the many spatial meanings of the universe and thus perpetuate a dynamic, even paradoxical universe. The earth itself is understood through centers, peripheries, and mediators. The centers are the points where revelation, communication, and passage between the many kinds of space occur. By establishing peripheries around the centers, the imagination defines fields within which relationships can be established so that critical reflection is possible.[51]

The dynamic spatial relationships of a cosmology are known through time. In all cultures humans experience qualities of time governed by solar or lunar movements, seasons of the year, labor (whether industrial, domestic, agricultural, or other), phases of life, and so on. The premier device for weaving these disparate times together is the calendar, which coordinates times, spaces, and ritual actions to provide expression and closure for the many aspects of the universe. Festivals are crucial moments in the calendar. Through sacrifice, dance, music, ritual combat, competition, and immoderation, festivals link qualities of time, space, and being. Participants think, feel, and act critically, in time and space, as they experience the destruction, renewal, and differentiation of life:

> Within the framework of cosmic periodicity, culture aims at a shuffled perfection, a stylized arrangement of all the possible qualities of being symbolized by diverse times. Toward this end, each mode of primordial reality finds its place on the calendar-round and returns to the center, but only for that calendrical moment that also celebrates it passing. Through the calendar of sacred feasts, the human appetite for being is satisfied in a piecemeal way.[52]

Thus, human history becomes the cycle of mythic history.[53]

Within this mythic context, human maturation (Sullivan's third category) emerges and evolves. The site of human origins is always a sacred starting point for the fabrication and transformation of humans. A soul (sometimes multiple) guarantees the continuity of the person as he or she experiences parts of reality. The body is both container and vehicle for many of these experiences. Complex symbolizations shape initiations that cultivate the development of person and community through cycles of growth and decay. Religious specialists assist in the more difficult phases (e.g., birth, puberty, illness, marriage, death).[54]

None of this would make sense without the final category: eschatology, which covers the destiny of the human race and of its individual members.[55] The broad category is meant to denote speculations about the terminal conditions of existence:

> [D]eath and eschatology are the final strain gauges of human and worldly significance. These endings test language, trying to the limit its capacity to reveal

and communicate primordial meanings. Whereas myths of creation and origin reach toward the imaginative limits of primal chaos or sublimity, images of demise measure language against the final, outer reaches of experience and against the very end—both termination and *telos*—of meaning itself. Subjected to this end, the creativity of first appearances goes on trial; the meaning of death and the end of time subject signification to its ultimate test. Can symbolism completely account for itself by revealing the meaning of the end?[56]

Rituals, sites, and stories collaborate to answer this challenge. Geographies of the afterlife bring closure and confirmation to the moral implications of space and time in the symbolizing world. Funerary rituals monitor and effect the transformation of a person into new spaces, times, and states of existence. For the community, the eschaton is a summation:

> The end is an essential religious element of the integrity to which individual symbols point, and it is the completion for which the symbolic condition as a whole yearns. . . . Eschatologies do not only comment on immediate social circumstances; they also assess human life and the material universe as states of being defined by constant confrontation with the obliterative condition of cosmic life. The fate of all creation, its status as a religious condition, appears in the signs of its decay, for creation is a terminal condition. The symbolic orders of space, time, color, sound, the food chain, the cycle of prey, social structure, and political hierarchy are the residual effects of the primordial catastrophe. Signs of this world's demise promise hope for a new emergent order.[57]

The new emergent order of the eschaton might take many forms. Time and space are dissolved, but as humans encounter the realm of absolute being, transformations abound. The festive cycle continues but without the constraints of differentiated time and space. There is feasting without saturation, dance without fatigue, music without end. The periodic destructions are themselves destroyed:[58]

> Historic being has not been for nought: the end transforms the *matter* of history and preserves, in transfigured forms, its significant achievement of having suffered change. The new mythical geography, which participates eternally in the transitional condition of immortal human beings, is the final age, a ceaseless feast, a world without end.[59]

In this study, then, "religious" does not mean gullibility or mystification. Religion here refers to a way of knowing the world that recognizes multiple perspectives and negotiates the difference integratively. Through symbol, rite, and centers, paradoxes become coherent wholes. Reflection on the world can move beyond western rationality. The logic of a critical mythic consciousness is not restricted to the mind; it includes the rest of the body, the emotions, spirits, dreams, and visions as well. The results can be innovative and critical, as well as passive and submissive.

This approach allows us to envision imperialistic religion and resistance religion without labeling either as pathological. In this broad paradigm, critical mythic thought can serve aggressors and subjugated people. The system is flexible enough—and reality is diverse enough—to allow for permutations limited only by the human imagination. Violence, appropriation, destructions, and sacrifice are all a part of the symbolized life.

Such a description of religion is an appropriate paradigm for examining both imperial cults and the text of Revelation. It helps us to move beyond an analysis that posits "religion" and "politics" as two separate sectors within society. This axiomatic separation has plagued the study of imperial cults for too long, leading to irrelevant arguments about whether the inhabitants of the Roman Empire really thought their emperor was divine, whether the worship of the emperors was religious, and so on.[60] Most studies were based on implicit modern western Christianizing theories of religion. Sullivan, on the other hand, based his hypotheses on the study of indigenous and other religions from several areas of the world. His morphology allows us to affirm that political administration of the Roman Empire was distinguishable from sacrificial ritual, but that the two were also intimately related.

This morphology also facilitates religious criticism as an academic practice. Most interpreters to date have dismissed imperial cults as degraded or false religion because they do not fit western definitions of religion. Such a procedure misses out on one of the great benefits of studying antiquity—the opportunity to gain a different perspective on our own contingent existence. An approach informed by the work of these religionists turns the tables. In a comparative framework, it is clear that imperial cults were religious. The important questions are: What kind of religious phenomenon are we dealing with? What are the implications for us of our encounter with this system? Unless the study of antiquity can interrogate modernity and question modern self-understandings, the task is not complete.

Edward Said and Postcolonial Theories

The model I have adopted is not perfect. Like most phenomenological approaches, it tends to produce a static reconstruction of a dynamic reality. Its focus on normative society can allow the interpreter to ignore marginal or deviant material.[61] Moreover, a phenomenological model often feigns objectivity[62] yet overlooks issues of domination and imperialism that undergird a particular religious system.[63] Because the topic of imperial cults and Revelation requires special attention to these sorts of problems, I need to supplement the model with two features from postcolonial studies. This section discusses the appropriateness of using postcolonial strategies on Roman imperial materials. Subsequent sections then describe discourse and contrapuntal interpretation in the writing of Edward Said.

Events of the last fifty years allow us—and perhaps compel us—to read texts from imperial settings differently than was formerly possible. Political developments during the last half of the twentieth century have resulted in new insights and new theories about the interrelationships of literature, power, and empire. The official dismantling of colonial empires after World War II resulted in the establishment of nearly one hundred new nations in areas previously ruled by European and American powers.[64] The results rippled through all sectors of societies, including academic institutions.

Aijaz Ahmad noted that the emergence of the term "postcolonial" was directly related to these events. The partition of Pakistan and the creation of Bangladesh in the early 1970s constituted a crisis in the status of nations in formerly colonized areas of south Asia. Among intellectual activists, these events led to theoretical discussions about the nature of the state in decolonizing areas,[65] and in this context of political science the term first gained currency.[66] The term soon became useful in other disciplines as western universities began to employ significant numbers of scholars from colonial and formerly colonized areas.

One crucial study was written by Edward Said, a Palestinian-American literary critic from the field of English literature whose interests span several disciplines. The publication of Said's *Orientalism* in 1978 is generally considered a turning point in the articulation of alternative perspectives regarding the relationships between texts and imperial power.[67] In *Orientalism*, Said set out to expose how the scholarly discourse about the Middle East helped maintain the political and economic subjugation of the Middle East to European powers. He argued that the academic practice of Orientalists allows us to understand "the enormously systematic discipline by which European culture was able to manage—and even produce—the Orient politically, sociologically, militarily, ideologically, scientifically, and imaginatively during the post-Enlightenment period."[68] European culture came to define itself against this imaginatively constructed Orient and greatly strengthened itself in the process.[69]

Since the publication of *Orientalism*, a corpus of postcolonial theories, methods, and studies in a variety of fields has accumulated.[70] These studies examine the relationships between power and knowledge in an imperial setting, with special focus on the experiences of those subjected to imperial rule. Diverse and at times irreconcilable points of view have emerged.

Said is, along with Gayatri Spivak and Homi Bhabha, one of the leading theorists in this recently developed and growing field of interdisciplinary research with primary attachments in the humanities and the social sciences.[71] It focuses on the practices, experiences, and perdurance of Euro-American forms of colonialism during the last two to three centuries. Although all academic disciplines and all institutions of learning embody certain kinds of political commitments, postcolonial studies emphasize political activism on behalf of peoples who were colonized by European or American nations.[72]

Given the modern focus of postcolonial studies, is it an appropriate way to approach ancient materials? There are reasons to be cautious. Because postcolonial studies have become fashionable within certain sectors of the American university, we should be suspicious. Postcolonial studies developed precisely as an alternative to the histories and literatures validated in European and American higher learning. Why, then, has postcoloniality become popular in those very circles? Is this another example of global capitalism's tremendous ability to coopt and to market its opposition? Is it a case of the university institutionalizing and neutralizing a subversive cultural theory?[73] Are we dealing with a survival strategy of immigrant intellectuals in the United States?[74] Or is this simply part of an imperialist pattern in which the west uses the experiences of the rest of the world in its effort to understand itself?[75] And whatever the cause, is it plausible that a Caucasian, third-generation American man like me could characterize aspects of his study as postcolonial? I do not think that the answer to any of these questions is obvious, and they remind us that the politics of scholarship are no less tangled at the turning of the millennium than at any other time.

Problems of content emerge as well. As already discussed, the origins of post-colonial criticism can be located fairly precisely, and this historical context is crucial for its practice. Nearly all of the theoretical and analytical studies have been devoted to topics relevant since the Enlightenment, and to problems forged with the hammer of nationalisms on the anvil of decolonization. But how might post-colonial analysis pertain to topics from ancient history?[76] Even Said, who seems to have the broadest interpretative ambitions, does not address empire as a panhistorical phenomenon. He confines himself to the peculiar character of imperialism since the eighteenth century.[77]

All of this suggests that a detailed and direct application of postcolonial methods to New Testament studies or Roman studies would be ill advised. There is an urgent need for a postcolonial reassessment of the history of New Testament interpretation since the eighteenth century, for these methods are well suited (perhaps even tailor-made) for that task. The ancient Mediterranean is a different case altogether. The dynamics of culture, knowledge, economy, religion, and power in the Roman world are too distant to be approached in exactly the same way.

My solution—or at least my resolution—is to posit that modern European and American empires and the ancient Roman Empire all belong to the larger category of "imperialism." For the purpose of this study, we can accept Said's broad definition of imperialism as "the practice, the theory, and the attitudes of a dominating metropolitan center ruling a distant territory."[78] Here Said uses "metropolitan center" as a technical term that many postcolonial theorists also employ to refer to a dominating center that controls extensive geographic regions. It is normally contrasted with "periphery" to indicate a complex differential in power between the dominating city and the rest of an empire. In discussions of the Roman Empire, the city of Rome functions as the metropolitan center (though I tend to use "imperial center"); the province of Asia would be one of many peripheral areas.[79]

At present, the methods and theories with the most promise for understanding ancient Roman imperialist topics are being developed in postcolonial studies. Because postcolonial methods were designed to examine a different historical period, they must be applied with less detail. However, I expect that the generic features of imperialism will make the transference appropriate.

An Imperial Discourse

One fundamental axiom for this study is that the exercise of imperialism is accompanied by an imperial discourse. "Discourse" requires definition because it has been used in many discussions in various disciplines, often imprecisely. This makes the task more complicated. First, I describe the term's usage and then I produce an intellectual genealogy for my definition.

The term is generally used to describe the systematic ordering of society in a way that validates the authority of certain institutions, behaviors, values, and identities. Such a discursive system embodies rules or expectations prevalent enough to be nearly invisible from within the system. These define the relationships of individuals and groups of people. A discourse normally involves a language or vocabulary that determines acceptable kinds of concepts and thinking. The system is supported by institutions and authorities that also play a role in devising and maintaining the system.

The work of Michel Foucault has been extremely influential for understanding discourse as espoused by Said and many postcolonial theorists. Foucault attempted to articulate a way of viewing the world that redefined such basic notions as truth, selfhood, and knowledge. He sought to define a theory that could explain how power normalizes certain social relationships but not others. He allowed no recourse in his explanations to alleged essences or to personal agency. Rather than appealing to such interiorities, he sought to imagine the world in terms of its exteriority. In Foucault's system, there is no defining center, no individual who creates, discovers, or explores. His study was rather "an attempt to define a particular site by the exteriority of its vicinity; rather than trying to reduce others to silence, by claiming that what they say is worthless, I have tried to define this blank space from which I speak, and which is slowly taking shape in a discourse that I still feel to be so precarious and so unsure."[80]

Said's *Orientalism* showed strong influences from the work of Foucault in the general notion of discourse as well as in some technical terms.[81] Said also employed new categories that were not a part of Foucault's system.[82] Said's most serious deviation was a reintroduction of personal agency into the analysis of discourse. Foucault wanted to define personhood as formed within the confines of discourse.[83] Said rejected this aspect, insisting instead that the "determining imprint of individual writers" must be taken into consideration.[84]

By the time Said wrote *Culture and Imperialism*, his dissatisfaction with Foucault had grown. According to Said, Foucault overextended his theoretical foundation when he tried to derive general theories of society and power from detailed studies of institutions of incarceration.[85] The result, according to Said, was an unacceptable totalizing of power projected from the prison onto all of society. Foucault's focus on the individual and the development of the microphysics of power did not lead to a broader understanding of colonial and metropolitan societies: "[I]gnoring the imperial context of his own theories, Foucault seems actually to represent an irresistible colonizing movement that paradoxically fortifies the prestige of both the lonely individual scholar and the system that contains him."[86] This in turn became a justification for political quietism on the part of sophisticated western intellectuals who, following Foucault, wanted a historical orientation that appeared to be in touch with the machinations of power in the world.[87]

I consider Said's critique appropriate. Foucault's definition of the self is a luxury that can be afforded only within the metropolitan center. For the victims of imperialism, to whom subjectivity has been denied and for whom identity has been defined in foreign terms, exteriority is no great improvement.[88] Discourse is a helpful analytic tool only if it is freed from its Foucaultian fetters. This study, then, will present discourse as a hierarchical system within which identities, knowledges, and values are defined and legitimated. Such systems are supported by institutions that have vested interests in their maintenance. I do not reject the role of individuals and groups in the formation or disintegration of such systems. Even if the efficacy of individuals tends to be exaggerated in popular American culture, individual action is a part of the dynamics of both critical thought and hegemonic dominance.[89]

Thus, when I write that imperialism is accompanied by an imperial discourse, I mean that the exercise of imperial power is accomplished with a more or less successful effort to define society in terms that make this power seem normal, or at least inevitable. In the Roman province of Asia, imperial cults were a crucial part of this discourse, and a careful examination of the existing archaeological evidence can pinpoint precisely how this was accomplished. That is the task of part I in this book.

Before that analysis, it is important to note that the concept of discourse also provides the justification for comparing archaeological and literary texts. Discourse in postcolonial theory is often detected through the analysis of literary texts or written documents, but this study will not be so confined. Foucault's analyses of discourse ranged far and wide through many kinds of materials as he sought the hidden powers that shape "reality." Though Said is a literary critic by training, his theoretical foundations also allow for a broader examination: "[Said's] method fragments the works of individual authors, jars them loose from their secure moorings in authorial intentions and 'universal' standards of truth and objectivity, and imparts to them a unity as enunciations of a discourse distributed across different disciplines, periods, institutions, and texts."[90]

Such fragmentations and realignments need not be confined to literature. As "a structure of attitude and reference," the imperial discourse is dispersed throughout various material or conceptual aspects of culture.[91] The imperial vision is maintained not only by sheer force but also by persuasion (though we must not forget that this takes place within a hegemonic context). The exercise of persuasion over a long period of time results in "the quotidian processes of hegemony," which find their expression throughout a society: in the physical transformation of the realm, in the emergence of new elites and new subcultures, and in artistic expression.[92] Here I find justification for my analysis of not only ancient literature but also coins, inscriptions, sculpture, and architecture. To confine ourselves to literature would not only restrict our findings; it would also deny the rich connections of those texts with their worlds. I violate these boundaries with trepidation but also with the hope of detecting previously unnoticed synthetic elements.

Contrapuntal Interpretation

In *Culture and Imperialism*, Said moved beyond his critique of Oriental studies in the west and broached the larger topic of the relationship between literature and imperial power. He also articulated a method that responded to criticisms of his earlier work. Dissatisfied with the totalizing, self-serving justifications of empire as well as those of Third World nationalisms, Said pioneered a "contrapuntal reading" that took account of both the official histories and the resistance histories.[93] Through this method he hoped to work toward a global but not totalizing theory.[94]

Said employed the concept of counterpoint as a metaphor for the interpretation of society. His use of the metaphor is based on western musical theory in which counterpoint denotes "one or more independent melodies added above or below a given melody" or a "combination of two or more related melodies into a single harmonic whole."[95] Like any good metaphor, this one leaves room for ambiguity. Does the metaphor suggest that even resistance serves the purposes of the imperialist harmonic whole? Does the metaphor privilege one voice instead of another?

Said changed the nuance of the metaphor later in his study to avoid the appearance of assuming that imperial power has total control of society. "[T]his global, contrapuntal analysis should be modelled not . . . on a symphony but rather on an atonal ensemble; we must take into account all sorts of spatial or geographical and rhetorical practices—inflections, limits, constraints, intrusions, inclusions, prohibitions—all of them tending to elucidate a complex and uneven topography."[96] So we must beware of placid social depictions that ignore dissonance. A contrapuntal reading of society might reveal an unruly, unharmonious ensemble.

The ambiguity of this metaphor is apt for at least two reasons. First, any social setting is composed of multiple experiences and readings. No single theory or interpretation will do justice to the historical experiences of the real people who make up the society under scrutiny.[97] Second, a text is connected to society in manifold ways: "Texts are protean things; they are tied to circumstances and to politics large and small, and these require attention and criticism. No one can take stock of everything, of course, just as no one theory can explain or account for the connections among texts and societies."[98]

A contrapuntal reading, then, is not necessarily aligned with one particular systematic theoretical orientation. It is the beneficiary of several theoretical traditions, but it focuses on the historical experiences of people as they maneuver within the localized manifestations of global forces.[99] The common theme is the imposition of power by foreigners in a global and historical perspective. This expansive scope requires a flexible theoretical orientation, because every text is formed and read in particular settings, and can have real effects on people's lives in specific settings.[100] This expansive scope is also required because the ancient materials show a range of compliant viewpoints and a range of resistant viewpoints. We should not confine our analysis to just two voices, the dominant and the resistant. All the materials should be taken into account.

Some reviewers conclude that Said did not succeed in his goal of developing a global theory attentive to historical specificity. Ernest Gellner criticized *Culture and Imperialism* over this issue of overextension. Gellner dissected Said's handling of colonial topics in North Africa and concluded that Said was more interested in his general thesis about literature in the service of colonialism than in actually grounding that theory in the historical struggles of the colonized people about whom he wrote.[101]

The eclectic theoretical foundation of Said's work has also drawn criticism. James Clifford saw it as a serious flaw that produced confusion in Said's analysis.[102] Ahmad saw darker forces at work: the lack of a systematic theoretical foundation was a sign that Said—and indeed most postcolonial intellectuals—had been seduced by the power of the western academy. According to Ahmad, Said and Co. pulled away from a Marxist political critique and offered in its stead a more palatable framework that sounded radical but had no real power.[103]

Even if Said overextended his argument, we should not overlook his central achievements. Said is a polemicist who pushed the argument to extremes in an attempt to make the whole world understandable. He is a literary critic who does not accept the prescribed tasks of literary criticism without question. Rather, he seeks to delineate the relationship of literature and power:

> What is important about Said's "contrapuntal reading" of works of literature—a reading in which ordinarily separate histories are allowed to play against each other, to produce not harmony but a complicated polyphony—is not its occasional bluntness or its sometimes overstated claims, but the range of insight and argument it makes possible. . . . It is a matter of learning how to find, in literature and elsewhere, what Said calls "a heightened form of historical experience"; which I take to mean finding history in places where it ought not to have been lost.[104]

For the purposes of a study on imperial cults and the book of Revelation in the Roman province of Asia, contrapuntal reading allows me to draw connections between the early Christian text and its first-century setting. The problem of overextension is ameliorated by the tightly focused scope of this study. The charge of eclecticism would be more serious in a study that presented itself as a treatise in political or economic theory. This book, however, is about the symbolic lives of communities and about the assertions about human communities that shape such systems of symbolization. To that end, a judicious synthesis seems preferable to a restrictive metatheory.

The Stakes

I hesitate spending too much space describing my motives for undertaking such a study because a good part of the enjoyment of reading a book, in my opinion, comes from the search for the author's axioms, blindspots, and agenda. Nevertheless, a few words are in order about why I think the historical topic warrants consideration some nineteen centuries later and why I have engaged these particular conversation partners (without their consent).

There is a fundamental issue at the heart of all the theorists I have cited. All of them ask, in various ways, if there is hope for the establishment of a just human community. Is it feasible? And, if so, upon what is it founded? I consider Said to be an ally because of his persistent critical vision and his empathy for those who suffer unjustly. Moreover, Said provides a method of interpreting history contrapuntally that helps integrate materials and voices normally confined to separate studies. As a practicing, believing Christian from the Mennonite tradition, I disagree with the secular assumptions of his procedure.[105] That is why religionists like Smith, Eliade, Long, and Sullivan supply the main framework for my historical task. All four are as urgent and compassionate as Said in their readings of the human condition, but their conclusions about the significance of religious experience in that condition are more similar to my own.

The same fundamental issue is at stake in our ancient materials. The worship of the Roman emperors and the book of Revelation both exhibit crucial concern for the proper ordering of human society. In the chapters that follow, I make the case that the two were at odds with each other in unequal battle. The vision of

Revelation, understood as a strident denunciation of official orthodoxies, is both appealing and terrifying. I cannot say that I fully embrace the text. I am committed, however, to supporting its extreme message as an unexpendable voice in the contrapuntal Christian canon.

If I thought that an examination of the relationship between imperial cults and Revelation should be limited to readers with a Christian commitment, however, I would have written a very different book. The pagan phenomenon and the Christian text, both of which seem bizarre to modern sensibilities, touch on central issues in the meaning of human experience. All governments validate their power by claiming to be operating in the best interests of those governed. All imperial powers legitimate their hegemony with proclamations of their good intentions for those they rule. To what extent are these claims justified? How should one act in the face of such claims? To these perennial problems, imperial cults and Revelation offer their respective responses and each is an affront to modernity in its own way.

I

THE LOGIC OF PARTICIPATION

The next six chapters survey the structures, values, and functions of emperor worship in the province of Asia. The temporal boundaries for the discussion begin with the Augustan period (31 BCE–14 CE) and end in the early second century CE. I begin with provincial cults of the emperors, move to the municipal cults, and then consider evidence for groups or individuals who worshipped members of the imperial family. A final chapter describes imperial cult religion, using the categories of cosmogony, cosmology, human maturation, and eschatology.

This progression moves in the opposite direction to that used by Christian Habicht (1973) in his excellent article on the worship of the emperors in this same period. His study began with individuals, moved to municipal cults, examined provincial practices (east and west), and ended with considerations of the emperor's own understanding of his status in society and cult. I work in the opposite direction to highlight not the self-understanding of the emperor but rather the functions of imperial cults in the Roman province of Asia.

2

PROVINCIAL IMPERIAL CULTS OF ASIA
UNDER AUGUSTUS AND TIBERIUS

By the end of the first century CE, Asia had established three viable imperial temples sponsored by the entire province. This chapter examines the available evidence for Asia's provincial imperial cults[1] during the reigns of Augustus and Tiberius. The next chapter completes the overview of provincial imperial cults by covering the rest of the first century. I want to develop as complete a picture as possible of these institutions based on the extant materials and to show the part played by provincial cults in the religious discourse of imperial authority in the province.

Rome and Augustus at Pergamon

The practice of establishing provincial temples drew the attention of Roman literati, alerting us to the fact that these institutions were considered an essential part of dominant imperial histories. Dio Cassius recounted the establishment of the first provincial temple at Pergamon in the context of a discussion of events from 29 BCE; he referred to Octavian as Caesar:

> At that time Caesar was attending to general matters, and he permitted the establishment of precincts to Rome and to (his) father Caesar—calling him the hero Julius—in Ephesos and in Nicea, for these were then the most distinguished cities in Asia and in Bithynia respectively. He ordered the Romans who

had settled among them to honor these two. But he allowed the foreigners—
whom he called Hellenes—to consecrate precincts to him, the Asians in
Pergamon and the Bithynians in Nicomedia. Beginning there, this (practice)
continued under other emperors, not only among the Hellenic nationalities but
also among the others, in so far as they are subject to the Romans. For in the
city (of Rome) and in the rest of Italy there is no one who dared to do such a
thing, however worthy of renown. Yet even there, various god-like honors are
given after their death to those who rule uprightly; and heroic shrines are even
built (to them). These things occurred in winter, and the Pergamenes also
received (the right) to hold games called "sacred" in honor of his temple.[2]

Dio's Romanocentric perspective is obvious in this excerpt: the empire is composed of Romans and foreigners. His historical distance, writing some two and a
half centuries after the events, requires us to treat some details with reserve, but certain
features of the text are important for our understanding of imperial cults in general. Dio recognized multiple imperial cult systems at work in the empire; three are
specifically mentioned here. He described the system in Rome in terms of hero
worship: god-like honors were appropriate for good rulers after death. He called
such a shrine a *heroon* (shrine for a hero), reserving the term *temenos*, or "precincts,"
for imperial cult temples in the provinces.

Dio mentioned two other imperial cult systems in the provinces of Asia and
Bithynia. For Romans living abroad, Augustus established in both provinces a
temenos with a double dedication: to Rome and to the hero Julius. This modifica-
tion of the system for Rome did not include honors for the living Augustus but rather
for his divinized adoptive father Julius and for the city of Rome. This implied fidelity to Augustus, and equated it with fidelity to Rome.

The foreign Hellenes were allowed to establish a third imperial cult system that
Dio thought would be scandalous if practiced in Rome because it included worship
of Augustus and of the goddess Rome. Dio also indicated his interpretation of the
primary meaning of the imperial cults of the Hellenes. Such cults indicated subservience to Rome. Thus, the implied reason for the existence of different systems of
imperial cults was that they involved different kinds of hierarchical relationships:
among Romans in Rome, between expatriate Romans and the imperial center, and
between subjugated foreigners and the imperial center.

The cults of Rome and Julius did not make a lasting impression. No archaeological evidence has been found for them, no other literary references to them
are preserved, and there is no sign that other temples were set up to follow this
pattern.[3] The only possible evidence consists of foundations at Ephesos that once
supported either a double temple or a double altar (fig. 2.1). The argument for
identifying these foundations with the cult of Rome and Julius, however, is circumstantial. The Ephesian remains represent the right historical period—last half
of the first century BCE. The location near the prytaneion (civic religious center)
and the bouleuterion (meeting place of the city council) would be appropriate
for a cult with governmental implications. Moreover, the foundations and the
modest courtyard are the earliest known example in Asia of a distinctive Italian
design, in which a podium temple is set near the back wall of a peristyle court-

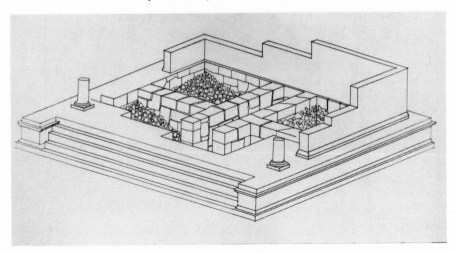

FIGURE 2.1 Axiometric reconstruction of the double foundation, Ephesos (*JÖAI* 51 [1976–77] 57).⁴ © The Österreichisches Archäologisches Institut, Vienna.

yard.⁵ Although identification as the temenos of Rome and Julius is likely, definitive proof has not been found.⁶

The provincial temple approved in 29 BCE for Pergamon for the use of Hellenes was much more influential. Dio Cassius remembered the temple as the starting point for imperial cult practice spanning several centuries. Some of his terminology was not precise, and he did not recount the historical setting that led to these innovations. For this information we need other sources. Dio neglected the fact that the temple for the Hellenes also had a double dedication. The official title of the temple was "of the goddess Rome and of Augustus,"⁷ but Dio mentioned only Augustus. This oversight was not unusual. A damaged inscription from Mytilene on the island of Lesbos, probably the oldest extant reference to the temple, omits Rome as well. The decree, issued sometime between 27 and 11 BCE while the temple in Pergamon was still under construction, proclaimed various local honors for Augustus at Mytilene and stipulated that copies of the Mytilene decree were to be set up in several major cities throughout the Mediterranean, including one copy "[in the temple being cons]tructed for him by Asia in Pergamon."⁸ Augustus was clearly the dominant figure in this religious institution.

The temple at Pergamon was dedicated by the whole province of Asia, not simply by a city or by an individual, although Dio did not clarify this point. A standard imperial procedure developed for the approval of such provincial temples; I discuss it later in this chapter in conjunction with Asia's second provincial temple established at Smyrna. More evidence for the procedure relates to that temple, and we do not know if the procedure was in place for the first provincial temple at Pergamon. Clearly Asian officials requested permission to initiate cultic honors for Augustus in some form: Tacitus said that Augustus did not prohibit Asia from building the temple and Dio wrote that Augustus allowed the Hellenes to do so.⁹ Modern interpretation tends to conclude that the Hellenes in Asia requested a temple for Augustus and that the princeps added a cult of Rome because he wished to avoid offending the elite sectors at Rome while he was in the process of consolidating his authority.[10] It is not clear who proposed Rome, however, because the Asian elite would have been aware of Roman sentiments[11] and could have requested a double dedication on their own. The temple of Rome and Julius was more likely the result of an amendment by Augustus, for it is hard to imagine the koinon of Asia requesting temples for the use of resident Romans.[12] Furthermore, because no lasting record of the temple remains, we may infer that the idea was not Asian but foreign.[13] The format reflected the Roman *divus* system in which good emperors were divinized after death by vote of the Senate. The emperor was then called *divus* (divinized one), not *deus* (god). Because no similar system existed in the Greek world Dio described it according to the closest analogy—hero worship.[14]

We may never know for certain who proposed which features. Apparently, to establish these temples, a complex negotiation took place between the emperor Octavian and a small group of the most prominent men of western Asia Minor. Because the unusual combination of temples was granted for both Asia and Bithynia, we may assume that the two provinces acted in concert. The provincial elites would have recognized the need to establish a cult recognizable to Asians and to Bithynians, but an equal or greater concern would have been to stabilize their relationship with Octavian. Less than five years earlier, Mark Antony and Cleopatra had spent the winter of 33/32 in Ephesos while tensions with Octavian were increasing. Early in 32, Antony and Cleopatra were joined in Ephesos by 300 Roman senators opposed to Octavian. This apparent attempt to form a government in exile failed; when Antony was defeated by Octavian in 31, Asia's future under Roman rule was very much in doubt.[15]

Octavian had his own problems. Control of the provinces was certainly one, but the question of support from the Roman elite was equally important. Octavian had effectively used religious propaganda against Antony, accusing him of assuming the royal pretensions of an eastern autocrat.[16] Would Octavian now raise suspicions in Rome about his own intentions by allowing the eastern provinces to worship him as a god during his lifetime?

This particular historical context makes the unusual arrangement of 29 BCE intelligible. Temples of Rome and Divus Iulius were ordered for Romans living in Asia and Bithynia and placed in the two cities where many of them resided. These cults were organized so that they would be acceptable to Romans in the Greek east by combining the divus system of divinization[17] with the eastern deification of the city of Rome.[18] In this way, worship at these temples by Romans inextricably tied loyalty to Rome with support for Octavian.

Temples built for the use of Hellenes drew on other traditions to consolidate Octavian's authority in western Asia Minor. The province of Asia had a history of cults for the goddess Rome at least to the early second century BCE.[19] A provincial festival honoring a Roman proconsul[20] and municipal games for another proconsul at Mylasa are attested from the early first century BCE.[21] Evidence from the middle of the first century BCE shows an Asian tradition of cults for Rome combined with cults for Roman officials.

An important precedent was set by a cult for Publius Servilius Isauricus, who had sided with Caesar during his lifetime, claiming the office of consul in 48 BCE. He served as proconsul of Asia late in Caesar's life from 46–44.[22] After Caesar's death, Isauricus supported Octavian, who was married to Isauricus's daughter for a short time. During this period Isauricus became known as a great benefactor in Asia. Magnesia on the Meander honored him for his donation to the temple of Artemis Leukophryne by setting up a statue of his father.[23] Pergamon named him as savior and benefactor of the city who restored its ancestral traditions and its democracy.[24] In Ephesos, he was honored with a cult "of Rome and of Publius Servilius Isauricus." The title is known from two epigraphic references to priests of this cult.[25] The references derive from the early second century CE, so this municipal institution survived at least a century and a half after his two years of service in Asia.

Such priesthoods and festivals that simultaneously honored Rome and a particular Roman official set important precedents for Asia's first provincial cult, but they also highlight the decision Octavian faced when Asians requested the right to build a temple for him in Pergamon. If Octavian approved the request, the Senate might use it against him as a sign of his desire for absolute rule. If Octavian refused cultic honors for himself, he could anticipate the continuation and probable proliferation of cults for Roman officials and would thus assist possible usurpers. By approving a cult for himself, Octavian began the process by which all ruler cults in Asia focused on the emperor and the imperial family. After his reign, no new cults of Roman officials were founded and cults of emperors spread.[26] Thus, a local cultic format turned the worship of the provincials toward the emperor and his family in Rome.

The provincial temple for Rome and Augustus at Pergamon has not been located. However, coins from Asia provide an image of what the temple may have looked like. A series of coins—silver cistophoroi minted from 20–18 BCE—appeared with a bust of Augustus facing right on the obverses. Three different reverses occur on these coins: a triumphal arch, a round temple of Mars, and the provincial imperial temple identified by the inscription *ROM.ET.AUGUST* on the architrave above the columns (fig. 2.2). Another inscription in the open fields on either side of the temple names the donor: *COM(mune) ASIAE*, "the koinon of Asia."[27] The temple is depicted with six Corinthian columns in front on top of a five-step crepidoma (foundation base). The corners and the apex of the roof are surmounted by palmette acroteria. Although perhaps not exact, this representation of the Rome and Augustus

FIGURE 2.2 The Temple of Rome and Augustus portrayed on a silver cistophoros of Asia. Augustus is on the obverse. *BMCRE* 1.114 #705. © The British Museum.

temple is probably accurate in broad outline, and it is certainly an image that spread throughout the province and beyond.

Images of military victory recur in the iconography related to the provincial temple at Pergamon. Other coins depicted the temple with the two central columns removed in order to show the statues inside.[28] Bronze coins of Pergamon from the years 4–5 CE began this practice during the Augustan period: two center columns were omitted to show Augustus in a cuirass (military breastplate) and holding a spear in his right hand.[29] A similar image appears on coins of the Tiberian[30] and Neronian periods.[31] An Asian tetradrachma from the reign of Claudius removed two more of the columns and depicted both statues within the temple (fig. 2.3). The standing Augustus is again clad in military uniform with spear in hand. To his left is the goddess Rome, her right hand raised to crown the victorious emperor, in her left hand a cornucopia.[32] These coins probably portray the statue accurately, for the public icon remained constant for at least a century and probably longer. The temple images thus focused on Augustus and his military victories. The founding of the temple probably related directly to his triumph over Antony at Actium, but the recurring image would have been appropriate throughout his career and provided important imperial imagery during the reigns of his successors as well.

Several new religious offices were created in Asia with the establishment of a provincial cult. The most prominent would have been the high priest of Rome and Augustus. The high priesthood should not be confused with the office of Asiarch. Although many studies have accepted the identification of these two offices, the literary and archaeological evidence for the Asiarchate shows that it was not a provincial office[33] but rather a municipal office with a wider range of duties sometimes related to imperial cults. The high priest, on the other hand, led the sacrifices at the annual provincial festival at the temple of Rome and Augustus at Pergamon and would have supported the sacrifices financially. This official is often mentioned in decrees from Asia's koinon, so he may have had particular responsibilities in the provincial council as well. Candidates for the position were elected by the koinon to serve in perhaps the most prestigious office in Roman Asia. The candidate pool was composed of a small percentage of the wealthiest male members of Asian society.[34]

A provincial temple like the one in Pergamon also required a neokoros, an official who underwrote the costs of maintaining the sacred temenos and sometimes assisted with ritual activities.[35] Although this office was not nearly so prestigious as a

FIGURE 2.3 Rome crowns Augustus. The reverse of a tetradrachma of Asia shows the statues within the temple of Rome and Augustus at Pergamon. The emperor Claudius is on the obverse. © The British Museum.

provincial high priesthood, the names of a few such officials have been preserved. An inscription from Pergamon honoring one of them raises several important issues:

> Οἱ νέοι ἐτίμησαν
> Γάιον Ἰούλιον Σακέρδωτα, τὸν
> νεωκόρον θεᾶς Ῥώμης καὶ θεοῦ
> Σεβαστοῦ Καίσαρος καὶ ἱερέα
> Τιβερίου Κλαυδίου Νέρωνος καὶ
> γυμνασίαρχον τῶν δωδεκάτων
> Σεβαστῶν Ῥωμαίων τῶν πέντε
> γυμνασίων, ἀλείφοντα ἐγ λουτήρων
> δι᾽ ὅλης ἡμέρας ἐκ τῶν ἰδίων,
> προνοήσαντα τῆς τε αὐτῶν καὶ τῶν
> [ἐφ]ήβων ἀγωγῆς, νόμους τε πατρίους
> [καὶ ἤ]θη κατὰ τὸ κάλλιστον
> [ἀν]ανεωσάμενον.[36]

The neoi honored Gaius Julius Sacerdos: the neokoros of goddess Rome and of god Augustus Caesar; priest of Tiberius Claudius Nero; and gymnasiarch of the 12th Sebasta Romaia for the five gymnasia, who supplied oil for the washings throughout the whole day at his own expense, who provided for their games [those of the neoi] and also for those of the ephebes, renewing the ancestral laws and customs according to what is most noble.

This inscription mentions one neokoros of the provincial temple, Sacerdos, a municipal aristocrat who served the city in several ways and was also priest for a municipal cult of Tiberius. The text focuses on his service as gymnasiarch for the games connected to the provincial cult Dio mentioned. The official name for the games is used here—the Sebasta Romaia.[37] We learn that the competitions of the neoi and the ephebes lasted one day, though other competitions probably extended the festival to several days. The position of gymnasiarch also seems to have been a municipal responsibility of the Pergamenes in conjunction with the provincial festival because the dedication is from a local organization regarding service to local groups and because the offices are civic (except perhaps that of neokoros).

The frequency of the Sebasta Romaia games is disputed, but this inscription helps narrow the options: they were either annual or biennial. The name in this inscription for the future emperor Tiberius was no longer used after 4 CE when he was adopted by Augustus, so the inscription must represent an earlier date. If the Sebasta Romaia were initiated immediately in 29 BCE, a four-year cycle for the festival would be impossible because the twelfth festival would have occurred later than 4 CE. If the festival was held every two years, the date for the inscription would be 7 BCE; an annual cycle would provide a date of 18 BCE. Neither date is supported by compelling arguments. A cult for Tiberius without any imperial nomenclature would be conceivable in 18 BCE, but this reference to a priest of that cult would be surprisingly early. The later date of 7 BCE would make a reference to the priesthood more probable. However, by 7 BCE, Lucius and Gaius were Augustus's clear choices as heirs, and a reference to a cult of Tiberius would be increasingly less likely.[38] So the date remains debatable.

The Sacerdos inscription also raises the issue of the language of divinization used in imperial cults. The reference to Augustus as θεός ("god") in a provincial cult setting during his lifetime is unusual. Municipal cults were not restricted in this way,[39] but provincial cults before Hadrian avoided the use of this explicit divine language out of deference to Roman expectations.[40] Augustus was normally described as a "son of god" in provincial documents that mention this temple before his death.[41] Municipal documents like the Sacerdos inscription were more flexible.[42]

One last office of the provincial cult requires comment. The Sebasta Romaia games required an agonothete to fund the competitions and lead the festivities. This prestigious position was higher in status than the neokoros but did not reach that of the provincial high priest. The high priest sometimes undertook the office of agonothete; several scholars have concluded that these titles were part of the same office.[43] However, the agonothesia was a lifelong office, whereas the high priesthood lasted only for one year. Moreover, the identification of the offices provides no explanation for the fact that some men are listed as high priest, and others as high priest and agonothete.[44] Three consecutive high priests of "goddess Rome and of Emperor Caesar Augustus, son of god," from the years 4–2 BCE illustrate both points. The first two men were described only as high priests; the third was both high priest and "agonothete for life." The agonothesia of the Sebasta Romaia was a separate office that involved leading one of the province's great athletic competitions.

In summary, Asia's first provincial cult was forged in 29 BCE in the aftermath of major struggles for control over the Mediterranean world. Asia had backed the wrong general (Antony) and then needed to affirm its support of the new ruler (Octavian). The unusual aspects of the arrangement—the double dedication to Rome and the emperor and the separate temple for resident Romans—in this historical context are the result of efforts to negotiate differences in cultic systems because of changing political realities. These cultic formats were not replicated later because the limitations of that historical situation were temporary. Nevertheless, the temple of Rome and Augustus had a great effect on the province and beyond. Several new offices were established that needed to be filled by members of the highest levels of Asian society and by the wealthiest citizens of Pergamon. A major new festival that included sacrifices and competitions became a stable part of Asia's festal cycles. Finally, the cult in Asia, along with the lesser known cult in Bithynia, became the starting point for an expanding phenomenon of provincial imperial worship throughout the empire. With the establishment of the cult of Rome and Augustus, new symbolic resources entered public life.

Asia's New Calendar

Within 20 years after his victory at Actium, the koinon of Asia sought greater means for honoring Augustus. Around 9 BCE, the members of the provincial council decreed a competition: whoever could suggest the highest honors for Augustus would be awarded a crown by the province. The winning proposal came from the Roman proconsul of the province, Paullus Fabius Maximus. The beginning of the proconsul's edict has been lost, but the extant portion records both his proposal and reasons for honoring Augustus (whom he calls Caesar):

[It is difficult to know whether?] the birthday of the most divine Caesar is a matter of greater pleasure or greater benefit. We could justly consider that day to be equal to the beginning of all things. He restored the form of all things to usefulness, if not to their natural state, since it had deteriorated and suffered misfortune. He gave a new appearance to the whole world, which would gladly have accepted its own destruction had Caesar not been born for the common good fortune of all. Thus a person could justly consider this to be the beginning of life and of existence, and the end of regrets about having been born.

Since on no (other) day could each one receive a starting point more beneficial for corporate and personal improvement than the day that has been beneficial to all;

And since it happens that all the cities of Asia have the same date for entrance into local office, which is an arrangement that has clearly been formed according to some divine counsel in order that it might be the starting point of honors to Augustus;

And since it is difficult to give thanks equal to such benefactions as his unless we devise some new manner of reciprocation for each of them;

And since people could celebrate more gladly the birthday common to all because some personal pleasure has been brought to them through (his) rule;

Therefore, it seems proper to me that the birthday of the most divine Caesar be the one, uniform New Year's day for all the polities. On that day all will take up their local offices, that is, on the ninth day before the Kalends of October, in order that he might be honored far beyond any ceremonies performed for him and that he might rather be distinguished by all, which I consider to be the greatest service rendered by the province. A decree of the koinon of Asia should be written encompassing all his virtues, so that the action devised by us for the honor of Augustus should endure forever. I will command that the decree, engraved on a stele, be set up in the temple, having arranged for the edict to be written in both languages.[45]

Maximus—the proconsul sent from Rome to rule the province—argued that the greatest honor Asia could give to Augustus would be to reorganize time around the birthday of Augustus. September 23 would be the beginning of every new year as well as the date when new municipal officeholders would begin to serve. This proposal would not have required a drastic change for most cities, for they tended to mark the new year at the autumnal equinox.[46] The proconsul's edict, however, was not couched in pragmatic terms about convenience for the cities. Rather, his rationale for reorienting time was based on the accomplishments of Augustus. From this official Roman perspective, the world was in disarray and headed for ruin until Augustus restored and transformed the world. Therefore, his birth was the most appropriate symbol for New Year's Day. The old world was given a fresh start, a new origin (ἀφορμή).

Another reason given for the proconsul's proposal was that local officeholders could assume their duties on the birthday of Augustus. The play on the word ἀρχή ("beginning" or "rule") in the edict was not frivolous. The "beginning" of their "rule" on September 23 affirmed the legitimacy of Roman imperialism. Local authority depended upon the regime of Augustus. The alignment of these local inaugurations with the birthday of the emperor promoted a vision of history based on the rule of Rome. The fact that most cities already inaugurated new officeholders at the equinox was said to have been no mere accident; some divine authority had preordained this in anticipation of the honors due to Augustus.

Finally, the centralization of the municipal calendars around the birth of the emperor was said to surpass even the ceremonies (θρησκεία) performed for Augustus. No matter how big the festival, an imperial cult involved only a segment of the population for a limited period of time. The calendar reform, on the other hand, would involve everyone every day. It represented the transformation of all life. This is one reason why the text emphasized both corporate and personal existence. All individuals and all communities were said to have been given new life through Augustus. The principle of reciprocity could be satisfied only through the reorganization of all facets of their lives.

The provincial council, as we might expect, responded positively to the proposal of the Roman proconsul. They composed a decree as he "suggested" and inscribed it along with his edict:

> A decision of the Hellenes in Asia; proposed by the high priest Apollonios son of Menophilos of Aizanoi. Whereas the providence that ordains our whole life has established with zeal and distinction that which is most perfect in our life by bringing Augustus, whom she filled with virtue as a benefaction to all humanity; sending to us and to those after us a savior who put an end to war and brought order to all things; and Caesar, when he appeared, the hopes of those who preceded [. . .] placed, not only surpassing those benefactors who had come before but also leaving to those who shall come no hope of surpassing (him); and the birth of the god was the beginning of good tidings to the world through him; and [when the highpriest was] Lucius Vulcacius Tullus and when the secretary was Pap[ias . . .] Asia passed a decree at Smyrna [that a crown should be given] to the one who could devise the greatest honors to the god; and Paullus Fabius Maximus the proconsul—sent for the well-being of the province by his [i.e., Augustus's] right hand and decision—has made myriad benefactions to the province, the extent of which benefactions no one could adequately express; and now that which was unknown until this time by the Hellenes he devised regarding the honor of Augustus: calculating time to have begun at his birth.

> For this reason, with good fortune and for salvation this was decided by the Hellenes in Asia. The new year will begin in all the cities on the ninth day before the Kalends of October, which is the birthday of Augustus. In order that the day be always aligned in every city, the Roman date will be used along with the Greek date. The first month will be observed as Kaisar(eios), as decreed earlier, beginning from the ninth day before the Kalends of October. The crown that was decreed for the one proposing the greatest honors on behalf of Caesar will be given to Maximus the proconsul, who also will always be proclaimed publicly in the athletic contests at Pergamon, the Romaia Sebasteia, with, "Asia crowns Paullus Fabius Maximus, who most reverently proposed the honors for Caesar." Likewise he will be proclaimed in the Kaisareia, the games celebrated in the city.

The rescript of the proconsul and the decree of Asia will be inscribed on a marble stele, which will be set up in the temenos of Rome and Augustus. The public advocates for the year will see to it that the rescript of Maximus and the decree of Asia will be engraved on marble steles in the leading cities of the districts. These steles will be placed in the Kaisareia.

The months shall be observed as follows: Kaisar(eios), 31 days; Apellaios, 30 days; Audnaios, 31 days; Peritios, 31 days; Dystros, 28 days; Xandikos, 31 days; Artemisios, 30 days; Daisios, 31 days; Panemos, 30 days; Loos, 31 days; Gorpiaios, 31 days; Hyperberetaios, 30 days.[47]

The decree of the koinon provides several more details about the new calendar. One important adjustment was that the first month of the year formerly named for Zeus (Dios) would be renamed in honor of Augustus (Kaisareios). The names of the other months of the year would be regularized as well: local municipal variations were to give way to a standard rotation of months.[48] Finally, the exact stipulation of days per month coordinated the new Asian calendar with the Roman calendar, ensuring that every Asian month would begin on the 23rd of the Roman month. In this way, every month of the year would begin with another smaller observance of the birth of Augustus.

The decree of the koinon exhibits a shift in focus from the existing portion of the proconsul's edict, though the missing portion of his edict prevents us from knowing its full extent. The language of benefaction is more pronounced in the koinon decree, with the result that Augustus is portrayed within a hierarchy of relationships rather than strictly as the founder of a new epoch. The hierarchy articulated by the koinon decree starts with Providence at the top, who ordains all of life and who filled Augustus with virtue. Augustus thus is able to be the benefactor of all humanity, and his primary accomplishments are said to be the cessation of war and the establishment of order. In the case of Asia, the hierarchy includes the proconsul as the one sent by Augustus. The proconsul mediates the benefactions of Augustus and adds his own for the benefit of the province. In this instance, the proconsul also mediates the proper response of the province to the emperor.

The decree presupposes that the next level of the hierarchy is filled by the koinon, whose members represent the cities and stipulate appropriate actions required of all the inhabitants of the province. These actions include appropriate honors toward those above them in the hierarchy, especially the proconsul and the emperor. As the winner of the competition to praise Augustus, the proconsul was himself awarded honors within the context of Augustan imperial cults. He would be publicly acclaimed both in the provincial games for Rome and Augustus and in the Pergamene municipal games for Augustus.

These texts were to be inscribed and posted in the provincial precincts of Rome and Augustus as well as in local imperial cult shrines in the district capitals. The display of the texts went further than this, however. Fragments from copies of the inscription have been found at Priene, Eumeneia, Apameia, and Dorylaia.[49] Of these, only Apameia is known to have been a district capital.[50]

The calendar reform was not an attempt to replace the calendars of the cities with the Roman calendar. Rather, a uniform system for reckoning time was added to older ones and all appear to have coexisted. The older systems probably remained predominant for most purposes, and the old names of months continued to be used in many places.[51] So the point was not to impose an exclusive framework for the experience of the passage of time. Rather, the new calendar added an important dimension to the old framework to develop, in Lawrence Sullivan's terms, "a shuffled perfection, a stylized arrangement of all the possible qualities of being symbolized by diverse times."[52] The new calendar expressed and enforced the growing importance of the province as a fundamental unit of organization, the increasing influence of Roman rule in the ordering of human communities in Asia, and the importance of Augustus in the understanding of time.

A Provincial Temple at Smyrna

In the middle of the reign of Tiberius (14–37 CE) Asians requested permission to build a second provincial imperial temple, even though no province had more than one such temple at the time and several appear to have had none. Roman historians took note of the request, and Tacitus has preserved a good deal of information about it, allowing us to discuss the occasion for the request, the procedure by which such cults were approved, and some meanings attributed to the cult.

According to Tacitus, Asia's request was a direct response to two court cases.[53] The first case, heard in 22 CE, began with charges of extortion (*repetundae*) against Gaius Silanus, proconsul of Asia, which were brought to the attention of the Senate by representatives of Asia. Roman senators soon brought additional charges against Silanus, including the crimes of sacrilege against the *numen* ("divine essence") of Augustus and contempt for the *maiestas* ("majesty, grandeur") of Tiberius. The opposition to Silanus grew among the imperial elite when his subordinate officers (a quaestor and a legate) supported the charges. Asia's most accomplished lawyers went to Rome to argue the case and to seek restitution. Tiberius took an active role in hearing the case and made it clear that he was seeking a guilty verdict. Tacitus recorded that the emperor asked pointed questions, allowed Silanus's slaves to be interrogated under torture, prevented the proconsul's friends from testifying in his defense, and even required the public reading of an Augustan indictment against a former proconsul of Asia. Silanus was found guilty, exiled to an island, and stripped of his property.[54]

The next year the province of Asia brought another case to trial in Rome. This defendant was Lucilius Capito, procurator of the imperial property in Asia. The provincials accused him of usurping the power of a military official by using troops against them. Tiberius again took an active interest in the case, opening the proceedings with a stern warning to the defendant about the seriousness of the charges. Capito was found guilty and condemned. Then Tacitus noted, "The cities of Asia, gratified by this retribution [*ultionem*] and the punishment inflicted [*vindicatum erat*] in the previous year on Gaius Silanus, voted a temple to Tiberius, to his mother, and to the Senate, and were permitted to build it."[55]

This statement by Tacitus provides another perspective on reasons for establishing a provincial imperial cult. In the third century Dio noted that the general phenomenon of imperial cults was a sign of subjugation to the city of Rome, which was probably one imperial view from the top of the imperial hierarchy. The perspective of the Asian elite in the early first century was somewhat different. In 23 CE, Tiberius and the Senate could be celebrated as the avengers of Asia, for they had punished those who afflicted the province and exacted restitution.[56] By decreeing a temple for their distant Roman allies, the Asians were simultaneously creating leverage against the lower-ranking Roman authorities who were closer at hand. This provincial temple was intended in part to build a direct connection to the central imperial authorities that bypassed appointees such as the proconsul and the procurator.

The province had taken a risk by bringing provincial officials to trial before the Senate and the emperor. If a defendant in such cases was acquitted, he and his allies remained in their provincial offices where they could take revenge on the accusers. Even when such cases were won, a province could acquire a reputation for being litigious and suffer consequences later.[57]

Tiberius was criticized for approving the Asian request for a temple. Rumors spread about his ambitions and vanity. Two years later, in 25 CE, Hispania Ulterior requested the right to build a temple to Tiberius and his mother Livia, citing the precedent set by Asia in 23 CE. Tiberius took this opportunity to defend himself before the Senate and to set future policy for provincial worship. According to Tacitus, Tiberius defended his approval of Asia's cult for two reasons: he was following the precedent of divus Augustus, who had allowed the temple to be built in Pergamon; and he permitted Asia a second provincial temple only because the Senate had been included in the dedication. As to future policy, Tiberius announced that the proliferation of provincial temples would trivialize the worship of Augustus. Hispania's request was refused and Tiberius grew increasingly disdainful of divine homage for himself.[58]

One year after Tiberius refused the request from Hispania Ulterior, Asia's approved temple came before the Senate again. A lengthy dispute had taken place in Asia about which city would have the right to provide a site for the provincial cult. In 26 CE, the cities had to send representatives to Rome for the Senate to hear their cases. Tiberius attended the hearing, which lasted several days. Eleven cities competed for the privilege, and the record of this argument supplements our understanding of the values inherent in imperial cults.[59] Four cities—Hypaipa, Tralleis, Laodikeia, and Magnesia—were disqualified as having too little strength (*parum validi*), in part a reference to the amount of municipal wealth needed to maintain a provincial cult. Such a temple should be placed in an impressive city with symbolic resources such as Ilion, which was not among the great cities but had a Trojan heritage.[60] Representatives of Pergamon argued that their temple of Rome and Augustus made them the natural candidate for a second provincial temple, but this argument was used against them; one temple was considered to be sufficient honor for the city. Prominent temples of Artemis in Ephesos and of Apollo in Miletos likewise damaged their petitions.

In the end the choice was between Sardis and Smyrna, and these cities argued their cause on two bases: loyalty to Rome and mythic genealogies that established kinship to Rome. Sardis representatives elaborated the common origins of the Etrurian and Lydian peoples through the two sons of King Atys, documented loyalty to Rome in the Hellenistic period, and noted the natural resources of Lydia.

Smyrna's representatives also cited traditions of consanguinity but focused on the dangers the people had faced to support Roman interests both in Italy and abroad. Smyrna's arguments carried the day. The provincial cult located there confirmed the city's grandeur, its sincere loyalty to Rome, and its blood relations with the imperial rulers.

The provincial temple has not yet been located, but the structure is shown on the reverse of a bronze coin from Smyrna (fig. 2.4). The architecture is schematic, showing the front of a Corinthian temple on a stepped crepidoma. The central space in the middle of four columns was left open to depict a statue of Tiberius sacrificing. The inscription indicates that the coin was issued while Petronius was proconsul (26–35 CE). The obverse contains two busts facing each other: Livia on the right and the Senate on the left. Thus, the coin confirms the unusual dedication of the temple as recorded by Tacitus. The format of the first provincial cult at Pergamon— Rome and the emperor—was not duplicated, but the triple dedication of the temple at Smyrna did preserve the general conception of that first cult: Tiberius was not worshipped alone but only in conjunction with a representation of Roman corporate authority (the Senate) and with a dynastic connection to Augustus (Livia). The iconography of the temple statue was significant as well. In contrast to the cuirassed Augustus, Tiberius was depicted as a priest engaged in sacrificial rituals. Whereas his predecessor was remembered as a conqueror who established a new order in the realm, the emperor Tiberius was portrayed by the provincials as one who carried on a tradition in a righteous fashion.

The procedures described in the accounts of Tacitus regarding provincial temples became the standard process for such institutions. Representatives of a province voted to initiate a cult of the emperor, and this decision was sent to the Roman Senate. The senators would hear the case and deliberate. The participation of the emperor would often determine the outcome of the hearing. So, to establish a provincial cult, the provincial elite needed to assess their own capacity for carrying the project through and the chances that they could navigate the machinations of politics among the elite at the imperial center. In some instances, it was a dangerous undertaking.

FIGURE 2.4 Livia and the Roman Senate are portrayed on the obverse of a bronze coin from Smyrna. The Senate is personified as a young man (left). The reverse shows the provincial temple at Smyrna and the statue of Tiberius as a priest sacrificing. © The British Museum.

3

PROVINCIAL CULTS FROM GAIUS
TO DOMITIAN

Gaius and Miletos

Dio Cassius wrote that the emperor Gaius ordered the Asians to build him a temple at Miletos.[1] The discovery of an inscribed statue base near the southwest corner of the temple of Apollo at Didyma provides information about the organization of this cult.

> [Αὐτοκράτορα Γάϊον Κα]ίσαρα Γερμανικὸ[ν]
> [Γερμανικοῦ υἱ]ὸν θεὸν Σεβαστὸν νεοπο-
> ιοὶ οἱ πρώντως νεοποιήσαντες αὐτοῦ
> ἐπὶ ἀρχιερέως Γναίου Οὐεργιλίου Καπίτωνος
> τοῦ μὲν ἐν Μειλήτωι ναοῦ Γαίου Καίσαρος τὸ πρῶ-
> τον, τῆς δὲ Ἀσίας τὸ τρίτον, καὶ Τιβερίου Ἰουλίου,
> Δημητρίου νομοθέτου υἱοῦ, Μηνογένους, ἀρχιερέως
> τὸ δεύτερον καὶ νεωκόρου τοῦ ἐν Μειλήτωι ναοῦ, καὶ
> Πρωτομάχου τοῦ Γλύκωνος Ἰουλιέως τοῦ ἀρχινεοποι-
> οῦ καὶ σεβαστονέωι καὶ σεβαστολόγου ἐκ τῶν ἰδί-
> ων ἀνέθηκαν κτλ.[2]

His first neopoioi dedicated (the statue of) emperor Gaius Caesar Germanicus, son of Germanicus, god Sebastos, from their own funds; when Gaius Vergilius Capito was high priest of the temple of Gaius Caesar in Miletos the first time—

his third (high priesthood) of Asia;[3] and (when) Tiberius Julius Menogenes, son
of Demetrios the lawgiver, was high priest the second time and neokoros of the
temple in Miletos; and (when) Protomachos of Julia, son of Glukon, was the
leader of the neopoioi and sebastoneos and sebastologos.

The inscription confirms that this was a provincial cult of Asia: the technical phrase
"the temple in Miletos" (τοῦ ἐν Μειλήτωι ναοῦ) and the equation of the high priesthood of the temple with the high priesthood of Asia make this clear. The statue
that once stood upon this inscribed base was probably commissioned in the first
year after the establishment of the cult, before the temple was even completed.

The inscription also provides significant information about the organization
of the cult. Three eponymous officials were named: the high priest, the neokoros,
and the archineopoios (leader of the neopoioi). The neopoioi of a temple were the
members of a committee charged especially with the maintenance and administration of the sacred facilities.[4] As the inscription and statue of Gaius were commissioned by the first neopoioi, these men were probably in charge of the construction
of the temple. The neopoioi are all listed by name and by city of origin in the ten
lines that follow the translated section. There were thirteen neopoioi for this temple,
including Protomachos, their leader. Louis Robert's study of their cities of origin
led to significant findings. He showed that the cities were not randomly chosen.
Each represented a *conventus*, an administrative district of Asia.[5] Thus, the construction was overseen, and probably financed, in a way that involved all parts of the
province. The archineopoios in this instance also held two other offices; he was
sebastoneos and sebastologos. The meaning of the former term is unknown; the latter
title was analogous to the office of theologos in other cults and designated the person who delivered a formal eulogy praising the emperor.[6]

Signs suggest that this cult went beyond the acceptable in a provincial cult setting. Dio's text says the emperor ordered the temple, which, if accurate, would have
been unseemly in the middle of the first century CE. The inscription confirms the
excessive character of this cult by using θεός to refer to Gaius. Moreover, no corporate figures like Rome or the Senate were worshipped along with the emperor. After his death in 41 CE, the emperor barely escaped the *damnatio memoriae* of the
Roman Senate, and the cult would have been discontinued at that time.

Dio also commented on why Gaius chose Miletos for a provincial temple: "The
reason he [Gaius] gave for choosing this city was that Artemis had preempted
Ephesos, Augustus Pergamon, and Tiberius Smyrna; but the truth of the matter was
that he desired to appropriate to his own use the large and exceedingly beautiful
temple which the Milesians were building to Apollo."[7] This text has led several scholars to conclude that Gaius wanted to appropriate the temple of Apollo at Didyma
for his provincial cult. B. Haussoullier first argued that Gaius ordered the province
to build a magnificent temple for him. As the Milesians were already rebuilding the
Didymeion for Apollo, Gaius had the koinon supply the necessary funds for the
project so that Apollo's temple could be used for the provincial imperial cult. According to Haussoullier, it is unclear whether Gaius wanted to be enthroned there
with Apollo or wanted to take over the precincts for himself. When Gaius died, the
province and the city dropped the unfinished project, which was no longer feasible

or desirable.[8] This scenario developed before the discovery of the Gaius inscription noted previously. With the publication of the inscription, Haussollier's hypothesis went into remission because of the references to the temple in Miletos (rather than Didyma).

Peter Herrmann has recently sought to revive the theory, pointing out that Didyma was within the territorial limits of Miletos, even though it was outside the urbanized center, and reviewing the circumstantial evidence of provincial involvement in the Didymeion rebuilding effort. His scenario was similar to that of Haussoullier: Gaius ordered the temple for himself; a small provisional temenos was established at Didyma, composed perhaps of only an altar in a designated area; and renovations were carried out to turn the Didymeion into a provincial temple.[9]

Although the Didymeion could have been designated as a provincial temple for Gaius, more likely it was not. Suetonius, who was a century closer to the events than Dio, noted that Gaius helped rebuild the Didymeion but did not accuse him of trying to take over the precincts, even though this would have suited Suetonius's polemical aims.[10] The inscription commissioned during the reign of Gaius by the official representatives involved in the project specifically mentions a temple (ναός, not τέμενος) of Gaius in Miletos. The reference to Miletos rather than Didyma is not the main problem in the phrase. This phrase must refer either to the alleged temporary temple (if so, we have to imagine an extra provincial temple built somewhere for Gaius) or to the Didymeion (if so, the venerable sanctuary of Apollo had already been completely coopted by Gaius). Neither of these situations is probable. More likely Gaius ordered a provincial temple for himself to be built in Miletos, but the Didymeion was not used for these purposes. Because he provided assistance for the rebuilding of the Didymeion, there may have been speculation that he hoped to be enthroned with Apollo just as he had requested to have his statue set up in the temple of YHWH at Jerusalem.[11] Dio either believed such speculation, reached the same conclusion on his own, or was simply confused about the actual events.

The short-lived provincial cult for Gaius provides a rare example of an imperial cult that failed. Financial resources and provincial organization were not the problem. The signs of exaggerated piety (i.e., the emperor's demand for a temple and the use of θεός) were unusual for a provincial cult but acceptable in municipal institutions. Because this third provincial temple was ordered within 15 years after Asia's second provincial temple was assigned to Smyrna, suspicions may have arisen among the imperial elite in Rome, especially as no other province had two such cults at that time. The cult was not viable because it was tied so closely to a single figure, who reigned briefly, was immediately discredited, and ultimately did not deserve such an honor.

Reorganizations

Two major developments took place in the provincial worship of Asia after the approval for the provincial temple at Smyrna in 23 CE and before the year 60 CE. First, the title "high priest of Asia" (ἀρχιερεὺς Ἀσίας) emerged.[12] Most secondary literature on imperial cults uses high priest of Asia as a generic term for the provincial high priesthoods of the province. If the hundreds of references to these officials are placed in chronological order, a different picture emerges. When Asia's first provincial cult was established in Pergamon, the main sacrificial official was called the high priest of Rome and Augustus in accordance with the dedication of that temple,[13] or simply the "high priest" in official documents and coins of the koinon, where the reference would have been clear.[14]

The first datable attestation of the title "high priest of Asia" comes from around 40 CE, found in the Miletos inscription for the statue of Gaius translated at the beginning of this chapter. There, Capito was said to be serving a third time as high priest of Asia. A damaged example of the title comes from 41 CE[15] and another is known from 44 CE.[16] After this, high priest of Asia becomes standard nomenclature for this provincial office.[17] The title is even used for the high priests of the temple in Pergamon, who were formerly called high priests of Rome and Augustus.[18]

The reason for this shift can be surmised, though there is no explicit proof. When Asia received the right to build a second provincial temple, several practical problems arose. First, "high priest of Tiberius, Livia, and the Senate" would be an awkward title for general use. More important, there were now two annual high priesthoods to fill, and there would have been questions of relative status between them. Should the high priesthood of the living emperor be ranked higher or lower than that of the deceased Augustus? Which of the two cities involved would admit to a less important temple? How would Tiberius, Livia, or the Senate be viewed in later decades? The solution seems to have been to adopt the title high priest of Asia for both provincial cults, thereby creating an equivalent ranking between the temples at Pergamon and Smyrna while minimizing the possibility of future embarrassments.

The new terminology signified an important shift in meaning. The high priesthoods were no longer identified by the object of worship but rather by those offering worship. The public rhetoric of the most prestigious imperial cult offices thus came to be framed in terms of the province's role. This process would have been inappropriate in the early Augustan period, during the subjection of the province to its new ruler. With the routinization of the relationship and the stabilization of foreign control over the course of 50 years, an assertion of provincial identity was no longer threatening because Asia was now firmly incorporated within the framework of the Roman imperial system.

Moreover, the new title avoided the need to identify individual rulers, a trend identified both for local imperial cults[19] and for the general phenomenon of emperor worship in the post-Augustan period.[20] The title thus lent itself to a corporate understanding of provincial worship and implied a more developed administration of the institutions. We do not have enough information left from the first century CE to determine whether this was the intention or the result of the new terminology, and it is not necessary to decide. The new title both reflected and shaped an evolving socioreligious phenomenon.

A second important development occurred in Asia's provincial worship during the second quarter of the first century CE: women began to serve for the first time as high priestesses of Asia. An inscription from Magnesia preserves the name of the woman and allows us to ascertain an approximate date. The inscription was dedicated by the boule and the demos of the Magnesians in honor of Juliane. Several of her offices were listed but the enumeration began with ἀρ[χιέ]ρειαν γε[νομένην] τῆς ᾿Ασία[ς πρ]ώτην τῶ[ν γυναικῶν] κτλ., "who first among women was high priestess of Asia."[21] Although the inscription is badly damaged, the restored text is quite defensible.[22] Juliane was the first high priestess in Asia's provincial imperial cults and quite probably the first high priestess in any provincial cult of the empire.

An approximate date for the inscription can be determined from one of the offices Juliane held. She was a stephanephoros, gymnasiarch, priestess of Aphrodite and of goddess Agrippina the mother for life,[23] as well as priestess of Demeter in Ephesos for life. The lacunae are more serious here, but the reference to Agrippina the mother is reliable, so the inscription could have been made only in two periods. Agrippina the elder was on bad terms with Tiberius, who had her arrested in 29 CE and banished to Pandateria, where she starved to death in 33. She was survived by three daughters and her son Gaius, who succeeded Tiberius as emperor. So one possible date for a cult for Agrippina the mother would be 37–41, during the reign of Gaius.[24] The priesthood could also refer to Agrippina the younger, however, the daughter of the elder Agrippina and the sister of Gaius. Agrippina the younger married the emperor Claudius in 49 and persuaded him to adopt her son Nero. She may have been involved in the poisoning of Claudius, which allowed Nero to ascend to the throne. So a cult for Agrippina the younger as imperial mother would be possible between 54 (Nero's ascension to the throne) and 59, when the emperor had her assassinated.[25]

Thus the date of service for the first provincial high priestess was clearly in the middle of the first century CE, sometime between 37 and 59. The precise significance of the participation of high priestesses in the provincial imperial cults, however, is debatable. Earlier writers assumed that "high priestess of Asia" was an honorary title awarded to wives of high priests and that it involved no actual participation in the sacrificial rituals.[26] More recently, scholars have agreed that high priestesses were participants in the provincial rituals, and the debate has focused on the nature of their participation: did these women serve alone[27] or only with a male relative?[28]

This complex issue does not need to be resolved for the purposes of this study.[29] Two points are relevant here. First, the appearance of high priestesses in the epigraphic evidence confirms that the provincial imperial cults were dynamic institutions that changed over time. Second, this change in the nature of the high priesthoods demonstrates that the provincial cults were one method for gender definition in public culture; imperial cults played a role in the process of gender construction in the first century. This second point reminds us that the provincial imperial cults were involved in the definition of personhood, Sullivan's third cornerstone of the religious life. The provincial cult materials deal especially with cosmology and, to a lesser extent, with cosmogony, whereas the definition of personhood is more pronounced in the imperial cult activities of groups. However, the meaning of human maturation is a consideration at the provincial level as well and should not be ignored.

The Temple of the Sebastoi at Ephesos

In contrast to the earlier provincial temples, the one established at Ephesos in the late first century CE is not mentioned in extant writings of the Roman historians. It is, however, the only temple of the three whose remains have been identified. Enough archaeological evidence has accumulated to provide a wealth of information about the building and the related institutions.

Thirteen inscriptions from the dedication of this temple have been discovered. The inscriptions were commissioned by cities from throughout the province and represent a much larger number of statue bases originally set up in the temple precincts by the cities of Asia.[30] All thirteen have similar texts, which appear in two variations depending on the status of the city. The formula for the subject cities began with a dedication to "Emperor Domitian Caesar Sebastos Germanicus." Then followed the name of the proconsul, the name of the demos that raised the statue, a reference to the temple, the benefactor who provided the statue on behalf of the city, and the name of the provincial high priest.[31] The free cities followed the same format but added a statement about their status after the city name, a statement about their relationship to Ephesos after the name of the temple, and the verb ἀνέστησαν ("erected") after the statement about Ephesos.[32]

The base commissioned by the city of Aphrodisias provides an example of the longer variant (fig. 3.1).

> Αὐτοκράτορι [[Δομι-]]
> [[τιανῶι]] Καίσαρι Σε-
> βαστῶι [[Γερμανικῶι]]
> ἐπὶ ἀνθυπάτου Μάρκ[ου]
> Φουλουίου Γίλλωνο[ς]
> ὁ φιλοκαῖσαρ Ἀφροδεισι[έων]
> δῆμος ἐλεύθερος ὢν κα[ὶ αὐ-]
> τόνομος ἀπ᾽ ἀρχῆς τῆι τῶν Σε[βασ-]
> τῶν χάριτι ναῶι τῶι ἐν Ἐφέσ[ωι]
> τῶν Σεβαστῶν κοινῶι τῆς Ἀσί[ας]
> ἰδίᾳ χάριτι διά τε τὴν πρὸς τοὺς [Σε-]
> βαστοὺς εὐσέβειαν καὶ τὴν π[ρὸς]
> τὴν νεωκόρον Ἐφεσίων [πό-]
> λιν εὔνοιαν ἀνέστησαν
> ἐπιμεληθέντος Ἀρίστω[νος τοῦ]
> Ἀρτεμιδώρου τοῦ Καλλι [ ]
> ως ἱερέως Πλούτωνος [καὶ]
> Κόρης καὶ νεοποιοῦ θεᾶ[ς]
> Ἀφροδείτης, ἐπὶ ἀρχιερ[έως]
> τῆς Ἀσίας Τιβερίου Κλαυδ[ίου]
> Φησείνου [[   ]]
> [[   ]]
> [[   ]]
> [[   ]][33]

To Emperor [[Domitian]] Caesar Sebastos [[Germanicus]]. When Marcus Fulvius Gillo was proconsul. The demos of the Aphrodisians, devoted to Caesar, being free and autonomous from the beginning by the grace of the Sebastoi, erected (this statue) by their own grace on the occasion of (the dedication of)[34]

FIGURE 3.1 Statue base with inscription for the Temple of the Sebastoi, dedicated by the Aphrodisians. The top stone with angled sides is from a different, unrelated statue base. Author's photo.

Asia's common temple of the Sebastoi in Ephesos, because of reverence toward the Sebastoi and (because of) goodwill toward the neokoros city of the Ephesians. Supervised by Arist[ion son of] Artemidoros son of Kalli[. . .], priest of Pluto and Kore and neopoios of the goddess Aphrodite, when Tiberius Claudius Pheseinos was high priest of Asia [[erasure]]

Several important facts can be gleaned from this group of inscriptions. The texts provide us with the full official name of the temple: Asia's common temple of the

Sebastoi in Ephesos. The inscriptions also allow us to date the dedication of the temple precisely to the year 89/90 during the reign of Domitian.[35] Moreover, the terminology shows that the exaggerated piety of the aborted cult of Gaius at Miletos was avoided. The term *theos* was not used for the reigning emperor, nor was the cult focused on one individual.

The temple of the Sebastoi at Ephesos was innovative in its own way. The cult differed from Asia's first two provincial cults because it did not include the corporate figures of Rome or the Senate. Instead, the "Sebastoi" were venerated, and the cult focused only on the imperial family rather than on another corporate object of veneration. So the third successful provincial temple instituted changes in its cultic format, but it maintained continuity with provincial cult expectations through its worship of the collective "Sebastoi" and by its standard language of divinization.

The inscriptions do not inform us of the specific Sebastoi who were venerated, but they allow us to draw some reasonable inferences. Domitian would obviously have been included. His wife, Domitia, could possibly have been worshipped alongside him: they were paired in at least one local cult from Tmolos;[36] she was honored as the New Hera at Stratonikeia;[37] and she appeared on an Ephesian coin of this period.[38] Domitian's brother and predecessor emperor, Titus (79–81 CE), was certainly included because fragments of his temple statue have been found.[39] The inclusion of Domitian's father, Vespasian (69–79 CE), is almost certain, though the evidence is circumstantial. As the first emperor to have his biological sons ascend to the throne,[40] Vespasian was a much more important figure than Titus. This supposition is confirmed by the erasures in these inscriptions. After the assassination of Domitian in 96 CE, the Senate condemned his memory and ordered that his name be removed from public documents. The personal names Domitian and Germanicus were chiseled off of the statue bases in the precincts of the temple of the Sebastoi, and on several bases the dedication was changed to read, "To Emperor *God* Caesar Sebastos *Vespasian*," rather than the original, "To Emperor *Domitian* Caesar Sebastos *Germanicus*." The Julio-Claudian emperors would not have been among those to whom the temple was dedicated: Augustus and Tiberius were already venerated in provincial cults of Asia, Nero and Gaius were unacceptable, and Claudius was too insignificant to be added some 35 years after his death.

So the cult certainly included Domitian and Titus and likely Vespasian as well. Domitia is a strong possibility, whereas other Flavian women remain theoretical possibilities. None of these people appears in the official name of the temple, however. The temple was designed to be appropriate for the long term, and this aspect of the institution served it well. After Domitian's death, the temple continued to function. The dedications to Domitian were excised from the public record and often replaced with dedications to the god Vespasian. Domitian's image would have been removed from the temple as well. With these minor modifications, the provincial temple at Ephesos continued to be a sacred site and a source of honor for both the city and the province. The image of the temple was displayed on Ephesian coins well into the third century CE (fig. 3.2).[41]

The language of the inscriptions shows that this provincial cult gave rise to discussions about the relationships of the cities under Roman imperialism. So it was

FIGURE 3.2 The reverse of this Ephesian coin from the third century shows the provincial Temple of the Sebastoi (right?), the Temple of Artemis (center), and the Temple of Hadrian (left?). *BM Ionia* 83 #261. © The British Museum.

a cosmological event, an opportunity to delineate and redefine the meaningful order of life in Roman Asia. The inscriptions constructed the following hierarchy, beginning at the top: the Sebastoi, Asia, the free cities, and the subject cities, with a reference to the proconsul as a mediating figure between the emperors and the province. All the cities were part of Asia; together they established a temple to the Sebastoi in Ephesos. So this provincial cult established both the corporate unity of the cities and their religious relationship to the imperial dynasty. Within Asia, the distinction between free cities and subject cities was confirmed.

The stilted language in the midsection of the inscription also reflects a more specific debate about the relationships of Ephesos and the other free cities. The earlier contention over which city would be awarded the second provincial cult that eventually went to Smyrna in 26 CE showed that the major cities considered such a temple to be a great honor. With the award of the third temple to Ephesos, the other free cities tried to mitigate the advantage gained by the Ephesians. This struggle is evident in the inscription's use of the language of benefaction. The free cities asserted that their rights and autonomy were granted directly from the emperors through imperial grace and then cast themselves as the benefactors of Ephesos in two ways. First, they asserted that they had awarded the temple to Ephesos by their own grace, thus comparing themselves to the emperors.

Second, the free cities employed traditional reverence/goodwill terminology of benefaction in their effort to subordinate the Ephesians. The two terms occur often in the epigraphic record of western Asia Minor with standard general meanings. Reverence (εὐσέβεια) was the proper attitude one displayed toward superiors, especially toward divine beings, who had acted graciously on one's behalf. Goodwill (εὔνοια), on the other hand, was the gracious attitude one manifested toward those in an inferior position.[42] Thus, the other free cities tried to place Ephesos in their debt by claiming that they had bestowed the temple on the city. Ephesos was to be the neokoros—merely the caretaker—for Asia's temple.

The strategy of the free cities was ultimately unsuccessful. The word neokoros appears for the first time as a title for a city with a provincial imperial cult temple in these inscriptions, and it is the last known attempt to use the title to downplay the importance of such a city. The Ephesians began to use neokoros as a title of honor

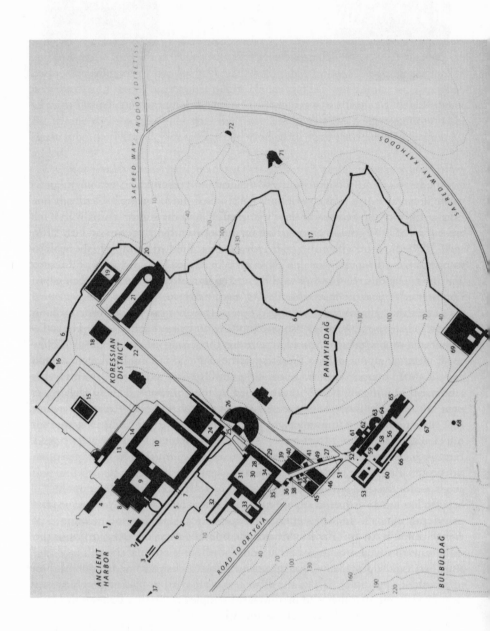

1–3 Harbor Gates
4 Warehouses
5 Street of Acadius
6 Byzantine city wall
7 Monument of the Four Evangelists
8 Harbor Baths/Baths of the Emperor
9 Harbor Baths/Gymnasium of the Emperor
10 Xystos of the Harbor Baths
13 Church of Mary
14 Southern stoa of the Olympieion
15 Temple of Hadrian Olympios/Olympieion
16 "Felsspalttempel"
17 Hellenistic city wall
19 Vedius Gymnasium
20 Northern gate
21 Stadium
22 Late antique fountain
24 Theater Gymnasium
25 Theater plaza
26 Theater

27 Embolos/Curetes Street
28 Neronic hall
29 Marble Street
30 Tetragonos Agora
31 West gate of Tetragonos Agora
32 Street from the west gate of the Tetragonos Agora
33 Sarapeion
34 Gate of Mazaeus and Mithridates
35 Library of Celsus
36 Altar of Artemis at the Triodos
37 Harbor excavation (500 m)
38 Gate of Hadrian
39 Latrine
40 Baths of Varius/Scholastikia Baths
41 So-called Temple of Hadrian
43 Heroon of Androklos
44 Heroon of Arsinoë IV/Octagon
45 Slope House 2
46 Slope House 1
49 Fountain of Trajan
51 Gate of Herakles

52 Memmius Monument
53 Temple of the Sebastoi
56 Upper Agora
58 Agora temple
59 Pollio Fountain
60 Fountain of C. Laecanius Bassus/Hydrekdocheion
61 Prytaneion
62 Double foundation
63 Bouleuterion
64 Basilica
65 Upper Gymnasium
66 Surge tank of Marnas Aqueduct/monumental fountain
67 Fountain on the road to the Magnesian Gate
68 So-called Tomb of Luke
69 East Gymnasium
70 Magnesian Gate
71 Shrine of the Seven Sleepers
72 Kybele sanctuary

FIGURE 3.3 Plan of the city of Ephesos. © 1995 by the President and Fellows of Harvard College. Reprinted by permission.

in their own civic inscriptions. Smyrna and Pergamon soon adopted the title for themselves on the basis of their older provincial temples.[43] In the second and third centuries, the term spread throughout the eastern Mediterranean as the coveted title of any city with a provincial imperial cult temple.[44] In the imperial setting of the late first century, the rhetoric of freedom and autonomy was becoming anachronistic. Free city status had been important in the Hellenistic ebb and flow of contesting regional powers.[45] Under the empire, it became increasingly problematic—an obstacle to good administration, as one emperor so innocuously described it.[46] Neokoros proved a better metaphor for an age of imperialism, providing degrees of honorable subjection and religious devotion.

Architectural and sculptural evidence adds to our understanding of the provincial cult of the Sebastoi at Ephesos. Excavators were examining an area near the Ephesian upper agora in 1930 in hopes of finding the site of the Parthian monument when they began to unearth the remains of a cella (figs. 3.4–3.6). It soon became clear that they had found the ruins of a medium-sized temple whose precincts were set atop an artificial terrace (85.6 × 64.6 m.) on the slopes of Mt. Korresos.[47] The temple was similar in broad outline to the images of earlier provincial temples in Asia known from coins: a Greek-style temple on a multistep crepidoma set near the middle of the precincts. In the Ephesian case, the temple was a tetraprostyle with a pseudodipteral colonnade (8 × 13 columns) on a six-step crepidoma. The interior measurements of the cella were approximately 7.5 × 13 m. The architectural order used for the temple is not known because few fragments of the superstructure have survived. The Corinthian order was normally used for such a temple in this region during the first century, but coin images of the temple appear to employ the Ionic order. Bluma Trell suggested that the Ionic order was simply a numismatic convention for temples on the Ephesian coins, caused by assimilation to the Ionic order of the Artemision, which was also portrayed on these coins.[48]

Underneath the terrace in a barrel-vault cryptoporticus, excavators found portions of one of the temple statues.[49] The extant fragments include a colossal head, the left forearm, and the left big toe (fig. 3.7). The original excavators identified the head as that of Domitian,[50] but a later monograph on Flavian portraiture showed that the head represented his older brother, Titus.[51] The identification was hampered because of the huge dimensions, which may have caused some distortion in the features,[52] and because the regional style did not imitate the standard imperial portrait types.[53] The head fragment measures 1.18 m. high; from chin to crown 0.74 m. The left forearm is approximately 1.8 m. long from elbow to knuckles. The left hand was clenched around a staff or spear, suggesting a military pose reminiscent of the statue of Augustus from Asia's temple at Pergamon.

The provincial temple was given a prominent location in the city. The precincts were located on an artificial terrace that provided a flat area above the slope of Mt. Koressos. The south side of the temple terrace was close to ground level, but the north side was raised approximately 10.4 m. above the descending slope, providing an opportunity for the construction of a monumental facade—a three-story stoa overlooking a plaza. The first story was executed in the Doric order. Behind the hall at this level was a series of small shops and a monumental stairwell ascending to

FIGURE 3.4 Model of the Temple of the Sebastoi at Ephesos. © The Kunsthistorisches Museum, Vienna.

the precincts above. The second story of the stoa was ornamented with engaged figures of deities on the columns, and the third story was probably Corinthian.[54] Only two of the engaged figures are preserved, and these have been reinstalled on a reerected portion of the facade (fig. 3.8). The extant statues depict Isis and Attis, so some have suggested that the second story facade was outfitted exclusively in eastern deities.[55] As there were originally 35–40 figures along the north facade, a wide variety of gods and goddesses probably were represented here.[56] Even though very little of this facade is preserved, this pantheon of deities clearly would have made a powerful im-

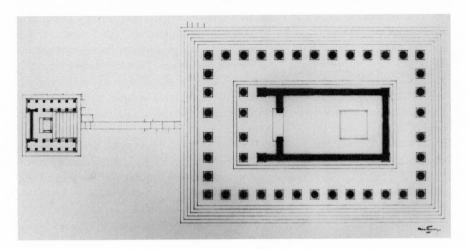

FIGURE 3.5 Reconstructed plan of the Temple of the Sebastoi. © The Österreichisches Archäologisches Institut, Vienna.

FIGURE 3.6 Temple of the Sebastoi, overview of precincts. Author's photo.

pression on the viewer, who would have perceived the unity of the empire and the divine support of the Sebastoi.

An annual festival probably coincided with the major sacrifices at the temple of the Sebastoi including competitions in athletics, music, drama, poetry, or other skills. The modern secondary literature normally assumes that Asia's provincial games, the κοινὰ Ἀσίας, were athletic events connected with the provincial cults of the emperors. Luigi Moretti challenged this assumption with convincing arguments, showing that Smyrna claimed to be the first to hold such games, even though it was not the first in Asia to have a provincial cult.[57] He also demonstrated that some cities held games called κοινὰ Ἀσίας long before those cities had provincial cults.[58]

For the provincial cult at Ephesos, evidence suggests that the city initiated its own municipal Olympic games in honor of Domitian as Zeus Olympios. The amount of data is small but convincing. An inscription from Iasos listed the numerous victories of the athlete Titus Flavius Metrobius,[59] among them a victory in the Ephesian Olympics. On the basis of another inscription about Metrobius, Moretti was able to date the reference to the Ephesian Olympics to about 90 CE.[60] Such games would have been discontinued after Domitian's death, so no other references to such games appear for about the next 35 years. Late in Hadrian's reign (i.e., around 125 CE) references to Ephesian Olympics reappear and accumulate rapidly (over 30 have been found). This evidence has led to the conclusion that the games were reinstituted at the beginning of the second quarter of the second century, this time to honor Hadrian Zeus Olympios.[61]

Provincial Worship in Roman Asia

The Temple of the Sebastoi finishes this survey because Asia's next temple signaled a turning point in provincial worship. That temple in Pergamon was granted by

FIGURE 3.7 Head and arm from the statue
of Titus, Temple of the Sebastoi. Courtesy of
the Efes Müzezi, Selçuk.

Trajan late in his reign around 113 CE. The format of the cult is not definitely known
because the evidence is incomplete: inscriptions and statue fragments suggest that
the cult was probably established for Trajan and Zeus Philios, but Hadrian appears
to have been included as well.[62] Whatever the format of the cult, the establishment
of a second provincial temple in Pergamon was a clear innovation that set the stage
for multiple provincial cults in major cities and for the proliferation of such institutions under the emperor Hadrian.[63]

During the period examined here, however, provincial cults in Asia operated
within other parameters. Within the specific historical context, these cults are important components of an evolving imperial discourse. The discourse defined relationships between the imperial center and the peripheral areas in a way that was
continually changing to meet new challenges. The provincial temples exemplify this
discursive trajectory. At Pergamon at the beginning of the empire, Augustus was
portrayed as the conqueror with Rome as his base of authority. At Smyrna some
50 years later, the emperor Tiberius was portrayed as the successor who maintained
justice within the imperial framework. The cult emphasized continuity by including Livia, the imperial mother, and the Roman Senate. The provincial cult of Gaius
at Miletos transgressed the boundaries of acceptability, as did the emperor himself,
and like him the cult was shortlived. By the late first century CE, expectations for a
provincial cult had changed so that there was no longer any need to include the Senate

FIGURE 3.8 Reerected north facade
fragments with engaged statues of
Attis (left) and Isis, Temple of
Sebastoi terrace. Author's photo.

or Rome in the cultic format; a dedication to the collective Sebastoi at Ephesos was
appropriate, though unacceptable a century earlier.

Even though Asia had three provincial cults by the end of the first century CE,
they were still rare compared to other forms of imperial cults. Asia's provincial cults
particularly dealt with cosmology: the maintenance and nourishment of the
province's relationship with Rome and with the centers of authority within the
imperial city. Because the provincial imperial cults were most clearly directed toward Rome, they were necessarily the most restricted of imperial cults. The number of the provincial cults, the language, the formats, and the procedures for establishing them all depended on Roman authority in a way that was not true for other
imperial cult institutions. Only the wealthiest members of the provincial elite could
fill the offices in such cults, and only a relatively small percentage of the province's
population would have attended the festivals. Such selectivity heightened the importance of these institutions and underscored a particular view of the world.

One result was a reordering of spatial imagination: in the new imperial geography, space centered on Rome. Another result was a temporal reorganization: meaningful time should be calculated by the actions of the Roman emperors. The calendar reform of the Augustan period was probably not very effective in this regard,

though it had great symbolic importance. The regular festivals of the provincial cults were probably much more influential in the life of the province because they created a cycle of annual competitions and festivity that marked the passage of time in imperial Asia.

In this process, the provincial cults also established a new provincial discourse that dealt with regional (rather than strictly imperial) issues. Cities found new ways to compete with each other within the imposed structures of Roman imperialism, seeking favorable positions within the imperial hierarchies. This civic competition could be quite contentious, but imperial cults provided one venue in which such problems could be negotiated and (temporarily) resolved. Roman imperial authority allowed these tensions to surface and also provided a framework within which they could be addressed.[64]

One of the most significant developments in the provincial cults of Asia was the emergence of the term neokoros in the late first century CE to describe a city with a provincial imperial cult temple. We can infer that the term became so prominent so quickly throughout the eastern Mediterranean because the metaphor expressed a fundamental aspect of urban life under Roman rule at that time, for neokoros—a caretaker of a temple of the Sebastoi—became the most coveted civic title. The worship of the emperors was becoming one of the most important characteristics of civic and municipal identity.

In these and other ways, provincial cults created, maintained, and refined meaningful order in the world. Although there were other functions of these institutions, the provincial temples served as crucial symbols of the cosmology that supported imperial rule, that defined the evolving identity of the province, and that promoted provincial obedience at various levels of society.

4

MUNICIPAL IMPERIAL CULTS

A Survey

When we move from the provincial to the municipal imperial cults, new difficulties appear. It is not always easy or desirable to disentangle provincial and municipal worship, so this chapter begins by explaining how these categories overlap. Another difficulty arises in extant documentation: even though there were many more municipal cults of the emperors, less information is available. This suggests that we are dealing with an aspect of imperial worship that operated within a different level of society with a distinguishable function. To handle the episodic nature of the evidence, I survey the contexts in which municipal worship is known to have occurred. In the next chapter I focus on two particularly well-documented cases of municipal worship from Aphrodisias and Ephesos to add depth to the survey.

Municipal Involvement in Provincial Worship

Municipal imperial cults were distinguishable from provincial cults in form and procedure, but the demarcation between municipal and provincial responsibilities was not nearly so clear. The categories aid comparisons but should not obscure the complexities of the topic. Moreover, I do not wish to specify every detail of municipal cults. I am more interested in the social groups that participated in these cults and how these cults structured social intercourse. So let us begin by blurring the categories.

In the previous two chapters several forms of municipal participation in provincial cults already surfaced. Every provincial temple needed a neokoros every year who would assist with the costs for maintaining the facilities. Thus, the pattern appears to have been that neokoroi lived in the city in which the provincial temple was located. For example, the inscription to G. Julius Sacerdos, discussed in chapter 2 called him the neokoros of the goddess Rome and of the god Augustus Caesar.[1] The scope of the inscription, as well as the offices that he held, suggests that the neokoria was a municipal liturgy. Another neokoros is attested for the provincial cult of Gaius in Miletos (discussed in chapter 3), even though the institution could not have functioned more than two or three years. This neokoros, Ti. Julius Menogenes, was probably a Milesian, for only he and the Milesian Capito are listed without their cities of origin; the other 13 provincials named in the text are all identified by the cities where they lived.[2] We also know that the prominent Ephesian Ti. Cl. Aristio was the neokoros of the Temple of the Sebastoi in the year after it was dedicated in his city.[3] Because few references to neokoroi of provincial temples have survived, we may surmise that it was not as prestigious an office as the provincial high priesthoods.

The athletic games established in Pergamon for the provincial Temple of Rome and Augustus required several officials, some of whom undertook their responsibilities on behalf of their city. The gymnasiarch was almost certainly a municipal responsibility. As noted in chapter 2, the reference to Sacerdos as neokoros of Rome and Augustus came in the context of honoring him for his service as gymnasiarch.[4] Again, there are few references to this office, suggesting it was less prestigious than the provincial high priesthoods.

The agonothesia for the games of Rome and Augustus was probably within the jurisdiction of the koinon. As I argue in chapter 2, the office was not simply one aspect of the provincial high priesthood, as some have suggested,[5] but rather a separate office, as the two have different terms. A list of decrees inscribed and displayed in Sardis from 5–2 BCE include official documents from Augustus, from the koinon of Asia, and from the city of Sardis.[6] The four koinon documents name the four high priests of Rome and Augustus from these years. Three of them were called "the high priest of goddess Rome and of Emperor Caesar Augustus, son of god," and one was also "agonothete for life of the great Augustan Caesareia [i.e., games in honor of Caesar] of goddess Rome and of Emperor Caesar Augustus, son of god."[7] This particular agonothete was from Thyatira. The other high priest and agonothete for life of the provincial temple in Pergamon known from this period was from Sardis.[8] So the agonothesia was a provincial office.

Provincial institutions offered other opportunities for the participation of cities and municipal elites. A dramatic example comes from the Temple of the Sebastoi at Ephesos. The surviving inscriptions from the dedication of this temple were set up by various cities of the province.[9] We can assume that many more such statue bases once graced the precincts of this provincial imperial temple. The inscriptions follow the same text until near the end, where each city names municipal benefactors who paid for their statues.[10] This feature provides us with a sample of a group of men from the municipal elites who facilitated the contributions of cities to the provincial imperial cult. The information is summarized in table 4.1.

TABLE 4.1 Municipal benefactors known from the inscriptions for the provincial temple at Ephesos

Individuals	Other service or honors listed	City	Bibliography
1 Cl. Menandros	first archon	Aizanoi	*IvE* 2.232, 232a (exact copies)
2 Aristo[ ] son of Artemidoros	priest of Pluto and Kore; neopoios of the goddess Aphrodite	Aphrodisias	*IvE* 2.233
3 Glykon son of Agathokleos	ἐργεπιστάτης (superintendent of public works)	Keretapa	*IvE* 2.234
4 Ti. Cl. Quirina Charmos, son of Kleandros	strategos	Klazomenai	*IvE* 2.235
5 T. Fl. Quirina Praxeos, son of Hermongenes	first archon; priest for life (from coin)	Philadelphia	*IvE* 2.236 *Münsterberg* 145
6 M. Cl. Agrippa	strategos	Silandos	*IvE* 2.238
7 [ ]	[ἀργυρ]οταμίας (city treasurer)	Teos	*IvE* 2.239 *BullÉp* (1967) 506
8 [ ]	[ ]archon[ ]	Kyme	*IvE* 2.240
9 Aulus Livius Agron	grammateus of the demos; financial officer (ταμίας) of the boule; son of the boule; priest and neokoros of [[Domitian]] Caesar and Domitia Sebaste and of their house and of the Senate for life	Tmolos	*IvE* 2.241
10 Athenagoras Lysimachos Boutos?		Tmolos	*IvE* 2.241
11 Lo[ ]	[a]rchon[ ]	[ ]	*IvE* 2.242
12 Timotheos son of Timotheos	archon	Caesarea Makedones Hyrkanioi	*IvE* 5.1498
13 Metrodoros son of Metrodoros	archon	Caesarea Makedones Hyrkanioi	*IvE* 5.1498
14 Menophilos son of Apollonios		Caesarea Makedones Hyrkanioi	*IvE* 5.1498
15 Menogenes son of Metrophanos/es?		Caesarea Makedones Hyrkanioi	*IvE* 5.1498
16 Menekrates son of Iucundus		Caesarea Makedones Hyrkanioi	*IvE* 5.1498
17 Phil[ ]	[ ]	Synaos	*IvE* 6.2048

The inscriptions yield a catalogue of 17 individuals, all men, who made it possible for their cities to participate in the provincial cult dedicated at Ephesos in the late first century CE. The names of 12 of them are completely preserved and 1 more is mostly intact. Two names are unknown due to lacunae, and two more are extremely fragmentary. Of the 17, it is clear that 5 were Roman citizens and 8 were not; the citizenship of 4 is uncertain. The inscriptions provide information on high municipal magistracies held by at least nine (and perhaps two more) of the men. The group of men included a grammateus of the demos, four archons (and perhaps two more), a strategos, a city treasurer, and a superintendent of public works. Two others are recorded with titles from offices related to temples and one other man (#5) is attested elsewhere as holding a priesthood. None of the men is said to have held a provincial high priesthood nor are any Asiarchs listed.[11] Although the individuals named here likely held other municipal offices that were not recorded, regional offices would probably not have been omitted in texts for this important provincial setting.

The resulting picture is fairly clear. The major public players were male members of municipal elites: men from the stratum of wealthy families who ran municipal institutions but whose influence did not extend far into regional, provincial, or imperial affairs. These particular donations on behalf of their cities were not especially expensive—a statue or two upon an inscribed base, sometimes financed jointly by two or three families. In return, their names were recorded on small monuments in the precincts of a provincial temple. Their history of municipal service and their local networks of personal connections gave them the opportunity to integrate their cities into the province's worship of the Roman emperors.

Municipal Imperial Cults in Temple Contexts

The preceding section demonstrates that "municipal" and "provincial" are not completely exclusive categories for the analysis of imperial cults. Certain offices and certain individuals connected these levels of organization. Clear distinctions between the categories also need to be recognized. The most obvious distinction involves procedure. Provincial cults were established through a particular process: the provincial council made its request to the Roman Senate, the Senate assessed the request and the preferences of the emperor, and a decision was rendered. An approval sometimes required modifications of the original proposal. The process was heavily influenced by the emperor and required the province to navigate a tangle of alliances and animosities within the imperial elite in Rome.

Municipal cults were not subject to this procedure. They could be instituted by local initiative and were funded from local sources. The city might send notification or even an embassy to Rome to announce the establishment of a temple, but this was not a requirement.[12] An inscription from Mytilene suggests that sending notices to other cities as well was not unusual.[13] The inscription announced the founding of games, sacrifices, and other honors for Augustus at Mytilene and was to be displayed in several major cities, including Pergamon, Actium, Brundisium, Tarraco, and Antioch on the Orantes.[14] The people of Mytilene also hoped to be allowed to display the text in Rome on wooden plaques in the house of Augustus and in the temple of Jupiter Capitolinus.

The career of Aulus Livius Agron, the ninth entry on table 4.1, takes us directly into the arena of municipal imperial worship. Along with his numerous civic duties and honors, he was also a prominent supporter of a local imperial cult at Tmolos. He served as priest and neokoros for life of an imperial cult established within the previous 10 years, during Domitian's reign. His titles reveal the format of the cult: ἱερέως καὶ νεωκόρου [[Δομιτιανοῦ]] Καίσαρο[ς] καὶ Δομιτίας Σεβαστῆς καὶ τοῦ οἴκου αὐτῶν καὶ τῆς συνκλήτου διὰ βίο[υ] κτλ., "priest and neokoros of [[Domitian]] Caesar and Domitia Sebaste and of their house and of the Senate for life."[15] The municipal temple included the range of important Roman figures: the emperor, his wife, their whole household, and the Senate.[16]

The erasure indicates the nature of this particular cult. When Domitian's name was banished from public memory after his assassination, only his personal name was removed from this phrase. The stoneworker who removed Domitian's name did not excise the name of the whole cult. He apparently assumed that the temple would continue to function, or at least that the phrases would not be offensive even if the cult ceased operation. The presence of the name of the cult was not an oversight on the part of the stoneworker; he found this unusual reference to Domitian buried deep in the midsection of this inscription. Nor would it have been too difficult to remove the rest of the phrase; four of the temple dedication inscriptions have three to four line erasures.[17] He chose instead to leave the name of Domitia and the references to the Flavian family and the Senate. All of this suggests that the municipal cult was much more than a means for currying favor with the current emperor. Most of the Flavian household and the Roman Senate were still worthy of veneration, even as dynastic politics shifted at the imperial center. This temple remained an important sacred site for the city of Tmolos, despite the demise of one deity.

Few temple structures in Asia have been positively identified as municipal temples for the members of the imperial family, so most of our information about municipal temples for the emperors comes from oblique references in epigraphic sources such as that just noted. The many references in inscriptions lead to several inferences. First, the inscriptions suggest that there were more temples to Augustus than to other emperors.[18] These cults for Augustus sometimes included the worship of Rome, following the model set by the provincial cult in Pergamon.[19] In other cases, however, temples employed other cultic formats. Miletos had a temple dedicated only to Augustus.[20] An inscription from Samos refers to a priesthood of Augustus, of Gaius Caesar, and of Marcus Agrippa. This priesthood implies a different format (the emperor, his lieutenant/son-in-law, and his grandson/adopted son), and it may not have been attached to a temple but to some other cultic setting.[21]

Temples of other emperors are epigraphically attested as well. A white marble block from the island of Kos bears the following inscription from the Claudian period (41–54 CE):

Τιβερίωι Κλαυδίωι
Καίσαρι Γερμανι-
κῶι Σεβαστῶι
Αὐτοκράτορι

τὸν ναὸν ὁ
δᾶμος ὁ Ἰσθμι-
ω<ι>τᾶν καθ(ι)ἐρ-
<ερ>ωσε.[22]

To Tiberius Claudius Caesar Germanicus Augustus Emperor; the city of the
Isthmiotans dedicated the temple.

The inscription exemplifies the municipal imperial temples that must have been
established in many places but for which little evidence has survived. The temple
was built by a small community, the quality of the engraving is not high, and the
reasons for the establishment of the cult are no longer clear. In fact, imperial temples
were not necessarily monumental complexes in the major metropolitan areas. We
should expect that most—if not all—small cities and towns had imperial temples,
some more modest than others, that complemented the array of religious institutions of each community.

Given the dearth of architectural evidence for municipal imperial cults, the
numismatic images provide valuable evidence for such buildings, though it is seldom clear whether these images were accurate representations. A series of images
appeared during the Claudian period on the coins of Hierapolis that represented a
municipal imperial temple in that city (fig. 4.1). The coins all name M. Suillios
Antiochos and portray Dionysian themes on their obverses—one series with a bust
of Dionysos crowned with ivy,[23] and another with Agrippina the younger as a devotee
of Dionysos.[24] The reverses all portray a hexastyle temple on monumental steps,
and three coins bear a description of the cult: ΓΕΝΕΙ.ΣΕΒΑΣΤΩΝ, "to the family
of the Sebastoi."[25] This legend on the reverse reflects a post-Augustan development
of the first century CE: the tendency to dedicate imperial cults to a collective or an
institution rather than to an individual.[26] In this case, the general term γένος,
meaning "family" or "race," provided a suitably inclusive category that could incorporate men and women from both branches of the Julio-Claudian dynasty.

Another image of a municipal imperial temple surfaces in coins from Laodikeia
during the Domitianic period (81–96 CE; fig. 4.2). These coins bear images of
Domitian,[27] of Domitia,[28] or of both[29] on the obverses. On the reverses are images
of a temple on three or four steps. The temple is portrayed frontally with six columns, or with the two middle columns missing to provide space for images of stat-

FIGURE 4.1 The reverse of this bronze coin from Hierapolis depicts a municipal temple
for the imperial family. Dionysos is on the obverse. Mid first century CE. *BM Phrygia* 229
#11, pl. 29.4. © The British Museum.

FIGURE 4.2 A municipal imperial cult temple at Laodikeia. The obverse shows Domitian in military attire. The reverse portrays a temple for Domitian and Domitia. Late first century. *BM Phrygia* 307 #185, pl. 37.6. © The British Museum.

ues.[30] The theme emphasized throughout is military victory. The bust of Domitian is clothed with a cuirass. When complete statues are shown in the temple, they portray the emperor in cuirass with a spear in his left hand and a trophy in his right. One reverse also has an inscription across the architrave frieze: ΕΠΙΝΕΙΚΙΟΣ, "contentious, warlike."

These Laodikeian coins portrayed a municipal temple for Domitian and Domitia. A comparison with the Domitianic cult at Tmolos discussed before shows how two contemporaneous imperial cults from different cities might portray the imperial couple. Both cults apparently included the emperor's wife. The format of the Tmolos cult was focused more on relations with the Roman elite, for it explicitly included the extended imperial family and the Senate. The Laodikeian cult may have included other members of the imperial family or the Roman aristocracy as well, but in its public iconography Laodikeia chose to emphasize the imperial couple and the emperor's military victories.

In some cases, municipal imperial cult activities were added to an existing temple cult and no new temple was built. A short-lived but impressive example of such joint worship comes from Pergamon, where the boule and demos honored the Pergamene Otacilia Faustina, daughter of Gaius Otacilius Faustus, during the Tiberian period. She was described as "priestess of [Athena] Nikephoros and Polias [and] of Julia, enthroned with (Athena), new Nike[phoros], daughter of [Germa]nicus Caesar."[31] The Julia who was the object of worship is also known to us as Livilla, the sister of emperor Claudius (41–54 CE).[32] She was born around 13 BCE to Germanicus (Drusus the elder) and Antonia the younger, and twice became a widow, of Gaius Caesar (d. 4 CE) and then of Drusus the younger (d. 23 CE).[33] In 31 she was condemned to death for complicity in the poisoning of Drusus.[34] The cult for her in Pergamon probably stems from the period beginning around 20 CE when her husband Drusus was heir apparent in Rome and could not have lasted more than decade, at least not beyond her condemnation in 31. In such a setting, a combined cult with Athena made sense and gave maximum flexibility in case of changing fortunes in the imperial family. For my purposes, however, the cult is an important example of the way an imperial family member could be associated with a major municipal deity. For the duration of her cult, Livilla would have been accorded some of the highest municipal honors. The festivals and sacrifices to Athena would have been offered to her as well.[35]

Other examples of joint worship, in which the worship of the imperial family was incorporated into existing cultic activity, come from the worship of Demeter in Ephesos. At least two major institutions for the worship of Demeter are attested from Ephesos.[36] One center was the Ephesian prytaneion, called the temple (ναός) of Demeter Karpophoros in one legal text.[37] The prytaneion served as the focal point for the administration of many municipal cults[38] and was also the location of the city's hearth and the center of the worship of Hestia Boulaia. Sacrificial activities for other deities were carried out there, and prayers of people who had finished their terms as prytanis were normally addressed to Hestia Boulaia, to Demeter, to Kore, to the undying fire, and to all the other gods.[39]

An inscription involving the worship of Demeter at Ephesos demonstrates joint worship of the goddess and of members of the imperial families. The text, found on a marble base that has been damaged so that the end of the text is missing, can be dated precisely to the year of the dedication of the provincial Temple of the Sebastoi at Ephesos because it records an official appeal to the proconsul of the province in 89/90 CE. The inscription reads as follows:

> To Lucius Mestrius Florus, proconsul;
> from Lucius Pompeius Apollonios of Ephesos.
>
> Mysteries and sacrifices, oh lord, are performed every year at Ephesos for
> Demeter Karpophoros and Thesmophoros, and for the gods Sebastoi by the
> mystai with great purity and according to established customs together with the
> priestesses, having been maintained for many years by kings and Sebastoi and
> the proconsuls for each year, as contained in their appended letters. For this
> reason, with the mysteries approaching also in your time, oh lord, it is necessary
> that those who must perform the mysteries appeal to you through me so that
> you might recognize their righteous [. . .][40]

In this case we have no evidence for naming a member of the imperial family as a new Athena. Rather, this example seems to incorporate imperial cult rituals alongside existing traditions. This could be accomplished quite simply through the addition of prayers or hymns, or (with a few more complications) through the addition of an altar and perhaps statues. The incorporation of imperial cult activities and objects was probably common in cultic settings. In an appeal to authorities such as this one to the proconsul, where great effort was made to establish the innocuous character of the rituals, the presence of imperial sacrifices (and perhaps imperial mysteries[41]) could only enhance the argument.

A second Ephesian institution involving Demeter was a group known as the Demetriastai Before the City, an officially sanctioned group that celebrated mysteries of Demeter outside the city walls. Although their sanctuary has not been located, it was presumably also outside the city. One inscription mentions some of the officials of this group: a priest for life (who, in this case at least, was also a priest of Dionysos Phleus), a hierophant, and a benefactor who underwrote the mysteries.[42]

A decree publicized by the Demetriastai provides an example of three members of the extended imperial family who were assimilated to various deities, rather than worshipped jointly alongside other deities. The decree was inscribed on a large stele of blue marble around the same time as the preceding example of the cult of Livilla at Pergamon. The beginning of the text is missing, and the surviving stone is broken in two. The existing portion of the decree lists the ways in which a benefactor—probably the Servilius Bassus mentioned later—had served the city and the group. He held (and paid the expenses of) the magistracy over the ephebes (κοσμητεία), the gymnasiarchia, the command of the night-watch (νυκτερινεία), and the office of superintendent of the water supply. The decree continues:

> Because of this the Demetriastai, who marveled at his goodwill toward them, judged that he should be given fitting honors in return. Since they are priests for life with a double portion and (with) aleitourgesia—(Servilius) Bassus of Artemis, Servilia Secunda of Sebaste Demeter Karpophoros, and (Servilius) Proklos of the new Dioscuri, the sons of Drusus—therefore: painted statues of them will be made; and these will be placed in a suitable location on land belonging to the demos with the appropriate inscription, after there is a decree from the boule and the demos.
>
> This has been decided by the Demetriastai Before the City; it shall be (enacted) just as it has been written.[43]

The three honorands all held important lifelong priesthoods, two of them for imperial cults. Servilius Proklos was named as a priest of the twin sons of Drusus and Livilla, and the two boys were venerated as "new Dioscuri." Servilia Secunda was a priestess of an imperial woman who was assimilated to Demeter Karpophoros. This might have been another example of a cult for Livilla (the mother of the twins), but it was more likely a priesthood for Livia because she provided the twins' living genealogical connection to Augustus and because there is ample evidence for other cults of Livia in Asia Minor during her lifetime.[44] In any event, the inscription can be dated after the birth of the twins in 19 CE and probably before the death of Drusus in 23 CE.[45]

Both of these Demeter inscriptions from Ephesos highlight the connections between municipal imperial cults and other levels of organization.[46] Just as the distinction between "municipal" and "provincial" was blurred by the participation of cities in provincial cults, so here we have a blurring of the lines between "municipal" and "group."[47] The decree of the Demetriastai mentions two imperial priesthoods—of Livia or Livilla and of the sons of Drusus—that should probably be classified as municipal because they provided aleitourgesia, exemption from other leitourgies. In other words, the city recognized the municipal importance of these priesthoods that involved only certain groups within the city. Moreover, their service to the city in these and other offices provided the rationale for requesting public land and for an official decree of the city for the erection of statues of these benefactors. Yet the priesthood of Sebaste Demeter Karpophoros was probably maintained through the Demetriastai, a group that did not include the whole city. We cannot rule out municipal administration because of the connection of Demeter Karpophoros with the prytaneion, but neither can we prove active municipal involvement because of the small amount of documentation.

Despite the lack of clear evidence about the structure of the institution, we can make certain observations. Through this imperial cult priesthood, the Demetriastai were able to contribute to the functioning of the city and to increase their own status within the city. The families of those who held these priesthoods were similarly affected: through participation in imperial cults, the Servilii made important contributions to the city and gained public honor in the city. Imperial cults were not the only way to gain honor in a city like Ephesos, but they were a prominent way. More important, the inscription reminds us that imperial cults were one of the only religious institutions with symbolic coherence within family, group, city, and province.

The request of the mystai of Demeter through L. Pompeius Apollonios to the proconsul L. Mestrius Florus in 89/90 is less clearly municipal. These imperial cult activities could simply belong to the rituals of a segment of the municipal population. They are included in this chapter on municipal cults for several reasons. The rituals of Demeter were a venerable tradition in Ephesos that had played a part in the city's well-being for centuries.[48] These rites were significant enough to require annual oversight from regional authorities. Even if the city was not involved in their administration, the festivals were a concern of the whole community in its relations with the provincial governor and with the divine realm. The imperial cults incorporated into this ritual complex acquired some of the same importance as the ceremonies of Demeter, and thus extended the meanings of imperial cults. Whereas provincial and municipal imperial cult temples tended to involve cosmological issues, imperial cults in a mystery setting would have assumed some of the meanings for which mysteries were known. Initiation and the development of human character would involve one spectrum of meanings; personal eschatology may also have been involved.[49] At the same time, imperial cults would have extended the significance of the Demeter rituals into the cosmological arena, as they forged new connections between the mysteries and imperial authority.

Municipal Imperial Cults Without Temples

Municipal imperial cults were not restricted to temple contexts. In fact, they are attested in all the major public spaces in the cities of western Asia Minor. The excavations of the north hall at Priene provide an example of a strong connection between imperial worship and the agora in the city center (figs. 4.3–4.4). The agora of Priene went through three major renovations, each based on a particular image of that area's function within the city. The first phase occurred at the refounding of the city in the fourth century BCE, when the major features of the area (agora, bouleuterion, Athena temple) were laid out in a pragmatic fashion using available space on the steep south slope of Mt. Mykale (modern Gülübahçe). This pragmatic approach was followed as other structures—such as an early north hall and the bouleuterion—were added with only an indirect connection to the agora. By the end of the third century BCE, however, other buildings around the west, south, and east sides transformed the area into an Ionic agora, in which functional considerations were giving way to Hellenistic demands for order and clearly demarcated public space. A third phase in which symmetry was imposed on the area was accomplished by the end of the second century BCE.[50]

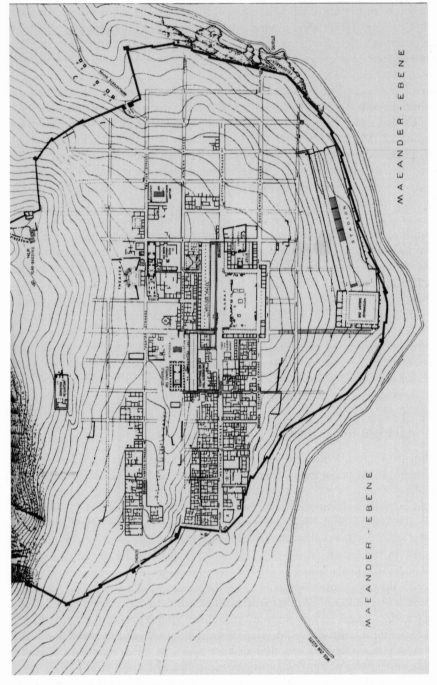

FIGURE 4.3 City plan of Priene. Reprinted, with permission, from Schede 1964. Courtesy of the Deutsches Archäologisches Institut, Berlin.

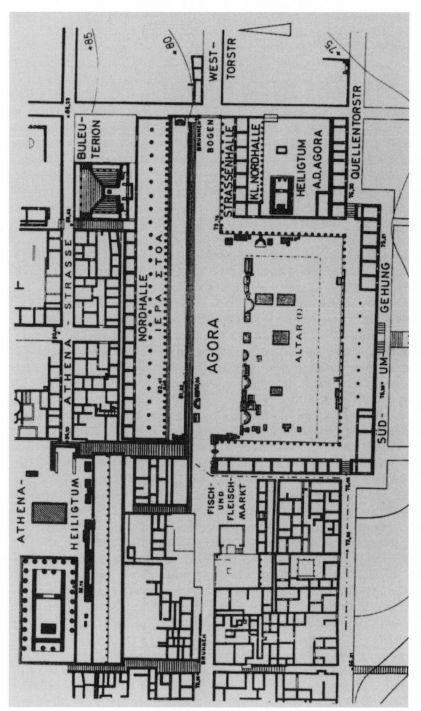

FIGURE 4.4 The Agora at Priene, ca. 100 BCE. Reprinted, with permission, from *IstMitt* 1993:392. Courtesy of the Deutsches Archäologisches Institut, Berlin.

The construction of a new north hall for the agora was an important part of this third phase. The new north hall was built sometime between 150 and 130 BCE as a two-aisled stoa with a row of 15 small rooms behind the aisles (fig. 4.4). The hall provided a stronger definition for the northern boundary of the agora by extending it further to the east and by hiding the bouleuterion's irregular use of space.[51] The north hall also provided new, more accessible space for the public display of honorific inscriptions. The antis walls of the Athena temple had previously been used for this purpose, with extant inscriptions dated from the time of Alexander to about 133 BCE, but this function appears to have been taken over by the new north hall. The small west and east sides were covered with honorific inscriptions, the oldest dating to around 130 BCE.[52] According to these texts, the walls of the north hall were known as "the most distinguished place in the agora."[53]

By the middle of the first century BCE, the north hall was known officially as "the sacred stoa in the agora."[54] There is no overt reason why the stoa should be called sacred except for the evidence from room 9, which is near the north-south axis of the agora.[55] Room 9 was one of three unusual rooms at the back of the stoa: each had an enlarged opening rather than a small door, giving it the character of an exedra, and each had marble revetment on the walls. Two inscriptions from the antae of room 9 lead to the conclusion that it was dedicated to the worship of Roman rulers. One inscription is a fragmentary copy of a letter or decree from the Roman proconsul that can be dated to the middle of the first century BCE.[56] The other inscription contained a long text from Asia's koinon, which mandated the reorganization of the calendars of the cities around the birthday of Augustus.[57] Line 67 of this second inscription required that the inscription be displayed in the Caesareia of the cities of Asia. Thus, room 9 likely served as a municipal imperial cult site for the city center.

Because the row of rooms was built about a century before the advent of the Caesars, the original function of room 9 is unknown. It may have originally been built as a shrine for the goddess Rome. Martin Schede, however, thought the cult of Rome was probably introduced later than the construction of the rooms. He suggested that Sulla's victories over Mithridates led to the renaming of the whole building as the sacred stoa.[58] Although this early history is unclear, by the late first century BCE the room probably had been given over to (or had come to include) the cult of Augustus. The room itself was not imposing, but the site of this imperial cult was among the most prestigious in the city with a crucial location in the civic center.[59]

The city of Miletos provides evidence for another kind of nontemple imperial cult that would have been a part of urban life in many cities of Asia. In this case, we have an example of a monumental altar in the courtyard of the city's bouleuterion (figs. 4.5–4.6). The foundations (9.50 m. wide × 7.25 m. deep) and superstructure fragments from the courtyard of the bouleuterion were first excavated in the fall of 1899. The foundations could not have been for the bouleuterion altar because such altars were normally located inside the building rather than outside.[60] The structure in the courtyard was clearly built later than the rest of the bouleuterion, so excavators concluded that they had uncovered the remains of a monumental tomb for a benefactor of the Roman imperial period.[61]

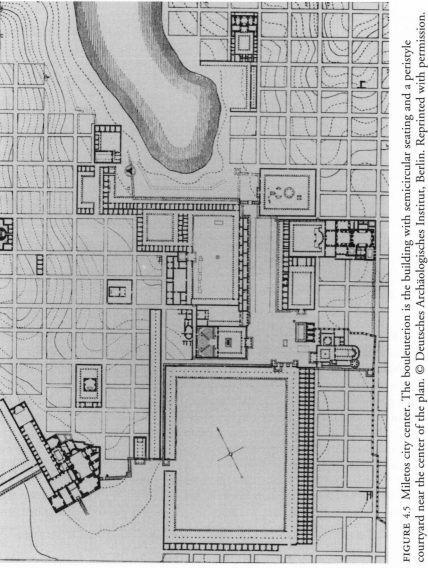

FIGURE 4.5 Miletos city center. The bouleuterion is the building with semicircular seating and a peristyle courtyard near the center of the plan. © Deutsches Archäologisches Institut, Berlin. Reprinted with permission.

FIGURE 4.6 Reconstruction of the imperial altar in the courtyard of the bouleuterion at Miletos. Reprinted, with permission, from *IstMitt* 1975:138. Courtesy of the Deutsches Archäologisches Institut, Berlin.

The problems of identification and reconstruction of the monumental altar were reexamined by Klaus Tuchelt in 1975. His comparative study showed that architectural and typological features ruled out the possibility that the building was a monumental grave or honorific monument. These features pointed instead to a monumental platform altar common to the region with walls on three sides and steps on the fourth side[62] that led to an interior space containing a rectangular sacrificial table.[63] Around the exterior were orthostats decorated with boukrania, garlands, and lion heads whose style suggests an early imperial date. Above the orthostat level were 12 sculptural reliefs: 4 on the back, 3 on each side, and 1 on either side of the front steps. The reliefs were separated by small columns. It is impossible to reconstruct the sculptural program from the few remaining fragments of reliefs, but the identification of a few figures is possible. One relief showed Leto, seated on a throne in archaizing style, with water nymphs from Mykale at her feet and with Artemis and Apollo nearby. There is evidence for at least one more Leto relief and one showing Tyro's sons, the mythic founders of Miletos.[64]

The evidence that ties the structure to the worship of the emperors is less direct than the evidence for other buildings in this chapter, but a fairly convincing case has been made.[65] There are two lines of argument. First, the propylon that gave access to the bouleuterion courtyard was inscribed with texts regarding donors to a local imperial cult.[66] The earliest texts are datable to the Augustan or Tiberian period,

and the latest ones come from the time of Nero. The presence of these lists at the bouleuterion is understandable if there was an altar of Augustus in the courtyard that was reached through this propylon. Second, the ornamental and architectural style of the structure in the courtyard enjoyed popularity in imperial cult settings during the early empire.[67] The best-known example is the Ara Pacis Augustae at Rome, similar to the building in the Miletos bouleuterion courtyard.

If Tuchelt's reconstruction is accurate, then we have valuable information regarding municipal imperial cults in Miletos. The altar was placed in a strategic governmental location directly in front of the bouleuterion. The boule was one of the quintessential expressions of ancient democracy as practiced in the cities of the Greco-Roman world. The altar of Augustus in front of the bouleuterion of Miletos made a dramatic statement about the importance and validity of imperial rule. The bouleuterion was no longer simply a municipal institution of an autonomous city; the building and the city were now within an imperial framework.

A second observation relates to the use of myth on this altar, which integrated empire into a local cosmology. The fragments of the sculptural reliefs suggest that the worship of Augustus was located within local myths. The few fragments point to the importance of local traditions, whether the narratives involved Olympians (Apollo, Artemis) or other less exalted figures (Leto, Mykale, Tyro). Therefore, we should not expect to find a uniform mythology of "imperial cult" in the Roman empire. Rather, we encounter a variegated religious landscape within which imperial cults could flourish.

Baths and gymnasia are other public spaces for which municipal imperial cults are well attested in Asia. Every city needed such establishments, not just for the cultivation of the body but also for the development of the whole human community. Baths provided settings for important social interaction. Gymnasia provided scientific, philosophical, cultural, civic, and religious training that was the foundation of urban life. We should not be surprised, then, to find these were also important contexts for the worship of the emperors.

Most of the major gymnasia known from imperial Asia had a large room off the exercise courtyards (fig. 4.7) that were usually rectangular, fitted with aediculae and tabernacle architecture, and reveted with marble. The rooms are sometimes called marble courts, but the name imperial hall ("Kaisarsaal") was coined after the excavations of the Vedius bath-gymnasium at Ephesos revealed an imperial period altar (Antonine) in front of the marble court.[68] Later, Fikret Yegül built a case that this specific architectural form in gymnasia was designated expressly for the purpose of imperial cults.[69] The circumstantial evidence is impressive but there are few clear attestations to confirm his conclusion.[70] The marble courts may have always been the site of imperial cults, but we should not overlook the evidence for imperial cults throughout such complexes.

The evidence from the great gymnasium at Pergamon illustrates the indirect nature of the data (fig. 4.8). A small temple once stood at the northeast end of the long narrow middle terrace; it was probably dedicated to Hermes and Herakles, the patron deities of the establishment. About 10 m. northwest of the temple was a small rectangular exedra with two Doric columns. Inside this exedra at the back was a podium (0.70 m. high, 1.70 deep) added in the Roman period. In the exedra the

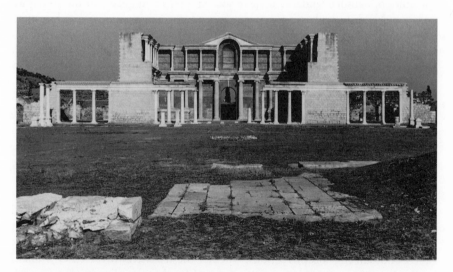

FIGURE 4.7 Reconstructed marble hall of the Sardis bath-gymnasium complex. © Archaeological Exploration of Sardis/Harvard University.

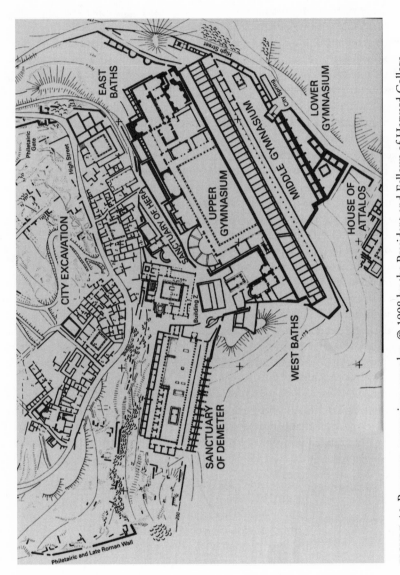

FIGURE 4.8 Pergamon gymnasium complex. © 1998 by the President and Fellows of Harvard College. Reprinted by permission.

excavators found an inscription with a dedication to Augustus and Livia, the θεοὶ Σεβάστοι, and to Hermes and Herakles. The podium may have supported statues of the divine imperial couple, but it is not completely certain that the inscription originally came from the room. Thus, we are assured that divine honors were offered to the imperial couple at the gymnasium, but the exact location of the shrine and the nature of these honors have not been determined.[71] Likewise, the upper terrace of the same gymnasium includes a room near the northeast corner of the terrace shaped more like a standard marble court. It has often been called an imperial cult room, but this description is based only on the dedication of the room to the emperor and to the city of Pergamon. The evidence on the upper terrace is suggestive but not unassailable.[72]

I do not suggest that there were no imperial cults in gymnasia; on the contrary, such cults were widespread in these contexts. The proliferation of athletic competitions in honor of the emperors and their families during the Roman period makes this conclusion unavoidable. Along with specific competitions known from the inscriptions of Asia, we should assume that most major imperial cults were accompanied by athletic games to round out the festivities.[73] The bath-gymnasium complex near the harbor at Ephesos apparently was built (or perhaps remodeled) for such purposes. When Ephesos received the right to provide a temple for the provincial temple of the Sebastoi, the city probably established Olympic games in honor of Domitian as Zeus. The bath building and palaestra were named the "baths of the Sebastoi" (or perhaps "baths of Sebastos"),[74] suggesting that the whole complex—and not just its two marble courts—was dedicated to the veneration of the emperor.[75]

The divine imperial family was recognized at baths as well. Lollia Antiochis paid for a local bathing establishment at Assos in the first half of the first century CE. The inscription noted that her husband Quintus Lollios Philetairos was priest for life of Sebastos God Caesar (Tiberius), and she dedicated the building to Aphrodite Julia (Livia) and to the demos.[76]

An inscription from Pergamon brings together several of the phenomena discussed in this chapter with startling economy. The inscription was found in 1929 in the Pergamene Asklepieion near the temple of Asklepios, engraved on a statue base in the early imperial period not later than the first century CE. The text came from the boule and the demos of Pergamon with the intent of honoring a certain Demetrios. The text describes him as

ἱερέ[α] τῆς τῶν Σ[ε-]
[βασ]τῶν Εὐσεβείας διὰ βί[ου,]
[κ]αθευρόντα πανήγυριν ἐ[ν]
[τῶ]ι τοῦ Σωτῆρος Ἀσκληπ[ιοῦ]
[τε]μένει Σεβαστῶν Σωτ[ή-]
[ρω]ν καὶ τελέσαντα τὴν ἀγ[ω-]
[νο]θεσίαν ἐκ τῶν ἰδίων [. . .][77]

priest of the Reverence of the Sebastoi, who founded a festal assembly for the Savior Sebastoi in the temenos of the the Savior Asklepios, and who completed the agonothesia from his own funds [. . .]

From this damaged inscription we learn that Demetrios, who was not a Roman citizen, was involved in local imperial cults in at least two significant ways. First, he was priest of a cult with an unusual format, a Romanizing imperial cult, imitating the sort of format one might expect in Rome, where his office would have been known as a *sacerdos Pietatis Augustorum*. Second, he initiated a regular imperial festival and served as its first agonothete. The festival was dedicated to the Sebastoi, probably Augustus and Livia, who are associated in this way with the city's international sanctuary. The epithet "Savior" assimilated the imperial family to the local deity Asklepios, in whose precincts the festival was held. This competition may have been dramatic or musical, for no gymnasium has been identified near the Asklepieion. The inscription shows, nevertheless, the implication of municipal imperial cults in organized competitions, the worship of other deities, the mediation of Roman influence, and the creative efforts of local elites to supplement the religious life of their cities and regions.

Imperial Cults and the City

Before moving on to consider two well-documented cases of municipal imperial cults, I offer a summary of the main features in the preceding survey. An examination of the epigraphic, numismatic, sculptural, and architectural remains demonstrates that imperial cults permeated community life. Various temples and small shrines for the imperial family were found in towns and cities, and imperial cults were part of worship at many temples of other deities as well. Municipal imperial cults were part of many institutions besides temples, such as the agora, the bouleuterion, the gymnasium, and the baths. Festivals normally involved processions beyond the sites of the sacrifices themselves, so all public spaces were involved in such activities at different intervals.[78] Imperial cults were an aspect of urban life encountered often and in diverse forms.

Second, municipal imperial cults were dedicated to a wider range of members of the imperial family than was true of the provincial cults. Wives of emperors played an important part, but possible successors to the throne were also emphasized. I already cited the example of Drusus, Livilla, and their sons. Others examples can be added to these, such as a dedication to "Marcus Agrippa, God Savior and Founder of the city";[79] Gaius Otacilius Chrestos's priesthood of Augustus and agonothesia of the children of Augustus (Gaius and Lucius);[80] or the temples for Augustus, Livia, and the sons of Augustus at Eresos on Lesbos.[81]

Third, several distinctive features are evident at the municipal level. The language of divinization operated differently at the municipal level from its use in the provincial cults. As Christian Habicht noted, the use of *theos* was unrestricted in municipal cults in Asia, even though it was avoided in provincial cults of the early empire.[82] The practice of joint worship—incorporating imperial worship into the cult of another deity—was widespread. There was also a marked tendency to assimilate the emperors and their families to specific deities, which was completely avoided in provincial cults of Asia from this period. Several examples have been noted in the chapter, but we should also note that there appear to have been regional variations. Mytilene, for example, seems to have been more prone to the practice of assimilation. References from there mention institutions honoring Augustus as Zeus Caesar Olympios Sebastos;[83] Julius Caesar Nero (brother of Drusus and brother-in-law of Livilla) as the son of the new *theos* Germanicus and of the goddess Aiolean Karpophoros Agrippina;[84] and his sister Drusilla as the new Aphrodite.[85]

Finally, municipal imperial cults were more closely attuned to local piety and local fashions. They were more flexible in terms of the possible formats and more easily integrated into a variety of contexts: sometimes they emphasized local heritage; other times they trafficked in Romanizing traditions. Administratively they were subject to local authorities. There was no need to petition the Roman Senate to establish such cults, and announcements about the foundation of such cults were sometimes sent to Rome and to other cities despite the non-Roman character of their formats. At the municipal level a variegated, decentralized (but not uncontrolled) series of buildings, officials, and rituals emerged that could be found in any community in Asia. For more details about the religious potential of such institutions, we need to look carefully at two instances with fuller documentation.

5

MUNICIPAL IMPERIAL CULTS
Two Case Studies

The preceding chapter produced a survey of municipal imperial cults in Asia based on available occasional evidence. This chapter presents two important cases with more definitive evidence. The Aphrodisian example provides insight into the arrangements and functions of a municipal imperial cult temple precinct, with epigraphic, architectural, and sculptural evidence taking us deeper into the phenomenon of imperial worship. The Ephesian example provides salient information about the relationship of the precinct to the city. Together, these two cases enhance our understanding of the importance of imperial cults in an urban center.

The Sebasteion at Aphrodisias

In 1979 an extraordinary structure came to light in Aphrodisias during the razing of a modern house near the ancient theater (figs. 5.1, 5.2).[1] As fragments of inscriptions, buildings, and sculptures appeared, excavators became convinced that a rare municipal imperial cult sanctuary had been uncovered. The evidence is convincing. There are multiple building dedications to Aphrodite—the city's main deity—and to the "gods Sebastoi," and statues from the propylon and reliefs that lined the precincts confirm these conclusions. This site could have been the Sebasteion mentioned in passing in an Aphrodisian inscription,[2] but there could have been more than one structure fitting that description in a city like Aphrodisias during the im-

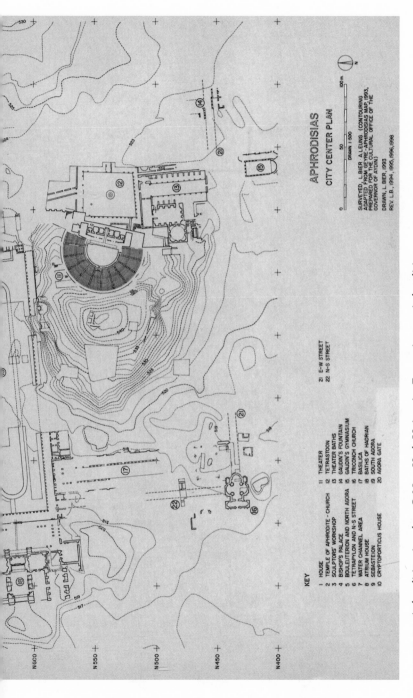

APHRODISIAS
CITY CENTER PLAN

0   50   100 m
DRAWN 1/500

SURVEYED, L.BIER A.LEUNG (CONTOURING
ADAPTED FROM GEYRE-APHRODISIAS MAP 1993,
PREPARED FOR THE CULTURAL OFFICE OF THE
GOVERNOR OF AYDIN)

DRAWN L. BIER 1993
REV L.B. 1994, 1995, 1996, 1998

KEY

1   HOUSE
2   TEMPLE OF APHRODITE - CHURCH
3   SCULPTORS' WORKSHOP
4   BISHOP'S PALACE
5   BOULEUTERION AND NORTH AGORA
6   TETRAPYLON AND N-S STREET
7   WATER CHANNEL AREA
8   ATRIUM HOUSE
9   SEBASTEION
10 CRYPTOPORTICUS HOUSE

11 THEATER
12 TETRASTOON
13 THEATER BATHS
14 GAUDIN'S FOUNTAIN
15 GAUDIN'S GYMNASIUM
16 TRICONCH CHURCH
17 BASILICA
18 BATHS OF HADRIAN
19 SOUTH AGORA
20 AGORA GATE

21 E-W STREET
22 N-S STREET

FIGURE 5.1 Aphrodisias city plan. © New York University Excavations at Aphrodisias.

79

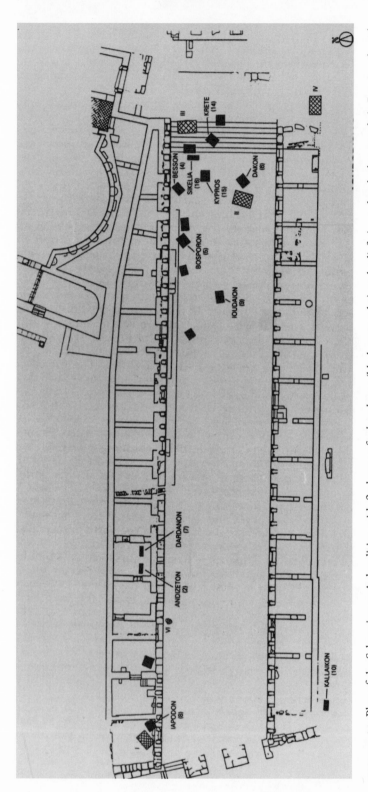

FIGURE 5.2 Plan of the Sebasteion at Aphrodisias, with findspots of *ethnos* bases (black rectangles) and reliefs (cross-hatched rectangles). Reprinted, with permission, from *JRS* 1988:52 fig. 1. Courtesy of the New York University Excavations at Aphrodisias.

perial period.[3] Because this site was clearly dedicated to imperial cult activity and the official title of the complex has not yet been uncovered, it has become convenient to refer to it as the Sebasteion.

The Sebasteion was accessible from a major north-south thoroughfare that ran from the theater perhaps as far as the temple of Aphrodite. The imperial cult complex was composed of five elements: a narrow rectangular paved courtyard (ca. 14 × 90 m.); two portico-like buildings, one on each of the two long sides; a propylon on the short west side; and a temple on the short east side.[4] For unknown reasons, the precincts projected east from the street at an angle that does not align with the city's grid.[5]

Construction on the site lasted several decades and was complicated by destructions and renovations. Analysts agree that work began under Tiberius and that an earthquake during the reign of Tiberius or Claudius damaged some buildings before the whole complex was completed. Construction was resumed and continued into the reign of Nero. Even though it was closely connected to the Julio-Claudian dynasty, the temenos continued in use long after the demise of that family.[6]

In spite of the extended period of construction, the entire Sebasteion complex was built according to a unified plan with a propylon, two porticoes along the sides of the precincts, and a temple opposite the propylon. The first building a first-century visitor would have encountered was the propylon—the monumental gateway between the street and the western end of the precincts (fig. 5.3). This two-story propylon was an innovative structure.[7] A viewer from the street would have seen three small stairways leading into the precincts that were separated by two square tabernacles with four columns each and no back walls. At the extreme ends of the propylon, alongside the outer stairways, were two more columns to mark the edges of the gateway. There were two stories of columns, the lower order Ionic and the upper order Corinthian. In general, the propylon created a transparency that allowed the viewer from the street to take in the propylon structure and to look through it for a partial view of the precincts.[8]

Inscriptions provide us with information about the programmatic character of the propylon. The architrave inscription indicates that the propylon was dedicated to Aphrodite, to the gods Sebastoi (θεοῖς Σεβαστοῖς), and to the demos by the same family that dedicated the north portico (more on them later). It also says that the donors provided the statues in the propylon.[9] Several of the bases from these statues have been found, and they show that the dedication was part of a discursive statement about the relationship of the civic deity Aphrodite and the Julio-Claudian dynasty. One statue depicted "Aphrodite, progenitor of the Gods Sebastoi."[10] Other bases found at a distance from the Sebasteion but probably belonging to the propylon held statues of Agrippina the elder (mother of emperor Gaius), her husband Germanicus, a rare Atia (mother of Augustus), Julia Sebaste (probably referring to Livia), Nero, and M. Aemilius Lepidus (husband of Gaius's sister Drusilla).[11] Aeneas, Lucius and Gaius, Ti. Claudius Drusus (first-born son of Claudius who died young), and others were included as well.[12] The meaning of the sculptural programme is clear enough, even though some of the statue identifications are unknown and a few of those mentioned might come from other contexts. The inscription and statues indicate that the complex commemorated the connection of Aphrodisias to the

FIGURE 5.3 Reconstruction of Sebasteion propylon with precincts and temple in background. Reprinted, with permission, from *Les Dossiers d'archeologie* 139 (June 1989) 49. Courtesy of the New York University Excavations at Aphrodisias.

Roman imperial dynasty by equating the city's principle deity with Venus Genetrix, the mythic progenitor of Julius Caesar and his successors.[13]

Upon entering the precincts, a visitor would have seen porticoes on the left and right sides of the paved courtyard (fig. 5.4). The term "portico," however, is only an approximate description for these structures because the interior arrangements and external ornamentation were unlike other buildings known to us from that era.[14] Contrary to normal expectation, the interior arrangements of the porticoes allowed for no hallway. Instead, there were separate rooms with little or no provision for access between them, and the rooms on the second and third stories may have been completely unused.[15] The exterior was unusual as well. The porticoes were quite tall for such close quarters—approximately 12 m.—and the colonnade was partially filled in by marble plates on the first story. On the second and third floors, relief panels completely covered the area between the engaged columns, leaving no windows or openings into the rooms.

The north portico was built soon after the propylon.[16] The north portico had two architectural features that distinguished it from its counterpart to the south. It was somewhat longer than the south portico (50 rather than 45 intercolumniations) and had a single constant width between columns (1.63–1.64 m.).[17] The architrave inscription indicates that the north portico was dedicated to Aphrodite, the gods Sebastoi, and the demos by the same family that provided the propylon. The donors were two brothers named Menander and Eusebes, and Apphias the wife of Eusebes. A later inscription informs us that the two buildings were subsequently damaged by an earthquake and had to be restored. The brothers were apparently dead by the time of the renovations, for the project was underwritten by Apphias,

FIGURE 5.4 Sebasteion courtyard, partially reconstructed; view from temple toward propylon. Courtesy of the New York University Excavations at Aphrodisias.

her daughter Tata, and her grandsons (also named Menander and Eusebes).[18] The later inscription from after the earthquake refers to the emperors as Olympians: Θεοὶ Σεβαστοὶ Ὀλύμπιοι.[19]

The south portico was built later than the propylon, for the point at which it joined the propylon took into account that the propylon had already been completed.[20] Two partial dedications come from the south portico. The most complete inscription was part of the western end of the architrave somewhere over rooms 9–12. It contains a damaged dedication and the names of benefactors:[21]

Ἀφροδίτηι star Θε[ ]ι Σεβαστ[..3–4..Τιβερ]ίωι Κλαυδίωι Κ[αί]σαρι star
τῶι δήμωι dolphin Τιβέριος Κλαύδιος Διογένης φιλοπολίτης ἅ
ἐπηνγείλατο Διογένης ὁ πατὴ[ρ α]ὐτοῦ καί Ἀτταλίς καὶ ὑπὲρ Ἀττάλου
τοῦ θείου τὸ καθ᾽ ἑαυτὸν μέρος ἀποκα[θ]έσστησεν.[22]

To Aphrodite, to The[ ] Sebast[. . . Tiber]ius Claudius Caesar (and) to the demos. Claudius Diogenes, loyal to (his) fellow citizens, restored that which Diogenes his father and Attalis (on behalf of Attalos the uncle) promised, as his own contribution.

The fragmentary dedication at the beginning is difficult. J. Reynolds concluded that the best possibility was "to Thea Sebaste (i.e., to Livia) and to Tiberius Claudius Caesar." A much more fragmentary inscription that was part of the architrave near the temple end of the south portico was recovered. This inscription included a damaged reference to Apphias and a dedication to Aphrodite, the Theoi Sebastoi, and to the demos.[23]

The fourth building of this complex—the temple—sat on a terrace at the east end of the paved court that was approached by a flight of steps.[24] It is the building about which the least is known. Enough pieces are preserved, however, to show that it was a prostyle podium temple with six Corinthian columns.[25] The combination of the terrace and the podium raised the temple considerably higher than the paved court, with the temple stylobate approximately at the same height as the Doric architrave above the first stories of the porticoes.[26] Fragments of the architrave inscription from the temple have come to light. Although they represent only a portion of the text, it is clear that Tiberius and Livia were named. The phrase [. . . . ὑπὲ]ρ Ἀττάλου . . . indicates that Attalis (on behalf of Attalos) and her family paid for this structure as well as the south portico.[27]

These four buildings—donated by two Aphrodisian families who may have been related to each other—defined a sacred space.[28] It was not modeled on typical Greek or Asiatic temple precinct designs, nor even on known Italian sanctuaries. The pieces of the ensemble are eclectic: the temple is Roman imperial, the porticoes are an unusual experiment with the Hellenistic stoa genre, and the propylon is an innovative Asian imperial development. The overall plan, however, is based on Roman models, particularly on the Forum of Julius Caesar and the Forum of Augustus. Both of these fora had portico-like sides leading to a temple near the back of the precincts. In the Julian Forum the temple was of Venus Genetrix; the temple in the Forum of Augustus was dedicated to Mars Ultor but also included Venus. The Forum of Augustus included engaged statues above the porticoes as well. These Roman plans were not simply copied. The Aphrodisians took the basic Roman outline and adapted it according to the limitations of this specific urban site and according to the expectations of local tradition. Thus, the architectural design was the result of a confluence of Roman, Hellenistic, and local influences.[29]

Each of the four buildings had its own significance for the functioning of the precincts: the propylon provided access to the sacred space, the porticoes directed the viewers toward the temple, the temple housed the sacred images, and so on. The synthesis of all these components, however, relied on the paved courtyard. In terms of the impact of the precincts on mortals, the court was the most important component. The buildings framed this space for the participants in the festivals. People gathered in this long, narrow container for the periodic sacrifices held here. The terrace where the sacrifices would have taken place was seven steps above the level of the crowd. The temple itself was raised even higher above the level of the viewers and was somewhat more distant. Thus, the courtyard was framed to direct the attention of the people forward and upward toward the imperial cult temple.

The porticoes were not utilitarian buildings: there is no evidence that the rooms on the ground floor were put to regular use, whereas the second- and third-story spaces were unusable and perhaps not even accessible. The primary function of the porticoes was public display, and for these purposes the sculptural reliefs on the second and third stories were crucial. About 10% of the original 100 reliefs in the north portico survive, mostly from the eastern and western ends that stood longer than the middle section of the portico. The shorter south portico held 90 reliefs, but about 75% of these have been recovered.[30] As the heights and widths of the stories varied, the known reliefs can be assigned to their original porticoes and their correct stories; some can even be assigned with confidence to particular rooms. An examination of these panels results in a fairly good idea of the sculptural programme that lined the precinct: the north portico focused on imperial rule throughout the world, whereas the south portico dealt with the emperors and the Greek world.[31] A brief consideration of the sculptures from each of these buildings provides valuable information on the use of mythology in a municipal imperial cult context.

The upper and lower registers of the north portico had distinctly different styles and subjects. Very few pieces from the sculpture of the upper (third) story have survived: of the 50 panels, only 3 are extant. Two of these are allegorical personifications: Hemera (Day) and Okeanos (Ocean).[32] They were found with their inscribed bases at the east end of the portico. Both figures were portrayed frontally with draperies that billow up behind their heads. The male Ocean is bearded and naked; the female Day is clothed. Their presence implies that the missing panels from the third story included also a Night relief and an Earth relief. Morning, Noon, and Evening are also possibilities.[33] A third relief from the upper register was quite different from these two Hellenistic allegories. The third relief depicts a specific historical moment: the accession of Nero to the throne. Nero wears military clothing and holds a spear; his mother Agrippina the younger (on the right) crowns him with a laurel wreath. This particular panel did not stand as long as the north portico, for it was found face down in the back northeast corner of the north portico's room 9, where it was reused as a floor slab. The dimensions of the panel indicate that it was displayed in the upper story; its reuse indicates that it was removed in 68 CE after the death of Nero.[34]

This leads to two possibilities for the contents of the poorly attested upper register of the north portico. One is that the upper register included a series of universalizing allegories, with an imperial series in the midsection.[35] A second possibility is that the upper register was purely allegorical, with the accession of Nero panel added when the new member of the dynasty came to power in 54 CE.[36] In either case, the upper register (i.e., the third story) at least sets out to portray the broad temporal and spatial categories of human existence and perhaps includes also the Roman imperial family as another defining category.

The reliefs of the north portico's second story are much clearer and more uniform. The sculptures in this register depicted a range of peoples and places of the empire in the following manner. Between each set of engaged Ionic columns was a lower panel with a statue base in high relief and an upper panel with an engaged statue above the base (fig. 5.5), creating the impression of a line of 50 statues. Each base had a mask with thick garlands draped on either side. Near the top of the base was an inscription identifying the figure above. The extant pieces record 13 national groups and 3 islands.[37] The seven or eight existing statue panels show that the groups and islands were personified as clothed females, with attributes specific to the subjects.

This is a peculiar group of statues, and J. Reynolds first recognized that the one theme tying most of them together was Augustan conquest. Nearly all of the known personifications from the second story of the north portico were defeated by Augustus.[38] R. Smith added nuance to this observation by pointing out the heterogeneity of the personified topics: some were administrative provinces, some were parts of provinces, and some were outside the empire. Even so, all the known references can be categorized in one of three ways: defeated in battle, defeated and added to the empire, or brought back into the empire under Augustus.[39]

Smith went on to look for models for such a series.[40] It is hard to imagine the Aphrodisians composing a series like this on their own because of the "bizarre subjects, stylistic homogeneity, and careful iconographic differentiation."[41] There are few literary references and even fewer archaeological attestations regarding groups of personified peoples or areas. The most likely candidate to have served as the model for this Aphrodisian series is either the Porticus ad Nationes or the funeral procession of Augustus.[42] The Porticus ad Nationes is known from Servius, who wrote that it was a building where Augustus erected images of all the peoples, each with distinguishing characteristics.[43] According to Dio Cassius, the funeral procession for Augustus also included images of "all the peoples (*ethne*) acquired by Augustus."[44] These and other examples show that there was a list of Augustan conquests, official or semi-official, and that models available at Rome depicted the peoples who had been defeated by Augustus. The Aphrodisians could have obtained drawings from Rome, or they could have had copies made by shops in Rome that were then sent to Aphrodisias.[45]

The peoples may have been arranged geographically on the north portico, but the evidence does not allow certainty: the findspots of the western *ethne* fragments tend to be in the western end of the precincts, and those of the eastern *ethne* toward the temple end, but some other findspots do not fit this pattern.[46] More important is the imaginary cultural geography propagated by the figures. Subtle distinctions in the representation of the various peoples and places distinguished those that were

FIGURE 5.5 Drawing of Piroustae statue with base and engaged columns. Reprinted, with permission, from *JRS* 1988:54 fig. 3. Courtesy of the New York University Excavations at Aphrodisias.

"barbarian" and those that were "Greek." The contrast is clear, for example, in the following two panels. Both are unidentified but show deliberate iconographic distinctions in terms of costume, pose, hairstyle, and so on.

The first panel presents a female figure in the Hellenistic tradition (fig. 5.6).[47] Though most of the head is missing, enough of the hair remains to identify a known ideal Greek portrait hairstyle gathered tightly at the back with one curl released onto the neck. The peplos is richly defined, though not quite accurate according to classical canons. The himation comes over the figure's right shoulder, across the chest, and onto the hanging left forearm.[48] The disposition is frontal with weight on the right leg. Both hands once held objects difficult to reconstruct. The raised right hand probably held a staff or spear; the left had a baton-like attribute. In sum, the panel presents a classic Greek figure who is free rather than subject to foreign powers. She

FIGURE 5.6 Unidentified ethnos or Greek island (*JRS* 1988, pl. 3). Courtesy of the New York University Excavations at Aphrodisias.

probably represented one of the three islands or perhaps another Hellenistic group or area whose name is no longer attested.

A second extant panel represents its subject quite differently (fig. 5.7).[49] The disposition is similar—frontal pose, weight on right leg, head in three-quarter view (though to the figure's right rather than left)—but the pose immediately indicates that this is a subject people or area, with the arms crossed and right hand grasping the himation. The arms are not bound to indicate captivity; rather, the clothing and hair reinforce the image of a semi-hellenized subject. The peplos has slipped down the right arm so that one breast is partially exposed. The hair is executed between the extremes of the tight Greek bun and a completely disheveled barbarian coiffure. The figure of a bull at her right is ambiguous: it could allude to a specific national stereotype, or it could simply heighten the barbarian features of the relief.

FIGURE 5.7 Unidentified ethnos with bull (*JRS* 1988, pl. 2). Courtesy of the New York University Excavations at Aphrodisias.

This panel was found near the base of the Dacians, but it could also have represented some other group or place at the margins of the Greco-Roman world.

In the north portico, then, there was an emphasis on the categories that defined life in the world where Roman power was exercised. There is even the suggestion that the edges of the Roman world are the edges of human civilization.[50] Within the civilized world, temporal, geographic, political, and cultural categories were elaborated in variegated detail through allegory and stereotype. The unassailable character of these categories was heightened by the relentless, uniform spacing of the engaged columns in the north portico and by the constant sunlight on this southern exposure. Such a world was brought into existence by the work of the gods and the conquests of Augustus.

Empire, deities, emperors, and conquest resurface in the reliefs of the south portico in new ways and to new ends. The reliefs of the second story are the best attested of the registers in the precincts, with all or significant parts of most of the 45 panels intact. The panels were devoted to scenes from Greek mythology. Some are known stories; others are references to unrecognizable narratives. In spite of the gaps in our knowledge, the cycle clearly was not governed by a rigorous programme. There is a culmination at the east end nearest the temple, where the last major scene is of Aeneas's flight toward Rome, and where images of Aphrodite and sacrifice predominate.[51] There does not seem to be a steady development toward this culmination in the rest of the register. The myth panels seem to cluster around certain figures or events, with popular figures such as Herakles and Dionysos more frequent than others.[52] The heroes and legends are not local; they participate rather in a more general, common Hellenistic mythology. Nor do the reliefs line up vertically to show a correspondence with panels in the register above them, though the vertical alignment of Aeneas's flight (second story) and the victorious Augustus (third story) over the center of room 1 seems intentional.[53]

The myth panels of the second story, then, present an episodic collection of images about the narratives that defined the Greek world, with an emphasis on Aphrodite near the end and her son Aeneas, who became both the ancestor of Rome and the tradent of Greek culture to Italy. In this sense, the south portico reliefs of the second story amplify the definition of Hellenic civilization contrasted with gradations of barbarity on the second story of the north portico and direct that definition of Hellenic civilization toward the Julio-Claudian emperors.[54]

The third story reliefs of the south portico were devoted to portraying the victorious emperors as Olympian gods. About a third of the 45 panels in the upper register presented members of the Julio-Claudian dynasty: Germanicus with a captive, Claudius overcoming Britannia, Claudius and Agrippina, Nero conquering Armenia (fig. 5.8), two princes (Gaius and Lucius?), and so on.[55] All the emperors are rendered in idealizing nudity that would be unthinkable in historical battle scenes commissioned in the city of Rome. At Aphrodisias the victories are cast in terms of Hellenistic mythic grandeur: the defeat of Britannia is designed as an Amazonomachy, and Nero's Armenian victory is overtly modeled on Achilles and Penthesilea (which also appeared at some point in the second-story reliefs). The use of myth is evocative rather than literal, however; Penthesilea died but Armenia was only vanquished. The purpose is to elevate the status of the Julio-Claudians rather than to create his-

FIGURE 5.8 Nero defeats Armenia; relief from Sebasteion
south portico, third story (*JRS* 1987, pl. 16). Courtesy of the
New York University Excavations at Aphrodisias.

torical allegories. One imperial woman was deemed worthy of her own panel.[56] She
was presumably Livia, shown sacrificing in a normal Hellenistic chiton with himation
over one shoulder (fig. 5.9). The damaged panel shows the bottom of a round altar
upon which she was probably pouring a libation.

Augustus occupied a crucial position in the third-story programme. The central panel of room 1 in the upper register is a crowded composition (fig. 5.10). A
naked Augustus stands left of center and a nike on the right, with a military trophy
between them.[57] At the base of the trophy we see a captive barbarian from the back
with his hands bound and head turned to the left.[58] Below Augustus's lowered right
hand is an eagle.

Another central panel, this one probably from room 9 or 10 based on the
findspot, featured Claudius in a dynamic context, with land and sea under his con-

FIGURE 5.9 Relief: Livia (?) pouring a libation; from the
Sebasteion south portico, third story (*JRS* 1987, pl. 22).
Courtesy of the New York University Excavations at
Aphrodisias.

trol.[59] In this scene a naked Claudius strides forward dramatically (fig. 5.11). Behind his head billows a drapery whose ends loop over his forearms. A smaller earth
figure has placed a cornucopia in his right hand; a sea figure has put the steering oar
of a ship in his left. The message is straightforward and clear: the exalted emperor
has brought prosperity to the world—fertility to the land and safety to the seas.

Other subjects were included in the third-story reliefs, all related to imperial
themes. The known subjects included Dioscuri flanking the Augustus with nike
panel, the goddess Rome and Ge (Earth), the goddess Rome and Aphrodisias personified, a veiled god, an Asklepios, a cult statue of Aphrodite, Aphrodisias crowned
by an allegorical figure, and several winged victories, including a nike (victory) of
the Sebastoi.[60] The register revolves around the Olympian accomplishments of
Augustus and his successors and the relationship with Aphrodisias.

None of the topics in either register of the south portico is based on Roman
models, as was the case with the *ethne* series of the north portico. The subject mat-

FIGURE 5.10 Augustus with nike, trophy, captive, and eagle; from the Sebasteion south portico, third story (*JRS* 1987 pl. 4). Courtesy of the New York University Excavations at Aphrodisias.

ter, the occasional compositional problems caused by poor design, and the imperial nudity all indicate that the south portico reliefs—as panels and as an ensemble— were an Aphrodisian project not intended for audiences at the imperial center but for consideration in this particular place in this province. Romans would not portray the emperor as an Olympian in an historical narrative relief, nor would they appreciate such bold claims to supremacy by the first citizen. In the Sebasteion, however, as viewers looked up from the paved court, they encountered the mythic dimensions of the Julio-Claudian dynasty. The members of the imperial family were gods, not replacements for the old deities but "a new branch of the Olympian pantheon."[61] These new Olympians were not foreign to the Aphrodisians but rather relatives through their common ancestor Venus/Aphrodite. Through this connection, the Aphrodisians created kinship between themselves and their conquerors. Hellenic was related to Roman, with "barbarian" as the category of the exotic other against whom both could be understood.

The reliefs from the porticoes are an integral part of the structural meaning of the precincts as a whole. The architecture, iconography, and dedications together present a synthesis of Roman, Greek, and Aphrodisian interests. The perspective of

FIGURE 5.11 Emperor Claudius over Land (left) and Sea (right); from the Sebasteion south portico, third story (*JRS* 1987, pl. 6). © New York University Excavations at Aphrodisias.

this municipal imperial cult, however, is thoroughly local. The Sebasteion provides us with a rare glimpse of a public statement on Roman rule from the provinces. This particular site may be more Romanizing than many others because of Aphrodisias's early history of fidelity to Rome,[62] but there are clear signs of appropriation in both directions, even as the power relationship is made manifest. The official narrative of Rome—the princeps who is first among the citizens as the natural heir of Rome's history and religion—was insufficient for this place. The Aphrodisians had to retell the story, recasting the emperor as the natural heir of Greek history and religion and redefining themselves as loyal relatives of the rulers.

In the Sebasteion, then, a crucial distinction between provincial and municipal imperial cults emerges. The provincial cults had limited contact with the lives of ordinary Asians in the early imperial period. The players in the provincial cults were the wealthiest members of the elite; the participants were limited mostly to the populations in the handful of largest cities where such festivals took place. This was appropriate because the functions of provincial cults were directed more toward the definition of the imperial center and the delineation of the hierarchies created in relationship to that center. Proper language from the center was employed; proper procedures were followed with the Roman elite. In these ways the relationship between imperial center and province was negotiated and corrected.

Municipal cults, on the other hand, were everywhere. The players included a wider range of local elites; the participants were the inhabitants of cities, towns, villages, and countryside. The functions of the municipal cults were directed at local conditions and responsive to local themes. They brought an opportunity for creativity unmatched by provincial cults or even by other established religious institutions. Proper language and proper procedure consisted of whatever the local authorities decided and enforced (with an eye on extramural reaction, of course). A municipal cult could absorb local piety and bring the imperial family closer to the subjects but at the same time avail itself of intercultural influences (from Rome and elsewhere) that are an unavoidable byproduct of imperialism. A whole new aspect of religious discourse was evolving in the empire, one with potential for symbolic coherence at several levels of community life.

An Augusteion at Ephesos

The Ephesians set up at least one early temenos for Augustus, but the precise location has been difficult to determine. An early hypothesis placed it within the precincts of the Artemision, but two recent proposals have argued that it was located in or near the upper agora. This example of a municipal imperial cult provides less information than the previous example about the precincts itself but a good deal more information about the relation of a precinct to the rest of its urban context. This section starts with a description of features of the upper agora pertinent to the argument about the Augusteion, beginning with the monuments that can be securely identified and moving to those that are debatable. A discussion of the place of the temenos in the city follows, and the chapter concludes with a comparison of the municipal institutions at Aphrodisias and at Ephesos.[63]

The upper city area was an important part of Ephesos during the Hellenistic period, but much of the evidence has been concealed or destroyed by later rebuilding (figs. 5.12, 5.13). The most important rebuilding project was a thoroughgoing renovation during the Augustan period in the area now known variously as the upper agora or state agora.[64]

The largest building in this area was a monumental basilica, a three-aisled hall 167.7 m. long and 16.3 m. deep that covered the entire north side of the agora.[65] The basilica opened onto the agora through 67 Ionic columns above a four-step crepidoma. Enough pieces of the exterior architrave have been found to provide a secure reconstruction of the entire dedication inscription.[66] The inscription was carved in Latin and then in Greek in one line along 80 m. of the architrave. The basilica[67] was dedicated to Ephesian Artemis; to Emperor Caesar Augustus, son of god; to Tiberius Caesar, son of Augustus; and to the demos of the Ephesians. The benefactors—G. Sextilius Pollio along with his wife Ofillia Bassa, their son G. Ofillius Proculus, and their other children—were members of one of the most

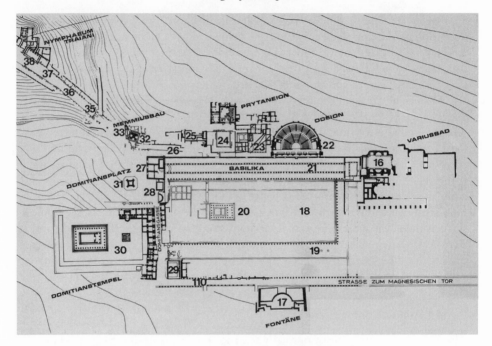

16	Upper Gymnasium	23	Double foundation and peristyle
17	Surge tank of Marnas Aqueduct/		courtyard
	monumental fountain	24	Prytaneion
18	Upper agora	28	Domitian plaza
19	South stoa of upper agora	30	Temple of the Sebastoi
20	Agora temple	32	Memmius monument
21	Basilica	35	Herakles Gate
22	Bouleuterion/odeion	38	Fountain of Trajan

FIGURE 5.12 Ephesos, plan of upper city. Courtesy of the Österreichisches Archäologisches Institut, Vienna.

influential families in Ephesos during the Augustan period. This inscription allows the building to be dated to the years 11–13 CE.[68]

At the east end of the basilica was a smaller room (approx. 12 × 16.3 m.) entered through the main aisle of the interior. The room has come to be known as the chalkidikum. Two inscribed statue bases were found here; one was made for a statue of G. Sextilius Pollio and the other for a statue of Ofillia Bassa.[69] Numerous other pieces of sculpture were found in this room as well, including a lifesize head of Augustus and many fragments from two overlifesize seated statues, one of Augustus and another of Livia (fig. 5.14).[70] These statues of the imperial couple and the local benefactors were probably displayed either in the chalkidium or in the hall itself, for stoas and halls such as this were often used for the display of paintings and statuary.[71]

Very little excavation has taken place along the western and southern edge of the upper agora (figs. 5.13, 5.15). The western end may have been marked by a

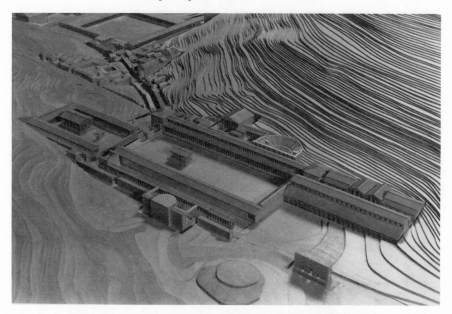

FIGURE 5.13 Model of upper city, Ephesos. © The Kunsthistorisches Museum, Vienna.

simple hall or perhaps just by a wall with a marble bench along its length. The long south side of the agora was defined by a building now referred to as the south stoa (160 m. long, one story, Doric order).[72] The corner where the south stoa met the eastern side of the agora provided one of two known entrances to the agora: a gate with a 6.75 m. wide opening and four Doric columns on its exterior.[73] The other known gate to the upper agora was located at the western end of the south stoa. It is very poorly preserved but clearly faced west, allowing traffic from the so-called Domitianic Street to enter the southwest corner of the agora.[74] The limited number of gates into the upper agora is peculiar. The gates served at least to highlight the monumental facade of the basilica as one entered the agora. The restricted access points may also indicate that this area had a strong sacral character.[75]

Three other monuments clustered behind the basilica are important indicators of the character of this part of the city: the prytaneion, the bouleuterion, and the controversial double foundation between them. A prytaneion could have several functions in any city. It was normally the site of the city's common hearth and the place where ambassadors and official visitors to a city were entertained. Beyond this the prytaneion might also play a role in governmental or religious institutions of the city. The main official, the prytanis, would normally play an important part in all of these.[76]

In Ephesos, a prytanis served for one year and would be particularly involved in four kinds of activities.[77] Two are relatively generic for this kind of office: the prytanis had to maintain the cult of Hestia and the eternal fire[78] and would also receive official municipal guests for dinner parties in the prytaneion.[79] Two other kinds of activities were more specifically Ephesian. One important responsibility

FIGURE 5.14 Overlifesize statues of Augustus (left) and Livia (right). Courtesy of the Efes Müzezi, Selçuk.

was to exercise oversight, along with the Kouretes, for mysteries of Artemis, which were celebrated every year to commemorate the birth of the city's most important goddess.[80] Finally, the prytanis was in charge of an official cycle of 365 sacrifices throughout the city for various deities.[81]

Thus, the prytaneion was one of the most important institutions in the array of activities that constituted the religious life of the city. It was approached from a street—now called the *clivus sacer*—that ran along the back side of the basilica. From the clivus one entered the peristyle courtyard (approx. 31.5 m. sq. including halls) in front of the prytaneion and confronted the six-columned Doric facade of the

FIGURE 5.15 Overview of upper agora, Ephesos. Author's photo.

prytaneion. The columns and the walls of the porch behind it were inscribed with the names of prytaneis and other officials who had completed their terms of service.[82] Two doors led from the porch into the building. One door led to side rooms on the left; the other led into the main room on the right. The main room (13.5 m. sq.) was probably the location of festive dinners and perhaps the site of the municipal hearth.[83] The other rooms probably served as meeting rooms or as storage for equipment associated with the activities centered here.

About 35 m. east of the prytaneion is a semicircular building with seating for about 1,400 people. The structure is less securely identified than the basilica or the prytaneion; even though it was among the first buildings to be excavated in the middle of the nineteenth century, its function is still debated. J. T. Wood unearthed part of the structure beginning in 1864 and gave it the name odeion because of its size and shape.[84] Further excavations were undertaken in the first half of this century,[85] but as adjacent buildings were explored in the 1960s and 1970s, a reevaluation of the semicircular building took place. Since that time, there has been a growing tendency to call the building a bouleuterion because several other buildings in the area seem to have civic or governmental functions. This building was larger than necessary to serve as the meeting place of the city's boule, which was composed of about 200 men, but it was not uncommon for a city to use its bouleuterion for concerts, orations, and other sorts of meetings.[86] Also favoring the identification as a bouleuterion are the absence of a scene building (suggesting deliberation rather than entertainment) and the posting of imperial letters on the scenae frons.[87]

The date of the bouleuterion is probably later than the period with which we are concerned. The building was dated to the middle of the second century CE due to a fragmentary dedicatory inscription from the years 160–169.[88] Wilhelm Alzinger pointed out, however, that this inscription could also have commemorated a remodeling, which would mean that the building was established closer to the first century CE.[89] There is also a possibility that a Hellenistic structure with the same function occupied this spot and was replaced by the current one. As no excavations have delved beneath the floor of the bouleuterion, this remains only a hypothesis. So the function of the building probably reflects the general character of this section of the upper city.

Between the bouleuterion and the prytaneion are the remains of a much more controversial precinct—one of two monuments yet to be considered. This 33 (east-west) × 28 m. precinct is fairly easy to describe, even though the visible remains are overlaid by a series of later renovations. It was composed of two main parts: a courtyard with Rhodian peristyle next to the west side of the bouleuterion, and a podium at the west end of the courtyard that supported two small structures. Limestone blocks from the stereobate of the podium are still in situ and show that the podium was built to hold two small structures side by side and facing east (fig. 2.1). Because it has not yet been established whether the small structures were altars or temples, I refer to the complex as the double foundation. A flight of at least seven steps along the front east side of the base led up from the courtyard. Marble orthostats lined the other three sides of the podium.[90]

Interpretation of the double foundation complex was made more difficult by early hypotheses that proved incorrect. The excavators tentatively labeled the complex as the municipal altar ("Staatsaltar") and dated it to the Hellenistic period on the basis of the peristyle colonnade.[91] Further evaluation showed that the Hellenistic date for the complex was wrong. The colonnade was Hellenistic, but it was brought there from some other older monument to be reused for the courtyard of the double foundation.[92]

The identification as a municipal altar has also been questioned, although none of the evidence has proved conclusive. Alzinger drew attention to the Italian character of the monument: the high podium against the back wall of a precinct was an unusual feature in Ephesian architecture during the Augustan period. The Augustan date and the double shrine suggested a connection with the cult of Rome and Divus Julius described by Dio Cassius.[93] The small scale of this precinct, tucked away in an important but less accessible area, would have been appropriate for the double cult specifically established for Romans.[94]

When these monuments were the only ones known, the area appeared to have the necessary prerequisites for a state agora, or the city's agora where governmental institutions were centered. In 1970, however, excavators unexpectedly found the remains of a moderate-size temple on the east-west axis of the agora (toward the west end) that greatly affected interpretation of this part of the city of Ephesos.

Because so much of the temple had been removed before excavation, there was very little evidence regarding the dedication of the temple.[95] Early publications offered a theory that the temple might have been dedicated to Isis or perhaps to several Egyptian deities.[96] Under normal conditions such a prominent location would not be expected for a temple of the Egyptian deities, but the peculiar situation of Ephesos in the late Republic gave the theory a certain plausibility. In the winter of 33/32 Mark Antony and Cleopatra stayed in Ephesos. Three hundred senators came to them there, and for a time it looked as if Ephesos might become the center of opposition to Octavian.[97] In this context a prominent temple to Isis in honor of Cleopatra might be plausible.[98]

The discovery of the agora temple gradually led to major reconsiderations of the whole area. Werner Jobst argued that the agora temple was dedicated to Augustus and that the entire upper agora area was related to this temple. His argument began with a convincing critique of earlier suggestions that the city's Augusteion was located near the temple of Artemis.[99] If the Sebasteion was not located near the Artemision, then where was it? Jobst pointed out that several pieces of evidence have been found in and around the upper agora, suggesting the presence of a Sebasteion there. One inscription honored a man who had put up a statue of Augustus and had consecrated the temenos (probably of Augustus).[100]

Another inscription is even more explicit and is important for several reasons:

ὑπὲρ τῆς τοῦ [κυρίου ἡμῶν]
Αὐτοκράτορος Τ[ίτου Καί-]
σαρος ὑγιήας καὶ διαμονῆς τῆς
Ῥωμαίων ἡγεμονίας ἀποκατεστά-
θη τὸ βλαβὲν περιτείχισμα τοῦ Αὐ-
γουστήου, κτλ.[101]

> On behalf of the health of our Lord Emperor Titus Caesar and (on behalf of)
> the permanence of the rule of the Romans, the damaged wall surrounding the
> Augusteion was repaired.

This interesting inscription mentions an Ephesian municipal imperial temple and
uses the unusual "Augusteion" in a Greek text. More important for the purposes of
this study, the inscription suggests some of the official motives for participation in
imperial cult institutions. The repair work is said here to be simultaneously a desire
or prayer for the health of the ruling emperor and a statement in support for the
continued rule of the Romans. Thus, the physical maintenance of the Augustus
precincts was to be understood as a symbol of support for the ongoing authority of
the current emperor Titus and for Roman imperial rule.

These and other inscriptions, along with the statuary mentioned before, lead
to the conclusion that a temenos of Augustus existed in or near the upper agora.[102]
Jobst made the case that the agora temple was indeed built for the worship of
Augustus. The case is circumstantial and will remain ambiguous until more direct
evidence surfaces. The overall redevelopment of the area is important, nevertheless.
A unified plan to organize the area was undertaken in the early Augustan period.
The agora floor was raised. A dramatic new basilica was constructed to ornament
the north side. The prytaneion was established nearby, as well as the double foundation precincts. Nearly all of the central institutions of Ephesian life were then in
this area, giving it the character associated with fora of Augustus in other cities.[103]
The main road from the Magnesian gate avoided cutting across this area but came
close enough to allow easy access.

The other alternative to the identification of the agora temple as the city's main
temple of Augustus is to turn instead to the double foundation. Peter Scherrer located the Augusteion at the double foundation precincts with the second structure
of the double foundation dedicated to Artemis.[104] This set-up would have allowed
the cult of the first emperor to be brought into the civic center in a relatively unob-
trusive manner. According to this interpretation, the agora temple then probably
served as the home for the cult of Rome and Divus Julius.[105]

Because neither of these two options is incontrovertible, a certain amount of
ambiguity must be maintained in this analysis. In either case, cults related to Rome
and Roman figures loomed large in this area. In terms of probability, the case for
the agora temple as an Augusteion is stronger: it takes more of the existing data into
account and is supported by parallels from other cities.[106]

Two Municipal Temples

These two municipal imperial temples at Aphrodisias and at Ephesos illustrate the
differences one encounters within the category "municipal imperial cult." The sanctuary at Aphrodisias was a fairly simple project whose sculpture is well preserved
and whose identification is secure. The architecture can be reconstructed, and there
is extensive information about mythic and global themes. The other temple, at
Ephesos, was part of a complicated series of buildings. Each building has its own

problems of interpretation and identification, and the coherence of the whole complex is debated. There is little or no information on the use of myth; instead, we are
rich in architectural evidence. Despite this imbalance, there is enough material to
allow profitable comparisons between them.

If we reflect on the two imperial cult sites discussed in this chapter, we see that
each is firmly grounded in its local situation. One way into this topic is to examine
the size of the two precincts. The Ephesian temenos of Augustus was much larger, so
large that the entire paved courtyard of the Aphrodisian precincts would have fit into
a little over half of the Ephesian basilica. We would expect no less, given the different
sizes and histories of the cities. Ephesos was one of the largest cities in the empire,
boasted a long history stretching back centuries, and had pretensions that Aphrodisias
could not afford. The Ephesian project reflects those pretensions with a huge temenos
whose dimensions exceeded 167 × 58 m. Aphrodisias had a much shorter history. It
was probably the result of a synoecism in the late Hellenistic period and began to flourish as a small city only in the early imperial period. With fewer resources and less of a
heritage in monumental architecture on which to draw, Aphrodisias constructed a
temenos that reflected Aphrodisian resources and aspirations.

In overall style, both municipal cults entered into the imperial traditions but did
so in different ways. Aphrodisias looked directly to Rome, the imperial center, for
inspiration, drawing specifically on the capital's forum tradition (particularly the Fora
of Julius and of Augustus) and on the Roman iconographic tradition of personified
nationalities. The Aphrodisians did not simply copy these imperial models but rather
used them to their own advantage. This Romanizing tendency of the Aphrodisians
was not a new development with the Sebasteion.[107] As a small, relatively young city
with strong ties to Rome, Aphrodisias demonstrated piety that had been developing
for some time and that was manifest in its municipal imperial cult.

The strategy of looking toward the capital is distinguishable from the strategy
used at Ephesos. The Ephesian precinct looked toward the developing urban imperial tradition of the eastern Mediterranean. The point of the Ephesian strategy was
to establish the place of Ephesos among the great cities of the empire. Its architecture shows more affinity with late Hellenistic tastes than with Roman styles. The
design of the basilica drew on the stoa and hall traditions of the Greek world, not
on the forum genre developing in the west. The agora temple shows similar choices:
the temple was built in good Hellenistic fashion, not according to Italian designs.

Finally, the Ephesian municipal imperial cult dominated the upper agora, the
sector where social organization was administered. Governance, sacrifice, and administration took place in this area, all within the shadow of the Augusteion. Perhaps the emperor loomed so large here because Ephesos was the provincial capital
and had a heightened sensitivity to the influence of the empire in everyday life. The
presence of imperial officials, the periodic visits of dignitaries, the processions and
ceremonies in Ephesos would have affected citizens' perceptions of imperial rule,
which would have found expression in their city imperial cults. Because there were
fewer imperial administrators and fewer imperial politicians in Aphrodisias, the
worship of the emperors took on a more distant and more abstract quality. This
may be one reason why the Aphrodisian temenos was dynastic and the Ephesian
temenos was limited to a specific emperor. Individual rulers made less difference in

the small cities of the province. The Aphrodisian elite certainly kept abreast of the developments within the dynasty, as shown by the wide range of imperial figures displayed as statues on or around the Sebasteion propylon. In Aphrodisias, however, changes in policy between emperors probably had less effect than in Ephesos.

With the passing of time, the temple of Augustus at Ephesos continued to be a powerful symbolic resource. When the city finally received a provincial temple under Domitian, the new temple was positioned directly west of the upper agora's southwest corner.[108] Was the site of the Flavian temple designed to show continuity and legitimation through proximity to the temenos of Augustus? Or was its elevated position above the temenos a sign of supersession? Such questions are probably not answerable some 1900 years later. The ruins of empire show clearly, however, that municipal imperial cults were part of a new discursive practice in Asia. These religious institutions provided a new range of options for the creative representation of identities within the imperial framework. They possessed considerable symbolic resources for incorporating human communities into the world created by the Sebastoi.

6

GROUPS AND INDIVIDUALS

The categories used in this study to examine imperial cults—provincial, municipal, group,[1] and individual—help us understand the phenomena, but, like all heuristic devices, they have limits. The first section of this chapter illustrates this through a discussion of hymnodes—male choirs that sang at religious events. Because some hymnodes cross at least three of these categories, and perhaps all four, they could have been included in chapters on provincial cults or municipal cults. I discuss them here because most of their activities took place in group settings, but they also illustrate the interconnections across the categories. The second section of the chapter presents imperial mysteries, an aspect of imperial cults that emphasized group settings more than others. The chapter closes with votive offerings individuals made for members of the imperial household.

Hymnodes in Imperial Cults

Singing, chanting, and reciting poetry are among the most widespread of religious practices. Evidence from Roman Asia provides examples of groups of singers known as hymnodes, who were specially trained to perform such duties for many deities.[2] The epigraphic references to hymnodes are mostly to men, and do not usually specify the cult to which the hymnodes belonged. Several refer to hymnodes of Artemis,[3] and some contexts suggest other cults, such as that of Apollo,[4] Zeus and Hekate,[5] and perhaps Dionysos.[6] Many other cults probably had such choirs.

Hymnodes were part of many imperial cults as well, and several documents increase our knowledge of such choirs. The following text is part of an inscription originally displayed at Hypaipa, near Ephesos. The inscription originally included at least three distinct texts, but it is now fragmentary at the beginning and breaks off at the end.[7] To make matters worse, the left side is damaged and some of the right side is missing as well. Despite the gaps, the inscription provides important information about the activities and organization of imperial hymnodes.

One of the three texts was a copy of a koinon decree from the provincial council of Asia from around 41 CE. Enough of the text is preserved to allow the following reconstruction:

> Decision of the Hellenes of Asia. Proposal of G. Iu. Anaxagoras, son of [. . .],
> loyal to Caesar [φιλόκαισαρ], high priest of Asia, and agonothete for life of the
> goddess Rome and of god Augustus Caesar, Zeus Patroos, emperor and pontifex
> maximus, father of the fatherland [πατρίς] and of the whole human race. Since
> it is appropriate to provide a public display of reverence and of pious consider-
> ation toward the imperial household during the year, the hymnodes from all
> Asia—coming together in Pergamon on the most holy birthday of Sebastos
> Tiberius Caesar God—complete a great work to the glory of the assembly,
> making hymns to the imperial house and completing sacrifices to the gods
> Sebastoi, leading festivals and hosting banquets [. . .].[8]

The end of this text provides a concise summary of the activities for which imperial hymnodes were responsible: they sang hymns to the imperial family, participated in imperial sacrifices, led celebrations, and hosted banquets.[9] The occasion for these activities is important as well. The gathering was in Pergamon for the birthday of Tiberius (Nov. 16). In 41 CE, however, there was already a provincial temple for Tiberius, Livia, and the Senate in Smyrna. So why did the hymnodes gather in Pergamon rather than at the temple of Tiberius in Smyrna? Another inscription (see next paragraph) suggests that these hymnodes began as a network of choirs from all Asia that gathered to sing the praises of Augustus at the provincial temple in Pergamon. Their duties apparently expanded as new emperors took the throne, new festivals arose, and more travel was necessary. The group retained their connection to the Pergamene provincial cult, though, and this reminds us that a provincial temple would have been the site of a cycle of festivals throughout the year for various members of the dynasty.[10]

The inscription reveals aspects of the organization of the hymnodes. The decree assumes the presence throughout the province of these hymnodes who gather on particular holidays, so we should imagine that many communities had similar male choirs who traveled to imperial cult festivals. A second text from the Hypaipa inscription—the dedication text that preceded the koinon decree—supports this supposition. The dedication text explained who commissioned the inscriptions and why. The extant portion began with a familiar rationale for participation in imperial cults, provided a date for the inscription by naming two local officials, and then recorded the people who commissioned the inscribed texts. The hymnodes responsible for the inscription would have been the local imperial choir from Hypaipa:

[. . . on behalf of the etern]al continuation of Tiberius Claudius Caesar Sebastos
Germanicus and his whole house. When the stephanephoros was Tiberius
Claudius Quirina Trypho, son of Asklepiodoros; when the grammateus of the
demos and neokoros and disperser of the imperial funds was Alexander son of
Apollonis.

The hymnodes dedicated (this) according to the decree that is in Pergamon
from the holy assembly, (the hymnodes) engraving the rights and privileges
given to them. Hosios son of Apollonios Herm[. . . oversaw this?][11]

Another organizational aspect emerges from this dedication text. The central
congress of the hymnodes from all Asia, called in the dedication text the holy synod,
ἡ ἱερὰ σύνοδος, met in Pergamon. The existence of this synod is probably confirmed by the third text from the inscription—the opening fragment of a letter from
the emperor Claudius. The name of the addressee is damaged, but the reconstruction is reasonable: "[to the hol]y [synod] of the hymnodes."[12] The imperial titulature
in the opening also provides a specific date for the letter between January 25 and
December 31, 41 CE.[13]

Thus, the probable events presupposed by the inscription's three texts follows
this sequence: the hymnodes of Asia convened in Pergamon, probably for the birthday of Tiberius. The koinon then issued its decree that praised the hymnodes for
their actions. A copy of the koinon decree went to Rome, and the emperor Claudius
responded with the letter, which is only partially preserved. The imperial letter from
Claudius approved of the celebration and may have stipulated conditions for its
continuation. Afterward, the synod of the hymnodes voted its own decree about
their newly approved rights and privileges. This synod decree was displayed in
Pergamon, probably in the precincts of the Temple of Rome and Augustus. The
hymnodes from Hypaipa ordered a copy of the decree to be engraved in their home-
town, and hymnodes from other communities certainly did the same.[14]

Three years later, in 44 CE, the proconsul Paullus Fabius Persicus issued an edict
with more information about the imperial hymnodes of Asia. The edict was issued
to resolve irregularities in the financial affairs of Ephesos. Much of the text focused
on financial administration related to the Artemision, which included questions
about funding for hymnodes of Artemis. This discussion required the proconsul to
clarify Ephesian funding for imperial cult hymnodes:

Likewise regarding the hymnodes—to whom no small part of the municipal
income is paid in order that this service be performed—it is resolved: the
ephebes, whose age and worth and ability to learn are better attuned[15] to such a
liturgy, shall provide this need without payment. Lest I seem to have judged the
case for all hymnodes everywhere, I exempt those singing hymns in Pergamon to
the god Augustus himself in the temenos dedicated by Asia. There the first
assembly gathered, not as though hired but voluntarily and without payment.
For this reason also the god Augustus preserved the privileges decreed later
regarding the succession of those who came after them, that their expenses be
defrayed not only by the Pergamenes, but by the whole of Asia, because such a
contribution would be a burden for a single city. Even though the city of the

Ephesians is freed from this expense and the service is transferred to the ephebes according to their proposal, they must see to it that the ephebes complete the duty carefully and with appropriate attention, singing hymns to the divine household in a fitting way.[16]

This edict provides useful information about the history of the hymnodes of all Asia. The reference to hymnodes comes in the context of a discussion of the organization of festivals for Artemis. We learn that, at least until 44 CE, the normal practice in Ephesos was for hymnodes for Artemis to be paid from municipal funds, and that this had become a burden to the city. The Ephesians requested[17] that they be allowed to free themselves of this expense by holding the ephebes responsible for the singing of hymns to Artemis, and the proconsul agreed. He stipulated, however, that his ruling did not free the Ephesians from their responsibility to send hymnodes to the provincial temple in Pergamon; in the process the proconsul provided historical details of those institutions. The gathering of hymnodes at the temple of Rome and Augustus in Pergamon began as a unpaid service. Pergamon probably financed many of their activities, for later it was decreed—with the approval of Augustus—that the costs should be underwritten not just by Pergamon but by all the cities. Persicus affirmed the ruling of Augustus and concluded that the Ephesians would still be responsible for the participation of their ephebes at the provincial imperial cult celebrations.

The next section of the edict is fragmentary but clearly moves on to the topic of hymnodes for Livia, who had been divinized by Claudius and the Senate three years earlier in 41 CE. Those who sang for her were to receive the same rights as those singing for Augustus, so the cities were probably liable for those expenses as well.[18] Thus, Persicus allowed the Ephesians to require their ephebes to serve at municipal festivals without payment, but required the city to maintain the delegations sent to Pergamon for imperial cult festivals during the year.[19]

The evidence is ambiguous regarding how long this arrangement persisted. On one hand, an inscription from around the third decade of the second century, consistent with the edict of Persicus, reports that when the emperor Hadrian visited Ephesos, the ephebes sang hymns in the theater while he listened.[20] On the other hand, more than a dozen references in the Ephesian inscriptions mention men called hymnodes, which would be an unusually small number if all the wealthy young men raised in the city served in this function as ephebes. Either everyone would mention it, or no one would mention it because everyone had served in this way.

The ephebes were not the only group of hymnodes involved in imperial cults; separate male choruses were apparently attached to provincial temples in Asia. References from the second or third century mention hymnodes "of the temple of the God Hadrian" at Ephesos.[21] A list of donors from Smyrna referred to the decree by which the city had been granted its second provincial temple (under Hadrian), along with sacred games, theologians, and hymnodes.[22] Another inscription notes that the hymnodes of the provincial cult in Smyrna included 24 men.[23]

These official decrees provide information about the organization and administration of certain male choirs. Information about the internal affairs of a particular group of imperial hymnodes comes from an inscribed altar of the early second century CE. In September 1885, the altar was found in the lower city area of ancient Pergamon, 3 m. below the nineteenth-century street level (fig. 6.1). The altar stood 1.045 m. high; it was a little over 0.5 m. wide and about 0.5 m. deep. All four sides were inscribed.[24] The front (side A) contained a dedication formula and the name of the group: "With good fortune. To Emperor Caesar Trajan Hadrian Olympios, Savior and Founder. The Hymnodes of god Augustus and goddess Rome (dedicated this)."[25] A list of the members followed this dedication. The bottom of the stone was lost, and parts of three lines have been erased in the middle, but at least 39 hymnodes were named. The erasures and lacunae probably named another four to six men who were members.

The other three sides of the altar are in better condition and contain texts that identified regulations for the activities of the hymnodes. Several comments on organization and ritual follow this translation:

SIDE B (to the right of side A)

With good fortune.
What the eukosmos provides during the year of his office.
In the month of Caesar on Augustan day, for the birthday of Augustus: one mina.
In the month of Peritios on the Kalends of January: one mina and one loaf.
In the month of Panemos on Augustan day, for Rosalia: one mina and one loaf.
On the third of the month of Loos for the mysteries: wine, one mina and one loaf.
On the next to the last day of the month of Hyperberetaios: one mina and one loaf.

The eukosmos will provide crowns for the hymnodes on the monthly celebration of the birthday of Augustus and on the other birthdays of the emperors. For the mysteries he (will provide): a crowning ceremony in the hymnodeion; crowns for the hymnodes and for their sons each day; and a round loaf, incense, and lamps for Augustus.

For those who pass away, the official will provide 15 denarii for incense, which he will receive back from the successor (of the deceased). The slaves of the undertaker will receive 12 denarii from the common (funds) for incense.

SIDE C (back side)

With good fortune.
What the priest provides during the year of his office.
In the month of Peritios on the Kalends of January: wine, table setting, one mina, and three loaves.
On the second of Panemos, for Rosalia: wine, table setting, one mina, and three loaves.
On the second of Loos: wine, one mina, and three loaves.
On the next to the last day of Hyperberetaios: one mina and three loaves.
On the 30th of the same month: wine (for the hymn sung) by the altar, and table setting worth one denarius.

The hymnodes being appointed from outside will give 50 denarii for the images of the Sebastoi.

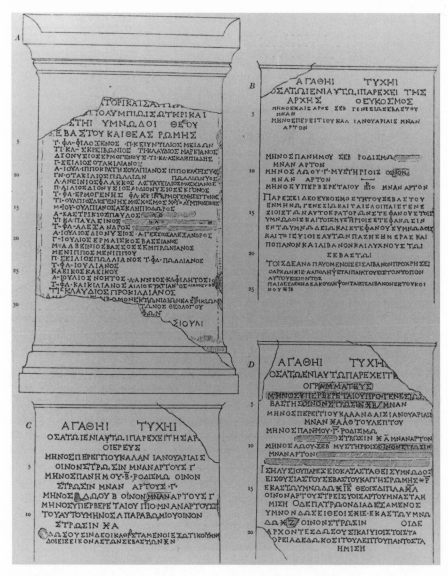

FIGURE 6.1 Drawing of an inscribed altar of the hymnodes of god Augustus and goddess Rome, Pergamon. Reprinted, by permission, from *AvP* 8,2 #374. Courtesy of the Deutsches Archäologisches Institut, Berlin.

SIDE D (left of side A)

With good fortune.

What the grammateus provides during the year of his office.

On the next to the last day of Hyperberetaios, for the birthday of Sebaste (i.e., Livia):
wine, table setting worth two denarii, and one mina.

During the month of Peritios on the Kalends of January: one mina, one denarius, and
nine asses in local coinage.

On the third of Panemos, for Rosalia: table setting worth one denarius, one mina,
and one loaf.

In the month of Loos on Augustan day, for the mysteries: wine, table setting, one mina,
one loaf [. . .]

[. . .]

> Upon admission, the appointed hymnode will provide 100 denarii for the
> sacrifices of Augustus and of Rome; 15 denarii for each hymnode (for the gods a
> double share of 30 denarii), wine, and three loaves; for sons, one loaf and one
> half mina. The one who succeeds his father (as hymnode) will give: to the gods
> 15 denarii; to each hymnode 7 denarii, wine, and table setting. The officials
> shall also refund 50% in local coinage to sons who have paid choral fees.[26]

These regulations reveal several aspects of the organization of the hymnodes of
god Augustus and goddess Rome. The exclusively male group had its own building
for meetings. The number of memberships was set at around 35–40, with new
members added only after the death of a hymnode. At least 34 of the men were
Roman citizens and 4 were not. With regard to admission, procedures for the incorporation of members were in place, but the sons of members received prefer-
ence, participating in some activities for a small fee and paying a lower price of admission to the group.

Three different officials are named in sides B–D: the eukosmos, the priest, and
the grammateus. It is difficult to discern any hierarchy. Fränkel suspected that the
order—starting at the front and moving to the right—provided a ranking, but his
calculations that the annual contributions of the three officials were roughly equivalent[27] seem to contradict that conclusion. The titles of the offices suggest functional
distinctions. Because "eukosmos" means "orderly, decorous, well behaved," this
official probably was responsible for general oversight, ensuring proper protocol.
The priest clearly would have been in charge of sacrifices, so the grammateus perhaps held administrative duties. Side A also mentions a theologos. None of the regulations requires him to provide anything for the meetings of the hymnodes. His title
shows that he was responsible instead for delivering sermons or encomia, praising
those worshipped in the meetings.[28]

The contributions listed on the altar show some distinctions between the offices, although the existing lists did not exhaust the responsibilities of these officers.
The contributions of the eukosmos consisted mostly of a mina (= 100 denarii) five
times a year, bread, wine, costumes (wreaths for the fathers, and sometimes for the
sons), and ritual paraphernalia for the mysteries. The priest also supplied money
for the feasts (one mina four times a year) and wine; his contribution of bread seems

to have been a triple portion, and he provided table settings three times. The grammateus gave a mina only three times; the other requirements for him were similar to those of the others (table settings, wine, bread).

The official name of the group does not quite match the official title of the provincial imperial cult institutions. The official title of the provincial temple in Pergamon began with Rome and then included Augustus, but by the Hadrianic period the goddess had receded in significance. The order of the deities in the official name of the hymnodes—Augustus first and then Rome—reflected this second-century context. Thus, the group's name, as hymnodes of "god Augustus and goddess Rome," placed the goddess in second place. More telling, however, there were no rituals or regulations listed for her veneration at all.

"Hymnode" should also not mislead us; the men were involved in other activities as well. For example, reference to care for deceased choir members appears twice, in the festival of Rosalia and in the guidelines for paying for funerary incense at the end of side B. The inclusion of sons and grandsons also gave the group a transgenerational character and a socialization function, frequent meetings no doubt encouraging business and economic collaboration.

From the extant texts a ritual calendar for the group can be constructed. In general, the hymnodes participated in three kinds of meetings during the year: four large festivals involving banquets and often lasting more than one day; a series of smaller annual gatherings (for which the only recorded donation is crowns for the hymnodes supplied by the eukosmos); and two types of occasional events at irregular intervals (funerals, admission of new members). If the hymnodes observed all the imperial birthdays, they met at least 19 times each year, about one meeting every three weeks. A glance at the dates shows that they had fewer meetings in certain periods. However, they met at least once a month, since the first day of each month was a celebration of the birthday of Augustus. The busiest periods were late September and May through June.

The calendar is laid out as in table 6.1, with the dates of the larger festivals in italics and parentheses indicating probable meetings.[29] The year began with a three-day festival ending with the birthday of Augustus on September 23. The celebration started with a large feast to commemorate the birth of Livia on September 21. Her actual birthday was January 30, but this group celebrated it in conjunction with that of Augustus.[30] The second day—the last day of the year—was spent at least in part at another banquet that included a special hymn sung at the altar. The donations for the third day, which was the actual birthday of Augustus, are relatively meager: a mina from the eukosmos but no food, wine, or table settings. Because September 23 was the date of the annual festival for Rome and Augustus at the provincial temple in Pergamon, the hymnodes were probably occupied there and elsewhere in the city at public gatherings on this auspicious day.

Two major festivals exhibited a distinctly Roman character: the Kalends of January and Rosalia, which were imported feasts, one for the beginning of the new year according to the Julian calendar and the other a three-day commemoration of the dead.[31] I discuss the final major festival, a three-day celebration of the mysteries, in the next section of this chapter.

How was this group connected to the provincial cult in Pergamon? Most scholars have concluded that these were the hymnodes for the provincial temple cult.[32]

TABLE 6.1 Reconstructed ritual calendar of the hymnodes of God Augustus and Goddess Rome

Date	Festival	Official	Donation
Sept. 21–23	Birthday of Livia (Sept. 21)	Eukosmos	Mina, one loaf.
		Priest	Mina, three loaves.
		Grammateus	Wine, table setting worth two denarii, mina.
	Day before birthday of Augustus, and last day of the year (Sept. 22)	Priest	Wine for the altar hymn, table setting worth one denarius.
	Birthday of Augustus, New Year's Day (Sept. 23)	Eukosmos	Mina, crowns for hymnodes.
(Sept. 30?)	Birthday of Titus	Eukosmos	Crowns for hymnodes.
Oct. 24	Apellaios Augustan day	Eukosmos	Crowns for hymnodes.
(Nov. 8?)	Birthday of Nerva	Eukosmos	Crowns for hymnodes.
(Nov. 16?)	Birthday Tiberius	Eukosmos	Crowns for hymnodes.
(Nov. 17?)	Birthday of Vespasian	Eukosmos	Crowns for hymnodes.
Nov. 23	Audnaios Augustan day	Eukosmos	Crowns for hymnodes.
Dec. 24	Peritios Augustan day	Eukosmos	Crowns for hymnodes.
January 1	Calends of January	Eukosmos	Mina, one loaf.
		Priest	Wine, table setting, mina, three loaves.
		Grammateus	Mina, one drachma, nine asses.
Jan. 24	Dystrios Augustan day (and birthday of Hadrian?)	Eukosmos	Crowns for hymnodes.
Feb. 21	Xandikos Augustan day	Eukosmos	Crowns for hymnodes.
March 24	Artemisios Augustan day	Eukosmos	Crowns for hymnodes.
April 23	Daisios Augustan day	Eukosmos	Crowns for hymnodes.
May 24–26	Rosalia, 1st day (and Panemos Augustan day)	Eukosmos	Mina, one loaf.
	Rosalia, 2nd day	Priest	Wine, table setting, mina, three loaves.
	Rosalia, 3rd day	Grammateus	Table setting worth one denarius, mina, one loaf.
June 23–25	Mysteries, 1st day (and Loos Augustan day)	Grammateus	Wine, table setting, one loaf [. . .].
	Mysteries, 2nd day	Priest	Wine, mina, three loaves.
	Mysteries, 3rd day	Eukosmos	Wine, mina, one loaf.
	Mysteries, each day	Eukosmos	Ceremony for hymnodeion; crowns for hymnodes and their sons; round loaves, incense, and lamps for Augustus.
July 24	Gorpiaios Augustan day	Eukosmos	Crowns for hymnodes.
(August 1?)	Birthday of Claudius	Eukosmos	Crowns for hymnodes.
August 23	Hyperberetaios Augustan day	Eukosmos	Crowns for hymnodes.
(Sept. 18?)	Birthday of Trajan	Eukosmos	Crowns for hymnodes.

Dates of larger festivals are in italic. Dates in parentheses indicate imperial birthdays that probably were observed even though the inscription does not enumerate them. I have listed Tiberius, Claudius, Vespasian, Titus, Nerva, Trajan, and Hadrian as possibilities, leaving out Gaius, Nero, his three brief successors from 68–69, and Domitian. The inscription uses dates from the Asian months. The corresponding dates according to the Roman calendar are conveniently summarized in Bickerman 1980:48 fig. 3.

Fränkel thought their hymnodeion might even have been located in the temenos of the Temple of Rome and Augustus,[33] but that seems unlikely because there is no reference to the provincial precincts in the texts from this altar. In fact, there is no reference to any provincial official or to any provincial imperial cult institution in the texts from this altar. The members, the festivals, and the finances take precedence; no mention of Asia, the province, the high priesthoods, the synod of hymnodes from all Asia, the agonothetes, the gymnasiarchs, or the Romaia Sebasta games appears.

Evidence suggest that these hymnodes were affiliated in some way with the provincial temple of Rome and Augustus. Their financial status as wealthy Pergamene men means they would have been expected to contribute to the provincial festivals. The donations required on the birthday of Augustus also suggest that the group participated in the public celebrations on that day rather than gathering separately at the hymnodeion. There are no donations for food or table settings on September 23, but every other day of all four major festivals—birthday of Augustus, Kalends of January, Rosalia, and the Mysteries—presupposes a common meal. Instead, the only donation listed on the birthday of Augustus is money for the group and crowns for the hymnodes.

An examination of the reconstructed ritual calendar shows that the main occasions—perhaps the only occasions—for participation in provincial institutions would have been on the monthly celebrations of the birth of Augustus. On these days the only recorded donations were the crowns from the eukosmos, probably part of the choir's costume. The hymnodes likely performed in public monthly on Augustan days. September 23 was also the climax to the three-day festival that began with a celebration of Livia's birth. On May 24 and June 23, the Augustan performances would have coincided with the beginnings of three-day festivals (Rosalia and the Mysteries, respectively). If the crowns were indeed a part of the choir's costume, we may conclude that the birthdays of the other emperors were also occasions for public performances. On at least some of these occasions, such as the birthday of Livia, the birthday of Augustus, and perhaps the birthday of Tiberius, the Pergamene hymnodes would have been joined by hymnodes from other cities throughout Asia.

Thus, the inscriptions from the altar of the hymnodes from Pergamon provide a rare glimpse into the internal workings of a group dedicated to the worship of the emperors. The hymnodes of the god Augustus and the goddess Rome were a wealthy, elite group of 35–40 men who engaged in religious practices together. Their regulations show no signs of direct control by the city or the koinon. They paid membership fees and made benefactions to their own group accounts. Yet the hymnodes also illustrate interconnections between provincial, municipal, and group imperial cults, because they represented the city and the province in one of the great symbolic events of Asia's year—the celebration of the oldest provincial imperial cult in the empire.

Imperial Mysteries

The imperial mysteries bear a double interpretive burden: problems associated with mystery cults and problems associated with imperial cults. Inquiry into mystery cults has a long history of publishing and contention.[34] A recent study has argued persuasively that academic discourse about "mystery religions" in the last two to three centuries has often served as a thinly veiled attack by Protestant scholars against Catholic theology and practice. Protestant scholars have tended to use mystery religions as an allegory for Roman Catholic Christianity, characterizing the mysteries as ritualistic influences that eventually corrupted pure primitive Christianity and prepared the way for the "Dark Ages."[35] Many studies of the ancient mysteries have been preoccupied more with a partisan interpretation of Christian history rather than with the stated object of inquiry.[36]

Interpretation of imperial mysteries also faces problems in the general interpretation of imperial cults. Specifically, there have been questions about whether the sentiments behind imperial mysteries were truly spiritual or simply political. These attempts to make the ancient world conform to parochial, modern definitions have not been convincing. H. W. Pleket pointed out the special pleading employed to dismiss the religious dimensions of imperial mysteries.[37] He argued that a wider definition of religion—one that recognizes the importance of ritual practice in the construction of an ordered world—allows us to place the imperial mysteries within the parameters of ancient polytheism.[38] Nothing in the existing evidence for imperial mysteries justifies separating them from other religious phenomena of their time.[39]

The evidence, as always, is less abundant than one would hope, especially for a single province. One source of information is the title "sebastophant" that begins to show up in imperial period inscriptions. Some historians of Greco-Roman religion likened this office to that of a theologos or an agonothete and thereby suggested that there were no true mysteries in the imperial cults.[40] However, the term sebastophant is built on the analogy of the hierophant in a cult like that of Demeter and Kore at Eleusis. At Eleusis the hierophant played a crucial role in the mysteries by performing sacred acts, speaking sacred words, and showing sacred objects. The sebastophant would have played a similar part in the imperial mysteries, especially in the revelation of the imperial statues.[41]

The office of sebastophant appears occasionally as a provincial imperial cult office, usually in a constellation of three specific offices: provincial high priest, agonothete, and sebastophant. For example, a damaged koinon decree from Smyrna, probably commissioned in the first century CE, referred to a provincial high priest who was also a sebastophant and agonothete of the Romaia Sebasta.[42] Five other inscriptions honor one man, T. Fl. Montanus, with three similar titles: "high priest of Asia of Asia's common temple in Ephesos, sebastophant, and agonothete for life."[43] His high priesthood was undertaken in Ephesos between 90 and 112 CE,[44] though he probably came from Akmonia.[45] One of the inscriptions appears to connect the three offices by embedding the titles sebastophant and agonothete between a reference to his high priesthood and the comment that he "served honorably as high priest" (ἀρχιερατεύσαντα ἐνδόξως).[46] As the same set of three titles occurs in a mid-first-century inscription from the theater in Aphrodisias,[47] it appears that one pattern of service in Asia was to serve in three distinct capacities—high priest of Asia, sebastophant, and agonothete of provincial games—in the same year and, presumably, in the same city.[48]

In the inscribed altar of the hymnodes of god Augustus and of goddess Rome from Pergamon, we find valuable information about imperial mysteries in a group (rather than provincial) setting.[49] As a local group, the hymnodes participated in a range of imperial cult festivals, one of which involved imperial mysteries. An examination of the texts on their altar indicates the importance of this holiday. The mysteries constituted one of the group's four major festivals during the year. Beginning on the Augustan day of the month of Loos, it was one of two events in which sons of members were certainly involved.[50] It was also the only festival that clearly required both a feast and crowns.[51]

There are also hints regarding the events of the imperial mysteries. The meeting hall assumed more importance during the mysteries than during the other three major holidays. Banquets were held here on each day for all four festivals, but we have references to a crowning ceremony inside of the hymnodeion only during the three days of the mysteries. The eukosmos also provided "a round loaf, incense, and lamps for Augustus,"[52] so small sacrifices to the first emperor were one of the most important activities that took place. Lamps served ritual purposes as well. The dramatic use of light and shadow was a standard feature of mystery rituals (and of ritual in general). The sudden illumination of imperial statues may have been a part of such rites.[53]

Thus, the altar inscription of this group leads to the conclusion that their mysteries were celebrated with a larger group (including hymnodes and sons), that the rituals inside the meeting hall were more elaborate than at other times with crowns for all of the regular members and also for their sons, and that the ceremonies involved daily sacrifices to Augustus and feasting. The inscription does not mention initiates or initiation or hint that there were sacral officials other than the priest. So the hymnodes cannot be classified as a mystery thiasos in the strict sense of the word. Rather, they were an elite group devoted to singing the praises of the divine imperial family in a number of contexts. Within their broad range of religious activities imperial mysteries were included.

In contrast to the Pergamene hymnodes of Augustus and Rome, some groups were organized around mysteries of other deities and added imperial mysteries to their regular cycle of holidays. Two examples from Ephesos illustrate the contrast with the Pergamene hymnodes. The first example comes from the base of a statue of Hadrian raised by a Dionysian group:

> Emperor Caesar Trajan Hadrian Sebastos—son of God Trajan Parthicus,
> grandson of God Nerva—pontifex maximus, holding tribunician power, consul
> for the third time. The initiates before the city (consecrated him) enthroned
> with Dionysos when the priest was Cl. Romulus, the hierophant was Cl. Eubios,
> and the curator [ἐπιμελητής] was Antonius Drusus. The statue was set up from
> personal funds by Theodotos Proclus the hymnode—son of (Theodotos) Proclus
> the mystagogue—with his children and (with) Athenodoros.[54]

The officials mentioned in this inscription reflect the group's structure as a mystery cult association. The initiates of Dionysos Before the City had a priest, a hierophant, a hymnode (probably for this thiasos), and a curator in charge of the mysteries.[55] Several related fragments mention a hierologos of the group.[56] The inclusion of Hadrian in this group's worship would have been a relatively easy transition. Although imperial mysteries are not explicitly mentioned, it is reasonable to conclude that they were celebrated for Hadrian as well as for Dionysos, as Hadrian is described as enthroned with the god.

The inclusion of imperial mysteries is more explicit in the worship of Demeter at Ephesos. I cited the evidence—an official request to the Roman proconsul—in the survey of municipal cults because the affairs of this group drew the city into provincial affairs.[57] One other aspect of the inscription is important: it asserted that imperial mysteries had been celebrated regularly in the city by the initiates of Demeter for some time.[58] This case of imperial mysteries added to an existing mystery cult organization suggests a pattern that was probably widespread in antiquity but barely surfaces in the surviving evidence.

These examples differ from that of the hymnodes of the god Augustus and goddess Rome in at least one important respect. The Ephesian groups were much less exclusive than the Pergamene hymnodes. The lists of Dionysian priests and mystai have been damaged, but we can assume that this group was much larger than the Pergamene hymnode association.[59] Clearly, mystery groups like these in Ephesos were more widespread than were imperial hymnodes. Thus, in the two Ephesian groups we see the process by which imperial mysteries included a larger segment of society. We have evidence not only for imperial mysteries celebrated once a year by the hymnodes but also for imperial mysteries permeating the celebrations for Dionysos, for Demeter Karporphoros, and for Demeter Thesmophoros, both in their private and public ceremonies. We may assume that such imperial cult practices went on in other religious groups as well.[60]

Families and Individuals

Before reviewing the evidence for family or individual worship of the emperors, I note that little material on these topics has survived from Asia. Such material would not be monumental and therefore was less likely to survive and be found. This does not completely explain the shortage of evidence because household altars and individual votives for nonimperial worship are not so rare. Another factor must be that imperial cults were less important in family and individual piety than was the case with some other religious institutions. This has led some scholars to conclude that imperial cults were not truly religious. True religion, so the argument goes, is a matter of the heart; only deeply felt, spontaneous emotion qualifies as genuine spirituality. This study relies on a different definition of religion. I am not trying to find out whether the Greeks really believed that the emperor was a god nor looking for signs that authentic emotion was the source of imperial cults.[61] This study constructs a description of the roles played by imperial cults within the larger polytheistic systems that defined urban life in the Roman province of Asia. Even if the amount of material for personal reverence is smaller, we need not conclude that imperial cults were not religious. No single cult covered all aspects of ancient religiosity. My goal here is to illuminate the specific contours of imperial cults as one fundamental part of Asia's socioreligious world.

The only clear evidence for household worship of the emperors in Asia comes from the first half of the second century CE, almost outside the limits set for this study. This later evidence should not be automatically projected back onto first-century practice. I include it here because it serves as an important reminder of the interdependence of household and city. At Miletos, the largest known group of household altars is composed of inexpensive pieces in various designs dedicated to Hadrian (for an example, see fig. 6.2). Because many are damaged, only an approximate range of their heights can be determined: 0.3–0.6 m. The inscriptions on the altars are formulaic, with only minor variations: "To Emperor Caesar Hadrian Sebastos Zeus Olympios, Savior and Founder," or sometimes, "Savior and Benefactor."[62] The excavators were so impressed with the number of these altars they speculated that every house may have had one.[63]

Because no other altars have been found for other emperors, perhaps these household altars for Hadrian were commissioned for a particular event, such as one of the emperor's visits to Asia, when all householders in Miletos—or at least those living in a certain area—were expected to purchase altars like these. As such, the altars provide an exaggerated example from one city rather than a picture of ordinary practice. The exaggeration, however, was probably based on a practice that was not abnormal. Some householders would have included imperial figures in family shrines throughout the imperial period.[64] Moreover, important municipal celebrations would have raised expectations for participation by some householders perhaps because of their locations along processional ways, because of the family's patronage connections, or because of the involvements of relatives.

Personal votive offerings to the emperor have been more widely discussed than family worship, even though the actual number of artifacts is small. The debate has centered on whether private prayers for divine assistance were directed toward the emperor, followed by votive offerings of thanks. In other words, was there an individual dimension to imperial piety, or was it purely "political"? One academic tradition has denied the personal dimension;[65] another has affirmed it on the basis of a few inscriptions.[66] The evidence for personal votives to members of the imperial family, however, is slowly accumulating, and the arguments against them are less credible. Nevertheless, a recent study concluded that votives naming emperors were actually *in honor of* those emperors but *offered to* some other deity, even though no other deity was named. According to the argument, the name was unnecessary because the identity of the god or goddess would have been obvious on the basis of the shrine where the votive was offered. When both a god and an emperor were named in the dative, the study described one phrase as a "votive dative" for the deity and the other (grammatically identical) phrase as a "dative of honor" for the emperor.[67]

Two inscriptions from Asia focus the discussion more profitably. One comes from near Ilion:

        Ἀντωνίαν τὴν
        ἀδελφιδῆν τὴν θεοῦ
        Σεβαστοῦ, γυναῖκα δὲ γε-
        νομένην Δρούσου Κλαυ-
        δίου ἀδελφοῦ τοῦ αὐ-
        τοκράτορος Τιβερίου, Σεβασ-
        τοῦ υἱοῦ, Σεβαστοῦ, μητέρα

FIGURE 6.2 Household altar from Miletos dedicated to
Apollo of Didyma and to Hadrian (*Milet* 1,7 #301).
Hadrian is called Zeus Olympios, Savior, and Founder
(of the city). Courtesy of the Miletos Müzezi.

δὲ Γερμανικοῦ Καίσαρος
καὶ Τιβερίου Κλαυ-
δίου Γερμανικοῦ
καὶ Λειβίας θεᾶς Ἀφρο-
δείτης Ἀνχεισιάδος,
πλείστας καὶ μεγίσ-
τας ἀρχὰς τοῦ θειοτά-
του γένους παρασχοῦ-
σαν, Φίλων Ἀπολ-
λωνίου τὴν ἑαυτοῦ
θεὰν καὶ εὐεργέτιν
ἐκ τῶν ἰδίων.[68]

Antonia (Minor) the niece of god Augustus, who was wife of Drusus Claudius the brother of Emperor Tiberius Augustus son of Augustus, mother of Germanicus Caesar and of Tiberius Claudius Germanicus and of Livia, goddess Aphrodite Ancheisias; she (Antonia) provided the largest and greatest beginnings for the most divine family. Philon son of Apollonios (honored) his own goddesss and benefactor, from his own funds.

This inscription follows standard conventions to express an extraordinary attachment to one member of the imperial family. Philon paid for the statue and base to honor Antonia Minor, daughter of Octavia and Mark Antony. Antonia's mother was the sister of Augustus, linking her to the first emperor. Antonia's marriage to Drusus—the younger brother of Tiberius—made her doubly related to the second emperor (Tiberius's adopted cousin through Augustus, and his sister-in-law through Drusus). She was on poor terms with her grandson, the emperor Gaius, and committed suicide in the first year of his reign (37 CE). This inscription comes from the reign of her younger son Claudius (41–58 CE). Thus, even though Antonia was a minor figure in the imperial cults of Asia, she was related to all the Julio-Claudian emperors until the time of this inscription.[69] The exuberant description of her as the most important ancestor of the imperial dynasty is understandable.

The most unusual aspect of the inscription, though, is the reference to Antonia's daughter Livilla as Aphrodite Ancheisias. Livilla was starved to death by Tiberius in 31 after she was condemned for the poisoning of her husband, Drusus, the son of Tiberius.[70] The next year some senators even proposed the *damnatio memoriae* because of her crimes.[71] The inscription's posthumous praise for Livilla is extraordinary even though she was Claudius's only sister, and it indicates the strength of the personal attachments of Philon to Antonia and her line.

The details of his relationship to the imperial family are not recorded. Philon was not an imperial freedman because his name indicates that he was not a Roman citizen, but he may have been an imperial slave. In any event, his attachment to his benefactress was unusual, referring to Antonia as "his own goddess." This discussion is not intended as a defense of genuine personal emotion in imperial cults that might therefore prove religious character. In some cases, strong individual affiliations could find expression in the institutions of imperial worship. Although these personal dedications are less numerous in the evidence than in some other cults, we should not infer that imperial worship was less religious. The religious functions of imperial cults focused more on community organization than on the individual.

An inscription from Aphrodisias illustrates how personal dedications allowed foreign imperial cult traditions to find expression in Asia. The inscription was found in a secondary context, reused for a late wall. The dedication itself probably comes from the mid-first-century CE, approximately contemporaneous with the previous example.

Θειότητι Αὐτοκρατόρων, Θεᾷ Ἀφροδείτῃ γενέτειρᾳ,
συνκλήτῳ, δήμῳ Ῥωμαίων, πολείταις, εὐχαριστῶν
Μᾶρκος Ἰούλιος Ἄτταλος ἀπελεύθερος Καίσαρος[72]

To the divinity of the Emperors, to the goddess Aphrodite Genetrix, to the Senate, to the demos of the Romans, (and) to the citizens (of Aphrodisias); in gratitude, Marcus Julius Attalus, freedman of Caesar.

Several features of this inscription are unusual in an Aphrodisian or Asian context. The first is the dedication to the "divinity of the emperors." Attalus was probably translating the Roman concepts of *divinitas* (divinity), *maiestas* (majesty), or even *numen* (divine power or status).[73] Such cults were common enough in Italy but unusual in Asia. The dedication to Aphrodite as Venus Genetrix was especially appropriate in Aphrodisias,[74] but the Senate and people of Rome are as yet otherwise unattested in Aphrodisian dedications. The reason for these oddities is that the dedicand was not an Aphrodisian but an imperial freedman who had moved to the city, probably to work on imperial holdings.[75] A personal dedication gave him the opportunity to express his gratitude in a manner more consonant with his culture of origin than with his adopted home. In the process, his personal votive functioned as an occasion for intercultural cross-fertilization and experimentation in imperial cults.[76]

Cultivating Personhood

Imperial cults were not confined to the municipal or provincial levels of public religion. The examples in this chapter show that many groups, families, and individuals were involved in the worship of members of the imperial family. Groups like the hymnodes of god Augustus and goddess Rome at Pergamon filled their year with imperial cult activities, whereas others like the Ephesian initiates of Demeter added imperial mysteries to their ongoing ritual calendar. Neither group was independent of its larger social setting. Their activities intertwined with municipal and provincial affairs in various ways. Yet these groups were involved in a distinguishable level of social interaction that implicated imperial cults in functions left relatively untouched by the provincial and municipal cults. Choir practices, esoteric rituals, mourning, remembrance of ancestors, the passing of winter, women's rituals, the agricultural cycles, the socialization of sons, household worship—all these were touched by imperial cults in group settings.

Imperial cult activity also involved personal votive offerings to members of the imperial family. They were not the most prominent aspect of imperial cult activities; votives tended to be offered more often to departed members of the dynasty than to those still living.[77] Whether these involved personal prayer or deep emotion is less important to this study than their distinctive roles. Extant personal dedications show signs of strong attachment to particular individuals in the imperial family. This level of imperial cult allowed experimentation and transplantation of foreign practices that would have been inappropriate at a communal level.

In the imperial cult activities of groups, families, and individuals, then, we see signs that the worship of the emperors affected the cultivation of personhood, one of the four primary features of a religious system, according to Sullivan. Personal maturation and rites of passage were generally a secondary aspect of imperial cults, for cosmological issues are more prevalent in the evidence at our disposal. A thorough handling of the materials, however, cannot overlook this level of religious expression in imperial cult institutions.

7

IMPERIAL CULTS AS RELIGION

The preceding five chapters examined specific imperial cults in their historical social contexts. I organized the analysis according to the people and groups that sponsored the cults: province, cities, groups, and individuals. This typology is imperfect, for many cults cross these categories; I have carefully pointed out the limits of such an analysis. The advantage is that we are forced to look more closely at the ways in which these institutions functioned in the lives of communities. With attention to social context, cultic format, and the demographics of participation, I hope to build a more nuanced explanation of the institutions.

The result is not a homogenous abstraction, but a reconstruction of imperial cults as one aspect of an evolving polytheistic system. Imperial cults did not compose an independent, mythic worldview; they were a distinguishable part of their broader, polytheistic cultural context. As such, they did not need to shoulder the whole burden for the religious life of the communities in which they were practiced. Rather, the worship of the imperial families and institutions constituted an identifiable feature of the larger symbolic world of Greco-Roman polytheism.

Imperial cults tended to fulfill particular needs within this polytheistic society. My goal in this chapter is to illuminate the religious profile of imperial cults in that setting, drawing from materials discussed in earlier chapters. The sections of the chapter are arranged in the categories of cosmogony, cosmology, human maturation, and eschatology, and the concepts of discourse and contrapuntal interpretation inform much of the discussion. In this way, it becomes clear that imperial cults made specific contributions to the religious system but introduced some serious problems as well.

Cosmogony

Primal cosmogony was not a primary concern in the imperial cults of Asia for several reasons. The Greco-Roman world already had developed interpretations of the ages before the advent of Roman imperialism. The existing stories sufficed for an explanation of prehistory.

Cosmogony could not be ignored, however, because stories about the origins of the world are intimately related to the structure of the contemporary world. In other words, cosmology makes little sense without cosmogony, for the trajectory of the meaning of this world cannot be traced without knowledge of its starting point. So an institution like the Roman principate—with so much power for shaping the world of the empire—needed to fit in the generative mythic structures of the Greco-Roman world. As those structures preceded the Julio-Claudian dynasty, the important issue was how Augustus, his family, and his successors were related to those stories about the beginnings. Could the emperors be connected to the mythic origins of the world in a satisfying, coherent fashion? Two strategies for addressing this issue are evident.

One cosmogonic strategy involved locating the imperial family within the Olympian branch of the pantheon, thereby tying them indirectly into the mythic narratives of the origins of the world. The practice of assimilating the imperial family to various deities—Augustus as Zeus, Livia as Demeter or as the new Hera, young princes as Dioscuri, and so on—was a part of this strategy. The sculpted panels of the Sebasteion at Aphrodisias provide dramatic examples showing the emperors depicted as a latter-day branch of the Olympians, offspring of Venus/Aphrodite. This practice did not give the imperial family a cosmogonic role; it simply explained the dynasty's connection to the beginnings. The Olympian imagery on the Aphrodisian reliefs was generated by other needs as well, including the development of a mythic connection between the city and the imperial center, the legitimation of local elites, competition among wealthy Aphrodisian families, and so forth. None of these motives would have sufficed without a compelling mythic explanation, however. Actions motivated merely by self-interest cannot survive long in a mythic discourse.

A second strategy supplemented the first and leads directly into the topic of cosmology. This second cosmogonic strategy depicted Augustus (and his dynasty) as the founders of a new world order. One of the clearest examples comes from the proposal to begin Asia's new year on the birthday of Augustus.[1] The proconsul's proposal to realign the calendar characterized the pre-Augustan period as a time of descent into chaos, the end of a degenerative process in which a disintegrating world was ready to fling itself headlong toward destruction. The birth of Augustus, however, represented the origin of a new age, the (re)creation of this world. Corporate existence and personal life were so profoundly affected that the birth of Augustus could be reckoned as the beginning of time. Thus, in his own lifetime he was becoming a mythic figure for the provinces. The present age was explicable only in terms of his life. The proconsul simultaneously raised Augustus to cosmogonic stature and equated the Roman imperial system with the cosmic structures of the world. The new calendar was supposed to reinforce this view in perpetuity.

Cosmology

These cosmogonic connections of the imperial house reinforced the primary religious concern of imperial cults: cosmology. In various ways, imperial cult institutions defined how space and time were to be experienced.

Imperial cults promoted a particular understanding of meaningful geography in which the city of Rome was central. The languages of divinization were one way in which this was accomplished. The most prestigious imperial cults were provincial institutions in which Roman ideas of divinity and acceptable honors were dominant. Living emperors were worshipped but not called θεός out of deference to Roman expectations. Overt divinization of living emperors was common in Asia only in local institutions. In the high-profile provincial temples, the religious traditions of Asia did not determine practice. For these cults the Asians needed to look toward Rome.

Procedures for the establishment of provincial temples supported this imagined geography. Asia could not simply establish an imperial cult on its own initiative. The koinon made a proposal that was subject to imperial scrutiny in Rome. Certain Asians would make the physical journey to Rome to present the province's case at the imperial center. The Senate and the emperor would craft a verdict, and then the advocates would travel back to Asia to deliver the decision. If arguments ensued, as was the case with Asia's second provincial cult, representatives would again go to the capital for resolution of the controversy. Thus, the provincial cults provided one important means for defining the broad structures by which geography was to be understood: Rome was the center of the world.

Imperial cults helped define meaningful geography within a province as well. The placement of provincial temples defined the most important communities in the region, so the cities competed fiercely for such privileges. In the period studied here, Roman authority validated the preeminence of Pergamon, then of Smyrna, and finally of Ephesos. Procedures for establishing local imperial cults added further nuance in the definition of space. Important civic institutions within the urban landscape, such as gymnasia, theaters, prytaneia, temples, and so on, might be enhanced through the addition of imperial cult activity. Cities such as Aphrodisias and Ephesos chose to establish new sacred sites and thus redefined the local topography. The petition of the mystai of Demeter to the proconsul L. Mestrius Florus in 89/90 CE reminds us, and reminded them, that even these local cults were not autonomous. At least some of them depended on the permission of Rome's representative for their ongoing imperial cult activity.[2]

The formats of imperial cults reinforced the imperial geography. The examples here have highlighted the many persons venerated in local imperial cults in Asia. The provincial cults were regulated according to other norms. The first two provincial cults included Rome or the Senate along with the emperor, whereas the third

included other members of the Flavian imperial dynasty. This corporate orientation suited Roman ideas of authority according to which the living princeps was
not to claim complete superiority within the Roman elite. Consequently, only once
during the early empire was a provincial temple in Asia designated for the worship
of an emperor by himself. This involved a cult for Gaius, which was discontinued
at his death. The three successful cults included corporate figures from Rome.

The diversity of persons and groups worshipped in imperial cults should not
obscure one central fact: all the objects of cult were Roman. In many manifestations, imperial cults all indicated a centered imperial geography. Reality revolved around the imperial city. Asia was defined as "provincial," subsidiary, dependent. The complexity of imperial cults allowed for a wide variety of maneuvers
in the definition of local geography, but the diversity clarified the fundamental
sacred geography of this world. The many variations rendered the main theme
unforgettable.

Yet a mythic consciousness requires more than a sacred geography. It also requires a definition of the meaning of time so that the unfolding of histories can be
properly understood. The evidence for imperial cults in Asia provides three important examples of this management of time. The first is the attempt to align the calendars of Asia with the calendar of Rome in 9 BCE. Greek cities had a tradition of
lunisolar calendars. The months corresponded to the cycles of the moon and were
named for festivals that occurred during that cycle. Various intercalations of days
and months were made, often ad hoc, to synchronize the lunar cycles with the solar
year.[3] The calendar used in Rome until the middle of the first century BCE was more
idiosyncratic, corresponding neither to the sun nor the moon. In 46 BCE Julius Caesar
completely renovated the Roman calendar on a solar model. Augustus instituted a
series of adjustments in 9 BCE that allowed the Julian calendar to function predict-
ably from 8 CE onward.[4]

Solar calendars have an advantage over lunar calculations because they maintain great regularity over long periods of time. Lunar calendars require complex
systems of exceptional days and months to keep community life—governance, festivals, agriculture, taxation, and so on—aligned to the seasons. The symbolic resources of a solar calendar for imperial authority are thus enormous. The comparative regularity of the solar year reflects nicely the imperial requirement of order and
conformity. At the same time that Augustus was perfecting the solar calendar of his
adopted father, his proconsul of Asia recommended that the province adjust its
calendars as well.

The realignment of Asia's calendars was not presented as a pragmatic proposal
because pragmatism was not the paramount issue. The proconsul's proposal and
the koinon's response demonstrated that the issue was the *meaning* of time. The
proconsul argued that time had been determined by the birth and achievements of
Augustus, and the koinon agreed. Augustus was a cosmogonic and cosmological
deity. He had saved the world from itself, ending warfare and returning order to
the world. The beginning of the year and the beginning of each month were to
become a commemoration of his birth. Augustus would make sense of time.

The new calendar was not intended as a simple imposition of Roman time but
rather as the means by which a local calendar would be calibrated. This bespeaks a

flexible hegemony, one that recognized the value of certain local traditions as long
as they operated within a Roman framework. Yet even this flexible hegemony met
resistance. The birth of Augustus was celebrated, but the old months of some city
calendars persisted well into the late empire. The proconsul's goal of organizing all
life around Augustus was unattainable. It was more feasible to allow for a range of
experiences in the province and to allow vernacular expressions of support for Rome.

A second example of how imperial cults molded the experience of time is through
festivals. In the ancient Mediterranean, festivals provided a complex set of benefits
that included respite from many kinds of work, commemoration of seasons of the
year, entertainment, and competition. The growth of imperial cults in the early
imperial period had a dramatic effect on ritual calendars. The number of regional
and local festivals increased greatly, and preexisting festivals took on new dimensions with prayers and sacrifices to the emperors added to the older traditions. Processions, sacrifices, athletics, gladiator battles, and musical competitions multiplied.
All levels of society were affected. Elite families now had more opportunities and
more responsibilities for public celebrations. Average and poorer Asians now had
more occasions to experience the benefactions of the elite and to increase their moral
responsibility to support the leadership of the elite. The logic of reciprocity within
the dominant discourse required such responses.

A third example of the effect of imperial cults on the provincial experience of
time comes from the inscribed altar of the hymnodes of Augustus and Rome. The
liturgical calendar on the altar reflects the multiple perspectives that could be incorporated in the mythic consciousness. The calendar manifested not a single systematic experience of the passing of time but rather a set of cycles that sometimes
merged but sometimes collided, producing juxtapositions of different qualities of
time. One cycle was the monthly birthday of Augustus based on the Asian calendar. Another cycle was marked by the irregularly spaced birthdays of various emperors. A third was the Roman calendar represented by the Kalends of January. At
least two other cycles were operative, although it is not clear how they should be
grouped. The major festivals (Augustus's birthday, Rosalia, imperial mysteries) could
belong together. Or the imperial festivals (Augustus's birthday, mysteries) could be
considered separately from cults for the departed (Rosalia, occasional memorials for
deceased hymnodes). Or perhaps the irregular funerals and inductions of new members constituted a separate cycle. In any case, the calendar drew the members into a
series of celebrations that covered a range of human experiences. The worship of
the emperors played a crucial part in this experience of time.

The hymnodes also illustrate one of the most distinctive features of imperial
cults within Greco-Roman polytheism, that is, the ability of imperial cults to function at all levels of society. The imperial cult activities of the hymnodes included
provincial, municipal, group, familial, and individual piety. Because the hymnodes
represent an exaggerated example of imperial piety, they clarify the complementary
role played by these cults. Imperial worship touched most or all aspects of life in
the cities of Asia, but it did not constitute the sum total of religious life. Rather,
imperial cults extended religious activities in new ways. No other symbolic system
had such a range of effective meaning. Other cults might be useful in municipal
religion, in household cult, in group activity, or in combinations thereof. Only

imperial cults could operate in all of these spheres while providing a cultic expression for the empire. The worship of the Olympians nearly approximated this range of applicability; thus, their worship was closely allied with that of the imperial institutions. The Olympians were not so directly connected to the practice of imperialism, however. Worship of them could not be tied so closely to one dynasty or one city. The emperors, their families, the Senate, and the city of Rome had redefined the structure of life in the Mediterranean world. Worship of them could be woven into all levels of the provincial experience of space and time as the preeminent expression of the dominant imperial discourse.

Human Maturation

A third cornerstone of the religious life is the process by which human beings mature throughout the course of life. The procedures for producing, nourishing, and defining men and women are legion. Sullivan gave special attention to images of the soul, treatment of the body, conception and birth, initiations and ritual, religious specialists, and authoritative religious knowledge. These issues are seldom addressed in discussions of imperial cults for three reasons. First, manifestations of these topics tend to be less public and more esoteric, so whatever evidence might have existed has mostly disappeared. Second, the evidence that does exist suggests that these were not central concerns in imperial worship. Finally, modern assumptions about the political (rather than "religious") nature of imperial cults have relegated these issues to the background. Thus, there is less material on human maturation through imperial cults than on any of the other three categories of analysis, but the ancient sources are not silent on these matters. In at least two areas concerns for the production of personhood are manifest. One is the construction of gender through the public service of specialists.

I have mentioned several religious specialists in this discussion. The priesthoods and high priesthoods, like Greek priesthoods in general, were not occupations.[5] Those who officiated in the imperial cult sacrifices were laymen and laywomen. These offices were sometimes held for life, but often they were for a limited time.

Literature on women and men in the Roman empire has grown exponentially of late,[6] and specific discussions pertain to women in imperial cults. Publications on gender and the worship of the emperors, however, have tended to focus on provincial high priestesses, especially on the provincial high priestesses of Asia. The older academic consensus was that provincial high priestesses did not actively participate in the provincial cults; rather, their titles were simply honorary, accorded to them because they were married to provincial high priests.[7] That consensus is now eroding; the more recent view is that provincial high priestesses probably participated in provincial sacrifices to the emperors but only as part of a married couple or with another male relative.[8]

The materials in the foregoing chapters show that within the full range of imperial cult activities, the public leadership of women appears to have been extremely limited. The questions about gendered participation in provincial cults raise important issues, but the overwhelming dominance of men in the available documentation for imperial worship in Asia cannot be disputed. We know that women served sometimes as high priestesses of Asia, as priestesses in some local imperial cults, and in local priesthoods of Livilla, Livia, and others. Men, on the other hand, still held the majority of the priesthoods and high priesthoods. Men also account for all the known imperial agonothetes, neokoroi, hymnodes, and municipal representatives to provincial festivals in Asia.

The imperial mysteries provide a possible exception. The late first-century request to the proconsul L. Mestrius Florus on behalf of the mystai of Demeter at Ephesos mentioned priestesses in the context of imperial sacrifices and mysteries.[9] The exact activities and individuals are not specified in the extant portion of the text, so the inscription reminds us that there is much we do not know. Nevertheless, the existing evidence is widespread and diverse enough to establish a not particularly surprising pattern: elite men were much more prominent in the public worship of the imperial family than were elite women. Women were relatively prominent in the provincial high priesthoods; they represent about 20% of the extant references to these high priesthoods.[10] There is little evidence for their leadership in other offices.

Beyond the small percentage of wealthy Asians who are reasonably well documented is the vast majority of men and women of Asia, about whom we have little direct information. A contrapuntal reading of the sources suggests that there were varieties of compliance and resistance. Given the small amount of data now available, inference is the only recourse in determining levels of participation. The preceding chapters have demonstrated that the vitality of the festivals, the distribution of imperial cults throughout urban areas, and the importance of imperial temples all imply widespread participation. The relatively small number of Roman troops stationed in the province supports this conclusion.[11] Imperial cults involved a wide range of Asians, and the men and women who attended the festivals learned that leadership in imperial cults was a predominantly male activity. So imperial cult activity reinforced cultural constructions of gender.

The ancient materials suggest another way in which imperial mysteries played a role in the constitution of human beings. The request of the mystai of Demeter to the proconsul Florus in the late first century CE noted that imperial mysteries had been performed in Ephesos for many years.[12] The Pergamene Hymnodes of god Augustus and goddess Rome, for whom we have inscriptions from the Hadrianic period, set aside the first three days of Loos (= June 23–25) for the observance of imperial mysteries.[13] No specific details of these rituals are preserved in either of these sources, except that they both involved sacrifices to emperors. We know further that a ritual of crowning took place inside the hymnodeion at this time and that lamps were needed on these days. Knowledge of the general character of ancient mysteries leads to the conclusion that these imperial mysteries at least involved initiations and other rituals that led to personal maturation along specific lines of development.[14]

The dearth of details about these particular imperial mysteries does not encourage speculation about the kinds of personal transformations involved. The existence of mysteries, however, confirms instances in which imperial worship played a role in the constitution of human beings. The hyperbole of the proconsul Maximus in 9 BCE about the birth of Augustus elaborated on a (more modest) facet of life in Asia:

We could justly consider that day to be equal to the beginning of all things. He restored the form of all things to usefulness, if not to their natural state, since it had deteriorated and suffered misfortune. He gave a new appearance to the whole world, which would gladly have accepted its own destruction had Caesar not been born for the common good fortune of all. Thus a person could justly consider this to be the beginning of life and of existence, and the end of regrets about having been born.[15]

In this view from the imperial center, Augustus was said to have transformed suffering into a new sense of community, reshaping the great structures of life and leading to a renewal that permeated the experiences of individuals.

Eschatology

Just as cosmogony illuminates the origins of this world and initiates reflection about its meaning, so eschatology provokes critical consideration of the ends of the world:

> Every complete mythology includes a terminal vision, for the end is an essential
> element of the integrity to which individual symbols point and the completion
> for which the symbolic condition as a whole yearns. The eschaton culminates
> symbolic life. Eschatologies assess humanity and the material universe. . . . The
> fate of all creation appears in the signs of its decay, because it is a terminal
> condition.[16]

The terminal vision normally includes a personal dimension and a cosmic dimension. The personal dimension explores and defines the experience of death. Geographies of the afterlife often describe the requirements for entering and inhabiting those distant terrains. A cosmic dimension of eschatology portrays the end of the age in a way that makes sense of this world. The eschatological destructions end spatial and temporal signification.

The personal eschatology of imperial cults is seldom addressed in the secondary literature, yet there are several allusions to it in ancient sources. The hymnodes of Rome and Augustus were involved in a wide range of religious activities, including funerals for other members of the group. These ceremonies were observed by the members of the chorus as an important rite of passage—both for the deceased and for the group—since the funeral signaled the need for the appointment and initiation of a new singer. The hymnodes also observed Rosalia, normally associated with the cults of ancestors, as a three-day festival beginning on the Augustan Day of the month of Panemos (i.e., May 24–26). The sources do not provide us with images of the soul or its passage through other worlds, nor do they allow an analysis of the rituals. That knowledge is probably lost forever.

Imperial mysteries provided another context in which personal eschatology would probably have surfaced. Once again we lack details, but mystery rituals addressed the challenge of facing death. Even though modern interpretations of the mysteries have often been hampered by uncritical Christianizing assumptions, there is at least general agreement that these rituals were related in some way to death and personhood.[17]

The apotheosis of the Roman emperor after his death is another context in which personal eschatology intersected with imperial cults. The ritual and concept of apotheosis were more important in the capital than in the provinces because divinization of living emperors was common outside of Italy.[18] The imagery of the emperor ascending to heaven in the chariot of the sun was also well known in Asia, however, and it affirmed a special geography of the afterlife for deserving emperors: they entered the realm of the Olympians. In this way the apotheosis of the ruler brought closure to the mythology of imperialism and provided the fitting conclusion to the idealized practice of hegemony. The ambiguities of ruling successfully over this world were resolved in the ascension of the ruler to the transcendent realm of the Olympians.

In cosmic eschatology, an important structural problem appears. The logic of imperial cults allowed for no termination of the world. These institutions were in fact dedicated to the prolongation of the current world. For example, the ancient materials emphasized dynasties. Modern analyses of imperial cults tend to focus on the worship of the emperor, so it is important to note how much of the surviving evidence transmits information about the worship of other members of the imperial household. As evidence accumulates, more and more names are added to the list of those for whom divine honors were offered. The list of people honored in imperial cults in Asia includes Augustus, his mother Atia, his wife Livia, his colleague and collaborator Marcus Agrippa, his grandsons Gaius and Lucius, his adopted son Tiberius, Augustus's niece Antonia the younger, both Agrippinas, Livilla, Livilla's two twin sons, her brother Germanicus, the emperor Gaius, Gaius's sister Drusilla, Drusilla's husband M. Aemilius Lepidus, the emperor Claudius, his son Drusus, Nero, Vespasian, Titus, Domitian, and Domitia. In addition, there were also corporate or abstract deities such as Rome, the Senate, the imperial household or family of the Sebastoi, the health of the emperor, and so on. Overall, then, "emperor cult" or "ruler cult" is too narrow a term to cover all the data. The emperor was certainly the most important figure, but the phenomenon as a whole was directed toward dynasties and the prolongation of the imperialist structures of this world. One fundamental goal of imperial cults was the continuation of the royal household and the maintenance of Roman hegemony.

Sources are clear about this commitment to the longevity of Roman imperialism. There is no need to worry about probabilities; the idea is overtly declared in the extant witnesses. The damaged text of the imperial hymnodes from 41 CE begins "[on behalf of the etern]al continuation of Tibe[rius Claudius Caesa]r Sebastos Germanic[cus and of] his [who]le house."[19] Forty years later, an Ephesian inscription echoed the same sentiments: "On behalf of the health of our Lord Emperor Titus Caesar and (on behalf of) the permanence of the rule of the Romans, the damaged wall surrounding the Augusteion was repaired."[20] Or we can can consult the following text from a small marble altar found in Phrygia: "Euphrastos, slave of Caesar, (prays) for the eternal continuation and victory of emperor Nerva Trajan Caesar Sebastos Germanicus Dacicus. Year 188 (= 104 CE), in the ninth month."[21] The discourse of imperial cults was committed to preventing the imagination from imagining the end of this world. This was a constant feature in the evolving imperial religious institutions.

This feature of the cosmic eschatology in imperial cults created a structural flaw in the religious system. This feature was unlike the relative lack of interest shown toward cosmogony and human maturation; those could be complemented by other religious institutions without serious dissonance. In contrast, the eschatology of imperial cults denied the symbolic character of Roman rule. The image of the emperor could not signify, could not point to a greater reality, because this symbolism would imply his own finitude. Imperial rule could not partake in the symbolic nature of all human projects because this would imply its eventual demise. Absolute being was attributed to an institution and to people who inhabited human space and time.

In this sense, the Roman Empire constituted a utopian vision that had the misfortune of succeeding. The transcendent claims for the emperor and his rule clashed with obvious contradictions in the experiences of real lives. Utopian vision became vulnerable to dystopian realities.[22] This vulnerability was due precisely to the exercise of Roman hegemony. The imperial discourse forced the religious system into an untenable position by requiring exemption of the imperial dynasty from the terminal conditions of existence. Imperialism violated the mythic consciousness, ignoring the limitations of language and symbol.

This systemic problem in a fundamental structure of the world was overlooked by many people for pragmatic reasons: the consequences of imagining the end of Roman imperialism were serious, perhaps fatal. The logic of participation was too strong. Imperialism's arrogance could not be condoned, however, by a critical mythic consciousness. This tension between cosmology and eschatology in the religious system provided the matrix within which John's religious criticism could take root. John's was not the only voice of opposition to Roman imperialism in the first century, but it has had greater influence, for better or for worse, over the course of centuries. His counterpoint to hegemony provides the subject of the second part of this book.

II

REVELATION, RESISTANCE

Part I concluded that imperial cults in Asia were concerned especially with the construction of a cosmology that reinforced Roman imperialism. That cosmology produced an imperial eschatology with fundamental defects. Part II argues that Revelation manifests a cosmology and eschatology that opposed the dominant discourse.

8

REVELATION IN SPACE AND TIME

The goals of this study are to produce a historically nuanced, systemic description of imperial cults in Asia for the general period when Revelation was written and to compare fundamental issues addressed in the cults and in the text. The preceding chapters analyze the imperial cult evidence from the province of Asia for the early imperial period (in this case, from Augustus to the early second century).[1] This chapter begins to build a comparison by establishing the spatial and temporal location of the text's author and audiences. Because the issue of place is fairly straightforward, I treat it briefly. After this, much of the chapter develops the main arguments regarding date. The chapter concludes that Revelation studies should focus less on alleged excesses in imperial cults under Nero and Domitian and more on the normative character of imperial cult activity.

Place

There is little debate regarding the geographical origin of the text because of indications in the text itself about the locations of the author and the addressees. John began by remarking that, when the first vision came to him (Rev 1:9–10), he was in the spirit on the island of Patmos, a small island approximately 50 km due west of Didyma. The long, narrow north/south axis of the island measures about 12 km; the widest part of the island—approximately 7 km—is in the north. In the first century, the island was sparsely populated. Administratively, it was part of the province of Asia. Although the text says explicitly only that he saw the visions there, scholars assume that John also wrote them and sent them from Patmos.

John was probably in exile on Patmos because of his disruptive message, for he wrote that he was on the island "because of the word of God and the testimony of Jesus" (1:9). This pair of phrases usually occurs in Revelation to indicate a message that provokes severe resistance.[2] Other passages use "testimony" in the same way.[3] Whether he fled to Patmos or was sent there by authorities is unknown.[4]

John addressed his text as a circular letter to churches in seven major cities of Asia: Ephesos, Smyrna, Pergamon, Thyatira, Sardis, Philadelphia, and Laodikeia. No clear statement in the text explains why these particular congregations were chosen. The first three cities were the most prestigious urban centers in the province. These three were on or near the Aegean coast, whereas the other four were further inland. Major roads connected the cities, but William M. Ramsay's theory that the cities were stations along a proto-Christian postal system is speculative and tendentious.[5] Six of these cities (all but Thyatira) received the right to hold provincial games (κοινὰ Ἀσίας) at some point in the imperial period.[6]

The naming of seven cities is important, for the number seven is one of the major devices used to organize material in Revelation. As a symbol in Revelation, the number seven represents perfection, wholeness,[7] the divine order that defines the cosmos and history.[8] Thus, the implication of writing to seven churches is that John's Revelation was intended for all the churches in the area, and explicit statements such as 2:23 support this conclusion. All the churches were to listen to the spirit speaking through John.[9]

The Returns of Nero

Most New Testament scholars have supported one of two possible dates for the composition of the book of Revelation: either somewhere near the end of Nero's reign (usually 68/69 CE) or late in the reign of Domitian (emperor 81–96 CE). Some recent publications have concluded that Revelation was edited in the late first century, using materials from earlier in John's life,[10] and this is probably the best reading of the evidence. Evidence for a Domitianic date is strong but not overwhelming. The reuse of earlier materials in Revelation probably accounts for the features that have led some to accept a date in the late 60s of the first century.

One feature of the text indicates that Revelation could not have reached its present form before 68 CE. Several ancient sources attest that many people did not believe reports of Nero's death in 68 CE and that they expected him to come back to retake the imperial throne. The fifth book of the Sibylline Oracles, a Jewish text written in the early second century CE, described Nero and his future return:

> One who has fifty as an initial will be commander,
> a terrible snake, breathing out grievous war, who one day
> will lay hands on his own family and slay them, and throw everything into confusion,
> athlete, charioteer, murderer, one who dares ten thousand things.
> He will also cut the mountain between two seas and defile it with gore.

But even when he disappears he will be destructive. Then he will return
declaring himself equal to God. But he will prove that he is not.[11]

Later in the text, Nero's behavior in Greece is chastised as shameless divine preten-
sion (5:137–42). His alleged flight to Persia in 68 is described (5:143–49) and his
future return at the head of the Persian forces is foretold (5:93–100).

Sibylline Oracle 4:135–48 treated the same theme in its own way. According
to this text, the return of Nero would occur sometime after the eruption of Vesuvius
in 79 CE, and it would have great consequences for the eastern Mediterranean. The
oracle is thought to have been written not long after the volcano erupted, that is,
during the last two decades of the first century CE:

> Know then the wrath of the heavenly God,
> because they will destroy the blameless tribe of the pious.
> Then the strife of war being aroused will come to the west,
> and the fugitive from Rome [i.e., Nero] will also come, brandishing a great spear,
> having crossed the Euphrates with many myriads.
> Wretched Antioch, they will no longer call you a city
> when you fall under spears by your own folly;
> and then pestilence and terrible din of battle will destroy Cyprus.
> Woe to miserable Cyprus, a broad wave of the sea
> will cover you when you have been tossed up by wintry blasts.
> Great wealth will come to Asia, which Rome itself
> once plundered and deposited in her house of many possessions.
> She will then pay back twice as much and more
> to Asia, and then there will be a surfeit of war.[12]

Others did not merely write about the return of Nero. A pretender to the throne
who claimed to be Nero wreaked havoc in Asia during the brief reign of Galba
(69 CE).[13] At least two other "Neros" appeared during the subsequent 20 years, one
in 79 and another in 88.[14]

These texts provide a context for allusions in Revelation to an eschatological
return of Nero. Revelation 13 records a seven-headed Beast representing Roman
power. One of the heads was mortally wounded but the wound was healed and the
Beast survived (vs. 3, 12, 14). The chapter ends with the riddle of 666—the number of the name of the Beast. Nearly all commentators acknowledge that this number represents the sum of the numbers associated with the letters in the name Nero
Caesar.[15] So the healing of a mortal wound could be an allusion to the mythic return of Nero.[16]

Revelation 17 more certainly employs the idea of the return of Nero. Here a
seven-headed Beast is described whose heads represent the seven hills of Rome and
seven kings (i.e., emperors). Five of the kings are said to have fallen, but one of the
seven would return as the eighth and final ruler (17:9–11). This allusion to the return of Nero in Revelation indicates that it could not have been written before 68 CE.
It does not help determine a latest possible date for the composition of the text, for
the motif of Nero's return continued to be used well into the second century and
beyond.[17]

"Babylon"

The use of the name "Babylon" in Revelation for the city of Rome also points to a date after 70 CE and probably to a date well after 70 CE. If this identification of Babylon with Rome was not clear to hearers before chapter 17,[18] in that chapter the Seer made the equation explicit through an angelic interpretation of John's vision. In Revelation 17 John described the vision of a drunken prostitute in lavish clothing. On her forehead was the name Babylon (17:5). Then the angel explained to John the meaning of this name. In the visionary logic of the dream, the seven heads were seven hills and also seven kings, a reference to the seven hills of Rome and to seven emperors (17:9). The woman represented the great city, which had dominion over the rulers of the earth (17:18). Chapter 18 then begins a series of oracles, taunts, and sarcastic laments regarding the destruction of the great prostitute. Thus, "Babylon" provided symbolic resources for a provincial castigation of the imperial center.

What kind of specific resources did it provide? Many scholars conclude that the connection between Rome and Babylon is that both destroyed the temple of Israel's god: Babylon's siege of Jerusalem resulted in the obliteration of Israel's first temple in 586 BCE, and Rome's siege of Jerusalem brought an end to the second temple in 70 CE.[19] So John could denounce Rome because of its attack on the Jerusalem temple. This would, in turn, require a date after 70 CE for John's Apocalypse.

Too little attention has been paid, however, to the theme of domination and diaspora, which is equally important in the image of Babylon. Two other Jewish texts, roughly contemporaneous with Revelation, provide illustrations of how the imagery could be exploited. Second Baruch was written in the late first century or early second century CE, after Rome had destroyed Jerusalem. The text reflects on this event by telling a series of revelations set around the time of the destruction of the first temple by the Babylonians in the sixth century BCE. The visions are attributed to Baruch, the scribe of Jeremiah.

Second Baruch does not dwell on the Babylonian destruction of Jerusalem (cf. 8:4–9:2). The text predicts and narrates the destruction rather quickly and then spends most of its energy wrestling with the long-term consequences of this new situation. Jeremiah is sent to Babylon to support the exiles (10:2). God promises Baruch that he will be preserved until the end of the age because he has not accepted what happened to Jerusalem and will even serve as a witness during the long period of Gentile domination (13:1–12). Through dialogues with divine messengers and startling visions, Baruch finally comes to understand that God has appointed the times of national humiliation and of vindication, whether these eras involve Babylon or Rome (32:1–9). The book ends with a lengthy letter from Baruch to the dispersed tribes of Israel, exhorting them to persevere in the age in which there is no temple. The implication for an audience living after the Roman destruction of the temple is clear: be faithful to the traditions and await God's vindication:

> Remember the law and Zion, the holy land and your brothers, and the covenant
> of your fathers; and do not forget the festivals and the sabbaths. And hand on
> this letter and the traditions of the law to your sons after you, just as your fathers
> handed (them) on to you. Be always regular in your prayers, and pray diligently
> with all your heart that the Mighty One may restore you to his favour, and that

he may not take account of your many sins, but remember the faithfulness of your fathers. For if he is not to judge us in the fullness of his mercy woe to all of us poor mortals (84:6–11).[20]

The apocalyptic text known as 4 Ezra provides another example of the way in which a Jewish author could connect Babylon and Rome through the experience of destruction and domination. In this text, another distinguished figure associated with the Babylonian period was appropriated—Ezra, expositor of Torah and advocate for restoration of the Judean community. The fictive time frame was 30 years after the first destruction (ca. 550 BCE; 4 Ezra 3:1). This setting allows the main character to wrestle with the issue of domination after destruction in a more pronounced fashion. Thirty years have passed, and those who destroyed God's temple seem to be faring quite well. In prayer Ezra asks:

Are the deeds of those who inhabit Babylon any better? Is that why she has gained dominion over Zion? For when I came here I saw ungodly deeds without number, and my soul has seen many sinners during these thirty years. And my heart failed me, for I have seen how thou dost endure those who sin, and hast spared those who act wickedly, and hast destroyed thy people, and hast preserved thy enemies, and hast not shown to any one how thy way may be comprehended. Are the deeds of Babylon better than those of Zion? Or has another nation known thee besides Israel? Or what tribes have so believed thy covenants as these tribes of Jacob? Yet their reward has not appeared and their labor has borne no fruit. For I have traveled widely among the nations and have seen that they abound in wealth, though they are unmindful of thy commandments (3:28–34).[21]

After further dialogues with the archangel Uriel about God's justice and God's plans for the world, Ezra has visions in which he encounters the eternal Zion in the form of a woman mourning over the destruction of the earthly Jerusalem (9:26–10:59), foresees the Messiah's judgment on Rome (11–12), views the coming of the Messiah and the eschatological reassembling of Israel (13), and receives the order to write scrolls about the public and the secret wisdom of God (14). Thus, the metaphor of Babylon in 4 Ezra does not simply label Rome as a destroyer of Jerusalem. It also reflects the urgent issue of theodicy that arises when there is no vindication of the victims over the course of time.

In Revelation the image of Babylon also allows the Seer to draw on Israel's prophetic heritage to develop understandings of Roman hegemony after the destruction of the temple. Revelation's use of Babylon differs, however, from the usage of 2 Baruch or of 4 Ezra because John did not explicitly refer to the destruction of the Jerusalem temple. The missing overt reference to the destruction does not require us to conclude that Revelation was written before 70.[22] John alludes to the destruction by invoking oracles from Scripture that refer to the first destruction but then shifts his audience's attention toward domination, exploitation, and injustice.

The use of biblical oracles in Revelation 18 provides an example. Jeremiah 50–51 provides the basic imagery for Revelation 18.[23] The Jeremiah oracles are a vicious series of pronouncements that call for vengeance against Babylon specifically because of the destruction of Jerusalem and the temple.[24] They lead into a final recounting of the Babylonian assault on Judah, the plundering of the temple, and the deportations of Judeans into exile (Jer 52). This section of Jeremiah had a formative influence on the shape of Revelation 18 because it establishes the destruction of the temple as one reason for the judgment of Rome/Babylon. Further on in the chapter, however, John drew on oracles directed against Tyre from Ezekiel 26–28. By applying the oracles about ancient Tyre to Rome, John was able to denigrate Rome also for its domination of the Mediterranean sea lanes and its economic exploitation of subject peoples.[25] John never referred to Rome as "Tyre," but only as "Babylon" because Tyre provided only images of economic exploitation. Babylon, on the other hand, provided the basic symbolic resources—destroyer of the temple and imperial oppressor. The other oracles provided John with the material he needed to elaborate his case against the empire.

John also used the Babylon image for rhetorical reasons. As in 2 Baruch and 4 Ezra, he tried to persuade his audience to be faithful while they awaited God's intervention. His definition of faithfulness, however, was distinctive from those of other texts. Whereas 2 Baruch emphasized festivals, sabbath, Torah, and prayer and 4 Ezra focused more on the intellectual and emotional issues of theodicy,[26] John's notion of faithfulness involved a stronger emphasis on withdrawal and separation.[27] In Revelation the lines between God's people and the rest of the world are drawn more clearly, the opponents are chastised more thoroughly, and the final destruction of evil is more central.

For the purposes of dating Revelation, then, the use of Babylon imagery is an important indicator. It requires us to date Revelation no earlier than the Roman destruction of Jerusalem in 70 CE. It also suggests that a date for Revelation in the late first century (or early second century) is more appropriate, because that takes into account the aspect of domination that was the logical consequence of the destruction.[28]

Seven Kings

The vision of Revelation 17 has affected discussions about the date of the text in another way. As the angel interpreted the meaning of the woman and the seven-headed Beast, John learned that the seven heads represented not only hills but also emperors. He learned that of the seven emperors, "Five have fallen, one is alive, the other has not yet come. And when he comes he must remain a little while" (17:10). Commentators have attempted to discern the identity of the sixth emperor—the one ruling at the time—to ascertain the period when the author of Revelation was writing.[29] The effort to list these seven has been complicated by two issues: it is not clear which ruler should be the starting point for enumeration[30] or whether every consecutive emperor should be included.[31] Scholars who conclude that Revelation was written in the late 60s start with Caesar or Augustus and exclude no one.[32] Those who conclude that Revelation was written in the last years of Domitian's reign begin with other emperors and often omit emperors for different reasons.[33]

The value of Revelation 17 for determining the date of composition has been exaggerated. Revelation 17 presents two insurmountable problems that call every enumeration into question. The first problem is the multivalent character of apocalyptic imagery. In the visionary realm, one symbol can signify more than one referent. The angel revealed to John that the seven heads represented both hills and kings. The inappropriateness of trying to produce lists of emperors from such imagery is clear from its results: we end up with one of the heads (= an emperor) present even though the Beast itself is absent (the Beast "was, is not, and is about to come up from the abyss," v. 8).[34] In the world of historians, emperors succeed one another. In the world of the Seer, we encounter more complicated relationships that defy historicizing descriptions.

The second problem in using Revelation 17 for enumeration is the apocalyptic practice of grouping rulers, calamities, visions, eras, and so forth according to specific numbers. In this case the fact that there are seven heads is more important than the attempt to identify each one. The seven rulers represent a full number, the completion of an era; the details do not need to line up so neatly. Particular members of a group are specified as important whereas others are not.[35] This is especially clear from analogous texts such as 4 Ezra 11–12, which includes a vision in which Roman imperialism is symbolized by an eagle with twelve wings, three heads, and eight more small subsidiary wings. Only three of the major wings and the three heads are important. The text describes Julius Caesar as the first wing (11:10–13a), and the second wing is clearly Augustus (11:13b–17). Then the third wing— Tiberius—receives one short sentence, and generalizations about the rest of the wings ensue (11:19–28). The identities of most of the twelve main wings and the eight opposing wings are irrelevant and do not match with known rulers.[36] The important part of the story resumes when the three heads—the Flavians Vespasian, Titus, and Domitian—awaken. Domitian is judged by God and the carcass of the eagle is burned (11:29–12:3a).

The apocalyptic method of 4 Ezra suggests that an enumeration of consecutive emperors for Revelation 17 is neither necessary nor advisable.[37] The important point is that the seven heads/kings identify Rome as the opponent and indicate that the end of Roman hegemony is near.[38] The only significant emperor is the one who will return (Nero), but the text makes no effort to tell us which head he might be. The practice of using special numbers for groups and the multivalent imagery of Revelation 17 are bound to confuse attempts to identify the seven rulers. The king "who is" will not help us deduce the date of Revelation.

Measuring the Temple

One last section of Revelation has figured prominently in debates about its date. Revelation 11 contains an enigmatic vision that begins with a command for the Seer to measure the temple of God, the altar, and those worshipping there. He is instructed not to measure the outer court because it has been given over to the nations to trample for 42 months (11:1–2). Following this command is a promise that two witnesses will testify. They will be killed by the beast from the abyss and their bodies left in the streets of Jerusalem. The general rejoicing over the demise of the witnesses will end when they are revivified and taken to heaven as an earthquake destroys a tenth of the city (11:3–13).

The bearing of this vision on the date of Revelation is related to the measuring of the temple in v. 1–2. Which temple is envisioned here? Some scholars conclude that it is the earthly temple in Jerusalem, and therefore the verses—and Revelation— were written before the Roman destruction of the Jerusalem temple in 70 CE. A recent historical reading of these verses has claimed that they included two predictions that turned out to be wrong: the Romans did not simply take the outer court but destroyed the whole temple, and their occupation lasted centuries, not 42 months.[39] According to this argument, these inaccurate predictions establish that Revelation was written before 70 CE when the predictions were proven wrong.

A modified form of this interpretation is espoused by some who prefer a late first-century date for the text. These commentators argue that the two verses come from a source that John later incorporated into his text. This source would have come from a Zealot prophet in Jerusalem in 70 CE who sought to encourage those trapped with him in the temple as the Roman troops advanced. Josephus recorded that such prophets were active until the final destruction, so perhaps Revelation 11: 1–2 is based on such a prophecy. The problems with this theory are many; it represents a case of special pleading to preserve a Domitianic date for Revelation. Aside from the obvious problems of how and why such a prophecy would have been preserved through the catastrophe in Jerusalem, there is also the issue of why John did not do a better job of molding the oracle to the course of later events.[40]

Other commentators have argued that the temple and altar in 11:1–2 are not the earthly temple in Jerusalem but the heavenly one.[41] This position can draw on biblical precedent, for the book of Ezekiel records a similar vision. In Ezekiel 40, the prophet was taken in a vision to see the heavenly model for the Jerusalem temple at a time when the Babylonian destruction had left no earthly temple standing. As a supernatural being measured the features of the outer court, the inner court, and the temple, Ezekiel took note so that he could instruct Israel on how the holy site and the holy people were to be restored so as to live in the presence of God (43:6– 12). Fourth Ezra provides a parallel use of the heavenly Jerusalem topos roughly contemporaneous with Revelation. One of Ezra's visions involves the revelation of the city of the Most High God, a transhistorical, spiritual reality of terrifying beauty. The text refers to it as Zion, an established city that transcends the historical vicissitudes of earthly Jerusalem (9:26–10:59, esp. 10:44–54).

The "heavenly temple" interpretation is not without its drawbacks. How could the outer court of the heavenly temple be given over to the Gentiles to trample for 42 months? This has led most commentators to conclude that the temple is an image for the people of God, specifically for the church; the outer court is the world[42] or that part of Israel that did not recognize the Messiah Jesus.[43] The community of faith is hemmed in but not destroyed, persecuted like the two witnesses but resurrected to new life.[44]

Because Revelation 11:1–13 is a notorious hermeneutical problem, the many questions about its meaning cannot be settled in this study.[45] None of the proposals is strong enough to make this a crucial argument for the time of composition. Moreover, the range of proposals takes too little account of the intertextual character of this part of Revelation.[46] There are clear signs throughout the section that John is reworking material from Ezekiel, whether in the eating of the scroll (Rev

10:9–10/Ezek 2:9–3:3), the command to prophesy (Rev 10:11/Ezek 3:4–11), the measuring of the temple (Rev 11:1–2/Ezek 40–43), the revivification of the witnesses (Rev 11:11/Ezek 37:1–14), or even the earthquake (Rev 11:13/Ezek 38:19–20). Added to this are allusions to Zechariah in the measuring of the temple (Zech 2:1–5) and in the description of the two witnesses (Rev 11:4/Zech 4). John was positioning his text among those of the prophets, comparing his message of judgment and preservation to theirs. Revelation 11 should not be pressed too hard for historical purposes. John was paying more attention to Scripture than to events.

The text of Revelation, then, provides some general indications about the date when it was written. The character of the visions does not allow for precision, but certain features point toward a late first-century date. The theme of Nero's return indicates a date after 68, and the name Babylon for Rome suggests that Revelation was written later than 70.

Irenaeus and Persecution Theories

Evidence about Revelation from outside the text supports a late first-century date but does not allow for great precision. Many commentators have relied heavily on a statement by Irenaeus regarding the date of Revelation.[47] He wrote, "For it [i.e., Revelation] was seen not long ago, but nearly in our generation, toward the end of the reign of Domitian."[48] This statement does not inspire great confidence because the time Irenaeus described as nearly in his own generation (σχεδὸν ἐπὶ τῆς ἡμετέρας γενεᾶς) was approximately a century earlier than when he was writing.[49] His effort to shorten the distance between himself and the author of Revelation is understandable in light of his polemical intent: he wanted to strengthen his claim to understand Revelation accurately. Irenaeus was not writing a history of the transmission of John's Apocalypse; he was arguing with Christian millenarian movements about the correct interpretation of Revelation. Moreover, Irenaeus left his historical judgment open to criticism by accepting the apostle John as the author of both Revelation and the Gospel according to John.[50] The testimony of Irenaeus can be used to confirm other strong evidence, but it cannot support much weight on its own.

Another kind of argument used to locate the Revelation of John in time concerns persecutions of the churches. In the writings of nineteenth-century New Testament scholars, the atrocities committed by Nero against members of the churches in Rome[51] provided a plausible social setting for Revelation. As the twentieth century began, the scholarly consensus about the date of Revelation shifted from the end of Nero's reign (i.e., ca. 68–70) to late in Domitian's reign (i.e., 95–96). One facet of this shift was the development of arguments for a Domitianic persecution of Christians. These arguments have largely been abandoned in recent years.[52] It is now clear that political executions in the imperial center increased late in Domitian's reign,[53] but there is no support for a systematic campaign against Christians in Rome or elsewhere.

The rejection of Domitianic persecutions in recent literature has not caused a return to a Neronic date for Revelation. Rather, there has been a general move away from crisis theories as a way of understanding Revelation. Adela Yarbro Collins made this move by arguing that John perceived an "incipient crisis" not yet manifest to others. Thus, there were elements of crisis but no full confrontation. The elements of crisis revolved around four themes: increasing alienation between Christians and Jews in the cities of Asia, a mutual antipathy between Christians and Gentiles due to Christian reservations about mainstream culture,[54] conflicts over wealth in western Asia Minor and in the churches, and the precarious legal situation of the churches in the late first century.[55]

Some Christians had also undergone experiences of trauma, most related to Roman rule. These included the destruction of Jerusalem, the massacre of Christians in Rome by Nero in the mid 60s, the growing pressure for Christians in western Asia Minor to participate in imperial cult activity, at least one example of martyrdom,[56] and the banishment of John to Patmos.[57] So, according to Yarbro Collins, Revelation was John's effort to shape a linguistic world that provided an imaginative retreat from the tensions of this incipient crisis:

> Through the use of effective symbols and artful plots, the Apocalypse made feelings which were probably latent, vague, complex, and ambiguous explicit, conscious, and simple. Complex relationships were simplified by the use of a dualistic framework. . . . Fear, the sense of powerlessness, and aggressive feelings are not minimized, but heightened. . . . By projecting the tension and the feelings experienced by the hearers into cosmic categories, the Apocalypse made it possible for the hearers to gain some distance from their experience. It provided a feeling of detachment and thus greater control.[58]

Elisabeth Schüssler Fiorenza did not actually abandon persecution theories; she recast them in terms of permanent, widespread imperial oppression. In this way she painted a much bleaker picture of Roman Asia, claiming that most of the inhabitants of the province were suffering under Roman exploitation:

> Many inhabitants of the cities of Asia Minor, staggering under the colonial injustices of oppressive taxation often combined with ruinous interest rates, were suffering from the widening gap between rich and poor. They were afraid of Roman repression of disturbances, paranoid prohibition of private associations, and suspicious surveillance by neighbors and informants. Whereas the vast majority of the population suffered from colonialist abuses of power, exploitation, slavery, and famine, some citizens in the senatorial province of Asia enjoyed the benefits of Roman commerce and peace as well as comforts and splendor of urban life and Hellenistic culture.[59]

In this generally repressive situation, according to Schüssler Fiorenza, the plight of Christians was even more difficult because their refusal to worship the emperors increased the threat of economic deprivation, imprisonment, and execution.[60] This imperialist setting gave Revelation its exigence, or urgency. John's rhetorical response, however, had to be calibrated to certain limitations: groups within the churches that had more positive opinions of Roman power, growing tensions between the churches and synagogues in Asia, and John's own theology.[61]

John's text can thus be understood as a rhetorical product of this exigence and these limitations. According to Schüssler Fiorenza, John did not provide an escape from this brutal reality; rather, he created a symbolic universe that allowed the churches to oppose the dominant symbolic system of mainstream society.[62]

Leonard Thompson engaged Roman social history more systematically than most Revelation scholars and argued there is no support for persecution theories or even deprivation theories:[63]

> There is little evidence to suggest fundamental conflicts either within the economic structure of the province or between the province and Rome. The writer of the Book of Revelation may urge his readers to see conflicts in their urban setting and to think of Roman society as "the enemy," but those conflicts do not reside in Asian social structures. The urban setting in which Christians worshipped and lived was stable and beneficial to all who participated in its social and economic institutions.[64]

The tensions evident in the text come not from the social setting but from the mind of John, according to Thompson. John was trying to provoke his audience, to alienate them from mainstream society.[65] What makes the text so powerful is that John did not simply reject dominant society. Rather, he reinterpreted the whole world, assimilating the public knowledge and transforming it.[66]

A contrapuntal approach is not antithetical to any of these options but draws on certain parts of them more than others. Thompson's reading of the broader social setting of Revelation in Roman Asia is the best available. There is no need to posit persecution or a widespread crisis in society to explain the hostility of Revelation toward Roman rule. We must also consider Schüssler Fiorenza's persistent attention to the discrepant social experiences of a small group like the churches.[67] Even if our evidence suggests that the overall situation was stable, we should not conclude that all the inhabitants were satisfied. Imperial authority always meets forms of resistance, because the encompassing claims of imperial authority cannot match the diversity of actual experiences and because imperial authority never legitimates the experiences of its victims. Given the amount and the character of the data left to us from first-century Roman Asia, we cannot expect to muster a complete account of that time and place. From the range of voices still available to us, we can, however, reconstruct their interaction.

Imperial Cults in the Text

The preceding review regarding persecution theories indicates a scholarly consensus that imperial cults were important in the formation of Revelation and a disagreement about their precise importance. Were imperial cults one of several traumas in an incipient crisis (Yarbro Collins), a major feature of the widespread oppression to which Revelation responded (Schüssler Fiorenza), or a normal part of life in a relatively placid province (Thompson)? The first step in evaluating this feature of the debate is to examine where imperial cults appear in the text of Revelation.

It is dangerous to say that anything in Revelation is clear. Nevertheless, it is safe to conclude that references to imperial cults within the text of Revelation come only in the last half of the book, specifically in chapters 13–19.[68] A brief overview of Revelation 13–19 demonstrates the importance of imperial worship in this part of the text. The first clear reference to imperial cults comes in Revelation 13. The chapter depicts two beasts, one from the sea and one from the earth. The Beast from the Sea appears first, coming with the power and authority of "the great Dragon, the ancient serpent, the one called Devil and Satan, who deceives the whole world" (12:9). The seven-headed, ten-horned Sea Beast astonishes the whole world when it recovers from a fatal wound to one of its heads. The world worships the Dragon and the Beast, noting the Beast's incomparable military ability. The Beast speaks great blasphemies against heaven and makes war on the saints. They are defeated and the Beast rules the whole world (13:1–8).

Commentators are virtually unanimous in their verdict that the Beast from the Sea represents the imperial power of Rome. There is also widespread agreement that the Beast from the Earth is in some way a symbol for the promotion of imperial cults.[69] The second beast receives its authority from the first beast and uses this authority to make the inhabitants of the earth worship the Beast from the Sea. The Beast from the Earth performs great signs so that the inhabitants of earth make sacred images of the first beast. They worship the images and receive the mark of the name of the Beast on their hands and foreheads (13:11–18).

So begins the confrontation between the Lamb and the Beast from the Sea, the dominant theme from this chapter until the end of chapter 19 that drives the plot to its dramatic conclusion. As the visions of that struggle unfold, the issue of proper worship is always near the surface. Revelation 14 opens with the Lamb standing on Mt. Zion, accompanied by the 144,000 faithful followers who have the name of God and of the Lamb written on their foreheads (14:1–5). An angel proclaims that the hour of judgment has come; all should fear God and worship the one who made heavens, earth, sea, and springs. A second angel announces the downfall of Rome: "Fallen, fallen is the great Babylon; all the nations have drunk from the wine of the wrath of her prostitution" (14:8). A third angel's call is the longest, warning that those who worship the Beast, who worship its image, and who receive its mark will drink from the undiluted wine of the wrath of God. Two divine judgments with harvest imagery follow (14:14–20).

A scene change takes us to the heavens. Seven angels come out of the temple bearing bowls filled with the seven last plagues of the wrath of God (15:1–8). The first bowl is poured upon the earth, causing boils to torment those who worship the image of the Beast and those who have received the mark of its name. The other bowls produce further plagues reminiscent of Moses' battle with Pharaoh before the Exodus. When the seventh bowl is poured out upon the air, a great voice from the heavenly throne says, "It is finished." There are tremendous earthquakes and hailstorms, and a third of the great city Babylon is destroyed. Yet people continue to blaspheme God (16:1–21).

The litany of catastrophes is then interrupted as one of the seven angels offers to show John the punishment of the great prostitute Rome. John is taken in the spirit to a wilderness where he encounters the great prostitute seated on the scarlet, seven-headed Beast.[70] The scene changes again as another angel announces that Babylon has fallen. Yet another angel calls upon God's people to come out from her, for she is about to suffer the judgment for glorifying herself and for living luxuriously. Laments follow from those who had become wealthy and powerful because of Babylon. Kings, merchants, ship owners, and sailors mourn the loss of the source of their livelihoods (18:1–19). Then the mood shifts as heaven, the saints, the apostles, and the prophets are told to rejoice over their vindication. An angel throws a millstone into the sea and proclaims the disappearance of Babylon forever. Heavenly crowds, the twenty-four elders, and the four living beings join the celebration and worship the one seated on the throne (18:20–19:10).

The time for battle finally arrives. The Word of God rides out of heaven on a white horse, followed by the armies of heaven. The Beast and the kings gather to make war but are quickly defeated. The Beast and the False Prophet (another name for the Beast from the Earth; 19:20) are seized and thrown alive into the lake of fire; their armies and allies are destroyed and left unburied for the birds to consume (19:11–21).

With the destruction of the Beast and the False Prophet, the topic of imperial cults disappears from the text. Satan is confined for 1,000 years, released, and finally cast in the lake of fire. The living and the dead are judged, and a new heaven and earth appear. The new Jerusalem descends to earth, and God dwells with humanity, wiping away every tear from their eyes (21:4).

Although a cursory retelling of the narrative of Revelation 13–19 can hardly explicate all the problems associated with these chapters, it is sufficient to establish the importance of imperial cults in this crucial section of the text. The section asserts that Roman imperial power is demonic and that people are deceived or pressured into imperial worship. Judgment is announced and depicted for those who participate. Those who refuse to worship the Beast are promised security. The worship of the emperors is not the only important theme in these chapters, but it is the defining activity that separates those who are condemned from those who belong to God. Imperial worship is contrasted to the worship of the creator. Imperial cults are portrayed as a deception, a blasphemous lie, one crucial aspect in the Roman practice of dominating and exploiting the world. As such, imperial cults are presented as a crucial aspect of demonic Roman hegemony.

Imperial Cults and the Date of Revelation

Because imperial cults play such a prominent role in the text of Revelation, it is natural that they have become part of the discussion about the date when Revelation was composed. When crisis theories were more prominent in these discussions, most thought that Revelation must have been written when there were exaggerated demands for worship of the imperial family. After scholars became more aware of the difference between John's perception of a crisis and the perceptions of others, there has been less need to posit major developments in imperial cults to explain the genesis of Revelation.[71]

When commentaries and monographs review the status of imperial cults under Domitian, the main ancient source is a paragraph from Suetonius.[72] In the paragraph Suetonius mentioned several divinizing tendencies of Domitian's reign: references by Domitian to his own divinity, gold and silver images (usually reserved for deities) dedicated to him in the Capitol, the use of "Lord and God" as his title in writing and in personal address, and renaming two months of the year after himself.[73] Although the paragraph in Suetonius has implications for religious practice, Suetonius was not writing primarily about imperial cult activities. These and other details about Domitian in the paragraph build a case for the excessive arrogance of Domitian, which was reflected also in Domitian's attitude toward his participation in the divine realm.

In fact, the only substantive issue commentators mention regularly in the debate about Domitianic imperial cult policy is the allegation that Domitian demanded to be called Lord and God. Most specialists now hold that this was an exaggeration, if not a fabrication, on the part of Suetonius.[74] Writers from the Domitianic period such as Martial and Statius did not use such forms of address, nor do the coins and inscriptions of Rome evince such practices.[75]

It is important to note that the secondary literature has been, by and large, a discussion about the worship of the emperors in Rome rather than about practices in Asia. One result of the analysis in part I of this book is that we can now base conclusions on materials more directly relevant to Revelation, that is, the evidence for imperial cults in Asia. When we turn from the imperial center to the province, it becomes clear that the title "Lord and God" is irrelevant to the question of imperial cults in Asia. There are no signs in the epigraphic or numismatic evidence from Asia that unusual divine titles were employed for Domitian. Even if the title were an issue in the imperial center, it was not important in the province of Asia.

Some other observations can be made regarding imperial cults and the date of Revelation based on the evidence from part I of this book. A survey of the imperial cult evidence from Asia suggests that the most innovative period was during the reigns of Augustus and Tiberius. There were several reasons for this creativity. One was that the Augustan period differed dramatically from the turmoil that had preceded it. The eastern Mediterranean had never before seen such an extended period of relative calm under one ruler. The institution and consolidation of imperial power under Augustus were certainly reasons for the flowering of imperial cults during his reign.

A second reason was the uncertainty regarding succession in the Augustan and Tiberian periods. For several years Marcus Agrippa seemed the most likely successor to Augustus. When Agrippa died in 12 BCE, Augustus had already ruled for 19 years after his victory at Actium. At that time it did not seem likely he would live and hold onto power for another 26 years. So several other candidates for succession came to the fore: Livia's son, Drusus; Augustus's grandsons, Lucius and Gaius; and finally Livia's son, Tiberius. Possible successors to Tiberius included one son of Tiberius who died in infancy before the death of Augustus; Tiberius's nephew Germanicus (died in 19 CE); another son of Tiberius (also named Drusus), who was poisoned in 22 CE; and other more distant male relatives. The end result was that for over three decades, the question of succession was constantly changing. In this setting, a great variety of imperial cults was possible and perhaps necessary.

The two periods in which scholars have tried to locate the composition of Revelation have not yet produced much evidence to suggest any great increase in imperial cult activities in Asia. The period of Nero seems to have been rather quiet with regard to imperial worship. The major known imperial cult monument of the period is the Sebasteion at Aphrodisias. The monument was probably begun in the Tiberian period and honored all the Julio-Claudians. Completion of the project extended into the reign of Nero, who is shown in a relatively reserved manner. One relief shows him in heroic form (fig. 5.8). Another is a subdued presentation of the emperor in military attire being crowned by his mother Agrippina the younger (fig. 8.1). The evidence shows that imperial cult practices in Asia during this period were not unusual for their time. They were certainly more restrained than the short-lived provincial cult of Gaius at Miletos.

The evidence for imperial cults in Asia from the Domitianic period also fit within the mainstream of imperial cult practice. There is no sign of the exaggerated claims alleged for this period. The Temple of the Sebastoi at Ephesos was well within the norm for provincial cults. Several members of the imperial family were worshipped, probably all of them Flavians. The living emperor Domitian was honored but not called θεός. When the Senate condemned him after his assassination, his name was

FIGURE 8.1 Nero crowned by his mother Agrippina; relief from the Sebasteion at Aphrodisias, north portico, third story (*JRS* 1987, pl. 24, #11). Courtesy of the New York University Excavations at Aphrodisias.

excised from inscriptions, and his image would certainly have been removed from the temple. The temple and its cultus, however, remained viable for at least another century and a half.

Thus, the most influential development in imperial cults of the last half of the first century CE does not have to do with excessive divinization. The signal development, first manifest in the dedications of the Temple of the Sebastoi but reflecting broader trends in society, was the use of neokoros as a technical title for a city with a provincial temple of the emperors. The power of this innovation was explosive. In a matter of years it changed the public rhetoric of empire in Asia. Within a century it had transformed the discourse of Roman imperialism in the eastern Mediterranean. From the late first century onward, the most prestigious self-designation that could be employed by a city in Asia was neokoros, indicating the presence of a provincial temple where the emperors and their relatives were worshipped.[76]

The production of Revelation, therefore, should not be tied to alleged excesses in imperial cult practices. Rather, we should turn our attention toward the fundamental developments taking place within mainstream imperial cult institutions and toward the role these institutions were playing in late first-century Asia. These developments do not provide a date for Revelation. They do provide access to the dominant discourse against which Revelation should be understood.

To summarize, then, the specific region of the Roman Empire to which Revelation was directed is clear from the text itself. This feature sets it apart from nearly every other apocalyptic text of its era. Efforts to specify exactly when Revelation was written have not succeeded in establishing a definitive date for the text. Internal evidence from the text of Revelation is most important in this regard, indicating a date after the death of Nero (68 CE) and after the destruction of Jerusalem by the Romans (70 CE). Moreover, the use of the name Babylon for Rome implies a date somewhat removed from the destruction of Jerusalem, when Jewish life was taking on the character of the first phase of the Babylonian exile, that is, no functioning temple, complete loss of sovereignty, and foreign domination.

External evidence indicates that Revelation was written well before the middle of the second century, for the text was known to Justin Martyr (d. ca. 160),[77] to Melito of Sardis (ca. 165),[78] and probably to Papias of Hierapolis (d. ca. 130).[79] If Irenaeus is correct, Revelation belongs to the late first century. As his historical judgment is questionable, some uncertainty should be maintained. The combination of internal indicators and external evidence points toward the period 80–100 CE as the most likely time for the composition of the text, though the Trajanic period (98–117 CE) is not unthinkable.

Evidence for imperial cults should not be used as a primary argument for one date or the other. Certain trends are distinguishable in the evolving discourse of imperial cults during the late first and early second century, but these are not dramatic enough to require that Revelation be considered a response to them. Moreover, it is not at all clear that John was responding to a particular historical event in this regard. The date of Revelation should be established on other grounds, after which consideration of imperial cult practices is appropriate.

Thus, Thompson was correct in describing imperial cults as a normal feature of everyday life in Roman Asia. The work of Yarbro Collins and of Schüssler Fiorenza reminds us, however, that mainstream views are not shared by everyone. We must take account of the discrepant experiences of any social setting. So the following chapters of this book build a structural comparison of issues that surface in imperial cults and in Revelation's discrepant interpretation of life in Roman Asia. A structural comparison does not require us to choose a particular date within the decades when Revelation was surely written. Roman imperial cosmology and eschatology were growing in importance, but their fundamental character was relatively stable in this period. Although I conclude that Revelation was probably written in the late first century, the following analysis is general enough to be applicable whether one is persuaded that Revelation was written in 69 or 96 CE. John's critique was not aimed at particular cults or institutions; it was directed at an imperial way of life.

9

CENTERING REALITY

Space and Time in Revelation

This chapter examines the way John's text centers spatial and temporal existence and contrasts this method with the centering strategies of the dominant discourse. The argument proceeds through three phases. First comes a description of the kinds of space one encounters in Revelation, followed by a consideration of the qualities of time revealed by John. Finally, I compare these conclusions with the work of Leonard Thompson, one of the few scholars to comment on the cosmological concerns of Revelation. The general lack of interest in these basic facets of the text is understandable. Revelation's view of the world is at odds with modern secular cosmologies and with most modern religious ones as well.

Three Kinds of Space

In a mythic consciousness space in the cosmos is usually associated with different types of beings.[1] Revelation presents at least three levels of spatial reality: heaven, earth, and the underworld (5:3).[2] Two topographical features are difficult to locate within this three-fold spatial schema. The wilderness and the lake of fire remind us that the imagery of Revelation often eludes systematization. But there is a relatively coherent imagined geography in the visionary's world.

Heaven is the most spectacular stratum in Revelation's universe. Although no precise mapping of the heavenly realm is afforded us, several of its features are mentioned. The most extensive description comes in Revelation 4. The scene begins at the throne of God, which is described only as having an emerald halo or rainbow.[3] In front of the throne are seven oil lamps, which are the seven spirits of God, and a glassy sea, clear and sparkling like crystal (also 15:2). Around the throne of God are 24 more thrones for elders who are adorned with white robes and golden crowns. Nearest the throne are four fantastic creatures.[4] Each has six wings that are filled with eyes, inside and out. One of the creatures looks like a lion, one looks like a bull, one has the face of a human, and one has the shape of an eagle (4:2–8). We are probably to imagine seven archangels around the throne as well (8:2), though they are not mentioned in chapter 4.[5]

The area around the throne is often noisy because of the startling sounds, thunder, and lightning. The activity in this area is mostly given over to worship. Night and day, the four creatures lead the heavenly liturgy with acclamations of the living God. The 24 elders bow down, cast their golden crowns down before the throne, and respond with further acclamations (4:8–11). In another text a huge crowd too large to number gathers before the throne. These people from all tribes and nations join the creatures, the elders, and the angels blessing God and announcing his victory (7:9–12).

The golden altar in front of the throne (8:3) is a prominent feature consistently associated with God's judgments against the world on behalf of his people. It is a horned altar (9:13), the sort one would encounter among the cultures from the eastern Roman empire (fig. 9.1). The altar speaks twice, once ordering an angel to dry up the Euphrates so that armies can cross and wreak havoc (9:14; see also 14:18), and once affirming the righteousness of God's judgments (16:7). The altar is described as the place where martyrs await vindication, pleading with God to end the delay and to avenge their cause (6:9–11).

The only reference to sacrifice on the altar is a complex image in Revelation 8:1–5 that develops the theme of vindication. The grammar is difficult, but the altar appears to hold burning incense, which is likened to the prayers of all the saints (cf. 5:8). An angel (presumably the one responsible for the fire on the altar mentioned in 14:18) receives additional incense in a censor. The angel lights the additional incense with fire from the heavenly altar to enhance the prayers of the saints. Then the angel casts the flaming mixture to earth, which leads to the blowing of the seven trumpets. Thus, the prayers of the saints help bring about God's judgment on the earth, which God accomplishes through angelic action.

One other possible allusion is related to sacrificial activity at the altar. The Messiah is also in the heavenly realm (19:11) with God at the throne (12:5), and the main image for the Messiah is that of the slaughtered Lamb. The author of Revelation makes no overt connection between the Lamb and the altar, probably because the Lamb has been slain from the foundation of the world (13:8) and because sacrifice will be irrelevant when the first earth comes to an end.[6]

Near the throne is the heavenly temple. At the end of the story of the two witnesses in Revelation 11, we learn that it is the place where the ark of the covenant is kept (11:19), though whether this is a heavenly ark or the ark that disappeared after the Babylonian destruction[7] is not clear. Angels (14:15, 17; 15:6) and martyrs (7:15) serve God in the heavenly temple. If Revelation 11:1 refers to the heavenly (rather

FIGURE 9.1 Example of a horned altar. The altar is in front of
a temple of Isis on Delos. Author's photo.

than the earthly) temple, then that chapter begins with a scene where the transcendent temple is measured.[8] This could, however, be an unusual reference to the earthly
temple[9] or perhaps a symbolic representation of the church (cf. 3:12).

In comparison, 4 Ezra 10 records a vision in which Ezra is allowed to see the
transcendent Mt. Zion, which is not affected by the vicissitudes of the earthly Jerusalem.[10] In Revelation, Zion is also a heavenly reality. After the judgment of humanity, Zion comes down to earth as the new Jerusalem, the place where God can finally dwell with his people (21:9–22:5; perhaps also 14:1–5).

Thus, in Revelation, the realm of absolute being is focused on the throne of the
Creator and the Lamb. There are also other splendid, lesser beings in heaven (the
creatures and the elders have already been noted). The Messiah's armies belong to

this realm (Rev 19:14; cf. 2 Bar 5:11) and an unspecified number of angels. The sun, moon, and stars are heavenly as well, though they are only occasionally personified or equated with angels as in other texts of the era.[11] The Dragon, the accuser of the saints, once dwelled here. Some special humans reside in heaven, particularly the martyrs, but their presence is characterized as anomolous (they are souls without resurrected bodies, 6:9–11) and unfulfilled (they long for vindication).[12]

The term earth is used broadly in Revelation for the middle realm below heaven, composed of earth in the limited sense (i.e., "dry land"), the sea, and middle heaven.[13] Middle heaven might also be considered a separate region because it is an intermediate zone between heaven and earth where flying beings deliver divine announcements (8:13; 14:6; 19:17). Because middle heaven is inhabited mostly by birds and is subject to the sorts of events that also occur in the human realm, one might more appropriately categorize it as one part of the earthly realm that has a distinct mediating function.

The rest of this realm is signified by "earth (dry land) and sea" (e.g., 10:2; 12:12; 13:1–14). The earth is said to have four corners (20:8), which are the sources of the four dominant winds (7:1). The earth is damaged by some of the judgments (9:3–4; 11:6; 16:1) and so is the sea (8:8–9). The sea receives relatively little attention, however, for humans are the main concern. Whereas the sea is a site of labor for some humans (18:17), it is the abode of other kinds of creatures (10:6). "Those who dwell on earth"[14] are the primary subjects and recipients of John's Revelation.

One of the distinctive features of earth, as the realm between heaven and the underworld, is that it is governed by time. One of the most powerful angelic figures in Revelation appears in chapter 10. The angel is described in a way that encompasses space and time, and it announces the end of temporal space. The angel comes down from heaven, places one foot on the sea and one on the land, and raises its hand to heaven. Its face is like the sun and its legs like columns of fire. When it speaks the first time, the seven thunders rumble, but John is not allowed to record what the thunders say. Then the angel "swore by the one living to the ages of ages— who made the heavens and the things in it and the earth and the things in it and the sea and the things in it—that time will be no longer" (10:6).

Toward the end of the text, John's audience encounters the end of this middle realm. When the Almighty appears on the white throne to judge the living and the dead, earth and sky flee from God's presence (20:11). The transitory realm cannot remain in the presence of the absolute. Temporal space is undone.

A second distinctive feature of the middle realm is that it is contingent. Events that transpire on earth are consistently represented as reactions to events in heaven. The Lamb breaks seals off a scroll in heaven and disasters occur on earth. Stars drop from the sky and effect earthly consequences. Angels blow trumpets in heaven and calamities strike the earth (Revelation 8 until at least chapter 11). The region of land, sea, and sky depends on heaven for its well-being and is subject to heaven's punishment.

Another part of Revelation's world appears to belong to the middle realm but is nevertheless difficult to locate. The wilderness provides a setting for two scenes in the text. The vision recorded in Revelation 12 describes a heavenly woman, who is hidden by God in the wilderness for her own safety. The Dragon is cast out of heaven and exiled to earth, where he attacks the Woman. The earth protects her, and the Dragon goes off to make war on her children. From this vision it appears that the wilderness is part of the earthly realm, though the events and actors are quite extraordinary. The other vision in the wilderness is recorded in Revelation 17. John is taken to the wilderness "in the spirit" by an angel. There he sees the Woman Babylon seated on the seven-headed Beast whose heads represent hills and kings. The Dragon, the Beast, and the Women of Revelation 12 and 17 are heavenly beings present in the earthly realm; thus, they play an important mediating role between these two levels of reality: they provide the correct understanding of life on earth. This hermeneutic is not available to everyone; it is known only in the spirit. Thus, the beings encountered in the wilderness—the Woman and Dragon of Revelation 12 and the Woman and Beast of Revelation 17—reveal the depths of what is normally known only superficially. The wilderness is a realm where mysteries are explained in the spirit.

The underworld receives the least attention of any of the three kinds of space. The abyss, one of its most prominent features, is not described, but its character as a place of confinement for evil creatures is clear enough. The abyss first appears in the text after the fifth angel blows its trumpet (Rev 9:1–11). A star that falls from heaven is given the key to unlock the entrance to the abyss. Once it is opened, smoke billows out and grotesque locusts are released on the earth. These locusts look like war-horses except that they have human heads, long hair, and golden crowns. They destroy vegetation and torment with scorpion-like stings those who do not have the seal of God on their forehead. The king of the locusts is the angel of the abyss, whose name is "Destruction" (Abaddon in Hebrew, Apollyon in Greek). The abyss occurs in the vision of the Seer also as the place from which the Beast of Revelation 17 arises to make war on the righteous (17:8; 11:7). After the death of the Beast, the Dragon itself is locked in the abyss for a thousand years.

This depiction of the abyss as a prison for evil creatures is in line with the usage of the term in Luke 8:31 and 1 Enoch 18:10. It is somewhat different, however, from the usage of 1 Enoch 10:13 and other texts, where the abyss is a place for dead humans synonymous with Sheol or Gehenna.[15] This difference is due to the fact that in Revelation, Death and Hades appear together as the abode of dead humans (1:18; 20:13) or as the bringers of death (6:8). As such, Death and Hades are an important aspect of Revelation's underworld.

The word "death" occurs often in Revelation in its more mundane sense as the end of human life without any personification. This is considered in Revelation to be the first death, not the second death after the general resurrection (2:11; 20:6, 14; 21:8). The second death is described as a lake burning with fire and sulphur. The Beast and the False Prophet of Revelation 19 are thrown in alive, without experiencing the first death, and are tormented forever before the angels and the Lamb. Later the Dragon is consigned to the lake of fire (20:10). Then Death and Hades are subjected to the second death (20:14) with all humans whose names are not written in the scroll of life (20:15).

The lake of fire is even more difficult to locate than the wilderness. This problem is not due simply to insufficient description. The lake of fire takes us to the limits of imaginative topography, as it signifies not simply extinction but the extinction of extinction. It cannot belong to earth or the underworld because it functions forever, long after the earth and sea have fled from the Almighty judge and are no more. It could perhaps be located in heaven, the realm of absolute being. But the status of heaven itself is in question once all things are made new. How can there be a heaven when the new Jerusalem has come down to the new earth, when God and the Lamb have vacated the transcendent realm to become the temple of God's people, when the divine and the earthly abide together on intimate terms?

The lake of fire cannot be systematically integrated into the three kinds of space. It remains a paradox. Heaven as the realm of absolute being cannot survive without a lake of fire that can destroy all symbolized existence. But neither can heaven long endure the smell of sulphur for it is a pollutant, a disturbing reminder of the final demise of its own signification. The paradox is not due to confusion or irrationality on the part of the Seer. This is the work of the critical mythic consciousness, pushing the fundamental categories of knowledge and experience beyond their limits. John signifies the end of signification; he symbolizes the end of his own symbols. This should not be confused with demythologization or with deconstruction. It represents, rather, the power of the mythic imagination to undermine its most cherished axioms. It is a practitioner's ferocious dissatisfaction with signification, the piercing gaze of religious criticism cast upon its own work. Our guide has taken us past this world of imagined space and time in search of an unattainable vista from which we can look back upon it.

Qualities of Time

Human experience is filtered through times. We live in many kinds of time blended through institutional contexts and through the work of the imagination. One of the most powerful organizers of time is the calendar. "Even as they keep the experience of the world intact, calendars experiment with sacred realities and redesign the meaning of the universe."[16] A cosmic periodicity "aims at a shuffled perfection, a stylized arrangement of all the possible qualities of being symbolized by diverse times."[17]

We know more about Asia's calendars and the role of imperial cults in them than we do about the calendar kept by the churches to which John wrote. The calendars of the cities and those of the churches would not have been exclusive. Through work schedules, community festivals, and family relationships, the churches would have participated in city calendars. In fact, most scholars would agree that John's opponents within the churches—"Balaam," "Jezebel," and the Nicolaitans—were more active participants in the round of annual festivals for various deities and rulers than John would have liked.[18] In Revelation, however, we glimpse a calendar and at least five different kinds of time.

Revelation immediately signals that the worshipping community is the crucial institutional setting for normative experiences of time. Revelation 1:3 pronounces a blessing both on the reader and on the gathered congregation that hears and heeds the message of the text. Moreover, John was quick to point out that his revelatory experience took place, or at least began, while he was in the spirit on the Lord's Day (1:10).[19] Whether there was a congregation on Patmos is not important for this point.

Proper worship is the locus for the understanding of times. John's text begins in worship and seeks a hearing in worship. Furthermore, Revelation is permeated by worship, hymns of praise and adoration, and liturgical language.[20] No other apocalyptic text can be characterized by such an strong emphasis on worship.[21]

So "worship time" is the first and most important kind of time in Revelation, unique because it spans heaven and earth. Worship goes on in the congregations on earth but only sporadically; in heaven it is continuous. Worship time builds a community that bridges the two realms. It also marks difference between those inside the church and those outside.[22] It is time organized around the throne of God, available in theory to all creatures but in practice only to those who participate with the churches and the angels in obeisance to God and to the Lamb. Worship time breaks the churches' earthly ties and substitutes heavenly ones.

Those outside the church worship the Beast of Roman imperial authority. For Beast worshippers, time is structured around the birth of Augustus and secondarily around the other emperors. As others ascend to the throne of the empire, their birthdays can be added to the festal calendar. The system meshed well with the rhythms of life in the cities of Asia, but it fit John's calendar poorly.

Worship time for the churches is distinctive in its dynamic stability, by which I mean that it is characterized by eternality and by motion. The constancy of the eternal God is emphasized in worship, manifest especially in the repeated acclamations of the One who was, who is, and who will come,[23] whose being goes on forever into the ages of ages.[24] Worship is also the time in which we encounter perpetual motion: there is ceaseless worship around the heavenly throne (4:18), and the martyrs serve God night and day in the heavenly temple before the throne (7:15). Worship signified life experienced completely in God's presence—never ending and always moving.

A second kind of time encountered throughout the book of Revelation is the Seer's experience of "vision time." In a style not unlike that of a shaman, John travels in the spirit through many qualities of space and time, encountering beings and realities inaccessible to most people. He comes into contact with different phases of historical time and records them in a disorienting fashion. The journeys validate his status as a prophet in the congregations, so his authority is based primarily on ecstatic experience.[25] The extensive allusions to authoritative writings, however, warn us not to draw too sharp a distinction between the ecstatic spirit traveler and the textual master, whose authority is founded on knowledge of an accumulated tradition.[26] John expected the hearers to recognize him on both counts, as visionary and as a master of tradition. The ecstatic element is nevertheless primary, for even his handling of authoritative texts is affected by his visions. He does not so much quote scriptures as build with them.[27]

Although all members of the congregations had direct access to worship time, their access to vision time was indirect, mediated by John and by other prophets such as Jezebel (2:20). The prophet traveled through times on behalf of the rest of the congregation, bringing back special knowledge of God's will in history. The retelling of the visions did more than transmit this knowledge. The oral enactment of Revelation in the churches approximated the revelatory experience[28] and gave the members a sample of other qualities of time. In the context of worship time, then, the congregations experienced other kinds of time that transcended everyday spatiotemporal realities.

One important feature of the Seer's vision time was a reinterpretation of "present time" as the period just before the destruction of the empire. In his retelling of the visions, John challenged the churches with a particular rendering of everyday time. John's label for present time was "3½ years," "42 months," and "1,260 days."[29] John's use of these equivalent phrases is an excellent example of his dual role as ecstatic and canonist. The figure is drawn from venerable tradition—the book of Daniel—as the time before God's final intervention in history. In Daniel there were 70 weeks of years (i.e., 7 × 70 years, or 490 years) that began with the decree to rebuild the Jerusalem temple. At the beginning of the seventieth week, the Anointed one would be cut off by a foreign king. Halfway through the last week, the Jerusalem temple would be defiled by the foreigner (Dan 9:24–27). At the end of the last 3½ years (= 42 months = 1,260 days) of the 70 weeks of years, the foreign king would be killed, the resurrection would occur, and judgments and rewards would be meted out (Dan 11:29–12:13). John took this authoritative text of Daniel and reworked the idea of 42 months in light of his visions, redefining the everyday time of his audience as the last great oppression before the eschaton. In the vision, present time became the prelude to history's denouement.[30]

The visions of John described the 42 months from several angles. The clearest description was as the time when the imperial Roman Beast was given authority to blaspheme against heaven and to make war on the saints (13:5–7). The present could also be described as the time when the Gentiles trample the outer court of the temple (11:2), the time when the two witnesses prophesy against those dwelling on earth (11:3–10), and the time when God protects the heavenly Woman from the Dragon (12:6, 14). This conjunction of images does not blend well because John envisaged the present as paradox: divine protection for those suffering defeat in the war with the Beast. Rather than imposing one interpretation on the present, John presented a collage of perspectives on the present, a range of readings on the situations of the congregations. His method reflected his jarring message; they were visions that barely fit together for times that barely cohered. Stated in other terms, they were visions of discrepant experiences that challenged the dominant discourse. A consistent theme, however, underlies these images: all of them offer the promise of protection in the midst of suffering in present time.

John provided his audience with an indirect experience of another quality of time that belongs to the period following present time. "Vindication time" belongs to the period after the 42 months. This period lasts 1,000 years; John calls it the "first resurrection."[31] Little space in the text is devoted to this first resurrection (20: 4–6), but a few points can be affirmed regarding it. The primary quality of the 1,000 years of time is, according to John, the vindication of the martyrs.[32] During the 42 months the souls of the martyrs plead with God from the heavenly altar, "O Ruler holy and true, how long will you not judge and avenge our blood against those dwelling on earth?" (6:10) At the end of the 42 months comes the time of their vindication. First the Beast of imperial Rome and the False Prophet who promoted its worship are defeated in battle and cast alive into the lake of fire (19:19–21). An angel comes down from heaven, binds the Dragon with a chain, and imprisons it in the abyss for the thousand years (20:1–3). The rest of the dead do not rise at this time; only the martyrs and those who refused to worship the Beast participate in the first resurrection. They are priests of God and of Christ and reign with them 1,000 years (20:4–6).

The focus on vindication becomes clearer when related and similar texts are surveyed. Revelation 20:11 alludes to Daniel 7:9–14, in which God sets up thrones and judges the little horn (Antiochus IV Ephiphanes, d. 163 BCE). The rest of the nations are allowed to live (as in Rev 20:4–6) but stripped of their dominion; finally one like a son of man comes on the clouds and is given dominion. The parallel with Daniel is only partial, however. In Revelation the figure of Satan is new, the throne scene occurs only after the Beast has been killed, the execution of the Beast is by the Messiah, others share in God's rule, and the idea of priesthood is added.

Other Jewish apocalyptic texts such as 2 Baruch and 4 Ezra provide further comparative material for the time between the destruction of Roman imperialism and the final judgment of humanity. Their handling of the theme is much different. In 2 Baruch, we are shown all history as a great thunderstorm, in which a series of 12 dark waters and bright waters are rained upon the earth (53–72). At the end of this series the Messiah binds and destroys the last earthly ruler (40:1–2). Then comes a period when the Messiah rules on earth, enjoyed only by those who survive to the end and who live in the land of Israel. Those who survive into this period will have Leviathan and Behemoth for food, as well as heavenly manna. The earth will produce crops beyond measure, aromatic winds will freshen the mornings, and clouds will supply dew in the evening (29:1–8). There will be painless births, and no one will die prematurely. The time is described as the end of corruption and the beginning of incorruption (73–74). When this period of messianic rule ends, the Messiah returns to glory, the souls of the righteous rise to their reward (30:1–5), and the wicked suffer the consequences of their actions (51:2). Fourth Ezra describes a similar scenario.[33] The Messiah appears and destroys the power of Rome. He saves the remnant of God's people and causes them to rejoice until the end of time (11:36–12:3; 12:31–34). This period lasts 400 years. Then the Messiah and all people die, returning the world to primeval silence for seven days. After this come the resurrection and the judgment of righteous and wicked (7:28–44).

Whereas 2 Baruch details the joys of the earthly rule of the Messiah, 4 Ezra shows less concern for the nature of this period than for the structure of the end of time. In contrast to both of these, Revelation gives no description of conditions during this time. In fact, it is not even clear that an earthly reign is intended in Revelation. John's audience is left to deduce the location of this reign as well as the status of life on earth. Death and Hades still hold the rest of the deceased until after the 1,000 years and perhaps add more souls to their collection (20:5, 14). The peoples of the world still exist, but they are no longer deceived while the Dragon is confined to the abyss (20:1–3, 8). Jerusalem is presumably repopulated by the saints as well (20:9).[34] Thus, John's description of the 1,000 years gave his audience access to "vindication time," cast in terms of earthly time but without its perennial evils.

The 1,000 years end with an incident otherwise unknown from the extant literature of that era: Satan is released from his captivity in the abyss to roam the earth again. He comes up from the underworld once more to deceive humanity. The Dragon and the kings of the earth gather to make war on the saints again, but fire falls from heaven and destroys the assault. History, or temporal existence in the space known as earth, is at an end (20:7–10).

John then exposed his audience to one more variety of time that I call, for lack of a better term, "new time." It might not even be appropriate to call it time, for the fundamental distinctions of this world are gone. In fact, this world itself is gone; there is a new heaven and a new earth. The sun and the moon, the two primary determinants of time, are eclipsed by the glory of God (21:23). Death, which gave time its poignant urgency, is dead. There is no night, no fear, no pain or suffering. There is, instead, a city. The city is a bride, though no wedding is portrayed. The city is shaped as a gigantic cella, though there is no temple. Language is stretched beyond its limits as the religious critic strains to describe the end of signification. Mythic symbolism describes its own demise. The method by which the fundamental notions of human experience were constructed challenges its own project to see what will survive.

This is not a universalization of worship time; heaven has not invaded earth, and there are no worship scenes described in the New Jerusalem. Neither is this a restoration of the primeval paradise. The many times have converged into an as yet indescribable reality. Heaven itself is changed as the absolute and the contingent realms flow together. The suffering endured by beings in both realms has been transformed into an eternal, righteous community.

John retold these visions of times for a purpose. The narration of present time, vindication time, and new time—learned by him in vision time and mediated in worship time—was an attempt to define the character of present time. Present time, properly understood, is for repentance and testimony. John maneuvered his audience to face two alternatives. Present time could be spent in ignorance and deception, like Jezebel of Thyatira (2:20–21), like the sleepers of Sardis (3:3), like the householder of Laodikeia (if the knock at the door is unanswered, 3:20), like those who worship the Beast (13:14), like Babylon herself (18:5–8). Or present time could be spent in endurance (1:10; 2:19; 2:25–26; 3:10–11; 6:11; 13:10; 14:12). Within this framework, the only logical response in the present time was to endure and to long for new time (22:17, 20).

Boundaries, Crossings, and Centers

The three spatial regions and the five kinds of time I outlined were not hermetically sealed, exclusive categories. Transgressions occur often and these crossings became a major feature in Leonard Thompson's analysis of the relationship of Revelation to its world. I consider Thompson's book to be one of the most important recent monographs on Revelation and so a consideration of his proposals is in order here. In brief, he argued that movement across boundaries in Revelation resulted in the transformation of the beings and objects that make the crossings. The transformations are consistent, operating according to certain principles. They display homologies and contrarieties among beings, objects, and events in Revelation; that is, they reveal relationships of similarity and dissimilarity among features of the text. So, for instance, the text exhibits homologies between God, the saints, the bride of the Lamb, righteous deeds, and so on through the color white and through certain garments.[35]

The homologies and contrarities operate across spatial and temporal boundaries and reverberate through different dimensions of the text (social, liturgical, psychological, etc.). The homologies especially, but also the contrarities, result in a blurring or softening of the boundaries in the text, according to Thompson. When the homologies and contrarities are charted, they reveal a deep consistency that undergirds all reality. For example, the Lamb and the Beast from the Sea (Revelation 13) share many features. Both are said to have been mortally wounded yet live on. Both are agents of higher powers, yet they receive honor and glory and power. Both become the central figure for a worshipping community. These homologies suggest that the Lamb and the Beast "form dyadic relationships, that is, they become doubles, split images of some more fundamental wholeness."[36] Another example is supplied by the major cities in Revelation. Rome/Babylon, the earthly Jerusalem, and the New Jerusalem are described in similar ways that point to "a common structure within good and evil in the Apocalypse."[37]

Thompson's analysis of boundary transformations leads to the conclusion that the Seer was trying simultaneously to provide an alternative to public knowledge (a sectarian activity) while speaking for the whole world (a cosmopolitan activity). Revelation does not merely castigate outsiders by drawing hard and fast boundaries, according to Thompson, for a unity transcends the boundaries and tensions in the text. The author tries to draw the Roman world into his framework and to speak for the unbroken wholeness that underlies all reality. This wholeness flows from God, upon whom everything and every power depends. God's dynamic power binds together all space and time, all "faithful followers, apostates, and infidels."[38]

The problem with this analysis is that it identifies boundaries while the centers remain invisible.[39] Boundaries cannot exist without centers,[40] and once those centers are named, much of the blur is dispelled.[41] Most of Thompson's main conclusions should be affirmed, including apocalypses are not necessarily generated by a crisis; apocalypses are not restricted in their appeal to one kind of social setting; and symbolic life is not epiphenomenal to "real" social forces at work in society. The specific point of disagreement here is whether Revelation attempts to speak *about* the world or *for* the world. Would the seer "be more faithful to his vision of an unbroken wholeness if he did subvert his cognitive exclusiveness"?[42] Revelation defines the centers of space and time quite differently from how imperial cults define them. We may conclude that Revelation did not attempt to speak for the world. Homologies did not soften boundaries; they reinforced them.

In part I, I argued that imperial cults constructed a cosmology with an imaginary geography centered on the city of Rome and a calendar organized around Roman dominion. Revelation, on the other hand, allowed no such geography of the earthly realm. The heavenly throne of God was John's center. The two great cities claiming dominion over John's congregations were Jerusalem and Rome, and John attempted to strip both of their claims. Whatever else we might make of the two witnesses of Revelation 11, we can be certain that they are portrayed as prophesying in Jerusalem, "which is called spiritually Sodom and Egypt, where their Lord was crucified" (11:8). "The Beast from the abyss," abruptly introduced into the narrative, kills the two witnesses whose bodies are left on the streets of Jerusalem. All the inhabitants of earth rejoice to be rid of the prophets, but after three days the two are raised from the dead and taken into heaven. An earthquake destroys a tenth of the city, killing seven thousand. The rest are terrified and give glory to "God in heaven" (11:13). Here Jerusalem is portrayed as the site where Jesus was crucified and the two eschatological witnesses were slain. The vision makes clear that Jerusalem has no more claim over the churches than any other earthly city.

Rome is also disqualified as unworthy to claim centrality, but the denunciation is much more strident. Rome is the seven-headed Beast coming up from the sea, the culmination of the four evil kingdoms of Daniel 7–12. The source of its power and authority is the ancient Dragon Satan (13:1–2). The imperial Beast deceives the nations, causes them to worship Satan and itself, speaks arrogant blasphemies against God and his dwelling place in heaven, and makes war on the saints (13:3–7). Later, judgment is pronounced. Rome will be devastated in an hour because of its economic exploitation, its violence, and its blasphemy (Revelation 18). Both Rome and Jerusalem are thus denied centrality. Even though the fear of God is still present in Jerusalem, there is no semblance of proper creaturely bearing in Rome. Rome is the enemy of God, not the center of reality.

In John's text the true center of space is the throne of God in heaven. The 4 living creatures, the 24 elders, the multitudes of angels, and the martyrs all gather around the throne (esp. 4:1–11; 7:9–17). The congregations of Asia are focused there in their worship, for the throne is the source of true knowledge (1:1–2) and righteous judgment (6–8; 15:1–8; 20:11–15). For John, then, nothing in this world of signification can be granted centrality. The ultimate center to be located outside the everyday world. The religious critic refused to sacrifice the integrity of absolute being by locating it in the contingent realm.

The centralization of time around worship in Revelation supports this spatial analysis. The time that makes sense of all the others is worship time. Present time, vindication time, and new time are elucidated in worship, the very time when one is oriented toward the spatial center: the One who is, was, and is to come. Revelation 21:5–6a combines the themes in a few words, weaving together space, true knowledge of the cosmos, and time: "And the one seated upon the throne said, 'Look, I make all things new.' And he says, 'Write! These words are faithful and true.' And he said to me, 'It is finished. I am the alpha and omega, the beginning and the end.'"

The verses also make clear that the throne itself is not the center. The "throne" is a circumlocution for the One who abides there. God—located specifically beyond the realm of symbolization—is the center.[43] The rest of Revelation 21:6 defines the nature of this center. "To the one who is thirsty I will give freely from the spring of living water," says the One seated on the throne. These apparently disconnected statements succinctly characterize the center of reality as the One who is active, faithful, and generous.

Yet this does not prepare the reader for the biggest surprise of the book. The goal of history is neither a return to the primeval paradise nor transport to the heavenly realm. Once the victory of God is complete and John's definition of space and time is vindicated, the center of space and time relocates itself. The throne of God and of the Lamb descends to humanity with the new Jerusalem (22:3). The goal of spatiotemporal experience turns out to be not the realm of absolute being but rather a crazy hybrid, the offspring of the marriage between a heavenly city and a slaughtered Lamb. The transcendent cohabits with the contingent, resulting in the unimaginable: walls with gates that are never closed, day without night, land without sea, habitation without temples, splendor without poverty, kings who offer their glory to the Creator, and nations that walk in the light of God's glory.

With these definitions of centers in place, the homologies created by boundary crossings appear somewhat differently. Four examples clarify the issues. The Lamb and the Beast from the Sea no longer appear as split images of a more fundamental wholeness.[44] The similarities in description—slain yet living, second in command to a higher sovereign, objects of worshipping communities—are not commonalities that depict the Lamb and the Beast as a dyad. Once the center is understood, the Lamb is the definition of reality, slain from the foundation of the world and living forever. The Beast is a blasphemous imitation bound for destruction.

Nor do the homologies between the cities of Revelation suggest "a common structure within good and evil in the Apocalypse."[45] Both Rome and the New Jerusalem are bedecked with jewels and precious stones; both the temple of 11:1–2 and the New Jerusalem are protected from incursions by unclean abominations. But this does not signal a fundamental similarity where "[n]ot only are distinctions blurred among past, present, and future, but also time and space are related as coordinates of a common order."[46] The centrality of the throne in John's definition of space allows us to affirm a much more dynamic situation. John has not simply staked out a different center to the world; he has asserted that there is no center in earthly space. The true center exists outside the earthly realm. Moreover, that center will shift as a result of its final victory. Distinctions in time are not blurred; rather, they are clarified. Roman imperial power is a masquerade. It belongs to the 42 months when time is spent either in deception or endurance; it does not belong to the time of eternal dominion.[47]

Revelation 12 provides two final examples. The chapter contains two boundary crossings from heaven to earth. A Dragon, the one called Satan and Devil, awaits the birth of a male child from a pregnant heavenly Woman because it wants to consume the infant. The child is snatched away to the throne of God, and the Woman flees to the wilderness where she is protected by God. The Dragon and his angels make war in heaven with Michael and his angels. The Dragon and his troops lose the battle and are cast to earth, where the Dragon attempts to pursue the Woman into the wilderness. The earth protects her, and the Dragon leaves to vent his anger on the rest of the Woman's children.

Commentaries manifest the contentious debate about the meaning of these images and this narrative. Our interest is in the two boundary crossings. Both crossings involve a heavenly sign (σημεῖον in 12:1 and 3) that is forced to earth. The Woman flees to earth for safety, where God and Earth both protect her from the Dragon. The Dragon, on the other hand, fights the heavenly hosts in a losing battle and is exiled to earth. The two transformations are radically different. The Dragon is frustrated in his aggression, sees that his days are numbered, and settles for venting his wrath on the Woman's children. He has become finite, doomed, and he rages in futility. The Woman is humbled in her descent. No longer clothed by the sun and the zodiac or standing on the moon, she is reduced to seclusion in the wilderness. She is dependent on God for her sustenance, but this is also for a short time (1,260 days or "time, times, and half a time," 12:6, 14). Her future is secure despite temporary setbacks.[48]

This narrative does not blur the spatial boundaries between heaven and earth or the moral boundaries between good and evil. The narrative transfers the locus of the conflict from heaven to earth. The two realms are connected by lines of contingency but in ways that reinforce a fundamental tension in the text: the Dragon is doomed and the Woman preserved. The heavenly origin of the problem, furthermore, suggests that resolution will also come from there and not from earth.

Other examples could be cited, but these four suggest the differences in our readings. Do the differences come from divergent methods and theories? Thompson's book worked from the text of Revelation toward social setting and relied heavily on Lévi-Strauss for his understanding of the function of myth.[49] I have worked from material related to social setting toward the text of Revelation and have relied heavily on Sullivan and the Eliade tradition regarding the function of myth. Method and theory are fundamental issues, but they do not—or at least they should not—confine analyses to parallel paths. The text of Revelation provides the intersection, and we both agree that at the heart of Revelation is a paradox: a slaughtered, living Lamb constitutes the deep structures of reality.[50] That image cannot speak for the world of Roman imperialism. The image has been recontextualized in many ways over the centuries, often in the service of Christian imperialism. In the Revelation of John— a literary product of a specific time and place—a crucifixion signifies behavior that Roman imperial authority will not allow. It means the end is near.

Recapitulation

Imperial cults in Asia from the first century CE give us access to crucial trends in public culture, where the most important spatial categories were oriented toward the city of Rome and the most important temporal categories were determined by the lives of the Roman emperors. Because this schema aligned with religious, military, governmental, and administrative definitions of the world, it had persuasive power.

This chapter charts the distinctive definitions of time and space in the Revelation of John. John's text contradicted the logic of participation. He tried to disabuse his audience of the notion that Jerusalem, Rome, or any earthly city could function as the geographic center of reality. He instead looked upward, defining God's throne as the meaningful center that infuses all other space with meaning. Similarly, the most important type of time in John's text was not dictated by the actions of the emperors; it was instead the time experienced in true worship. During worship one learned the true meaning of all other times and experienced some of them to some degree.

In this structure of meaning, we see the outline of a practitioner's religious criticism. Rather than settling for the flawed eschatology of imperial cults in which one prays for the eternal reign of the Roman emperor, John chose a thorough eschatology

that held strictly to the integrity of absolute being and demanded the eventual demise of all symbols. This entailed a rejection of the powerful and relatively stable
cosmology of his social setting. He fashioned instead a more dangerous definition
of reality, with space and time organized around the absent throne of God while
the churches waited for an unfilled future on a not-yet-created earth. In this way
the present was portrayed as paradox, not as wholeness. The tension was resolved
not through a return to the primeval or through transport to the realm of the absolute. Instead, John envisioned the end of the times and spaces of this world and the
establishment of a new species of existence. His perspective was so extreme that even
the current center of present time and space—worship directed toward the throne
of God—was relativized in light of the future.

It is not evident that such an inherently unstable cosmology can support the
life of a community, but success and longevity do not appear to have been major
concerns for John. These weaknesses in John's religious system were mitigated to
some extent by his use of mythic traditions, which lent a semblance of continuity
to his project. But that is the topic of the next chapter.

10

WORKING WITH MYTH

Myths are often treated as abstractions, as stories that can be detached from the cultural and political systems within which they develop. Although such an approach enables structural and narrative analyses, it can overlook the contexts in which mythologies are useful. This chapter examines the use and the usefulness of myth in imperial cult settings and in John's Revelation. My comparison does not presuppose that John ever saw sites such as the Sebasteion at Aphrodisias or other imperial cult artifacts. The slight possibility of direct contact is irrelevant to my argument. I conclude that the imperial cult evidence gives us access to various levels of the dominant discourse in Roman Asia. John's text provides an opposing mythic interpretation of Roman imperialism. The archaeological and literary texts can be compared at the discursive level in a contrapuntal interpretation.

This approach shows that John's use of mythic traditions gave his project some continuity with the world he devalued. John established an eastern Mediterranean ethos for his congregations and articulated an understanding of history informed by the traditions of Israel. This resulted in a particular kind of continuity that could challenge the reigning verities of his day.

The Specificity of Myth

Mythic traditions derive from someplace; they are not neutral. A community's important stories tell us about that community's identity. In the Sebasteion at

Aphrodisias, we encounter a standard Greco-Roman pantheon. Zeus, Aphrodite, Dionysos, and Herakles play prominent roles, along with other gods and goddesses. There are also representations of corporate entities (especially cities and peoples), images of celestial phenomena like the sun, personifications of land and sea, imperial men as gods, and imperial women in dignified human form. This range of imagery was not arbitrary. The figures were executed and displayed to indigenize Roman rule through two crucial strategies. One was the mythic connection of the Aphrodisians to the Romans through their common relationship to Aphrodite. Through the invocation of Aphrodite's son Aeneas, Greek culture was defined as the source of Rome's greatness and the Aphrodisians were able to align themselves with the foreign rulers. The other strategy was a sculptural representation of civilization along a continuum from "Greek" to "barbarian." The definition of "civilized" that included Greeks and Romans could be contrasted to "barbarian" through a complicated set of gradations.[1]

A variant on this use of mythology to indigenize imperial cults (thereby integrating Roman imperialism into local traditions) can be seen in the altar sculptures from the bouleuterion at Miletos as well.[2] The Milesian sculptures also employed Olympians who had regional significance—in this case Apollo and Artemis rather than Aphrodite—but they took the imperial institutions even deeper into local myth by invoking Leto, Tyro, and others. Imperial cult mythology was flexible enough to be worked into almost any local mythology, as is the case with any successful imperial discourse.

Revelation, on the other hand, working with Jewish mythic traditions, did not allow the integration of imperial cults or of other local traditions. Several important studies on Revelation have examined John's use of Jewish scripture[3] and his use of general mythic traditions.[4] What tends to be overlooked in such discussions is the specific, Jewish character of the traditions of John's communities. John did not define space as centered on Jerusalem, but his use of mythology marked his communities with an identity from the periphery of the empire.

The contrasts are numerous. In John's Revelation there is no pantheon in the strict sense. Around the throne of God is a cast of thousands, but they are all creatures. Some of these figures would have been understandable outside of a church or synagogue setting. Death, Hades, dragons, multiheaded beasts, and stars would have been familiar images to anyone in the cities of western Asia Minor.

The most frequently encountered supernatural figures in Revelation—angels—would have been unusual for a Gentile audience. Philo tried to explain them by describing angels, demons, and souls as three different names for one underlying reality. There are good and bad demons, good and bad souls, and good and bad angels.[5] More frequently, Jews and Christians compared angels to nikes (cf. figs. 5.10, 10.1). The evidence is later than the first century, but there were clear attempts to portray angels as the personification of victory.[6] Angels in Revelation and nikes were both associated with warfare but had different functions. Revelation and other Jewish literature told of legions of angels fighting in cosmic warfare, whereas nikes appeared in art as solitary or paired figures representing military victory. More important, angels in Revelation are one of the primary means of communication between God and humanity, sometimes having an appearance and authority going far beyond that of the nikes in imperial art and mythology (e.g., Rev 10:1–11).

Other aspects of John's mythology would have been less accessible to average Asians of his time. The abyss in Revelation might have been likened to Tartarus, though their functions were different. A concept like the eschatological return of the primeval monsters Leviathan and Behemoth would have been much more foreign to a Gentile audience.[7] References to the tree of life, Jezebel, and Balaam entailed specific and thus more esoteric allusions to Jewish tradition.[8] Satan as the major cosmic antagonist of Revelation would have been foreign to Gentiles as well. This figure developed in the history and literature of Israel from an adversarial member of the heavenly entourage to an independent figure challenging the authority of God.[9] In Revelation he led a revolt in heaven. The angels led by Michael defeated Satan and his armies and cast the rebel forces to earth, where Satan pursued those who fear God (Rev 12).

Perhaps the most important contrast is in the image of the supreme god. The image of Zeus on his throne was already well defined before the first century CE (fig. 10.1). The premier expression of the scene had been created by the sculptor Pheidias in the fourth century BCE for the temple statue at Olympia.[10] The bearded Zeus was portrayed there by a chryselephantine statue. He was seated with a staff in his left hand and with a nike standing in the palm of his outstretched right hand. The image, widely acclaimed for its grandeur, was widely disseminated through coins, jewelry, sculptures, and paintings.

The image of God on his throne in Revelation was not articulated in this way. There is no description of the transcendent One. God is never portrayed in an iconographic fashion and barely speaks in the text. Even the description of God's throne in Ezekiel 1:22–28, from which John drew some details, was more prone to anthropomorphism. Whereas Ezekiel could describe the glory of God as similar to a human form (albeit like burning metal), John could only describe the scene with general comparisons: the throne is like precious stones, and around the throne is something like a halo or rainbow (two motifs from Ezekiel 1).[11] Other Jewish scriptures provided more details for John's imagery. The lightning and thunder come from the description of God's presence at Sinai in Exodus 19:16. The seven spirits are related to Zechariah 4:1–10. There is probably influence from the

FIGURE 10.1 Zeus enthroned in his temple at Olympia. A small carnelian ringstone from the Roman imperial period shows a standard image of Zeus Olympios. A nike is in his left hand and a scepter in his right. To the left of the temple are two stars; a star and a crescent moon are on the right. © Bibliothèque nationale de France, Paris.

thrones and the divine judgment scene of Daniel 7:10–11 as well. So even though the image of God is portrayed in Jewish terms, the ineffable appearance of God in John's vision report sets it apart from mainstream society[12] and from its literary predecessors.[13]

Three observations are important here. First, the Roman Empire included many distinguishable religious systems. The stories of the Libyan deities were not the same as the stories of the gods and goddesses of the Egyptians, Israelites, Syrians, Greeks, Italians, or Gauls, to name a few. There were many mythologies in the Mediterranean basin, each with a venerable heritage. Second, these national mythologies, though distinctive, were not self-contained, isolated units. Some had common prehistoric origins that resulted in family resemblances across systems. Moreover, centuries of Hellenistic imperialisms and then Roman hegemony in the eastern Mediterranean created pressure to homogenize mythologies in certain ways. When John was writing, there had been centuries of comparison and cross-fertilization among Mediterranean mythologies.

The similarities must not distract us from a third observation: myths are more than abstracted patterns. They are maleable, deployable facets of the interactions of communities existing in time and space. The Jewish mythology of Revelation constitutes a rejection of the elevation of Greek culture evident in monuments like the Sebasteion. John's use of mythology from the eastern Mediterranean did not encourage his hearers to move toward the center of Greco-Roman society. John's Asian audience was urged to adopt or to maintain an identity from the edge of the empire, an identity closer to the barbarian end of the spectrum.

Mythic Patterns

Given that the Sebasteion and Revelation worked from different mythic traditions, the two approaches to their own traditions shared some common methods for organizing stories. Enough of the south portico of the Sebasteion has survived to allow some conclusions about its mythic method. The clearest organization of the reliefs was the division into two registers, one each on the second and third stories. The second story contained scenes from Greek mythology; the third story contained reliefs devoted mostly to subjects involving the imperial household. Neither the second nor the third story reliefs followed a linear development, nor is there a unitary conception into which all the pieces can fit. Clusters of scenes may have provided focal points in the facade, but the evidence is not complete. There appears to have been an increase in the connections between scenes at the east end as viewers drew nearer the temple. At that end were more references to the relationships between Rome and Aphrodisias, with Aeneas and Augustus at the center of attention.[14]

This arrangement, in which the sculpted subjects were "neither haphazard nor systematically connected,"[15] is reminiscent in some ways of the organization of Revelation. The visions of John are connected through a variety of devices: single narrator, recurring characters and imagery, consistent vocabulary, specific numbers, and so on. The whole of the text, however, does not immediately reveal a systematic organization that governs the parts, so nearly every commentator produces a different schema that purports to reflect the development within the material.

These arrangements of material in both Revelation and in the Sebasteion reflect their provincial origins. A unitary sculptural relief narrative like the adornment on the column of Trajan at Rome suited the purposes of the imperial center but would have been less convincing to those ruled by the center. The discrepant experiences of subject peoples require more ambiguity. In the case of the Sebasteion, the ambiguity was harnessed in support of foreign rule. In Revelation the ambiguity of organization allowed the Seer to develop an alternative perspective to Roman dominion.

At a level deeper than the connections of one scene to the next, a mythic pattern has been established for Revelation.[16] It is often referred to as the "combat myth," but I prefer to call it a pattern and reserve "myth" for stories as they were actually told (or at least written). The mythic pattern is a generic framework that structures particular myths in several ancient Near Eastern cultures. The myths tend to be stories about kingship and victory over the forces of chaos and destruction. The elements of the pattern have been elaborated by modern scholars.[17] One scholar has listed the following elements in the pattern:

> Appearance of dragon or pair of dragons
> Chaos and disorder
> The attack
> Appearance of the champion
> The champion vanquished
> The dragon's reign
> The recovery of the champion
> Renewed battle and victory of the champion
> Fertility of the restored order
> Procession and victory shout
> Temple built for the warrior god
> Banquet (wedding)
> Manifestation of the champion's universal reign[18]

This pattern provides the broad structure for stories in a wide range of east Mediterranean cultures. Greeks employed the pattern for the story of the birth of the twins Apollo and Artemis, whose mother, Leto, was threatened by the serpent Pytho. Another variation on the pattern appears in Egyptian mythology in the stories about Isis, Osiris, Horus, and Typhon.[19] Some parts of the pattern appear in Babylonian stories of Marduk and Tiamat, in Canaanite stories of Baal and Yamm, and in Accadian, Hittite, and Ugaritic myths.[20]

Scholars generally agree that this mythic pattern informs Revelation as well but disagree about what to make of this conclusion. Yarbro Collins focused on Revelation 12, where the pattern is most evident. In chapter 12, the details have the most in common with the story of Leto and Pytho.[21] Yarbro Collins went on to argue that the entire text of Revelation is structured around repetition of the pattern: the different elements appear at various places as the text circles back to the pattern in order to reinforce it.[22]

More recently, David Barr has suggested a different use of the mythic combat pattern in Revelation. He argued that the pattern provides a framework for the last half of the book, that is, the visions of Revelation 12–22. Barr called this section the "war scroll" because it depicts spiritual forces in a cosmic battle that will determine the fate of the world. Thus, the mythic pattern provides the structure for a story that brings Revelation to its dramatic conclusion: the audience (Rev 2–3) is instructed that true worship of God (Rev 4–11) allows them to enjoy the benefits of the Messiah's victory over chaos and evil if they persevere to the end (Rev 12–22).[23]

Barr's explanation of the use of the mythic pattern in Revelation represents an advance in several ways, especially because it does not require a complicated series of recapitulations involving pieces of the combat pattern.[24] Instead, the mythic pattern supplies the plot for a large section of Revelation, which is more in keeping with analogous stories from the ancient Near East. The influence of the pattern can probably be extended to include Revelation 4–11 as well.[25] Yarbro Collins noticed the role played by stories about the assembly of the gods as a prelude to stories about divine battles with monsters and suggested that Revelation 4–5 is modeled on that kind of heavenly assembly scene.[26] If so, then the heavenly throne vision that begins in Revelation 4 would be the opening scene in the mythic combat pattern. It would function as the scene in which the champion appears before the divine assembly and accepts the challenge of subduing the monstrous antagonist. For the purposes of this chapter, however, we do not need to accept such wide-ranging influence of the mythic pattern on Revelation. Even a minimal interpretation that restricts the pattern to Revelation 12 shows that the mythic pattern plays a crucial role in the text.[27]

Why is the use of this mythic pattern important? Discussions of the pattern's role have sometimes wandered into discussions of whether John was adopting a pagan myth for his text. This issue is a red herring. The combat pattern was already present in John's scripture in the stories and songs that portray Israel's God as the divine warrior,[28] and it was a pattern common to several cultures.[29] The point is not whether John borrowed from "paganism." Rather, John was drawing on a pattern known to many peoples. John was expressing a widely held conviction about the nature of reality that allowed him to make a broader appeal to Jews and Gentiles. While the details of his mythic traditions were specifically Jewish, the pattern made his vision cycle less idiosyncratic and gave his text more continuity with this world than his cosmology and eschatology would suggest.

The pattern is also important because it reflected an eastern Mediterranean understanding of reality. The combat pattern was well known in the Roman imperial period, but it came from the east. John did not confront the imperial discourse by inverting its own stories: he did not pick up the idea of a world saved from self-destruction that is manifest in Asia's Augustan calendar,[30] nor did he adopt the agrarian utopia found in the literature of the imperial center.[31] John employed an eastern, provincial mythic pattern to challenge Roman imperial hegemony. He told different stories and used them to label Rome as the agent of chaos and destruction.

Myth as History

The modern idea that myth and history are mutually exclusive does not work well when applied to the Roman Empire. On the contrary, myth and history appear to have had much in common. The Sebasteion at Aphrodisias and Revelation both presented mythic histories that found their fulfillment in specific human beings. The Sebasteion represented the Julio-Claudian emperors and their wives as the culmination of the history of Greek culture and thus as the apex of world history. Revelation presented a different interpretation of meaningful history. In Revelation Jesus fulfilled Israel's history, as the one who would bring world history to its proper conclusion. The two mythic discourses disagreed over the central figures of history.

Both Revelation and the Sebasteion connected mythology and historical figures through established paradigms from the past. The Sebasteion used established mythic models to present specific historical events in the lives of the emperors. For example, the panel of Claudius subduing Britannia recalled the general theme of battles with Amazons (fig. 10.2). The defeated province is clad in a short tunic with her right breast uncovered and her right arm raised to ward off the death blow (or

FIGURE 10.2 Emperor Claudius subdues Britannia; from the Sebasteion at Aphrodisias, south portico, third story (*JRS* 1987 #6 pl. 14). Courtesy of the New York University Excavations at Aphrodisias.

perhaps to plead for mercy). Claudius, wearing only a cloak and an idealized Corinthian helmet, stands behind her with his right arm raised to strike her.[32]

The panel that shows Nero defeating Armenia is even more precise in its use of myth as history (fig. 5.8). Here the sculptor used a well-known subject—the death of Penthesilea at the hands of Achilles—with Nero portrayed as the heroic warrior and Armenia as the queen of the Amazons.[33] In both Aphrodisian sculptures, myth shaded into allegory as an interpretation of historical conquests. In both cases, however, the myth provided an allegory with only limited application. The original myths ended in the deaths of the antagonists, but in imperial discourses regions are normally "incorporated" rather than destroyed. Perhaps those details were irrelevant. The allegories could have simply provided mythic grandeur for the military exploits of the emperors, provoking an impression rather than detailed parallels. Or, perhaps, from a provincial perspective the mythic deaths expressed something of the province's ambiguous experience as a highly valued—yet subjugated—area.

Revelation drew on scriptural parallels in similar ways. The clearest examples appear in the messages to the seven churches. Balaam and Jezebel were not the actual names of leaders in the churches but names of notorious Gentiles in the narratives of the mythology of Israel. Their common characteristic was that they convinced Israel to worship other deities. John invoked these mythic models (2:14, Pergamon; 2:20, Thyatira) and applied them to specific church leaders who were advocating a more accommodating stance toward mainstream culture. He thereby sought to discredit his congregational competitors by equating them with the great deceivers of old.

An important distinction between the sculptures of the Sebasteion and the Revelation of John was that the sculptures spoke only of the past whereas the apocalyptic text extended its description into the future. In these predictive revelations, John still drew on established paradigms as interpretive devices. The exodus model, a favorite, served in both the descriptions of the disasters brought on by the first four angelic trumpets (Rev 8:7–12) and those brought on by six of the bowls of the last plagues (16:2–11). The exodus model allowed John to emphasize judgment as well as divine protection and liberation.

Furthermore, John did not confine himself simply to invoking models. John created powerful new images through a recombinant mythic method whereby pieces of various models were conjoined in novel ways.

For example, in Revelation 4:6–8 John described four living beings near the throne:

> Around the throne, and on each side of the throne, are four living creatures, full
> of eyes in front and behind: the first living creature like a lion, the second living
> creature like an ox, the third living creature with a face like a human face, and
> the fourth living creature like a flying eagle. And the four living creatures, each
> of them with six wings, are full of eyes all around and inside. Day and night
> without ceasing they sing, "Holy, holy, holy, the Lord God the Almighty, who
> was and is and is to come." (NRSV)

The vision of the four creatures around the throne clearly draws on two visions of the throne of God: Ezekiel 1:4–21 and Isaiah 6.[34] John was not content with either of these received traditions, however, and conflated aspects of each to create a new vision distinguishable from the previous two. The four creatures derive from Ezekiel 1 yet they are described differently. John's creatures no longer have four faces each (of a man, a lion, an ox, and an eagle). They have no wheels nor do they fly around as a unit.[35] In Revelation each creature is either a lion, an ox, a human, or an eagle. They have six wings like the seraphim of Isaiah 6 rather than four, and they lead in the three-fold doxology of the seraphim, which is also amended to include John's distinctive description of God as the one who transcends time. The four beings in Revelation become distinguishable figures, and somewhat less fantastic (though this is certainly a relative distinction).[36] In this way John simultaneously related his messages to those of two classical prophets and asserted his own authority to relay the messages of God to God's people.

The description of the Beast from the Sea in Revelation 13:1–2 provides a second example of John's innovative mythic method, developing new directions from the scriptural text using mythic patterns known from several eastern Mediterranean cultures. The base text for John's elaboration was Daniel 7, in which Daniel recorded a dream of four successive world empires leading up to God's eschatological intervention. The empires came as four beasts—one like a lion, one like a bear, one resembling a leopard, and one undefined. Rather than fitting the Roman Empire into this schema, John created an image of the Roman Empire as a different beast that arose from the sea. It had all seven heads and all ten horns of Daniel's beasts and resembled them in some way (a leopard with the feet of a bear and the mouth of a lion).

This new beast also resulted from a combination of the Daniel 7 beasts with another mythic pattern. Several ancient Near Eastern cosmologies had stories about a serpent monster—usually with seven heads—who inhabited the sea and the cosmic waters under the earth. In some of these cosmogonic stories, this mythic sea monster battled a deity.[37] The most common name for the serpent was Leviathan. In Jewish tradition Leviathan was paired with Behemoth, a land monster.[38] These two were said to have been created by God on the fifth day of creation but were being preserved until the messianic age, when they will serve as food for the great banquet.[39] In Israel's scriptures, the symbolism of this sea monster could be used to characterize oppressive empires such as Egypt (Isaiah 51:9–11; Ezek 29:3–5; 32:2–8) and Babylon (Jer 51:34–37).[40]

John superimposed this Leviathan imagery, rich in cosmogonic, eschatological, and political symbolism, on the Danielic image of oppressive world empires. The result was no longer an exegesis of Daniel but rather an exegesis of Roman authority. Mythic themes and characters flowed together to label Rome as the ghastly embodiment of all of history's oppressors, one of the great sources of chaos in the world, and a mythic opponent of Israel's God. The empire was the culmination of the history of evil in the world.

John's recombinant method was not a peculiar personal approach. John was following in the tradition of certain Jewish apocalyptic writers. The author of Daniel had the freedom to rewrite earlier prophets in light of new revelations, and so Jeremiah's 70 years became 70 weeks of years in Daniel 9:2–27.[41] Apocalyptic literature—and perhaps personal visionary experience—created an authority that allowed the author to take great liberties with received traditions. It is not a stable mode of interpretation nor does it lend itself to institutionalization of authority. It is neither bound to canonical conformity nor is it cut free from tradition. As a mythic method, it lends itself well to a resistant stance. The allegory of the Sebasteion sculptures, on the other hand, was not a risky proposition. The canon was coopted for empire. The sculptures did not express a critical exegesis of Roman authority; they were instead a vernacular apology for imperialism.

Perhaps the most important difference between imperial cult discourse and the book of Revelation is in their mythic appraisals of the role of violence in history. One of the earliest known images from the worship of the Roman emperors comes from the provincial cult in Pergamon established within two to three years of Octavian's victory over Mark Antony at Actium (31 BCE). The image of the temple statue was disseminated widely, and it was an image of Augustus the conqueror (fig. 2.3). Coins minted by the koinon in honor of this provincial temple emphasized this military theme with triumphal arches and a temple of Mars.[42] Municipal cults drew on military themes as well, as in the Laodikeian cult in which Domitian was described as a warrior.[43] Another example comes from the koinon decree regarding the calendar reforms under Augustus. Here the emperor was described as "a savior who put an end to war and brought order to all things."[44] Military dominance is not the only theme found in the imperial cult materials but is certainly one of the most important ones. Armed victory had created the empire, and military strength sustained the imperial system.

The author of Revelation was aware of the importance of military conquest in the dominant discourse but appraised it differently. The vision in Revelation 13 introduces the Roman Empire as the seven-headed, ten-horned beast.[45] After the description of this beast, we are given a popular response in verses 3b–4: "The whole earth was amazed by the Beast. They worshipped the Dragon for he had given authority to the Beast, and they worshipped the Beast saying, 'Who is like the Beast? Who is able to make war against him?'" In verses 7–8 the unparalleled dominion of the beast is described: "It was given to [the Beast] to make war against the saints and to defeat them. Authority was given to him over every tribe and people and tongue and nationality. All those who dwell on earth worshipped him, everyone whose name was not written in the scroll of life of the Lamb, the one slaughtered from the foundation of the world."

In this vision of the imperial Beast, the themes of worship and warfare are intertwined in different ways around the character of the Beast and the Lamb. The demonic pretender to world dominion is worshipped for his ability to defeat all opponents. The figure who is truly worthy of receiving worship and dominion, on the other hand, is described precisely as the one who was victimized and defeated. These verses go on to indicate that the significance of the slaughter of the Lamb goes beyond the bounds of history. The victim has been slaughtered from the foundation of the world; this act constitutes history itself. The meaning of history is revealed in the one who suffers violence, not in the one who inflicts violence.

The theme of military confrontation moves this section of Revelation to a climax in 19:11–21. Here the protagonist takes up arms, not as a Lamb but as a warrior on a white horse. A barrage of mythic texts is again aimed at John's audience, this time to declare Jesus as the Messiah promised by the traditions of Israel. But the struggle is brief: after the long anticipation of this moment, there is no battle scene. And the Warrior is oddly equipped—there is blood on his himation before the battle, and his only weapon is a sword coming out of his mouth. The two antagonists—Beast and False Prophet—are seized and cast into the lake of fire; the rest of the opponents are killed by the sword of the Warrior's mouth. (Then why did he need support troops from heaven?) Even at the denouement of the conflict, in the moment of vengeance, there is an ambiguity to the violence that allows John to circumscribe the role of violence in history. Only the Messiah fights the battle; the saints do not take part.[46] In the middle of the confrontation, John still reminds his audience of the churches' peculiar conception of the Messiah as the one whose blood was spilled. John allowed his audience to envision the end of imperialism, but he did not allow them to usurp the role of avenger. If anything, the battle is revelatory: it clarifies who is king of kings (19:16), who judges justly, who makes war (19:11).[47]

Neither did John allow his audience to imagine that the destruction of imperial Rome was the final battle with evil. The victory against Rome brings a respite but not the eschaton. The battle with Rome is separated from the final destruction of evil through the intervention of a thousand-year period during which Satan is imprisoned (20:1–6). This is one of many surprises at the end of John's narrative. Some of John's contemporary writers expected a messianic age at the end of history and before the resurrection,[48] but none of the texts known to us has a second battle after that age. This provides important insight into John's religious criticism. I argued earlier that John's commitment to the purity of transcendence did not allow him to center reality around any earthly time or place. In the same way, John refused to identify any earthly power with transcendent evil. The battle with empire had eschatological characteristics and implications, but it was not the eschatological battle. John's was a thorough critique, allowing earthly authorities to be neither divinized nor demonized.[49]

One of the most striking agreements in the mythic methods of Revelation and of imperial cults surfaces in the subject of violence related to gender imagery. The Sebasteion at Aphrodisias—as one example of a mythic interpretation of the emperors—promoted a patriarchal vision of life in the Mediterranean world. Revelation—another mythic appraisal of empire—did the same. Both the sculptures and the text presented corporate entities as women who were attacked and destroyed by masculine figures. In the extant panels from Aphrodisias, Armenia and Britannia were struck down by the emperors because of their opposition to empire. John's vision also portrayed violence against a corporate female image in his report of the destruction of Babylon, who claimed to be a queen but was depicted as the great prostitute (Rev 17–18, esp. 18:7–8). So in an imperial cult setting deified emperors slay women who resist. In Revelation are oracles of God's judgment on a blasphemous woman who rules and declares herself independent.[50]

Furthermore, the Sebasteion and Revelation both use the theme of the faithful wife. Agrippina the younger appears in two crucial places in the Sebasteion panels, first in full regalia as the wife of the divine Claudius as a commemoration of the ideal of marital harmony (fig. 10.3)[51] and in another panel crowning her son Nero as the successor to Claudius (fig. 8.1).[52] As wife and mother she provided the cru-

FIGURE 10.3 Claudius and Agrippina. The relief shows the imperial couple; from the Sebasteion at Aphrodisias, south portico, third story (*JRS* 1987 #3 pl. 8). Courtesy of the New York University Excavations at Aphrodisias.

cial link that legitimized the accession of the new emperor; in this way the bridal imagery supported hegemony. The topos of the bride appeared in Revelation also in the final chapters as a description of the new Jerusalem (19:7–22:5).[53] God had prepared this bride for her marriage to the Lamb, but legitimation is not the crucial function. Revelation superimposes ideals of marriage onto the consummation of history, using the bride and groom as a way of imagining the utopian union of humanity and deity. Thus, Revelation pursued subversive religious goals in its masculine and feminine imagery but within the limits of the same gender conventions that characterized an imperial cult discourse like that enshrined in the Sebasteion.[54]

Finally, both Revelation and the Sebasteion were executed in ritual settings. The Sebasteion was an elaborate attempt to structure a public ritual through the definition of space. The mythology was integrated into the propylon, porticoes, and temple that surrounded the courtyard. Even if much of the sculptural programme is no longer clear, the temple end emphasized sacrifice, Augustus, and Aphrodite. Empire and city converged as one neared the altar and the temple.

John's text was associated with a different architectural form: the house. The churches did not have the luxury of designing a space for their activities. They performed their rituals in spite of their architectural settings. Unusual demands were made on the structures by the rituals, and the rituals at times must have been modified as a concession to the necessities of space.[55] John persevered nonetheless, writing a lengthy text to be read in the context of this uneasy negotiation of ritual space.

The specific ritual for which he wrote was the Lord's Supper. Two arguments support this claim. First, the language of worship permeates the book in the frequent use of hymns and acclamations of God. Beyond the formal elements of worship, however, there are also phrases, interjections, blessings, and short doxologies. All of this builds the case for a general worship setting in Revelation.[56] A second argument points specifically to the Lord's Supper ritual. David Barr, in a comparison of the language of Revelation with the instructions in Didache 9 for celebrating the Eucharist, lists more than 20 parallels. A good number of the parallels come from the end of Revelation, especially from Revelation 22, suggesting that John expected that his Apocalypse would precede the taking of communion on the Lord's day. In effect, he was defining how communion should be understood through his narrative.[57] The ritual of the Lord's Supper would confirm the mythology John laid out. The east Mediterranean orientation, the reworking of Israel's mythology, the understanding of world history, the destructions of evil, and the marriage feast of the Lamb were all compressed into the ritual consumption of the Messiah's body and blood. Revelation, like the Sebasteion, led its audience to sacrifice.

Even though his cosmology was weak and his eschatology overwhelming, John attempted to locate his audiences in a particular place in this world. They were to draw on the traditions of Israel for their understanding of the current state of affairs. Israel's traditions could, however, be deployed in many ways. The way John used these traditions provided his audiences with a place in this world. If they accepted his critical reading of history and society, what kind of communities would they become?

11

COMMUNITIES WORSHIPPING HUMANS

The preceding chapter outlined the ways in which John used mythologies to define the meaning of history and to promote a particular identity for the congregations within that history. How did John imagine this system would be expressed in the life of a community that worshipped Jesus? How was it to be different from mainstream society? This chapter looks more specifically at the character of the congregations as John understood them by exploring leadership and organization, the character of apocalyptic personhood, and outsiders.

Organization of Churches

According to John's text, "church" was the fundamental unit of the movement to which he belonged, but Revelation makes clear that these churches were related to each other. The messages of Revelation 2–3 were directed toward particular congregations but were sent to all seven churches because all were actually being addressed in each message. Thus, near the end of each message comes the refrain, "Let the one who has ears hear what the spirit says to the *churches*" (emphasis added). This thought is emphasized again in the center of the seven messages. In the mid-section of the middle message (the fourth one, to the church in Thyatira), we are told that Jezebel and her followers will be punished and "*all the churches will know* that I am the one who searches heart and minds" (2:23, emphasis added). So Revelation is addressed to a network of churches that are praised or upbraided in the presence of all the other churches.

Did John have a concept for that larger network beyond the plural "churches"? He did not employ ἐκκλησία ("church") with a universal meaning in order to speak about this movement. Other texts for churches in this area—such as Colossians and Ephesians or the letters of Ignatius—could use the singular "church" in this larger sense, but that was not the case with Revelation.[1] In Revelation, church has the local meaning "congregation." This term is used almost exclusively in the first three chapters of Revelation. Church appears 20 times in Revelation, 18 related to the messages of Revelation 2–3.[2] The other two occurrences of the word frame the entire text: the epistolary opening of 1:4 and Christ's confirmation of the text's authority in 22:16. Church was an important concept for John, but it does not describe the movement in which he participated.

The term that gives us clarity about John's concept of the movement is βασιλεία, "kingdom, sovereignty, rule, empire." John considered the churches to be an alternative to the earthly rule of kings and emperors.[3] In the doxology of the epistolary opening, John described his movement as a kingdom: "To the one who loves us and freed us from our sins by his blood, and made us to be a kingdom, priests for his God and Father, to him be glory and dominion forever and ever. Amen."[4] Then in the scene around the heavenly throne at the crucial moment when the Lamb takes the scroll, the 4 living creatures and the 24 elders fall down and sing:

> Worthy are you to take the scroll and to open its seals.
> For you were slaughtered
> and you purchased for God by your blood from every tribe and tongue
> and people and nation,
> and made them for our God a kingdom and priests.
> And they shall reign upon the earth. (Rev 5:9–10)

In these two acclamations about the significance of Jesus' death, John relates that death to the establishment of a kingdom. This terminology placed the churches into direct opposition to the Roman Empire—which was called Rome's "kingdom over the kings of the earth" in Revelation 17:18[5]—and in opposition to the kingdoms of kings who supported the Roman beast (17:12, 17). John considered the churches to be an alternative sovereignty, a polity resisting the imperialism of his time. It was not a choice between religion or politics; it was a choice between legitimate and illicit authority.

Revelation 1:5b-6 and 5:9–10 refer to the churches also as priests for God. In these texts John reworked a statement about Israel in Exodus 19:6 and applied it to the churches. Exodus 19:6 comes at an important point in the narrative of the formation of Israel. The Hebrews had arrived at Mt. Sinai. Moses went up the mountain and YHWH instructed him:

> Thus you shall say to the house of Jacob, and tell the Israelites: You have seen
> what I did to the Egyptians, and how I bore you on eagles' wings and brought
> you to myself. Now therefore, if you obey my voice and keep my covenant, you
> shall be my treasured possession out of all the peoples. Indeed, the whole earth is

mine, but you shall be for me a priestly kingdom and a holy nation. These are
the words that you shall speak to the Israelites. (Exod 19:3b–6)

John used a modified form of Exodus 19:6 to describe the churches as a kingdom
and priests. His articulation followed neither the Hebrew מַמְלֶכֶת כֹּהֲנִים ("kingdom
of priests" or "priestly kingdom") nor the Septuagint's βασίλειον ἱεράτευμα ("royal
priesthood"). He divided up the two features of the phrase to define the churches as
βασιλείαν καὶ ἱερεῖς ("a kingdom and priests"), shifting primary emphasis toward the term βασιλεία.

In what sense did John consider the saints to be priests? Commentators mention three possibilities, but we need not choose between them: John's imagery is
multivalent, and the functions of priests were not monodimensional. The saints were
priests in the sense that they enjoyed the unmediated presence of the deity,[6] they
extended the redemptive work of the Messiah to the rest of the world,[7] and they
offered true worship to God.[8]

To this list we should also add a neglected facet of the imagery: a reinterpretation of the notion of ritual purity. For example, 1 Peter 2:9 uses the same Exodus
text as it is reflected in the Septuagint and proclaimed the churches to be a "royal
priesthood." The author of this text drew on the idea of a priest's ritual purity and
used it to describe the churches as a people set apart from the world to God (esp.
1 Pt 2:7–11). Priestly purity as a metaphor for social and ethical distinction would
fit well with John's understanding of the church and of sainthood.

So priesthood added the elements of divine presence, a redemptive role among
the nations, proper worship, and purity of purpose. Kingdom, however, was a more
important description for John's movement because it tied in more directly with
John's view of the meaning of human history. History for John was the story of the
ultimate success of God's kingdom despite opposition from the kingdom of this
world. At the sounding of the seventh trumpet voices in heaven shouted:

> The kingdom of the world has become
> (the kingdom) of our Lord and of his Christ.
> He shall reign forever and ever. (11:15b)

The heavenly response to this acclamation shows that Revelation does not envision a gradual transformation of this world into the kingdom of God. The 24 elders
fall down before the throne of God, worship him, and say:

> We thank you, Lord God, ruler of all, who is and who was,
> that you took your great power and ruled.
> The nations [τὰ ἔθνη] raged,
> but your rage came,
> the time of judging the dead;
> giving the reward to your servants the prophets and the saints and those who
> fear your name, both small and great;
> and destroying those who destroy the earth. (11:17–18)

Revelation shows how the kingdom of this world becomes the kingdom of God
and of his Christ (11:15). The kings of the earth play an important role in this pro-

cess. The proper role of kings is to acknowledge the Christ who rules over all kings (1:5; 19:16). In reality, however, they are deceived by the seven-headed Beast because it is empowered by the Dragon. They gather together to oppose the Christ and his heavenly armies, but when that climactic battle begins, they are quickly destroyed. After the thousand years and the demise of the Dragon, there is a hint that the kings of the earth will finally realize their proper vocation and bring their glory to God in the new Jerusalem (21:24). In the end, God, his Christ, and his followers reign forever (22:5). The churches represent a movement that is a new kingdom under the authority of the worthy ruler. Divine rule will be fully established when the Messiah brings vengeance and justice to the rebellious kingdom of this world.

The relationship between the churches and the historical Israel is raised because John applied Exodus 19:6 and other biblical passages about Israel to his movement. John did not use the term "Israel" for the churches, even though he considered scriptural references to Israel to refer to the churches. Israel is used in Revelation only to describe institutions from the mythic past: the 12 tribes of Israel (7:4; 21:12) and Balaam's deception of Israel through Balak (2:14).

What then was his perception of the relationship between the churches and the historical Israel? The best description comes to us in the image of the eschatological new Jerusalem. The new Jerusalem that comes down out of heaven from God has a high wall with two distinct features: 12 gates, each bearing the name of a tribe of Israel, and 12 foundations, each bearing the name of an apostle. The image as a whole refers to the people of God.[9] Although the image is not an allegory, the two features of the wall have their own significance. Entrance to the city is through Israel, but the city is not built upon Israel. The heavenly Jerusalem is a standard feature in Jewish apocalyptic, appearing as a transcendent phenomenon that predates the historical Israel.[10] So it is not quite accurate to say that John understood the churches to be the true Israel.[11] The churches were the people of God,[12] founded on the apostles of the Lamb. Historical Israel played a crucial part but did not define the transcendent reality.

Members of the movement in which John participated were known as ἅγιοι, "holy ones, saints" (usually plural) or δοῦλος, "servant, slave" (usually singular). This observation is important, in view of the common modern practice of calling these people "Christians," a word that does not appear in Revelation. John's most frequent general term was holy ones, found in narrative,[13] in hymnic material,[14] in admonitions,[15] in a lament,[16] in a judgment oracle,[17] and in an editorial aside.[18] Thus, the churches were composed of people who were holy, just as God (4:8; 6:10) and Christ (3:7) were holy. A complementary term that can be used for members of the movement is servants. Although both terms connote complete dedication, "servant" is often associated especially with the prophets, so it can imply special duties of certain church members in Revelation.[19]

An examination of John's references to officials helps us better understand his view of the movement. Several kinds of church leaders are mentioned in Revelation, the most important being the prophets, who revealed the message of God to his people about the ultimate meaning of their lives and of history (10:7). These prophecies were to be heard and kept by the churches (1:3; 22:7). Others might claim to be prophets (2:20 regarding Jezebel), but John makes clear that he is a prophet without explicitly using the title. His scroll is a scroll of prophecy (1:3; 22:7, 10, 18), and an angel says to John, "I am a fellow servant of yours and of your brothers the prophets and of those who keep the words of this scroll" (22:9).

The role of the prophet is closely bound with that of the witness (μάρτυς) and the issue of testimony (μαρτυρία). All five occurrences of "witness" in Revelation designate someone who dies for the faith: Jesus (1:5; 3:14), Antipas (2:13), the two witnesses of Revelation 11:3, and a group (17:6). The term does not yet connote the technical sense of a martyr, however, because testimony in Revelation does not refer specifically to dying. Testimony is the faithful adherence to—and proclamation of—the truth of God; death is often the result, according to John.[20] Thus, it is especially the prophets who proclaim the word of God and the testimony of Jesus.[21]

Other leaders are also mentioned in Revelation. The first one we meet is the reader mentioned in 1:3, who would have supplied the voice for this text when it was first heard in the churches of Asia.[22] Apostles are also mentioned, but with a certain ambivalence. The names of Jesus' 12 apostles are written on the foundations of the wall around the new Jerusalem (21:14), but people in the churches who called themselves apostles were to be treated with suspicion (2:2). Teachers appear only in negative settings: Balaam taught Balak to place an obstacle before the sons of Israel (2:14); Jezebel taught and deceived the servants of God to commit adultery and eat meat sacrificed to idols (2:20, 24);[23] and the teaching of the Nicolaitans is something for which the Pergamenes should repent (2:15).

A comparison of Revelation with earlier Pauline discussions of leadership provides further perspective on John's view of the nature of the churches. In 1 Corinthians 12:28 Paul wrote that the most important leaders provided by God to the churches were apostles, prophets, and teachers—in that order—followed by an unranked group of those with gifts for deeds of power, healings, assistance, direction, or tongues. John, on the other hand, ranked prophets highest, treated apostles with suspicion,[24] and portrayed teachers only negatively. Revelation ignores the rest of the functions Paul mentioned. Likewise, the description of specialized activities (not strictly officials) in Romans 12:6–8 mentions prophecy, service (διακονία), teaching, encouragement, giving, and administration. Revelation speaks favorably of the first two but emphasizes endurance rather than encouragement; John did not address giving and administration. Similar results come from a comparison of Revelation with Ephesians 4:11, which counted apostles, prophets, evangelists, pastors, and teachers among the gifts given by Christ to his church. Revelation affirmed that the original apostles were a benefaction and emphasized the contemporary work of prophets but questioned teachers and ignored evangelists and pastors.

Several other terms for the churches and their leaders popular in the first or early second centuries are not recorded in Revelation. John did not use such terms as Christian,[25] bishop, deacon,[26] elder,[27] widow,[28] body of Christ, or sons of God. These omissions do not tell us whether the seven churches of Asia had such positions and concepts. Some congregations probably included some of these offices and used some of these terms, though the case must be argued for each term individually. The comparisons make clear, however, that John was promoting a particular perspective on the churches. John either disliked the term Christian or did not know it. He repeated the common practice of known writers from first-century congregations of referring to their groups as churches and the members as the holy ones.[29]

John was learned in the Jewish scriptures, but in Revelation he undermined other teachers. His emphasis was not on mastery of a canon but on direct revelations from the risen Jesus (sometimes through the mediation of an angel) that informed and shaped his scriptural knowledge. He showed no concern in his text for church offices or for differentiated leadership. He advocated instead a kind of theocracy in absentia, a divine empire, in which messages from the distant throne of God were delivered through the prophets to all the holy ones. Thus, John could summarily refer to the membership of the churches as "his [God's] servants the prophets, the saints, and those who fear his name" (11:18).[30]

This vision is not exactly an egalitarian utopia.[31] John's view of the churches was utopian because of its weak cosmology, but the relative lack of differentiation was not a democratization of the churches, especially in contrast to the Pauline body of Christ imagery. John's view was rather a relativizing of earthly distinctions in the presence of the Creator's divine holiness. Around the throne of God are only creatures. Among the creatures, however, important distinctions are still maintained. The line between the saints and the rest of the world is crucial. The boundary between the churches and the angels is less clearly drawn. Angels and saints are all part of the group of creatures who worship God, but the churches appear to be limited to the saints.[32] Among the saints, the venerable 12 apostles of the past and the past and present prophets are the most important.

Apocalyptic Personhood

One of the pillars of the religious life is human maturation, that is, the constitution and development of persons. As we examine the congregations addressed by Revelation, we must also ask what kind of individuals John was trying to mold through his text. When John wrote about the saints, what kind of persons did he envision?

Because this study is comparative, we note first that our evidence regarding the constitution of human beings in Revelation is different in kind from the evidence for imperial cults. The imperial cult materials name hundreds of officials: mostly high priests and high priestesses but also priests, priestesses, neokoroi, agonothetes, hymnodes, and others. We have references to imperial cult rituals as well that involved a larger segment of society: sacrifices, processions, concerts, mysteries, competitions, festivals, and so on. Revelation has few such references to individuals or rituals.

Imperial cult activities reinforced a view of public culture that was male-dominant and subservient to Rome. John roundly denounced this public culture of obeisance to Rome in Revelation 13:11–18 especially and throughout chapters 13–19. John's criticism of public culture was framed in terms of authority and obedience, however; his critique did not overtly treat issues of gender.

This patriarchal character of John's Revelation has engendered criticism on several counts. Tina Pippin argued that the Apocalypse is a misogynist text that is dangerous to women. In the text women are excluded from the utopian city, for the faithful are described as virgin males who have not defiled themselves with women

(Rev 14:4), and the eschatological city is itself a bride whom the male followers "enter" (double entendre intended). But that is not the most serious problem, according to Pippin. As the text unfolds, only four female images play an important role and all of them are subject to male control: "Jezebel," who is castigated and condemned; the Woman Clothed in the Sun (Rev 12), who is stranded in exile once she has given birth to a male; the Great Whore (Rev 17), who is to be burned and eaten; and the Bride of the Lamb, who is submissive and silent.[33] Thus, Revelation is portrayed as a fantasy of male power, where women's voices and values are suppressed and where female images are subjected to horrendous treatment. Political domination is subverted, but male domination remains intact.[34] In a more wide-ranging investigation of the effects of Revelation on readers, Catherine Keller concurred:

> The poetics of power, of conquest, of swords and iron rods pitted against female flesh, penetrates the significatory field of the Apocalypse. A feminist ethic cannot "veil" the misogyny of its metaphors, even if, as Elisabeth Schüssler Fiorenza stresses, this *is* the one book of the New Testament dedicated to justice.[35]

Such readings of Revelation as a misogynist text are based on an inadequate treatment of the text's symbolism. This problem has four aspects. First, scholars have selectively used feminine imagery in the text. The statement that there are four important female images in Revelation—all dominated by males—omits at least one. Ge ("Earth, Land") is a well-known figure from Greek mythology (cf. fig. 5.11); she is also mentioned in Scripture.[36] She appears in Revelation 12 as a positive character, who acts on her own to protect the Woman Clothed by the Sun. Only two other characters in Revelation are able to oppose Satan actively and successfully: the Messiah and the archangel Michael. The lack of scholarly discussion on this fifth female character seems not to be a sign of conscious selectivity but rather a case of modern lack of interest in the first-century mythic world in which Revelation participated.

Scholars have not thoroughly compared the male and female imagery of Revelation. The threats against Jezebel and her children (2:22–23) have not been compared to the threats made against the followers of Balaam (2:14–16); or the destruction of the Whore (17:16) to the destruction of the Beast, the kings, and the soldiers (19:17–21); or the passivity of the Bride (21:2) to the passivity of Antipas (2:13). The assertions that Revelation refers only to one actual woman has not been compared to the number of actual men mentioned.[37] *If* we are going to analyze the imagery in this manner, then we should at least be comprehensive and conclude that Revelation is not simply misogynist; it is also misandrist and probably misanthropic.[38]

A second aspect of the problem with method and symbol is that there is little or no recognition of the difference between the sign and that which is signified. The female images represent a variety of relationships between symbol and referent that should affect interpretation. Jezebel is a derogatory epithet for a historical human; the Woman Clothed in the Sun and the Bride represent transcendent entities; Ge as the personification of the earth and Babylon as a personified city draw on standard Greco-Roman mythic traditions; and the Whore is one part of the symbolization of an imperialist power. If one wants to understand how these images affected the lives of real women and men, then one cannot simply treat the images as an undifferentiated group.

A third aspect of the problem is that particular symbols are isolated from the narrative and then interpreted in an atomistic fashion. The main characters in John's narrative are regularly subjected to shifting symbolization; that is, a particular referent is symbolized in different ways at different points. For example, the Great Whore is cited as an example of the extreme misogynism of the narrative because of violence against a female image. The Whore, however, is but one part of two of the symbolizations of Roman hegemony. An earlier symbolization depicts Roman hegemony as the Beast from the Sea, which is paired with a subordinate Beast from the Land (Rev 13). These two beasts derive from Leviathan/Behemoth mythology, which have unstable gender associations. The beasts are usually male, but Leviathan is female in 1 Enoch 60:7–9.[39] After this, the symbolization of Roman rule shifts to a complex, double image: the Great Whore riding on a beast reminiscent of the Beast from the Sea (Rev 17). Then Roman hegemony is manifest as Babylon (Rev 18), and finally it becomes a Beast served by a False Prophet (Rev 19). Within the context of John's narrative, an image such as the Great Whore should not be reduced to a cipher for gender because it is one part of a series of symbolizations that cannot be simplified into a single gender code.

This shifting symbolization also occurs for the referents Jesus (epiphanic figure, slaughtered lamb, heavenly warrior, then back to slaughtered lamb) and the people of God (churches, saints, perhaps 144,000 from the tribes of Israel, perhaps 2 witnesses, Woman Clothed in Sun, perhaps 144,000 male virgins, God's people, military camp of the saints, heavenly Jerusalem, inhabitants of heavenly Jerusalem). When John's shifting individual images are isolated, the result is a facile connection between gender and symbol that is not true to the complexity of the text.

A fourth aspect of the symbol and method problem is that some images are simply misread. The Woman Clothed in the Sun is not left in exile. John noted that her time in the desert would be temporary protection until the final intervention of God (12:6). The resolution of her desert sojourn is found in a different symbolization, for there is some continuity between the Woman and the Bride. Another example is the assertion that John forces women to choose between two stereotypical roles, the whore or the bride. The image of Jezebel, however, allows another role. In his denunciation of the historical woman who is the referent of this symbol, John does not deny the woman's status as a prophet among the saints. He wrote that she *called* herself a prophet (2:20). When that language is used in these messages, the hearer expects the phrase, "but she is not." This is the same pattern he used to denounce would-be apostles (2:2) and those who called themselves Jews but were not (2:9; 3:9). However, John does not deny "Jezebel" her prophetic status. In the manner of his denunciation, he confirmed the role of women as prophets in the congregations of Asia.

To understand gender in John's constructions of apocalyptic personhood, then, we cannot rely on four selected and isolated symbolizations. We must put these in the broader context of his view of the world and his suspicion about claims to authority.

John's text represents the world as a place of deceptions and hidden truths. There is danger of deception from insiders such as pseudo-apostles (2:2), prophets (2:20), and teachers (2:6, 14–15). The problem, however, is not limited to the churches. Satan is characterized as the one who deceives the whole world (12:9) through Roman rule (18:23, using the image Babylon). The main agents who actually accomplish the task of misleading the masses are the provincial and local elites of the empire, indicated through the shifting symbolizations of the Beast from the Earth (13:14) and the False Prophet (19:20).[40] Once Roman hegemony is destroyed, Satan himself is confined for a thousand years so that he will not deceive the nations (20:3, τὰ ἔθνη). After this millennium, he is released and deceives the world once more, precipitating the final destruction of evil (20:8–10).

In this world of beguiling appearances, hidden truth can be known through revelation. The messages to the churches contain several examples. The Smyrniote congregation knows distress and poverty, but they are actually wealthy (2:9). The Sardis congregation appears to be alive, but the Risen Christ declares they are dead (3:2). The Laodikeian congregation considers itself to be wealthy and self-sufficient, but the truth is that they are wretched and miserable (3:17). True knowledge comes from above, where mysterious songs are sung that can be learned only by the faithful (14:3). Ultimately this revelation is about the mysterious Messiah (1:1), whose name is written but cannot be known by anyone else (19:12). Those who embrace this knowledge receive a new name that only they can know and they feast on hidden manna (2:17).

Given that the world is a place of deception and hidden truth, John did not proclaim a blind obedience to esoteric knowledge but called instead for a hermeneutics of suspicion about claims to authority. He commended his audience for questioning the authority of people who claimed the title apostle (2:2), and the faithful are continually represented as the minority among those who have not been fooled by the authoritative claims of Rome. The messages to the seven churches end not with a command to submit but with a call to discern: "Let the one with an ear hear what the spirit says to the churches!"

John even raised questions about his own authority by recounting twice his temptation to worship improperly the angelic medium of his revelations (19:10; 22:9). These two sections certainly enhance the persuasiveness of his message by emphasizing the glorious character of his visions. At a deeper level, however, the twin accounts show the vulnerability of the author as the prophet is tempted to abandon the core of his message, deceived not by evil desire but by the sheer grandeur of the experience. Both episodes occur after the truth of the revelations is affirmed, and both angelic responses emphasize the necessity of discernment that results in proper worship: "You must not do that! I am a fellow servant with you and your comrades who hold the testimony of Jesus. Worship God! For the testimony of Jesus is the spirit of prophecy" (19:10 NRSV). The angelic responses denigrate authority based on status: angels, prophets, and saints are all fellow servants. The validity of the message is the crucial factor. Discerning the true message results in true worship.

The primary exhortation in the book is to endure,[41] which is a function of living in a world of deception and discovering the hidden truth about reality. Thus,

the crucial characteristic of apocalyptic personhood in John is struggle: persever-
ance in the truth in the midst of a deceived world, refusal to submit to false claims
of authority, or, in John's words, holding to the testimony of Jesus.

Did John describe this style of personhood differently for men and for women?
Clearly not. Throughout his text John refers to the saints in terms that do not dif-
ferentiate for gender. To counterbalance the selective use of feminine imagery by
some interpreters of Revelation, we need only to look at the other places where the
faithful are described to see that John is remarkably egalitarian in regard to gender
among the saints. There is no hint of gender discrimination among the slaughtered
souls under the heavenly altar (6:9–11), for the Romans and local authorities did
not desist from torturing or executing female members of the churches.[42] The
unnumbered multitudes of martyrs around the heavenly throne is not an exclusively
male image (7:9–17), and the voice from the throne instructs all God's servants—
not just men—to sing to God (19:5).

The suggestion that women have no place in John's utopia because the new
Jerusalem is portrayed as a bride is equally unconvincing. The names of those written in the scroll of life since the foundation of the world certainly included men
and women, just as the rest of those who dwell on earth included astonished men
and women (17:8). Or should we suppose that only men came through the final
judgment (20:11–15)? When one examines the whole text of Revelation—rather
than four isolated images—it is clear that John's vision of the saints has a greater
degree of equality between the sexes than other canonical writings such as the
Deuteropauline Epistles, the Pastoral Epistles, or 1 Peter. Compared to the imperial cult officials or the imperial hymnodes named in part I of this study, Revelation holds up well on the issue of gender.

I do not mean that John's use of gender imagery, judged 19 centuries later by
academicians, is not problematic. Ideas of female impurity, images of violence against
women and against men, and patterns of male domination have been destructive
for women and men, in John's day and in ours. They are not, however, the focal
points of John's views on personhood, nor do they constitute the total of his religious criticism. As secondary aspects of Revelation's symbolization, they are meant
to nurture communities of individuals who question the authorities of this world.
John did not anticipate modern questions about the use of female imagery, but his
critique of Roman imperialism contained underutilized resources for examining
gender and language.

Violence in Revelation is related to the question of gender. I have tried to disentangle the two, to show that they are not identical. Revelation's eschatology should
not be reduced to a battle of the sexes won by male violence. What message about
violence did John convey?

According to Revelation, apocalyptic personhood includes the renunciation
of force.[43] The saints were challenged to be victorious, but human victory was
redefined as nonaggression. They do not participate in either the final battle against
Roman imperialism (19:14–21)[44] or in the final destruction of the Dragon (20:9).
The saints are the victims of aggression; the only humans who make war in Revelation are those who are deceived by the Dragon.[45] The responsibility of the saints
is to keep the testimony of Jesus[46] by holding onto what they had (2:25; 3:11;

14:12) or remembering what they had abandoned and repenting to regain it (2:5; 3:3).

Three reasons support this rationale for a nonviolent stance. First, John believed that violence is a divine prerogative. The mythic combat pattern was appropriate for John's narrative: the God of Revelation is a warrior.[47] God's right to judge derives from his status as the creator of all things (4:11) and from his unique ability to deliver righteous judgment (19:1–2). Violence, vengeance, and justice belong to God alone; they are beyond human competence.

Second, John makes clear that the victories won by the saints are epiphenomenal to the victory won by the Lamb (12:11). According to the paradoxical nature of victory in Revelation, the Lamb's victory came not through violence but through suffering.[48] Hence, John introduces the Lamb by juxtaposing messianic and sacrificial allusions in 5:5–6; the conqueror is the one who was slain. This unlikely image of a slaughtered living lamb then serves as the primary symbol for Jesus, overshadowing both the epiphany of the Risen Christ (1:12–16) and the appearance of the Warrior (19:11–12). Even in the eschaton after the violent destructions of Rome and the Dragon, Jesus is portrayed as the Lamb. The spilling of his blood established the kingdom composed of the churches (1:5–6). The Lamb's blood is said to generate human reality, for he is slain from the establishment of the cosmos (13:7) and the names of his followers are written in the scroll of life from the establishment of the cosmos (17:8).

The Lamb's blood even stains the image of Jesus as Divine Warrior, whose garments are bloodied before the battle (19:13).[49] The subservience of the warrior imagery to the sacrificial imagery is heightened in a vision of the saints in heaven who had been victorious over the Beast (Rev 15:2–4). These saints sing the song of Moses—an allusion to the poem about the Divine Warrior in Exodus 15—and the song of the Lamb, whose justice and truth are revealed particularly in his death. This heavenly medley juxtaposes two songs that force John's audience to remember that their victory has been established by Jesus' death, and not by divine acts of aggression. Apocalyptic personhood requires imitation of the Lamb but not the Warrior.

Third, personal eschatology of individuals must be taken into account. John's deployment of the Jewish ideas of resurrection and judgment are crucial to his promotion of human nonviolence as a part of apocalyptic personhood. Resurrection and judgment allowed John to redefine the cycle of life through which a person moves. He asserted that two deaths are possible—a bodily death and consignment to the lake of fire after resurrection. Everyone is subject to the first death, but those who have been faithful in the testimony of Jesus (20:4–6) and who have not lived immoral lives (21:8) escape the second death.[50] John could thus make the paradoxical assertion that the conquerors will be conquered in life (2:10; 13:7). The conquered conquerors, however, are promised the ultimate prize: fruit from the tree of life (2:7), immunity from the second death (2:11), affirmation from Jesus before his Father and the angels (3:5), eternal life in the presence of God forever (3:12), and a place with the Risen Christ on his throne (3:21; cf. 5:10 and 20:6).

These three foundations of John's apocalyptic nonviolence—vengeance as a divine prerogative, the redefinition of victory as endurance of suffering, and hope beyond death—condense into one heavenly acclamation in Revelation 12:10–11:

Then I heard a loud voice in heaven, proclaiming, "Now have come the salvation and the power and the kingdom of our God and the authority of his Messiah, for the accuser of our comrades has been thrown down, who accuses them day and night before our God. But they have conquered him by the blood of the Lamb and by the word of their testimony, for they did not cling to life even in the face of death." (NRSV)

So John envisioned churches composed of individuals who lived in a world full of deception. They were encouraged to test authorities to find the hidden truths about this life. Prophets, teachers, emperors, and apostles were liable to mislead. Women and men who saw through the lies knew that, appearances to the contrary, God had already won the battle with the Dragon through the blood of the Lamb. They needed only to hold onto the truth to escape the second death and to participate in the reign of the Lamb.

This definition of apocalyptic personhood extended the traditions of Israel. Death, violence, and male domination were essentially foreign to God's intentions for humanity (Gen 3–4). They were a temporary disruption in human experience, a part of "the first things" that God would wipe away along with every tear (Rev 21:4). The apocalyptic extension of Israel's traditions looked forward to the new Jerusalem in which the tree of life was again available to humans, not just for the prolongation of life but also for healing (22:1–5).

Outsiders

The heading for this section—"outsiders"—perhaps casts the issue of boundaries and belonging in stark terms. John's conception of his group in society included views on humanity, on the composition of society, on the place of the churches, and on categories of outsiders, all overlaid with questions of Jewish identity and with disagreements among insiders.

When John wanted to refer to humanity in general, he occasionally used terms such as "the whole world" (οἰκουμένη)[51] or "the whole earth."[52] More often he used the generic term "people"[53] or "those who dwell on earth."[54]

In texts where humanity is described by subcategories, we see a rudimentary social theory at work. John often described humanity or a significant portion of it using a phrase such as "every nation, tribe, tongue, and people" (14:6).[55] These are overlapping distinctions among earth's inhabitants. People (λαός), like "crowds" in 17:15, indicates a group that belongs together but does not indicate what binds them together. Tongue (γλῶσσα) is a category of language and culture. Nation (ἔθνος) denotes cultural distinctions related to birth and nationality in a way that is not strictly true of language. Tribe (φυλή), on the other hand, normally refers to a subunit within a society (as in the case of Israel) or within a city.

John recognized other distinctions in status, power, and financial resources that he tended to articulate in binary oppositions: great and small,[56] wealthy and poor,[57] free and slave.[58] The material in Revelation 18–19 shows that the Seer was aware of other social positions (discussed in the next chapter). At this point it is sufficient to note the polarizing effect of the rhetoric. John portrays the extreme limits and ignores the middle ground, suggesting a theory of society as a place where resources are distributed unequally. He treats even imperial offices with little precision. All rulers are "kings," all courtiers are "great ones," and all military officers are "chiliarchs."[59] The Seer apparently felt no compulsion to recognize the nuances of status and power. He could paint society with a broad brush because he considered the options to be limited and clear. People are defined within standard categories involving biological, social, financial, and governmental distinctions. The fine points are irrelevant when the disparities are acknowledged.

In the midst of this human population, the churches cross the standard categories. They have been selected from these groups to be a kingdom and priests.[60] They are God's people, destined to rule with God and the Lamb.[61]

In view of this perspective on the world and the churches, it is surprising how little is said overtly about Israel or things Jewish. One glaring exception is the synagogue of Satan found in two of the messages (2:9, Smyrna; 3:9, Philadelphia). In the message to Smyrna, certain Jews of that city are demonized for their blasphemy; John strips them of their self-designation as Ἰουδαῖος.[62] Likewise, some Jews in Philadelphia are said to be lying when they call themselves Jews, and the risen Christ promises that they will finally recognize that the churches were correct. John did not claim the name "Jewish" for the churches in his text, however, and did not describe humanity as a polarity of Jewish/Gentile.[63]

John has a general term for those who do not fear God: the ones whose names are not written in the scroll of life.[64] John mentions two types of outsiders. One is the participant in imperial cults, that is, one who worships the Beast from the Sea.[65] This conflict between the churches and those who worship the Beast dominates the latter half of the book. This is not two equal communities facing off; John portrays it as a small network of faithful witnesses against everyone else. The destiny of the Beast worshippers is the lake of fire (19:21; 20:15).

The second type of outsider John identified is the immoral person. Two lists suggest his ethical concerns. Those who have no part in the New Jerusalem include cowards, the unfaithful, the detestable, murderers, fornicators, sorcerers, idolators, all liars.[66] An earlier vision adds thieves to the list.[67] The ethical concerns are emphasized only in Revelation 9 and late in the book, before and after the confrontation with Rome. While Rome holds dominion over the Mediterranean, John's attention is fixed on participation in imperial cults as the primary threat. Before that section and afterward, a wider view of outsiders that includes the ethical concerns prevails.

Four examples in Revelation present ambiguous insiders who challenge John's definitions of the outsider. All are mentioned in the messages to the seven churches, and there is just enough information to generate much secondary literature on the difficult subject of their identities. One set of ambiguous insiders included those who called themselves apostles. The Ephesian church was commended for testing these claims and rejecting them.[68] Without further information, we can only speculate that these were traveling apostles like those mentioned in Didache 11:3–6.

The second and third examples of ambiguous insiders were labeled in Revelation with symbolic names. "Jezebel" referred to a prophetess in the church at Thyatira

(2:20). "Balaam" may have signified a prophet in the message to the church at Pergamon (2:14), although it is hard to tell whether the name represented an individual or a general attitude. Both labels invoke the names of notorious Gentiles who caused Israel to engage in sacrifice to other deities. Both references in Revelation mention the problem of consumption of meat sacrificed to deities, so we have a general indication of the challenges represented by these insiders. Jezebel and Balaam advocated a religious stance that placed fewer restrictions upon the churches regarding participation in mainstream culture. A more accommodating attitude toward sacrificial meat would allow greater freedom in socializing, in employment, and in public activities. Whether the teachings associated with Balaam and Jezebel permitted full participation in imperial cult rituals is unanswerable, given the state of our information. They certainly advocated practices that violated John's sense of the boundaries between the churches and those outside.

A fourth category of ambiguous insiders is the Nicolaitans, who were mentioned in the messages to Ephesos and to Pergamon. Early church tradition identified these people as practitioners of irregular sexual practices. Clement of Alexandria knew two versions of the story, both of which linked this group to the Nicolaus mentioned in Acts 6:5.[69] One version said Nicolaus gave his wife away to another man as a libertine; the other said he did so to demonstrate his complete asceticism. The historical value of Clement's record is dubious but might well preserve an accurate memory that the Nicolaitans were known for maintaining different sexual standards than those espoused by John and some others.

Modern scholarship, on the other hand, has tended to group the Nicolaitans with Jezebel and Balaam as proponents of cultural accommodation.[70] There is insufficient information to allow for a definitive conclusion, but commentators have tended to overlook the fact that the Nicolaitans appear to have had a recognizable name, which suggests a founding figure (Nicolaus), identifiable followers, and social organization. In spite of the meager evidence, we should assume that the Nicolaitans at least represented a distinguishable option among the churches of Asia and recognize that they are portrayed with a different level of social complexity than is the case with Jezebel or Balaam. Whether the issue was sexual or culinary or both, we cannot know.

An examination of discussions of outsiders in Revelation, then, reinforces the idea that John understood the churches to represent God's kingdom, chosen from among the peoples of the earth. The citizens of this kingdom faced hostility and death threats but were not to respond with violence. Their task was to maintain the testimony of Jesus even at the cost of their lives, for they knew that the Lamb had already defeated their enemies and that the second death would not harm them. Outsiders lived in a world of deception, and society was divided between those with resources and those without. Some within the churches disagreed with John, including at least a contingent more involved in mainstream culture and perhaps another group that promoted a more lenient sexual ethic. The churches John addressed were defining their place in society in various ways. In everyday existence, life in a polytheistic milieu gave rise to various tensions. In John's view, the encounter with imperial cults was the most urgent.

12

WORSHIP AND AUTHORITY

This chapter is devoted to the distinctions in John's text between "good" and "bad" authority. It is not a chapter on the politics of Revelation; it goes deeper than politics. I have sought throughout this study to avoid applying modern notions of "political" and "religious" to the ancient data, because this pair of categories is poorly equipped to define Roman imperial societies. Our "politics and religion" suggests styles of community life that characterize modernities to various degrees, but have little to do with the Roman Empire.

So I have framed this study in terms of mythic worldviews, also a modern western category. This approach is more disciplined in its attempt to understand and represent the variety of ways in which humans know and shape the world. Furthermore, I have paid particular attention to theorists who study the nature of worldviews and experiences in areas like native South America (Sullivan), African America (Long), India (Eliade and, to an extent, Wilfred Cantwell Smith), and other decolonizing regions (Said). This method hardly guarantees objectivity. It simply expresses my bias in favor of analysis that recognizes relationships of domination and resistance in societies.

In this chapter I consider what is meant by "worship," compare the authority of the deified Jesus with the authority of the Roman emperors, and examine the roles assigned to the rulers of this world by Revelation.

Worship as a Category

So far in this study I have used "worship" rather loosely for a variety of activities and institutions. The English term only approximates ancient practices. When asked to define or describe worship, most contemporary westerners probably would not include blood sacrifice, libations, or food offerings in their answers. Yet in the ancient world, these rituals were at the core of community life.

Blood sacrifice was fundamental to community life in ancient Mediterranean societies, but its precise function is currently a matter of scholarly debate. One important proposal described animal sacrifice as a ritualized action that created community through the public display of death. The ritual supposedly originated in pre-agricultural hunting communities. As societies evolved beyond that phase, the ritual remained tied in some ways to its prehistoric past. According to this view, sacrifice was both a recognition of the paradox that one must kill in order to live and a way of dealing with the danger posed to the community by unrestrained killing. The central act of slaughter evoked feelings of awe, guilt, and fear. Corporate participation in the display of death created a shared guilt that bound the community together. At the same time, the death of the animal confirmed, by contrast, the superior power of the undying gods. Death brought the community together in an experience of finitude, transgression, and the wholly other.[1]

Another set of scholars has rejected this evolutionary approach and focused instead on the power of animal sacrifice to organize a specific sociocultural system.[2] According to this view, blood sacrifice did not put death on display but rather disguised it through a complex series of rituals. These activities—especially the division and consumption of sacrificial meat—created boundaries in society that evoked a cosmic order. Those boundaries defined mortal and immortal, human and animal, and concomitant subdivisions:

> If the act of slaying lies at the heart of the *thusia* [i.e, blood sacrifice], it resides
> there like a subversive threat that is repeatedly conjured away. It is a defect
> against which care is taken to construct and organize the delicate balance of a
> rite which embeds life in death. It admits that we must slaughter animals in
> order to eat, yet at the same time it aims to banish acts of murder and savagery
> from what is human.[3]

More recently objections to the idea that death is the central element of blood sacrifice have arisen. Extensive examination of Greek vase paintings that depict sacrificial rituals suggests that feasting and revelry were more important for the participants than the actual slaying of the animal. The slaughter was only one aspect of the larger process of dedicating a gift to the deities and of sharing a meat meal. According to this view, the meaning of sacrifice resides not in the death of the animal but in "the exploration of the concepts of *dôron* (gift), *timê* (honor), and *charis* (grace), in the mechanisms by which honors done to the gods bring joy and benefits to both gods and men."[4]

Fortunately, we do not need to adjudicate among these theories of the meaning of sacrifice in this context. The purpose in summarizing them here is to highlight the fundamental role sacrifice played in ancient worship and to indicate its importance in the life of communities like the cities of Asia. It should not surprise us, then, that one of the main internal problems addressed in Revelation's messages to the seven churches was precisely the question of sacrificial meat,[5] for the consumption of such meat raised important issues about theological and social commitments.[6]

The consumption of sacrificial meat could take place in a number of contexts. Such food could be eaten in the context of the sacrificial ritual itself, in dining quarters affiliated with a particular sanctuary but dedicated to different kinds of gatherings (e.g., birthdays or meetings of professional guilds), in restaurants unaffiliated with a temple, at home after purchase at a market, and elsewhere. An absolute ban on the consumption of sacrificial meat by church members in all these settings would have had a dramatic impact on the integration of the churches into their social contexts.[7] This issue was not primarily social in Revelation. It was a question of proper worship. In Revelation, insiders who violated expectations regarding sacrificial meat were signified as "adulterers," for they had disregarded the exclusive claims of their God. Nearly all outsiders would have been worshippers of the traditional deities, but they were not castigated as adulterers because the initial commitment to faithfulness had not been made. These people needed to repent[8] and were excluded from the new Jerusalem.[9]

Revelation contains many examples of activities that approximate modern western ideas of worship. Three are associated with sacrificial temple activity but they occur in highly symbolic settings. The first two involve the verb λατρεύω ("serve, worship"), which normally refers to ritual duties executed in a sacred context. The verb is used in Revelation 7:15 in reference to the unnumbered multitude from every nation, gathered around the heavenly throne, who worship God in his temple continually, night and day. Similarly, God's servants will worship him in the new Jerusalem (Rev 22:3), although there is no longer any need for a temple (21:22). The other sacrificial form of worship described in Revelation would have been familiar to anyone of that day. An incense offering is kept lit on the altar of the heavenly temple, its smoke ascending and mingling with the prayers of the saints.[10]

These three examples do not occur in present time: two happen in heaven and one in the future. For acts of worship in present time, John most frequently used the verb "to bow down" (προσκυνέω). Bowing down was an act of subservience. It might involve kissing the feet or the hem of the garment of the one before whom one bowed; sometimes kissing the ground was appropriate. All these actions recognized the complete authority of another, whether a deity or a powerful human.[11] So the physical act of submitting to authority might take place before rulers (especially eastern rulers),[12] before deities, or before divine images.

Revelation reflects all of these usages. People who bowed down to deities other than Israel's God or to statues of divine beings were chastised[13] because only the God of creation[14] and the Lamb[15] were worthy of such obeisance. Revelation referred often to those who bowed down to the emperors and to images of Roman authorities.[16] (I discuss this topic further later.) There is also a peculiar promise made to the angel of the church in Philadelphia that those from the synagogue of Satan would one day bow down at its feet.[17] But John was twice warned against his (understandable) temptation to prostrate himself before an angel who revealed God's truths to him. Both incidents end with the admonition to bow down only to God.[18] Thus, for John, one crucial aspect of worship was allegiance. Bowing down was a physical enactment of submission to divine authority.

Another aspect of worship that permeates Revelation includes words spoken or sung to God or the Lamb. At least 17 examples of spoken worship appear in Revelation. Two of these statements by the author, one near the beginning of the text and one near the end, chart the course for the text as a whole. The first one (1:5–6) provides the starting point by ascribing glory and might (κράτος) to Jesus as the one who washed the saints from their sins by his blood. As a result of Jesus' actions, the saints were made into a kingdom and priests to God.[19] Jesus is addressed by the author again at the end of the text, this time in the form of an impassioned plea for Jesus to return soon.[20] Thus, the two examples of worship provide a frame for the text, the first one confirming the deeds of Jesus and the last one pointing to the consummation of Jesus' mission. As such, they model the intended response of the audience. The hearers are to move from an understanding of the work of the Lamb to a longing for his return.

Between these two statements of worship are a host of statements about God, or addressed to God, embedded at a deeper level of the text. These statements are made by other characters within the visions the author narrated.[21] Many of the statements occur in the context of bowing down to God, which links them to the preferred body posture of worship in Revelation. These statements provide several reasons for worshipping God. God's authority flows first of all from his status as the creator of all things[22] and his transcendence of time.[23] Beyond this, John cites God's actions as worthy of worship. God's vindication of his servants occasions spoken worship in 11:17–18. Stated conversely, God is worshipped because he judges evil in the world.[24] And finally, the imminent arrival of the marriage feast of the Lamb leads to shouts of "Hallelujah!" and to rejoicing.[25]

Worship in Revelation, then, acknowledges beings who have authority. Worship is enfolded in the meaning of sacrifice; it entails submission and obedience; it enjoins acclamations, blessings, praise, and thanks. Jesus, who performs many acts that evoke worship of God, is also considered worthy of worship in Revelation.

The Authority of the Lamb

As in contemporary imperial cults, so in Revelation there was relatively little interest in reopening the accepted cosmogonic narratives to introduce new characters. Allusions are made in Revelation to Jesus' prehistory, or existence before his earthly life. The Risen Christ described himself as the first (1:17) and as the beginning or source (ἀρχή) of creation (3:14). His slaughter is also said to have taken place from the establishment of the cosmos (13:8). Whether these scattered references portray Christ as the first created being or as an instigator in creation itself is uncertain. Clearly, however, cosmogony and the role of the Christ in those events are not primary issues in Revelation.[26]

In chapter 7 I noted that imperial cult evidence manifests at least two strategies used to make limited connections between the emperors and cosmogonic stories. One

strategy (and I do not use the term in a deprecatory fashion) was to include the imperial family within the category "Olympian," either by assimilating members of the
imperial household with specific deities or by describing the family as a new branch
of the Olympians. A second strategy was to portray the emperors, especially Augustus,
as the mythic founder of a new world order and to assert that the present structures of
existence came into being through the deeds of the deified emperors. Both strategies
parallel Revelation's explanations of the importance of the deified Jesus. But the parallels are not exact and highlight differences in the dominant and resistant discourses.

Revelation obviously did not attempt to connect Jesus with the Olympian deities. Rather, the text drew a fairly clear connection (taking into account the visionary character of the narrative) between Jesus and the God of Israel in the context of
worship. Five hymnic passages arranged in two sets in Revelation 4–5 make the
connection. The offering of worship in these five texts forms a crescendo with three
rhythms. The recipients of worship display one rhythm. The first and second statements are adoration of the One seated on the throne, but the third and fourth statements turn toward the Lamb. The final statement brings these two figures together
with a final ascription of glory and honor to God and the Lamb together. A second
rhythm is evident in those who offer worship: first the 4 living beings, then the 24
elders, then myriads of angels, all earthly beings, and eventually all creation.

A third rhythm characterizes the physical actions associated with these five
hymnic statements. The third rhythm grows like that of the worshippers. This third
rhythm is less carefully worked out and less important; it nevertheless complements
the two previously mentioned. The first hymnic piece begins with ceaseless praise
spoken by the four living beings. The second involves bowing down to God; the
third follows with bowing down to the Lamb. The fourth and fifth return to speaking, but in the fifth member of the series the use of "forever and ever" reminds the
hearer of the ceaseless praise in the first member.

The five worship statements in Revelation 4–5 can be charted according to these
factors to show the complex progression (table 12.1).

These three overlaid cadences—of recipient, worshipper, and action—draw
together the One seated on the throne and the Lamb as the two beings uniquely
worthy of worship. This strategy is parallel in some ways to the Olympian descriptions of the deified imperial household: both move a human into the category of
beings who can be appropriately worshipped, and both move that human into the
highest category of being. There are some obvious differences as well. The two dei-
fications take place within distinct religious systems with different limitations. A
standard Greco-Roman pantheon allows for a number of divine beings, whereas the
traditions of Israel were restricted in this respect. Augustus and his successors were
normally compared to the figure of Zeus, the high god in a polytheistic system. Oddly
enough, Revelation did not try to maintain a monotheistic ethos by simply identifying Jesus with the one God. In a system that ought not to allow a second deity,
Jesus was declared worthy of honors equal to God, even though he was not identified with God.

John did not attempt to work out the relationship between the Lamb and the
One on the throne through discussions of ontology or through abstract reasoning.[27]
His vision report works through the logic of worship and of apocalyptic symbol.

TABLE 12.1 Progression of worship in Revelation 4–5

Verse	Recipient of Worship	Offered by	Action of Worship	Content
4:8	God	4 living beings	Ceaselessly saying	Holy, Holy, Holy, the Lord God Almighty, who was, who is, and who is to come.
4:11	God	24 elders	Fall before God, cast thrones down before God	You are worthy, our Lord God, to receive glory and honor and power, for you created all things, and by your will they existed and were created.
5:9–10	Lamb	4 beings and 24 elders	Fall before the Lamb and sing	You are worthy to take the scroll and to open its seals, for you were slaughtered and by your blood you ransomed for God saints from every tribe and language and people and nation; you have made them to be a kingdom and priests serving our God, and they will reign on earth.
5:12	Lamb	4 beings, 24 elders, and myriads of angels	Saying with a great voice	Worthy is the Lamb that was slaughtered to receive power and wealth and wisdom and might and honor and glory and blessing!
5:13	God and the Lamb	Every creature in heaven, on earth, under the earth, in the sea	Saying	To the one seated on the throne and to the Lamb be blessing and honor and glory and might forever and ever!

The symbolization of the deified Jesus in 5:5–6 has several themes, but the main characteristic is paradox:

> Then one of the elders said to me, "Do not weep. See, the Lion of the tribe of Judah, the Root of David, has conquered, so that he can open the scroll and its seven seals." Then I saw between the throne and the four living creatures and among the elders a Lamb standing as if it had been slaughtered, having seven horns and seven eyes, which are the seven spirits of God sent out into all the earth. (NRSV)

The paradoxical themes in this text are derived from the scriptures of Israel and combine several facets of Israel's hopes. Two themes relate specifically to the hope for a Davidic ruler. The lion of Judah can be traced back to Genesis 49:8–12 and evokes images of a powerful ruler capable of protecting God's people. The root of Jesse alludes to Isaiah 11, where there is an anticipation that the Davidic line will establish justice, end hostilities throughout all creation, gather God's people, and will bless all nations. These images of a Davidic ruler are then juxtaposed to that of a sacrificed lamb (Rev 5:6), drawing on texts such as Isaiah 53, where the redemptive suffering of the servant of the Lord is described.[28] John's portrayal of Jesus as the sacrificed lamb would have been understandable within other sectors of the first-century churches. The added features of seven horns and seven eyes distinguish it from other known proto-Christian texts.[29]

Even as John synthesized in Jesus such images as the Davidic ruler, Servant of the Lord, and the sacrificial Lamb, he refused to homogenize them. Instead, we are left with startling, unresolved juxtapositions: a lion who appears as a lamb, a slaughtered lamb that lives, a victor who is vanquished. The result is a complete redefinition of omnipotence. Strength and authority belong not to the one who has practiced violence but rather to the one upon whom violence has been inflicted. The image of victory is thereby completely inverted.[30] This point is driven home throughout the rest of the text by the primary identification of Jesus as "Lamb that was slaughtered." He is characterized by his sacrifice of himself on behalf of others, from the foundation of the world[31] and into the time of the new Jerusalem.[32]

The same style of recombinant imaging of Jesus appears in Revelation 7:16–17, where the significance of the "Lamb" is stretched in new ways: "They will hunger no more, and thirst no more; the sun will not strike them, nor any scorching heat; for the Lamb at the center of the throne will be their shepherd, and he will guide them to springs of the water of life, and God will wipe away every tear from their eyes" (NRSV). The text begins with a quotation from a salvation oracle that belongs to another poem about the servant of the Lord (Isaiah 49:1–13). This promise of release from want and from suffering leads immediately into an allusion to the role of the Davidic ruler as shepherd from Ezekiel 34:23. The Revelation text then circles back to Isaiah 49:10 with the promise that the Lamb will lead them to springs of waters. Rather than simply quoting Isaiah 49, however, John used the verb ὁδηγήσει ("he will lead") from Psalm 23 (Ps 22:3 LXX) and thereby injected the image of the Lord as shepherd. John's section then ends with a quotation from another salvation oracle that comes from Isaiah 25:8 and promises that the Lord of Israel will make a feast for all peoples on his holy mountain. The shame of God's people will be removed as he wipes away the tears from every face.

Thus, John's imagery in Revelation 7:16–17 compresses the Lamb, the Davidic ruler, the servant of the Lord, and the promise of salvation to all peoples into one poignant passage. The theme of fulfillment ties the pastiche together, with the streams of living water satiating thirst and the feast on the holy mountain satisfying hunger. The result is less shocking than the lion/lamb image of Jesus in Revelation 5:5–6, but the element of paradox is still strong. In Revelation 7:16–17 the Lamb is again the ruler and connected to the heavenly throne, but this time the Lamb is also the shepherd who leads the flock. The theme of fulfillment does not rule the image because it is only a promise of fulfillment, not the fulfillment itself. The tension of the paradox remains.

The dissonance of these images grows out of John's resistant stance in relation to his setting in imperial society. His creative combination of religious traditions elicited doubts about the accepted imperial definitions of reality. Who is worthy of worship? What was the true nature of authority? Was it won by the powerful? Was it guaranteed to the faithful? Such images of Jesus could not be based in the institutions of Roman imperial society in Asia (or elsewhere). The matrix within which such a Jesus made sense was in churches, or more specifically, in the kinds of churches John envisioned and I outlined in the previous chapter. The paradox expressed an experience of the churches in which the bold claims made in worship were not manifest in everyday life. One could witness to the hidden truth and await vindication.

The second cosmogonic strategy noted in imperial cult evidence was the portrayal of Augustus as the founder of the imperial world order. The shape of the world known to the inhabitants of Roman Asia was a reflection of the actions of the first emperor. Thus, the day of his birth could be called "equal to the beginning of all things"; he was worthy of the highest honors imaginable.[33] This intimate connection of cosmogony and cosmology is evident as well in the hymnic material about the Lamb in Revelation 5 but on a very different scale. The 4 beings and the 24 elders began to sing the praises of the Lamb as the founder of a new sovereignty: "You are worthy to take the scroll and to open its seals, for you were slaughtered and by your blood you ransomed for God saints from every tribe and language and people and nation; you have made them to be a kingdom and priests serving our God, and they will reign on earth" (Rev 5:9–10 NRSV). The Lamb's blood sacrifice founded a new kingdom from among all the nations. The myriads of angels concurred. "Worthy is the Lamb that was slaughtered to receive power and wealth and wisdom and might and honor and glory and blessing!"[34] Finally, all creatures joined in, offering joint worship to the One on the throne and to the Lamb.[35]

The authority of the Lamb, then, was based in his execution of God's will and in his execution. His kingdom had been won not by inflicting suffering but by enduring suffering. Such a view was so at odds with dominant views of reality that it could best be expressed in paradoxical imagery: the king of beasts as a slaughtered lamb that shepherds the nations.

Pretenders to the Throne of God

Having emphasized that only God and the Lamb were worthy of worship, John offered in Revelation 12–13 an alternative interpretation of Roman imperialism. This task was not easy. Rome had controlled the entire Mediterranean basin for at least a century and certain regions for much longer. If Revelation was written toward the end of the first century CE, then this political system had survived even the demise of the Julio-Claudian dynasty. John had to explain why a transcendent God would tolerate an apparently successful, apparently unstoppable superpower that did not acknowledge the Creator and had destroyed the temple of God in Jerusalem.

John's dissenting portrait of imperial society contained four features. The first was a broad characterization of present time as an era of harassment and hostility.[36] In Revelation 12, John described in visionary terms some of the effects of the coming of Jesus. A heavenly woman who represented (in some way) the people of God gave birth to a male child.[37] John signaled that this child was the Messiah by reference to Psalms 2:9—the child was about to shepherd all the nations with an iron rod.[38] Satan, in the form of a great red dragon with seven heads and ten horns, was ready to consume the child, but God intervened, taking the child away to the heavenly throne.

War erupted in the heavenly realm. The Dragon and its angels fought with the archangel Michael and his angelic troops. The defeat of the Dragon became the occasion for rejoicing and for fear. The inhabitants of the heavens could rejoice because the Dragon was cast down to earth (12:9) and its time was short (12:12); they were rid of the cosmic antagonist and his destruction was imminent. The earth and sea, however, were now vulnerable to the Dragon's great wrath.[39] When it could not harm the woman (who was divinely protected in the wilderness), the Dragon stormed off to do battle with the rest of her offspring, identified as the ones who keep God's commands and have the testimony of Jesus.[40]

In this way, John recast the present time of his audience not as a period of imperial prosperity but as Satan's last desperate opportunity to take revenge on those who feared God. The ultimate victory of the saints had been decided by the sacrifice of the Lamb and by their own testimony (12:11), but they would need to weather the last storm.

Within this broad framework, John could develop the second aspect of his view of imperial society: his conclusion that Roman imperial authority was demonic. He communicated this through the next phase of his vision. After the Dragon was thwarted in its attacks on the woman in the wilderness, it went to the shore of the sea. A beast arose from the sea, and commentators almost unanimously identify this beast with Roman hegemony. In fact, this Beast from the Sea symbolism borders on allegory.[41] A strong argument for the identification comes from the fact that the imagery in this part of John's vision is based on Daniel 7:1–7, where a series of four beasts arise out of the great sea. Each of the four Danielic beasts—a lion with wings, a bear with three tusks, a leopard with four heads and wings, and a powerful creature with ten horns—signified a world empire that conquered the eastern Mediterranean during the first millennium BCE.[42]

In Revelation, the Roman Empire was portrayed as a composite of all these tyrannical empires.[43] In scriptural terms Rome was the ultimate empire, combining all the destructive characteristics of its predecessors. The seven heads and ten horns also gave the image of Rome cosmic proportions beyond previous historical empires, for this indicated a physical resemblance with "the great Dragon, the ancient serpent, called Devil and Satan."[44] But John left nothing to the imagination here. He wrote that the Beast from the Sea received its power, throne, and great authority from the Dragon, not from Jupiter or some other Olympian.[45] Moreover, in an overt reference to imperial cult activity, John wrote that the whole world began to bow down before the Dragon and the Beast.

Revelation 13:11–18 introduced a third aspect of John's view of imperial society: the demonic authority of local elites who collaborated with Rome. A second beast arose, this time from the earth. This beast was a subordinate figure, but it played an important role in the imperial system. The Beast from the Earth was subordinate in the sense that its authority came from the first beast and it promoted the worship of the first beast. The second beast played a crucial role as the figure responsible for organizing and enforcing obedience. Thus, the Beast from the Earth was no mere lackey or a neutral figure: John described it as having the appearance of a Lamb but the voice of a Dragon. It was the junior partner in this demonic system.

Efforts to identify the referent of the symbol of the Beast from the Earth are generally similar but with significant differences in the details. There is widespread agreement that the symbol is related to local officials involved in the imperial cults of Asia. The disagreement is evident when scholars become more specific. Did the Beast from the Earth refer to priests and priestesses in the local imperial cults?[46] To anyone involved in the regulation and maintenance of imperial cults?[47] To the koinon?[48] To imperial cult officials or Roman government of the province?[49] To imperial cults and pagan worship in general?[50] To everyone who promoted imperial cults or imperial propaganda?[51]

Most of these proposals are too limited. The analysis in part I of this book has shown that imperial cults in Asia permeated Roman imperial society, leaving nothing untouched. So it is almost impossible to separate imperial cults from public religion, from entertainment, from commerce, from governance, from household worship, and so on. Furthermore, by focusing on certain officials, we tend to overlook the fact that the families wealthy and prominent enough to provide officials for imperial cults tended to be the same families that provided candidates for governmental positions. Governance and piety were not independent sectors of society, nor did the leaders in these activities compose distinct groups. The mythic world encompassed all of this and more.

Perhaps the best summary of the referent for the Beast from the Earth came from Yarbro Collins:

> The vision about the beast from the earth (13:11–18) would have called to
> mind the leading families of Asia Minor, who had control of both political
> office and the various priesthoods. These families, as well as the general
> populace of the region, were very enthusiastic in supporting and even extending
> the worship of the emperor.[52]

The Beast from the Earth was not quite an allegory, but the range of its referents is clear: it signified the network of people and overlapping institutions in Asia described in part I of this study.[53] The elite families mentioned in part I led sacrifices, underwrote festivals, built temples, voted honors, and so forth as part of their full range of civic duties. The elite families mobilized the masses in support of the emperor and enhanced their own standing in the process.[54] In terms of social mechanisms, John's description of how the empire worked is not so different from modern scholarly reconstructions: distant Roman power provided the rule and the authority, while local elites collaborated in the pacification and stabilization of their regions.[55] What is distinct in Revelation is the condemnation directed both at the authority of Rome and at the authority of the distinguished families of the province.

The fourth aspect of John's rendering of imperial Asian society is the question of legitimacy. There were both demonic and godly forms of authority in John's world, but how were they authorized? What was the difference in their natures? How could one tell which was legitimate? Worship is not the answer here, for both forms were legitimated in worship. John made the contrast in the following way. The authority of God and the Lamb was proper because it was based on God's nature as transcendent creator and on Jesus' actions as redemptive sacrifice. The authority of the Dragon and the Beast from the Sea was based on deception and force.

The theme of deception appears at crucial junctures in Revelation 12–13 (and throughout the book). When the Dragon is finally identified clearly as Satan, he is described as "the one deceiving the whole world."[56] The primary activity of the Beast from the Earth is also to deceive, which it accomplished through the great signs it worked: causing fire to fall from heaven, giving voice to the statues of the first beast, and so on.[57] These tricks led people to worship the Beast from the Sea.

In the two-beast vision of Revelation 13, Rome has a more specific function that also leads people to blasphemous imperial worship. Here the Beast from the Sea is said to be unmatched in its ability to make war. It can force its will upon the whole world. Even an apparently fatal wound to one of its heads cannot stop the beast. On this particular point (military supremacy), John is not parodying imperial theology. Monuments like the Sebasteion sculptures[58] or the images of Augustus from the first provincial temple at Pergamon[59] confirmed John's argument. Roman authority was based on the ability to subdue its enemies. John was portraying in a reasonably accurate manner one of the basic presuppositions of imperial cult activity. The emperors could not, and should not, be resisted.

John's rendering of imperial cult activity in Revelation 13 reeks with hyperbole,[60] but he consistently reinforced his exaggerated denunciations of imperial cult practice with more subtle literary devices. Legitimate spoken worship results in acclamations such as "You are worthy, our Lord and God, to receive glory and honor and power," or "Worthy is the Lamb that was slaughtered to receive power and wealth and wisdom and might and honor and glory and blessing!"[61] The invincibility of Roman power, however, can evoke only rhetorical (and perhaps ambivalent) questions such as "Who is like the beast, and who can fight against him?"[62] Furthermore, the physical response that comes from an encounter with the One on the throne or with the Lamb is to fall down, often as a part of bowing down in worship.[63] When people encounter the "glory" of Roman authority in Revelation, however, they are amazed and then sometimes deceived into bowing down to worship.[64]

The distinction is highlighted by the theme of mimicry. The One on the throne has his agent the Lamb and the spirit of prophecy; the Dragon has his agent the Beast from the Sea and his False Prophet.[65] The One on the throne and the Lamb are worshipped together (15:3–4), as are the Dragon and the Beast from the Sea (13:4). First the 144,000 servants of God are sealed on the forehead to preserve them through suffering (7:3); then those who worship the beast are sealed on the forehead and the hand in order to avoid suffering (13:16–17). The Lamb was slaughtered yet lives; one head of the Beast from the Sea was fatally wounded yet the beast still lives. In these and other examples, the satanic forces can only mimic the true God. Imperial cults, according to John, are nothing but a blasphemous imitation of the worship due to the One on the heavenly throne. They grow up around an illegitimate authority. The cults are based on deception and violent opposition to God rather than on obedience.

The Case against the Empire

Late in his text John reported visions of the judgment of Babylon. The symbolization of the imperial center shifted from a seven-headed beast to a grotesque caricature of a prostitute, which then shifted into the image of Babylon personified as a woman. In content, the visions move from a revelation of the true nature of Roman rule (Rev 17) to laments over Rome's destruction by allies and rejoicing by heavenly enemies (Rev 18) to a narrative of the final confrontation between Rome (portrayed once again as a beast) and the Messiah (Rev 19). Although it is beyond the scope of this chapter to examine the complexities of John's intertextual method in this section, the imagery and social commentary cannot be explained without a recognition of this background.[66]

The image of the great prostitute had its literary roots in Jewish prophetic literature, where several corporate entities were represented in this way.[67] The metaphor functioned in various ways in oracles against Nineveh, Tyre, and even Jerusalem. As the capital of the Assyrian Empire, Nineveh gained a reputation for its aggressive expansion. This reputation was reflected in Nahum 3:4, where the symbol of the prostitute emphasized the ability of the imperial center to seduce and enslave whole nations. The image could also be used in other ways against a sea-faring empire like that of the Phoenicians. Isaiah 23 contains oracles against Tyre, one of which likened the city to a prostitute. The theme of seduction occurs in this text as well, but the purpose is not to enslave nations. Here seduction is a part of Tyre's effort to entice the nations and regain its mercantile empire. Used against Jerusalem in Ezekiel 16, the image provided the opportunity for accusations of unfaithfulness. Jerusalem had not simply been unfaithful to YHWH by worshipping other deities. The prophet claimed the city was the worst kind of prostitute, pursuing other lovers out of wanton desire rather than for payment.

Thus, in Israel's tradition, the metaphor of "prostitute" for a corporate entity proffered great resources as a rhetorical weapon against Roman authority. One part of this was its potential for polemic against polytheism. The point in Revelation was not, however, to brand Rome as particularly polytheistic. Polytheism was not a sector of Greco-Roman society but rather its fabric. From John's point of view, Rome had exaggerated the error and arrogance of polytheism to blasphemous heights by adding the exaltation of the emperors to it.

"Prostitute" extended John's objection to Roman imperialism beyond the strictly cultic contexts. Through the metaphor, John could make the necessary connections between cult, commerce, politics, and empire in his critique. The reservoir of meaning inherent in the image of the seven-headed beast was limited mostly to the signification of strength and violence. The image of the prostitute, on the other hand, provided symbolic resources for denouncing idolatry, political domination, and economic exploitation. Revelation 17 made the transition between these symbols when the familiar beast and the newly revealed prostitute appeared together. As John's text began to detail the blasphemy of Roman rule in Revelation 18, the beast receded and the prostitute became the focal point.

John drew on several prophetic texts in this section of Revelation to develop this broader critique of Roman hegemony. The textual influences on Revelation 18 are many. Much of the chapter draws on prophetic denunciations of Tyre and Babylon, but two texts greatly influenced the structural elements of Revelation 18. One of these is Ezekiel 26–27. These two chapters contain sixth-century BCE oracles directed against Tyre. The Ezekiel section opens with the accusation that Tyre rejoiced over the Babylonian destruction of Jerusalem, seeing in the tragedy a chance to increase its market share of regional commerce (Ezek 26:2). Pronouncements of divine judgment on Tyre ensue (26:3–14). The prophet then described the reactions of other rulers to the sudden destruction of Tyre: they tremble and lament (26:15–18). The oracle ends with a declaration by YHWH that he will indeed bring that imperial city to a dreadful demise (26:19–21).

In Ezekiel 27, the prophet takes up an extended lament in which the island city of Tyre is described as a sea-going ship. The beautiful materials and craftsmanship of the vessel are praised (27:3–11). A long series of statements details the cargo and trading partners of the city/ship. As the rowers head out onto the high seas, however, an east wind sinks the vessel, sending it to the bottom of the Mediterranean Sea (27:25–27). The pilots and sailors of the region stand at the shore and mourn the loss of Tyre (27:28–36).

> Who was ever destroyed like Tyre in the midst of the sea?
> When your wares came from the seas,
> you satisfied many peoples;
> with your abundant wealth and merchandise
> you enriched the kings of the earth. (Ezek 27:32a-33)

Whereas Ezekiel 26–27 provided economic aspects of John's critique of Rome, Jeremiah 50–51 supplied the basis for three important images in Revelation 18. These two chapters of Jeremiah consist of a long series of oracles, this time directed at the historical imperial city of Babylon. In Jeremiah 51:7 we are told, "Babylon was a golden cup in the Lord's hand, making all the earth drunken; the nations drank of her wine, and so the nations went mad" (NRSV). In John's vision, the responsibility for the madness of nations has shifted. Now Babylon is a prostitute offering a golden cup of wine to the inhabitants of earth.[68] The calls to flee Babylon and to rejoice over the city's demise (Rev 18:2–4) also come from Jeremiah, although other prophetic texts are at work here as well.[69]

Finally, the symbolic action of the strong angel in Revelation 18:21 is a reworking of the ending of Jeremiah 51. After writing the oracles against Babylon, Jeremiah instructed a royal official to take them along to Babylon as he traveled in Zedekiah's entourage. After arrival at the imperial center, the official was to read the oracles, then tie a stone to the scroll, cast the scroll into the Euphrates, and say, "Thus shall Babylon sink, to rise no more, because of the disasters that I am bringing on her."[70] In John's vision report, this image is developed further: an angel casts a millstone into the sea and declares, "With such violence Babylon the great city will be thrown down, and will be found no more."[71]

I cite these texts from Ezekiel and Jeremiah to demonstrate that John was not simply quoting or interpreting Scripture. He was rather refashioning it for his own times. From Ezekiel 26–27 come the theme of judgment on a maritime empire and the structural element of laments over a fallen empire. From Jeremiah 50–51 come the elements of the call to flee Babylon, the gold cup intoxicating the nations, and the stone thrown into the waters. Jeremiah also contributed useful themes of utter destruction of an imperial center,[72] vengeance visited on the destroyers of Zion,[73] and a denunciation of idols and the worship of deities other than the Creator.[74] From these texts, from pieces of other texts, and from the symbolic potential of the prostitute, John offered an alternative reading of his imperial setting.

This alternative reading depicted levels of complicity for the peoples of the empire, the merchants, and the kings. The kings of the earth are represented as having the most intimate relations with the great prostitute of Roman hegemony. These petty rulers received their authority from Rome and had the most direct complicity with the prostitute. Thus, in contrast to the other characters in the vision report, only the kings were said to have committed fornication with the prostitute, for they are guilty of abusing their power.[75]

When the lament of the kings is compared with that of the princes in Ezekiel 26, two observations can be made. First, the Revelation lament of the kings is briefer, probably because the kings receive significant attention elsewhere (Revelation 17:12–14; 19:19–21). Second, the nature of their lamenting is different. In Ezekiel 26:16–18, the princes of the coast are severely distraught. Even though the reasons are not stated overtly, there is an implication that they fear the same fate might await them.[76] Revelation is more cynical. The lament of the kings suggests that they are grieving their own loss because of the judgment that fell on Babylon. They stand at a distance, abandoning the prostitute because of her torment, so their true motivations are revealed. In this way John opposed the rhetoric of imperial harmony, benefaction, and loyalty found in the dominant discourse. According to John's visions, the empire was held together by greed and self-interest.

At the other extreme from the kings is the general populace of the empire. The general population was not absolved of guilt, but their participation in imperial society reflects manipulation as much as personal initiative. The peoples of the empire had become drunk from the wine of her harlotries;[77] they had been deceived by the sorcery of the great merchants.[78]

Between the kings and the people, two other levels of complicity surface. One group—the one that received the most attention from the seer in this chapter—is composed of the merchants, "the great ones of the earth."[79] There is only a fleeting reference to merchants in Ezekiel 27:36, but in Revelation 18 their importance has greatly increased. They are described as those who made themselves wealthy from the prostitute, not as those who fornicated with the prostitute or as those who became drunk from her wine.[80] The merchants also fear her torment and stand at a distance, but their lament evoked memories of the prostitute's splendor and the sudden disappearance of her wealth.

The second group whose status is somewhere between the kings and the people consists of the shipowners, pilots, and sailors. These receive little attention. Their presence is probably attributable to the prominence of shippers in Ezekiel 27:28–36 and to their connection with the merchants of the Roman Empire. It was, after all, Roman control of the sea lanes that made their international commercial activities possible.

A closer look at John's vision report shows that he specifically described the merchants as those who profited from the power of the prostitute's στρῆνος.[81] The precise meaning of the word is difficult to assess, for it appears only a few times in existing literature and the contexts yield different results: arrogance,[82] wantonness,[83] eager desire.[84] In Revelation 18:9 it is normally translated as "luxury" and suggests a self-absorbed, extravagant lifestyle made possible through the exploitation of international markets in the so-called pax Romana. The verb στρηνιάω occurs later in the chapter, confirming that this is a central issue. In fact, it is one factor that the prostitute, the kings, and the merchants have in common: they are all motivated by their own desires for self-aggrandizement and self-gratification. In a passage asserting that God will pay back the prostitute double for her sins, a voice from heaven specifies two of her main transgressions: "As she *glorified herself* and *lived luxuriously*, so give her a like measure of torment and grief."[85] So too the kings are not simply those who have committed adultery with the prostitute but also those who have lived lives of luxury and wanton excess (οἱ στρηνιάσαντες).

One last aspect of the accusations against Rome becomes explicit at the end of Revelation 18. We have already seen how the discourse and practice of Roman authority were criticized for deceiving the whole world (Rev 18:23). In Revelation 18:24 John returned to a theme that recurs throughout the book: Rome's violence against God's people and indeed against all humanity. The superpower has spilled the blood of the prophets, the saints, and all those slaughtered upon the earth. Thus, in Revelation 19:1, the rejoicing begins in heaven over Rome's demise. The blood of God's servants is avenged.

The actual narrative of the destruction of the seven-headed Beast is abbreviated: the Messiah—the "Word of God"—rides out with his heavenly troops to do battle;[86] an angel calls to the birds of middle heaven to feast on the impending carnage;[87] and the enemies are defeated.[88] The kings and troops fighting alongside the Beast are killed, but a special punishment awaits the Beast and his False Prophet. There is no first death for them; the two are cast alive into the lake of fire.

The Kings of the Earth

The brevity of John's narrative about the destruction of Rome is no accident. John was primarily concerned to present before the churches the character of his opposition to empire. His opposition was religious: Rome had claimed a status that belonged only to God. In its arrogance, the imperial city had enslaved the nations through military force and through the seduction of their rulers and their aristocratic families. The complicity of the kings extended Roman rule throughout their world, and the price of resistance was paid in blood. Meanwhile, the excesses of the privileged few were funded by an international trading system that trafficked especially in luxuries and accumulated large amounts of capital in the hands of a few. The masses marveled at the power of the beast (Rev 13:3–4) and were deceived by the magic of the marketplace (Rev 18:23).

In John's system, then, there was no legitimate place for earthly empire. His religious criticism was specifically aimed at Roman imperialism, but the character of his critique had broader implications. John was not just anti-Roman; he was anti-empire. The violence required to establish hegemony is not the prerogative of humans; Rome's use of military force was a blasphemous usurpation of God's right and ability to judge justly. The economic inequities of empire were the result of corporate and personal immorality; they merited the condemnations of God. So in John's text, imperial cults are not an aberration; they are the fitting manifestation of imperialism. They take us to the heart of the confrontation over who is king of kings.

If there is no place in John's system for an empire—a "kingdom over the kings of the earth" (Rev 17:18)—we might well ask whether there is allowance at least for kings of the earth. John did not answer that question directly in his text. He laid out no political theory; he spoke as a religious critic from a mythic worldview. The kings of the earth are uniformly portrayed in a negative light. They are the subjects of oracles of judgment;[89] they are manipulated by demonic spirits;[90] they cavort with the great prostitute;[91] they attempt to make war against the Word of God.[92]

It is more than a little surprising, then, to meet them one last time in the new Jerusalem: "The nations will walk by its light (i.e., the light of new Jerusalem), and the kings of the earth will bring their glory into it."[93] This single hopeful statement regarding the kings of the earth draws on Israel's hopes for Jerusalem; it may even be a meditation on the meaning of Isaiah 60 or Psalm 68. The literary background and utopian character of Revelation 21 suggest that the statement offers us insight into John's view of the true goal of earthly rulers. It is an idealized vision but one that nonetheless leaves the audience an opening to consider the role of earthly authorities.

The kings of the earth, however, were not John's primary concern in Revelation. He showed more interest in two other issues. One was the question of who would be worshipped as the king of kings. This is the heart of the conflict in Revelation, and it is the reason that the throne is the central symbol.[94] John insisted that Jesus Christ was the ruler of the kings of the world,[95] that the Lamb was the king of kings and lord of lords.[96] The Christ shared this status with the One seated on the throne,[97] and proper worship could be offered only to them. Rome's claim was a challenge to the authority of the One on the throne, and that challenge expressed itself in cultic, political, and economic terms.

The other central issue in Revelation is the kingdom of God and of his Christ. This kingdom was composed of churches, the realm in which the authority of the king of kings was recognized. It was a kingdom defined by suffering and endurance in this world.[98] Like the Roman Empire, this kingdom transcended national, ethnic, and linguistic barriers. In contrast to the Roman Empire, its inhabitants were priests and servants of God,[99] and its purity was compromised by any other cultic attachment. John set high standards. They were so high that to keep them would make it almost impossible to survive under Roman authority in imperial society. That was precisely John's point.

13

REVELATION IN THIS WORLD

John's vision for the kingdom of God and his Christ has not yet been realized. Perhaps he would be surprised to learn that it has taken so long, or perhaps not.[1] His text has nevertheless remained viable across millennia. But how has John's religious criticism been received and deployed by later groups?

Elisabeth Schüssler Fiorenza noted that among Christian communities in recent times, Revelation tends to be emphasized by groups at the margins of mainline churches and theology. Among these marginal Christian groups, three reading strategies have emerged for interpreting Revelation.[2] Each strategy can lead to various conclusions, but the generalizations provide a broad orientation to the usefulness of Revelation. One of the strategies has been biblical literalism. This approach to Revelation assumes that John was writing about specific events of the interpreter's time in cryptic codes. By interpreting the language literally and cross-referencing it with other biblical prooftexts, such readers decipher the text and then construct a timetable for the end of history, which is usually imminent. John's critique is thus reinterpreted and applied to contemporary events. His dreams help people imagine the end of this world, thereby relativizing contemporary power relations in particular ways for particular purposes.

Others have read Revelation with the assistance of interpretive strategies based in liberation theology.[3] These readers have been inspired by Revelation as they struggle for justice in specific contemporary settings. For them, the Apocalypse provides a biblical model for Christian action that opposes oppression. Rather than viewing Revelation as a coded blueprint for the end of the world, these communities find in the situations of the first-century churches religious direction and motivation for their modern political praxis. John's religious criticism thus becomes a model to be emulated rather than a secret message to be decoded.

Feminist critical thought provides a third strategy for reading Revelation in some Christian communities. Rather than treating the Bible as literal prediction or liberation prototype, such readers examine the way that language and symbols affect women's struggle against patriarchal oppression. This strategy has led some to reject Revelation because of its divine machismo; others attempt to highlight patriarchy within the text and to salvage other aspects of the Apocalypse.[4] In these communities John's religious criticism is emulated and even used against the text in certain ways.

It has not been my goal in this study to produce an interpretation of Revelation for Christian communities, but the topic deserves comment. The materials covered in this book and my method of treating them have the most in common with the second and third strategies. My contention that Revelation is an anti-imperial text meshes well with liberation interpretations of the Apocalypse, and my description of John's critique adds precision to reconstructions of the first-century struggles. If Revelation is to serve as a prototypical Christian manifesto, a description of John's first-century setting is one crucial step in developing a movement that holds on to the testimony of Jesus.

Certain kinds of Christian feminist interpretations are also amenable to this study of imperial cults and Revelation. As John tried to move his congregations away from participation in the imperial discourse of Roman Asia, he brought a host of other assumptions about proper authority and conduct into question as well. John's religious criticism did not extend far into gender relations, but I would say that his break with dominant culture tended to undercut the patriarchal authority of that culture. In his visions, then, we find a mixed picture: certain features of patriarchal authority were not questioned even as John painted a relatively egalitarian view of what it means for women and men to hold the testimony of Jesus. The implications of his religious criticism for gender relations remained underdeveloped in the text.

Few Revelation specialists have attempted to interpret the Apocalypse for a contemporary, "not-necessarily-confessing" audience, for it is not clear why a modern audience should consider this ancient text if Revelation's authority as Scripture is not the starting point for the investigation. David Barr took up the challenge. He argued that Revelation is a crucial part of the western cultural heritage and is important especially in American culture. So he set out to provide an American audience with the historical and literary tools necessary for an informed reading of the text.[5] A modern western audience, approaching Revelation as a narrative from the first century, would likely scrutinize the ethics of the ancient critic. Is Revelation finally just a story about the triumph of power? Does God win simply because God is stronger? Is the Apocalypse ultimately an immoral story? Barr maintained that it is not immoral. Revelation's religious criticism is not based on a glorification of power. Rather, the Apocalypse describes coercion as self-destructive. The real conqueror is Jesus, who suffered instead of inflicting suffering.[6]

Catherine Keller has also written on Revelation for a general western audience. The cultural significance of the Apocalypse weighed more heavily on her because of her suspicions that the text was a self-fulfilling prophecy of destruction.

> Perhaps, I have wondered, it is not mere coincidence that the last book of the holy book of the Western world envisions a cataclysmic end, given that the West seems in its modernity hell-bent on producing some literal form of that end. Odd, I thought, that Western modernity has espoused an optimistic millennialism of progress while busily facilitating the most demented of ecological or nuclear dooms. I became curious about the nature of the link between the multiple readings of a divinely authored denouement and what one might dub the *man*made apocalypse of the late second millennium C.E. Expectations seek, after all, to realize themselves. So the religious habit of imagining the world out of existence would not seem to be irrelevant to the material habits of world-waste running our civilization.[7]

Keller's reason, then, for reading Revelation is that the text might be responsible for the problems that threaten us all, especially environmental ruination, weapons of mass destruction, and international consumer capitalism. Keller argued that the real problem runs deeper than these particular destructive practices. The real problem is the style of John's religious criticism. Revelation has imprinted the modern west with what she called the apocalyptic pattern, "a habituated and reactive tendency, collectively instilled and readily acted out in individual bursts of self-righteous certainty: we may 'do an apocalypse' in our most intimate relations as well as in our most visionary politics."[8] It is a pattern characterized by an either/or morality of good versus bad, by a need to purge the evil from the world once and for all, by the expectation of a violent showdown in which good triumphs even though the world is destroyed in the process, and by the establishment of a pure, permanent utopia.

The difficulty in dealing with the apocalyptic pattern is that we are all inside the apocalypse. Most westerners, Keller claimed, adopt the apocalyptic pattern unconsciously.[9] Biblical literalists are aware of the pattern and try to retrofit it onto modern politics. Others aware of the pattern try to fight it but do so in an apocalyptic way that simply inverts and maintains an apocalyptic style of life.[10] Still others are satisfied with defending Revelation; they soften the text's harsher aspects without holding the text responsible for the effects generated by its style of religious criticism.[11]

In a cultural setting where there is no direct route out of the apocalyptic pattern, Keller argued that the best we can do is to examine Revelation from a counter-apocalyptic perspective. Counter-apocalypse involves a recognition of one's own participation in the apocalyptic pattern even while trying to break the habit. Counter-apocalypse has an ambivalent appreciation for the pattern: it tries to steer clear of the dualism but is drawn to the commitment to justice.[12]

Keller's formulation is important for us because she addressed a fundamental problem in the interpretation of Revelation. The apocalyptic pattern permeates western and American cultures, affecting personal and global policies while undergoing almost no critical scrutiny. Furthermore, her reflection on the apocalyptic pattern was motivated by some of the same issues that are a catalyst for my study. Imperialism, injustice, righteousness, suffering, religious commitment, environmental degradation, and governance were problems in John's day as well, but we are now much closer to matching the hyperbole of his imagery. These issues have been constantly reformulated over millennia, but not solved. The body count is still rising.

In my work on Revelation I have not adopted the counter-apocalyptic position. Such a posture seems to me to draw the connections between John and ourselves too directly. My strategy has been to emphasize the foreignness of Revelation in hopes of pitting the modern apocalyptic pattern against its alleged ancient source. Modern popular interpretation of Revelation exercises great power over readers—even trained readers—and it often prevents us from encountering the text or understanding the character of John's religious criticism. We think we already know Revelation's contents and perspective, even though very few features of the apocalyptic pattern appear in John's text. Revelation contains no references to an Antichrist; God contends with a cosmic antagonist (Satan) and an earthly empire (Rome). No final conflagration destroys the earth; heaven and earth finally flee when God makes all things new, long after the final confrontation with the Beast. Revelation contains no references to hell; there is a lake of fire into which death itself is thrown. Nor does Revelation promise an eternal dwelling in heaven; the new Jerusalem comes down to the new earth, and God abandons heaven to take up residence below.

So I do not try to hold Revelation accountable for its reception throughout history. A more profitable approach, I think, is to interrogate the interpretive communities that have used Revelation in the light of John's religious criticism. For that reason I have recontextualized Revelation by comparing it with unfamiliar materials—coins, inscriptions, sculptures, buildings from the early Roman Empire related to the worship of the emperors—to carve out a strange vantage point on the text and on ourselves. My hope is that, by situating Revelation among other first-century artifacts, we will better understand its alien character and will learn to appreciate it more fully in its foreignness.

This strange vantage point—comparing the text to its chosen adversary—leads to several conclusions about Revelation as a practitioner's religious criticism. From the traditions of Israel and from the experiences of the churches, John fashioned a narrative of resistance to Roman hegemony. The narrative was a jarring ride through dreams and nightmares, leading its audience through self-criticism, heavenly liturgies, disasters natural and unnatural, imperial oppression cast in mythic terms, divine intervention, a final reckoning, and utopia. Its point of view was provincial but its cosmology weak, so John's critique offered no illusions of national revival or political supersession in this world. John's religious criticism emphasized instead a powerful eschatology, allowing his audience no accommodation to this world if they would attain the new earth.

The grounds for John's religious criticism allowed his text to transcend its particular historical setting and to be applied to many other situations. The ambiguity of his symbolization facilitated the process as well, for these enigmatic images might well allude to any number of experiences. The basis of John's criticism, however, was this assertion: there is only one authority worthy of human service. This assertion moved his work beyond the confines of his times and turned it into a hypothesis about the relationship between deity and hegemony. For this reason I have argued that John's text was not simply anti-Roman; it was anti-empire.

John's corollary hypothesis about the insidious, imitative character of evil finds perverse support in the history of the reception of Revelation by the churches. The very "kingdom" for which John wrote turned his text into a tool of empire. In the hands of some Christian communities, the Apocalypse has thus become a dark parody not far removed from the image of the Beast from the Sea that threatens its subjects with death, or the Beast from the Earth that looks like a lamb and speaks like a dragon. An old axiom takes a tragic turn: imitation becomes the sincerest form of deception. I argue, however, that this use of the text should not invalidate John's religious criticism but rather confirms aspects of that critique in a disquieting fashion. In a world of deception, Revelation would still call readers to vigilant discernment.

This strange vantage point leads to religious criticism of the academic variety as well, raising questions about the discipline of New Testament studies. Commentators have almost unanimously concluded that imperial cults were a fundamental issue in the book of Revelation. But if this is so, why has most of the evidence for imperial cults been ignored for so long? Hundreds of pieces of evidence—inscriptions, coins, sculptures, altars, and buildings—have been found and published that are related to imperial cults in the province where John's churches were located. Yet only a handful of these have been noted in the scholarly discussions of the Apocalypse of John.

One reason for this problem is the difficulty of integrating archaeological data into traditional New Testament studies. What appears at first glance to be a simple question about additional data quickly raises issues of method and theory. How shall we draw diverse media such as literature, inscriptions, and coinage into one analysis? How are we to imagine the connections between them? And if the literary text comes from a small, unorthodox movement like the churches whereas the archaeological evidence comes from the elite leaders of mainstream society, do the problems become insurmountable? I think the challenge can be met. This study has endeavored to do so using an amended phenomenological approach.

A second question about the discipline of New Testament studies has to do with imperialism. If the central figure of the Christian faith was executed on a sedition charge by the occupying forces of the Roman Empire, and if the early churches took root and grew in an imperialist setting, then why is there so little theorizing in biblical studies about empire and religion? This issue is especially acute in Revelation studies, dedicated to the explication of a text of divine judgment on the Roman Empire. Yet only a few New Testament studies ask about imperialism and religion, and those studies tend to be labeled "politicized."

I suspect that the reasons for this second problem are less defensible. This second question, like the first one, raises difficult conceptual issues. (What counts as religion? as politics? What is power? How do these operate in human communities?) But the second question raises another more disturbing issue. The countries where the discipline of New Testament studies has flourished during the last two centuries are precisely the countries that have claimed large sections of the earth as their empires.[13] Has the discipline of New Testament studies been a tool of imperialism? Or perhaps this line of questioning absolves the churches too readily. Maybe the churches defined both biblical studies and imperialism over a much longer period. In any event, it is inconvenient—to say the least—to explore these issues because the inquiry threatens to undermine fundamental structures of contemporary life in the west. Could the western academy withstand a studious attention to hegemony? Could Christian churches tolerate a thorough accounting of their abuses of power? Could the modern west survive if it attempted to atone for its domination? John would not dodge these questions.

My main reason, then, for framing this study for a not-necessarily-confessing audience is that Revelation provides an opportunity to fashion a strange vantage point from which to view ourselves as those confined not to the apocalyptic pattern but to various forms of modernity. John's Apocalypse is not the main source of the problems facing humanity. It is one of the texts that has been useful in the creation of these problems, but it is also a text from within the western tradition that challenges the very foundations of modernity. Religious criticism (of the academic variety) of the modern world becomes possible.

When we recognize our place among those who are to be interrogated by our own inquiries, the ancient materials present at least three challenges. One is in the definition of humanity. To an age that strives for individual freedom, John would respond that autonomy and self-gratification are not suitable human goals. Humanity, according to John's text, finds satisfaction in obedience and worship. The just community gathers around the one true authority. It is established by the righteous sufferer and maintained by adherence to that suffering. Or to cast this in the terms laid out in the first chapter of this book, the experience of ultimate signification is born in the encounter with suffering, oppression, and death. That experience of radical contingency has the potential for exposing mundane signification and for transcending it. It might be the basis for a new critical language that leads toward new forms of human society.

John and the practitioners of imperial cults would have agreed with this criticism of modernity. John and his opponents all testified that worship is a fundamental human activity, that personhood and community are unthinkable without obedience and sacrifice, that divine service is our highest goal. There was no argument among them on this point, only on the proper object(s) of worship.

In fact, most of humanity throughout most of history would agree that religiosity is a fundamental aspect of the human experience. Only recently in the modern west has this idea been abandoned at the intellectual and societal levels.[14] In this period the problems of violence, technology, ecology, and imperialism have been exacerbated so that our species might now extinguish itself, taking many other species along with us. These problems did not appear with modernity, but they have assumed monstrous proportions during this period. The ancient world, then, is agreed: we moderns have lost our moorings.

John would probably go beyond the mere affirmation of worship, however, and declare that the search for freedom is illusory. The choice facing humanity is not between freedom or bondage, he might say, but rather between servitude that builds community or servitude that destroys. That is why proper worship, and not just worship, was a central issue in Revelation. The service of empire is blasphemous and destructive.

We will seriously misunderstand Revelation on humanity and worship if we ignore the second challenge—the renunciation of force as the basis for community. The apocalyptic pattern has trained us to expect violence in victory, to turn to coercion to win a just war, to extol servitude for everyone except those who rule. Revelation will have none of this. The only real victory in Revelation is the sacrificial death of Jesus. All other victories are subsidiary and are won by stubborn confession of that death. Victory belongs to the victim. Even the final confrontation with the Beast is not really a battle: the name of the "warrior" is the Word of God; his only weapon is the sword of his mouth; no fighting is recounted; the only blood mentioned is the warrior's, shed before the confrontation.[15] Imperialism finally meets its match: resolute weakness.

The practitioners of imperial cults would not have agreed with John on this issue. Imperial cults were devoted to the worship of another authority, one that forced itself on the Roman Empire upon pain of death. In fact, Revelation's assessment of power is so contrary to normal human practice that most churches throughout history have not agreed with John either. The use of Revelation to promote Christian imperialism is located at this juncture: the proclamation of John's challenge to embrace servitude, accompanied by the rejection of John's challenge to renounce force. The celebration of God's weakness in Revelation is thereby transformed into a triumphalism of the worst sort, a parody of true worship, a just war. It is the genesis of the apocalyptic pattern.

No wonder John's third challenge is seldom recognized. Revelation's positions on humanity, society, and power are so foreign that few people bother to consider the epistemology that supported them. Revelation's knowledge of the world was not founded on anything resembling a western mode of rationality. It was a pneumatic epistemology, experienced in the spirit. It was based on the claim to an unmediated experience of the wholly other, on a confrontation with the complete contingency of human life. This experience of ultimate signification evoked awe and adoration. In its presence John collapsed as though dead. This revelation of the Other calls all human projects into question: empires, prophets, apostles; democracy, control of the means of production, free trade, human rights, self-determination. Even John's own narrative was vulnerable, so vulnerable that he resorted to curses at the end in a vain attempt to preserve the text from emendation or censorship.

To the world of modernities, then, Revelation challenges any epistemology that signifies only in the mode of western rationality. The loss of a mythic consciousness is the loss of a critical perspective, the loss of a religious criticism based on the sense of otherness engendered by signification and suffering. Mythic ways of knowing the world are not offered here as a panacea, for hegemonic discourses also employ myth to great effect. After all, both Revelation and Roman imperialism presupposed that communities are located in a mythic world that defines the order of life and the meaning of human suffering. The most destructive imperialisms in history, however, have been secular and have occurred during the last hundred years. That should concern us.

These three challenges are the reason for the ambiguous image embedded in this book's subtitle, "Reading Revelation in the Ruins." In this study of Revelation I have attempted to read the Apocalypse in the archaeological evidence, in the ancient ruins, in the remains of the Roman Empire. But the comparison of Revelation with these materials threatens the contemporary world of the interpreter as well. It would undermine the so-called civil society; it would attempt to reduce modernities to ruins. From this strange vantage point the text provides different ways of imagining our world, of illuminating its tragedies and of suggesting its potential, by confronting us with the meanings and ends of empires.

GLOSSARY

ACROLITHIC: Describes a statue with wooden torso and stone extremities (legs, arms, and head). The wooden torso made the statue lighter; it was overlaid with expensive materials.

ACROTERION: An ornament placed on the roof of a temple, either at the top of the gable or at the corners of the roof.

AEDICULA: A small decorative pavilion used in the ornamentation of a facade. Such facades often formed the background for a theater stage or for a monumental fountain. Used interchangeably with "tabernacle."

AGONOTHETE: An official who sponsored athletic or musical competitions.

AGORA: The market or forum of a city; one of the centers where commercial, administrative, and sacrificial activities would occur.

ALEITOURGESIA: The status of being exempt from liturgies for a particular period of time due to a person's other public service.

ANTAE: The ends of the long walls of a cella when these walls project beyond the shorter perpendicular walls of the cella.

ARCHITRAVE: The horizontal architectural element above the columns of a temple or other building.

ASIARCH: A male official in the province of Asia. The responsibilities of this office are disputed. The widely held view that the Asiarch was identical with the high priesthoods of Asia is rejected in this study, in favor of the view that an Asiarch was a special category of agonothete.

BOUKRANIA: Sculptural reliefs of the skulls of bulls, a common decorative motif in sacrificial settings.

BOULE: The city council.

BOULEUTERION: Meeting hall of a boule.

CELLA: The main building of a temple. The cella housed the statue of the deity and was the deity's dwelling place.

CHILIARCH: A military commander.

CHITON: A simple tunic worn by men or women in the Roman imperial period. It was pulled on over the head and gathered at the waist with a belt.

CHRYSELEPHANTINE STATUE: A statue overlaid with gold and ivory.

CISTOPHOROI: In the Roman imperial period, silver coins minted by the koinon of Asia.

CREPIDOMA: The foundation platform upon which a temple was built.

CRYPTOPORTICUS: A vaulted passage that is underground or hidden within the substructure of a building.

CUIRASS: Military breastplate; often used for statues of emperors.

CULT: An institution or group of institutions dedicated to sacrificial activity. This usage should not be confused with modern sociological or popular definitions of the term "cult."

DEUTEROPAULINE EPISTLES: 2 Thessalonians, Colossians, and Ephesians. The Pauline authorship of these texts is debated.

DIVUS: Latin term for a divinized emperor. There was no equivalent term in Greek.

ENGAGED COLUMN: A stone surface carved so that the semicircular shape of half a column protrudes from the surface.

ENGAGED STATUE: A stone surface carved so that part of a statue protrudes from the surface.

EPHEBE: A young male in his late teens from an aristocratic family, who was being educated for civic leadership.

EPONYMOUS: An eponymous office is one used in inscriptions to provide the date of an event.

ESCHATON: The period after the resurrection and judgment in certain forms of Jewish or Christian eschatology.

ETHNOS: A national group. The plural sometimes means "Gentiles" in Jewish texts.

EXEDRA: A concave area set back in a wall. It is similar to an apse but is larger and usually not covered.

FINDSPOT: The precise location where an artifact was discovered. This may be close to or distant from the place where an artifact was orginally used.

GRAMMATEUS: The highest municipal official, who normally served for a term of one year.

GYMNASIARCH: An official charged with providing for the upkeep of a gymnasium for a specific period of time.

HEROON: Shrine for the worship of a hero.

HEXASTYLE: A style of temple with six columns in front of the cella.

HIEROPHANT: One of the major leaders in mystery cult rituals. Responsibilities would have included sacred actions, speaking, or the revelation of sacred objects.

HIMATION: A cloak worn by men or women during the Roman imperial period. A himation could be draped around the torso and arms in several ways and was often worn over a chiton.

IN SITU: Refers to artifacts found exactly where they were used in antiquity.

INTERCOLUMNIATION: The distance between two columns in a colonnade. The distance is measured from the center of the columns.

KOINON: The council of a province. One of the duties of a koinon was oversight of provincial imperial cults.

LIBERATION THEOLOGY: A form of Christian theology that began in the late 1960s in Central America and has since been embraced in several areas of the world. It is characterized by a strong concern for justice and sometimes combines a Christian commitment with a Marxist analysis of society and economy.

LITURGY: A form of public service in Greek cities that especially involved financial donations to support a variety of specific activities, such as choruses for festivals, athletic games, upkeep of gymnasia, and so forth. Liturgies are sometimes indistinguishable from magistracies.

MAGISTRACY: A form of public service in Greek cities that especially involved personal effort, such as serving as a city official. A magistrate normally paid for some or all of the expenses associated with the office, but there was often a civic budget that underwrote costs. Magistracies are sometimes indistinguishable from liturgies.

NEOKOROS: An official with special responsibilities for the maintenance of a sacred precinct. Beginning in the late first century CE, the term could also be used to describe a city with a provincial imperial cult temple.

NEOPOIOS: A member of a group of neopoioi who made administrative decisions concerning the facilities and holdings of a temple.

OBVERSE: The side of a coin placed into an engraved template before being struck on the other side (i.e., on the reverse). The obverse normally was adorned by the image of a deity or a member of the imperial family.

ORTHOSTAT: A stone slab placed upright on one of the thin edges, usually at floor level.

PALAESTRA: A training facility for the body and mind. These were usually smaller than gymnasia and included rooms of various sizes around a colonnaded courtyard.

PASTORAL EPISTLES: 1–2 Timothy and Titus. These are generally thought to have been written in Paul's name after his death by a later admirer or disciple.

PENTAETERIC FESTIVAL: A festival held every four years, that is, in the fifth year since the previous festival.

PERIPTERAL: A temple design in which there is a colonnade on all four sides of the cella.

PERISTYLE: An outdoor courtyard or garden that is surrounded on all sides by colonnaded halls.

PEPLOS: A garment worn by women. It consisted of a large rectangle of cloth, folded in half parallel to the body on one side. Large pins were used to fasten the two halves of the cloth above the shoulders, and a belt gathered the robe at the waist.

PODIUM TEMPLE: A temple on a raised base having steps only on the front side.

PROPYLON: A large or monumental gate leading into an enclosed area.

PROSTYLE: A temple with columns in front of the cella.

PRYTANEION: Official building for the prytanis of a city, town, village, or sanctuary.

PRYTANIS: A civic or sanctuary official, usually elected annually. The functions varied widely from place to place. They often included responsibilities for rituals, for government, or for hosting visiting dignitaries.

PSEUDODIPTERAL: Describes a temple that has a single colonnade on all four sides that is made to appear as though it had a double colonnade.

REVERSE: The side of a coin that was struck after the blank coin was placed into an engraved template. A wide range of designs adorned reverses. See obverse.

REVETMENT: Stone panelling, usually of marble, that covered a wall made of less expensive material.

SCENAE FRONS: The facade that defined the back of a stage in the interior of a theater or odeion.

SCENE BUILDING: The building behind the scenae frons, hidden from the view of those seated in the theater or odeion.

SEBASTOLOGOS: An official who delivered eulogies in praise of the emperor.

SEBASTONEOS: Meaning unknown.

SEBASTOPHANT: An imperial cult official similar to a hierophant. Responsibilities would have included sacred actions, speaking, or the revelation of sacred objects.

SEPTUAGINT: The Greek translation of Jewish scriptures. LXX is the standard abbreviation.

SISTRUM: A small percussion instrument like a rattle that was used in the worship of Isis.

STEREOBATE: The hidden foundations of a building.

STEPHANEPHOROS: Title of certain officials who were also granted the privilege of wearing a crown.

STOA: A hall with a colonnade along one long side. Such halls were one to three stories high and often incorporated a series of small rooms at the back of the hall, opposite the colonnade.

STRATEGOS: A leader or commander in the military; or, a high municipal magistracy, especially in the cities of western Asia Minor.

STYLOBATE: The top of a crepidoma.

SYNOECISM: The consolidation of small neighboring communities to form one larger town or city.

TABERNACLE: A small decorative pavilion used in the ornamentation of a facade. Such facades often formed the background for a theater stage or for a monumental fountain. Used interchangeably with "aedicula."

TEMENOS: The precincts of a temple or other sacred site.

TETRAPROSTYLE: Describes a temple with four columns in front of the cella. Tetraprostyle temples sometimes have a peripteral colonnade that stands in front of these four columns and continues on around the whole temple.

THEOLOGOS: An official who delivered sermons or encomia, praising the deity or deities for whom the rituals were performed.

THIASOS: A group dedicated to the worship of a particular deity or group of deities.

YHWH: The four main letters from the personal name of the god of Israel; also called the Tetragramaton. It has become customary to refrain from writing or pronouncing the full name out of reverence.

NOTES

1. Religious Criticism

1. For examples of studies about several regions using a wide variety of methods, see Geertz 1980; Valeri 1985; Hardacre 1989; and Olupona 1991.

2. I will not invest space in a recitation of the history of the interpretation of imperial cults, for a good deal of that history is not particularly enlightening. Price 1984b constituted a fundamental turning point in the interpretation of imperial cults. He also provided a helpful summary of some of the problems (11–19).

3. Although the use of male pronouns for generic concepts is dated, I have chosen to retain them in quotations without the conventional "[sic]." Grammar and the politics of gender are important issues, but they are not my main concern in this study.

4. Cantwell Smith 1963:38. Pagan and early Christian authors did not use the Latin *religio* to signify a system of doctrine, a set of practices, or institutional considerations. They shared a rough consensus of *religio* as a personal encounter with the transcendent. During the Middle Ages *religio* was not a prominent term. The notion of a dynamic response to the living God lived on instead in the concept of "faith." When *religio* does appear in medieval texts, it tends to take on the meaning of rites, especially those associated with the monastic life (1963:19–32).

5. Cantwell Smith 1963:42.

6. Cantwell Smith 1963:44.

7. Cantwell Smith 1963:47.

8. Cantwell Smith 1963:44–48.

9. Cantwell Smith 1963:48–50. The first of the four meanings comes closest to Smith's definition of "faith."

10. Cantwell Smith 1963:51. Smith proposed that we examine religion in terms of two categories: the cumulative tradition and faith; cf. Cantwell Smith 1963:154–92; 1979:3–19. I think his critique of the intellectual history is more helpful than this proposal, at least in terms of its potential for research on historical topics like the Roman Empire.

11. Eliade 1965:95–102.

12. For example, the final lines of 1965:74.

13. Eliade 1965:91–92.

14. Eliade 1965:12–20.

15. Eliade 1965:21–48. In an archaic social system, according to Eliade, there are no profane actions. Any action whose connection with the celestial archetypes is broken becomes meaningless and superfluous. Only modern societies can conceive of profane actions; p. 28.

16. Eliade 1965:21.

17. Eliade 1965:35.

18. Eliade 1965:51–92.

19. Eliade 1965:154.

20. Eliade 1965:148.

21. Eliade 1965:149.

22. Eliade 1965:150–51.

23. Eliade 1965:152 n. 11.

24. Long 1986:58.

25. The contrast with Cantwell Smith here is only partial. Smith's notion of faith is personal but not individualistic. He emphasized that religious studies deals with persons and their responses to the transcendent but also examines the cumulative historical traditions within which those persons are located.

26. Long 1986:24.

27. Long 1986:97.

28. For an analysis of Long's work, see Carrasco 1991.

29. Long 1986:68–71.

30. Long 1986:71.

31. Long 1986:5.

32. The term is coined in response to Said's advocacy of "secular criticism." See n. 105.

33. These two forms of religious criticism—one by the practitioner and another by the academician—are different in character. The practitioner's critical perspective grows out of a participant's experience in a particular religious tradition. Academic religious criticism is based on the nature of its subject matter (the study of religion) and raises critical questions about the academy, its disciplines, and society.

34. Long 1986:73.

35. Long 1986:79–96.

36. Long 1986:6.

37. Long 1986:162.

38. Long 1986:163.

39. Long 1986:164–71.

40. Segal 1987 called this an unanswered question in Long's work.

41. Long 1986:138, 139.

42. It would be unfair to compare them without recognizing that their projects had different agendas that affect their applicability to this study. Long's primary concern for religion since contact limits its usefulness for earlier periods. Eliade's phenomenology is too general

for the kind of analysis I am pursuing. Smith's "cumulative tradition" shows some promise on historical topics, but the relationship between faith and the tradition is ambiguous when dealing with modern topics. When dealing with ancient topics, I fear the problems would multiply.

43. Sullivan studied with Eliade and later taught at the University of Chicago. I find his morphology of religious life more convincing than Eliade's patterns in religion because it is more systematic and because Sullivan's analysis is historically defined and geographically circumscribed.

44. Sullivan 1988:2–9. Cf. Long 1986:79–96.

45. Sullivan 1988:22.

46. Sullivan also used the terms beginnings, creation, and archaeology for this category. I prefer cosmogony because it avoids confusion: in this study archaeology is used often in a very different way, and creation might suggest the biblical account in Genesis.

47. Sullivan's term for this is actually "the human condition," covering the human constitution, human growth and decay, and religious specialists. I have tried to simplify this and make it more descriptive by using "human maturation" for this category.

48. Sullivan 1988:22. A review of the secondary literature on myth is beyond the scope of this study. Edmunds 1990 provides a useful survey of the major interpretive traditions.

49. Sullivan 1988:620.

50. Sullivan 1988:24–110, 615–23.

51. Sullivan 1988:111–52, 623–25.

52. Sullivan 1988:634.

53. Sullivan 1988:153–227, 625–34.

54. Sullivan 1988:230–385, 634–60.

55. This generic use of the term should not be confused with technical uses of "eschatology" in discussions about Christian theology.

56. Sullivan 1988:660–61.

57. Sullivan 1988:549–50.

58. Sullivan 1988:467–614, 660–82.

59. Sullivan 1988:614.

60. See n. 2.

61. J. Smith 1978:292–94.

62. Capps 1995:153–56.

63. Sullivan dealt with these issues especially in his discussion of eschatology, where he described how ideas about the end have been used by South Americans against colonial powers and against Enlightenment sciences; see esp. pp. 2–9, 549–614, 672–82.

64. Said 1993:194.

65. The use of technical terms like "decolonization" and "postcolonial" is not intended to suggest that colonization has ended or that its influence has disappeared.

66. Ahmad 1995:12–28.

67. Seidman 1996:314.

68. Said 1978a:3.

69. Said 1978a:3. One crucial criticism of Said's book was that he had indulged in the kind of academic practice he denounced. Reviewers faulted him for simply responding to the imperialist metanarrative of Orientalism with a different metanarrative, rather than building a new kind of analysis. See Clifford 1988:271.

70. Williams and Chrisman 1993 provide a helpful selection of important texts in this tradition.

71. These three represent distinctive orientations. Said tends to draw eclectically from a range of oppositional theorists such as Fanon, Foucault, and Gramsci. Spivak is more closely

aligned with Derrida and poststructural theory. Bhabha brings expertise in psychology to his analyses.

72. Some (e.g., Ashcroft et al. 1989; Mohanram and Rajan 1996) would narrow the scope of postcolonial literature or theory to cover only the cultures and histories of those areas that were part of the British Empire.

73. Said 1993:321.

74. So Ahmad 1992:195–97.

75. Ashcroft et al. 1989:172–73.

76. The problems and potential for Roman studies are explored in Mattingly 1997. For the area of biblical studies, see Donaldson 1996.

77. Among the features that distinguish modern imperialism are the following: a propensity for dominating distant lands without necessarily ruling adjacent territories; enhanced technologies of travel, communication, and warfare (1993:282–310); the cultural invasion of the provinces by the dominant power (1993:221); and the existence of a developing global capitalist economy. Accompanying this form of imperialism is a discourse that assumes the authority of the western observer; a hierarchy of spaces focused on European centrality; and the relegation of the non-European to a secondary racial, cultural, or ontological status (1993:58–59).

78. Said 1993:9.

79. "Peripheral" is not primarily a geographic designation. Geographic distance from the imperial center is only one of many factors that come into play. The province of Asia was more closely aligned with Roman authority than were some other areas geographically closer to Rome.

80. Foucault 1972:17.

81. See for example Said 1978a:3, 272–74. Ahmad 1992:167 criticized Said vehemently for invoking Foucault's carefully constructed system while running roughshod over the finely honed distinctions.

82. For instance, the relationships of discourse, vocabulary, and figures/tropes (Said 1978a:71).

83. Gane and Johnson 1993:9. In the same volume, Bevis et al. (1993:208–9) argue that Foucault began to valorize the role of the subject more highly in his later writings.

84. Said 1978b; 1983:14–16.

85. Said 1983:243–45. The same sort of criticism could be leveled against Said's project, which is based primarily on studies in comparative literature.

86. Said 1993:278. See Spanos 1996:147 for a defense of Foucault against Said's accusations.

87. Said 1983:245. His criticism was not reserved for followers of Foucault. "As for intellectuals whose charge includes values and principles—literary, philosophical, historical specialists—the American university, with its munificence, utopian sanctuary, and remarkable diversity, has defanged them. Jargons of an almost unimaginable rebarbativeness dominate their styles. Cults like post-modernism, discourse analysis, New Historicism, deconstruction, neo-pragmatism transport them into the country of the blue; an astonishing sense of weightlessness with regard to the gravity of history and individual responsibility fritters away attention to public matters, and to public discourse. The result is a kind of floundering about that is most dispiriting to witness, even as the society as a whole drifts without direction or coherence" (1993:303).

88. Said 1993:167–68; Gallagher 1994:14.

89. Said 1983:14–16.

90. Prakash 1995:203.

91. Said 1993:xxiii. Due to the nature of my investigation, I take "culture" to be a broader phenomenon than does Said in *Culture and Imperialism*. I do not restrict the term primarily to literature and the arts as he does. Rather, culture is used either for the worldview

of a community or for the set of relations and practices generally acceptable in a given community. Culture refers to a domain of community life that is not static; on the contrary, it is continually evolving. The changes are sometimes accidental and sometimes intentional but never unequivocal. In Friesen 1996 I analyzed an example of the evolving nature of culture and its complex affiliations with the material and affective aspects of life in a colonial setting.

92. Said 1993:109.

93. Said 1993:xxv, 66.

94. Said 1993:194.

95. WWWebster Dictionary. Available http://www.m-w.com/dictionary.htm, May 28, 1999.

96. Said 1993:318.

97. Said 1993:xxiv.

98. Said 1993:318.

99. Said 1993:xxv, 259, 318.

100. As this statement suggests, Said expressed deep ambivalence toward postmodernism, which he characterized as a luxury of western intellectuals. The issue of the relationship between postmodernism and postcolonial theory is disputed. For a summary, see Williams and Chrisman 1993:13.

101. Gellner 1993. Several of Gellner's other criticisms are not quite so germane. They are directed more toward the positions that Said staked out earlier in *Orientalism* but abandoned by the time he wrote *Culture and Imperialism*.

102. Clifford 1988:268–71, in a review of *Orientalism*.

103. Ahmad 1992:195–97.

104. Wood 1994:45.

105. The title of this chapter, "Religious Criticism," comes from my argument with Said's advocacy of "secular criticism." According to Said, secular criticism eschews abstractions and denounces appeals to mystical authority. He accused many literary critics of ignoring the political and economic settings of texts and of mystifying the social relations of literature. Such mystification reminded Said of religious practices, which he normally assesses in a negative fashion; Said 1983:3–25, 290–91. The first part of this chapter outlines a different understanding of religion. Religious criticism is founded on the conclusion that a mythic consciousness can be the source of mystification or of critical thought, depending on the particular circumstances.

2. *Provincial Imperial Cults of Asia Under Augustus and Tiberius*

1. In this study, "cult" refers to an institution or cluster of institutions dedicated to sacrificial activities. It should not be confused with the modern sociological usage of the term "cult," which is used for small, deviant religious organizations.

2. Dio Cassius 51.20.6–9. Translation adapted from Loeb.

3. The lack of supporting evidence raises some suspicions about the reliability of Dio on this point, but it is highly unlikely that he would devise such an unusual arrangement.

4. For a plan of Ephesos, see fig. 3.3.

5. A Greek design would normally include monumental steps on all sides of the shrine, and the building would be placed near the center of the courtyard. Alzinger 1972–75:249–53; Hänlein–Schäfer 1985:264–65; Jobst 1980:253–56, 258.

6. Scherrer 1989:98–101 rejected the identification, favoring instead the temple foundations near the center of the Ephesian upper agora. See chapter 5.

7. For example, a copy of a koinon decree found in Hypaipa and dated 2 BCE–14 CE referred to an official from this temple as high priest "of goddess Rome and of Emperor

Augustus, son of god;" *IvE* 7,2.3825 l. 11–13 (= *IGR* 4.1611). In Greek, the name Augustus is rendered as Sebastos. Throughout this study, I attempt to use Sebastos whenever possible to reflect the Greek as accurately as possible. Since the Latin Augustus is so established in English practice, however, I make an exception and use the Latin form for the name of the first emperor. In the names of other emperors, Sebastos is used in this study as the transliteration of that Greek name. Although this sometimes sounds odd in English, I am willing to risk some dissonance to preserve distinctions made in the ancient sources. I also refer to the goddess as "Rome" rather than the traditional "Roma" to reflect in English the fact that the city and the goddess shared the identical form of the name in Greek.

8. *IGR* 4.39a l. 12 (= *IG* 12,2.58 and *OGIS* 456): [ἐν τῷ ναῷ τῳ κατασ]κευαζομένῳ α[ὐ]τῷ ὑπὸ τῆς Ἀσίας ἐν Περγάμῳ.

9. Tacitus *An.* 4.37; Dio 51.20.7 (quoted previously).

10. Suetonius *Aug.* 52 reports that Augustus's policy was to refuse cultic honors for himself unless Rome was included, but that general statement may or may not apply to the first known request of this sort.

11. Bowersock 1965:115.

12. Dio is ambiguous here: Augustus "allowed" these to be built, but he "ordered" their use by Romans living in the provinces.

13. For a detailed discussion of the possible initiatives and emendations in this process, see Habicht 1973:55–64.

14. Price 1984b:75.

15. A description and references regarding this historical setting can be found in Knibbe 1980:756.

16. Some of the issues are reflected in texts like Plutarch *Ant.* 24.4; 26.5; 54.9; 60.3–5.

17. Price 1984a:83–84.

18. Habicht 1973:59.

19. Mellor 1975:13–26, 195–98.

20. Habicht 1973:61 noted a pentaeteric festival (one held every four years) for Q. Mucius Scaevola, proconsul in 94/93. The attempt to found similar games for a successor (L. Valerius Flaccus) was unsuccessful.

21. Games for C. Marcius Censorinus, *CIG* 2698b.

22. *Kl.P.* 5.143 #30.

23. Robert and Robert 1948:39–42.

24. *IGR* 4.433. This was probably due to his restoration of the Asklepieion's right of asylum.

25. *IvE* 3.702; 7,1.3066. Both priests of this cult also served as prytanis, suggesting that the cult of Rome and Isauricus was located near the foundations tentatively identified as the site of the temenos of Rome and Julius. It is also possible that the double temenos was dedicated to the proconsul rather than to Caesar.

26. Price 1984b:51.

27. Sutherland 1970:36, 103; pl. 12–14. *RPC* 1,1.2216–2220 (pl. 98–99).

28. Pick 1929:30; Price 1984b:178 n. 37.

29. *BM Mysia* 139 #242, pl. 28.

30. *BM Mysia* 140 #256, pl. 28; *RPC* 1,1.2369 (pl. 105); ca. 30 CE with Augustus referred to as ΘΕΟΝ ΣΕΒΑΣΤΟΝ, "god Sebastos/Augustus."

31. *RPC* 1,1.2372 (pl. 105).

32. *BMCRE* 1.196 #228, pl. 34; *RPC* 1,1.2221 (pl. 99). See also *BMCRE* 2.96 #449, pl. 43 (silver tetradrachma, mint unknown, reign of Vespasian). *BMCRE* 3.12 #79, pl. 3 (silver tetradrachma, reign of Nerva) has a similar image with small differences in the statue of Augustus.

33. Deininger 1965:41–50 has been the most influential recent proponent of the identification theory, and he is followed by most modern writers. Magie 1950:449–50 concluded that Asiarchs were municipal officials in charge of festivals and competitions. Kearsley has written several articles arguing that the Asiarchate involved municipal governance; her 1996 article provides entry into her writing on the subject. Friesen 1999 supports the view of Magie. See also http://www.missouri.edu/~religsf/officials.html.

34. On provincial high priestesses, pp. 68–70.

35. For the evolution of this office, see Friesen 1993:49–53. The term came to have a technical meaning in provincial imperial cults late in the first century CE; see chapter 3.

36. *IGR* 4.454.

37. Minor variations include "the great Sebasta Romaia" (*IGR* 4.498, Pergamon), the "Romaia Sebasta" (*OGIS* 458 l. 58–59, 9 BCE), and "the Romaia Sebasta established by the koinon of Asia in Pergamon" (*IGR* 4.1064 = *SIG* 3.1065, Kos, 37–41 CE).

38. Magie 1950:1297 n. 57.

39. See chapters 4–5.

40. Price 1984a:84–85.

41. E.g., *Sardis* 7,1.8 l. 75–76, 83–84, and 100–1 (koinon decrees from 4, 3, and 2 BCE).

42. E.g., *IGR* 4.975 (Samos), though this may be later than 14 CE. *IGR* 4.1608 uses θεός for Augustus in the Claudian period.

43. Most recently, Herz 1992:110–12.

44. *Sardis* 7,1.8 l. 75–82, 83–88, and 99–119.

45. *OGIS* 458 l. 3–30 (= IvPr 105). Parts of this translation were adapted from Johnson et al. 1961:119; Lewis 1974:11–12; and Price 1984b:55.

46. Magie 1950:480–81.

47. *OGIS* 458 l. 30–71. The rest of the inscription (l. 71–84) gives further instructions on the institution of the new calendar, rules for intercalation, etc. My translation adapts some parts from Lewis and Reinhold 1955:64–65; Lewis 1974:12–13; and Price 1984b:54.

48. The Macedonian calendar was used as the standard; Bickerman 1980:47–51.

49. *IvPr* 105 is the largest existing section.

50. Robert 1949.

51. Magie 1950:1343 n. 40 for examples.

52. Sullivan 1988:634.

53. Tacitus *An.* 4.15.

54. Tacitus *An.* 3.66–69.

55. Tacitus *An.* 4.15. Translation adapted from Hadas 1942:153.

56. The inclusion of Livia is left unexplained in the text. Her ties both to Augustus and to Tiberius made her an important figure to be considered, even though there is no evidence she played a role in these particular trials.

57. Brunt 1961:217, 220, 224–25.

58. Tacitus *An.* 4.37–38. Suetonius *Tib.* 3.26 overlooked the early decision of Tiberius in favor of Asia's second provincial temple and presented Tiberius's later position of disallowing divine honors as his general policy.

59. Tacitus *An.* 4.55–56.

60. Halikarnassos was also rejected, in spite of its claim to be free of earthquakes.

3. Provincial Cults from Gaius to Domitian

1. Dio 59.28.1. Gaius reigned from 37 to 41 CE. He is more familiarly known by the name Caligula.

2. Robert 1949:206.

3. Herrmann 1989:193–94 understood this section to mean that Capito served as high priest of the provincial temple of Gaius and as high priest in another provincial imperial temple (either at Pergamon or at Smyrna) in the same year. It is much more likely that the section means that Capito's high priesthood of Gaius in Miletos was his third term of service as high priest of Asia because there are no other known examples of someone elected to two different provincial high priesthoods in one year. For the standard conventions in recording high priestly service, see the chart in Friesen 1993:172–88. More recent information is available on the World Wide Web at http://www.missouri.edu/~religsf/officials.html.

4. *PW* 16:2433–39; *Kl.P.* 4:56–57.

5. Robert 1949:212–38.

6. Robert 1949:210; Pleket 1965:340.

7. Dio 59.28.1. Translation adapted from Loeb.

8. Haussoullier 1902:272–79.

9. Herrmann 1989:193–96.

10. Suetonius *Gaius* 4.21–22.

11. Tacitus *Hist.* 5.9.

12. Friesen 1993:79–81; Campanile 1994:151.

13. *Sardis* 7,1.8 l. 75–76, 83–84, 89–90, 99–101.

14. *BM Lydia* 251 #104–105 (Sardis); *IvPr* 105 l. 31, 78–79; *IvE* 7,2.3825 (Hypaipa).

15. *IvE* 7,2.3801 II l. 4–5: [τοῦ ἀρχιερέως τῆς Ἀσί]ας κτλ. reconstructed in a standard koinon formula.

16. *IvE* 1,1.17 l. 70–71. The title is almost complete even though the context is severely damaged.

17. Two inscriptions could possibly be earlier than the 40s of the first century CE but are probably later. *IvE* 4.1393 uses the title (the reconstructed lacuna is reliable) but can be dated only between 14 CE and about 114 CE. *IGR* 4.1524 (Sardis) was inscribed no earlier than 26 CE and no later than about 120 CE.

18. E.g., *IvE* 4.1393; *IGR* 4.577 (Aizanoi), 1238 (Thyatira); *AvP* 8,3.30. A variation on the old title for the Pergamene official is still used in *AE* 1994:501 #1643 (45–54 CE), but it eventually disappears from the archaeological record.

19. *PW* 1896 2:479–81.

20. Price 1984b:57–59, 245–48.

21. *IvMag* 158 l. 5–6.

22. For a discussion of the problems, see Friesen 1993:86–87.

23. κα[ὶ θεᾶς Ἀγριπ]πείνης [μητ]ρος διὰ (β)[ίου?]. These offices are listed in *IvMag* 158 l. 7–11.

24. Herz 1992:103–4.

25. *OCD* "Iulia Agrippina;" *Kl.P.* 1.148 #2–3; Corbier 1995:187–92.

26. Deininger 1965:41, 154; Rossner 1974:102.

27. Kearsley 1986.

28. Wörrle 1992:369–70; Bremen 1996:114–41.

29. For a searchable database of the known references to high priestesses of Asia, see http://www.missouri.edu/~religsf/officials.html.

30. It is impossible to know how many statue bases once occupied the precincts. For the purposes of estimation, it is probable that the extant sample is somewhere between 10%–50% of the statues commissioned by the cities. If the 13 inscriptions represent half the original total, then there would have been around 25. If the 13 represent about 10% of the original total, which I think is closer to the actual situation, we would have to imagine 125–150 statues adorning the precincts.

31. *IvE* 2.232–32a (Aizanoi), 234 (Keretapa); 235 (Klazomenai); 238 (Silandos); 239 (Teos); 240 (Kyme); 241 (Tmolos); 242 (fragment, city unknown); 5.1498 (Makedones Hyrkanioi); 6.2048 (Synaos).

32. *IvE* 2.233 (Aphrodisias); 237 (Stratonikeia).

33. *IvE* 2.233. The published transcription has 2½ lines erased at the end. Personal examination of the statue base indicated that 3½ lines had been erased. See also Reynolds 1982:167–68 #42.

34. The translation "on the occasion of" assumes a dative of cause, due to the analogy of similar inscriptions. My addition "(the dedication of)" is based on similar groups of dedicatory inscriptions. The reasons are laid out in Friesen 1993:42–44.

35. A general date of 88–91 is indicated by the terms of service of the proconsuls and provincial high priests in the inscriptions. The specific date 89/90 is based on (1) the clustering of eight or nine of the thirteen inscriptions at this time and (2) the inclusion of the neokoros of the temple in the two inscriptions from 90/91. For details, see Friesen 1993:44–49.

36. *IvE* 2.241, discussed in chapter 4.

37. *IvSt* 2,1.1008.

38. Keil 1919:118 #12.

39. The statue is discussed later in this chapter.

40. Cf. Corbier 1995.

41. E.g., *BM Ionia* 91 #305 (reign of Caracalla).

42. For examples and elaboration, see Friesen 1993:39.

43. Friesen 1993:57–58.

44. See Friesen 1995:236–45 on the relation of the title neokoros to the phenomenon of city titles in the eastern Mediterranean. The emergence of the technical term neokoros was a turning point in the public discourse of the eastern empire.

45. Jones 1971:40–64.

46. Pliny, *Ep.* 10.93.

47. Keil 1932:53–61.

48. Trell 1945:58–59.

49. Bammer 1972–75:386–89 suggested that the statue may have stood outside in the precincts, but this is highly unlikely. The statue was acrolithic, having marble extremities and a wooden torso, so it would have deteriorated rapidly if exposed to the elements. It is also clear that the statue was displayed next to a wall because the back of the head was hollowed out to decrease its weight.

50. Keil 1932:59–60. Inan and Rosenbaum 1966:67 and pl. 16 #1 accepted the identification as Domitian.

51. Daltrop et al. 1966:26, 38, 86, and pl. 15b.

52. Inan and Rosenbaum 1966:67.

53. Daltrop et al. 1966:26.

54. Vetters 1972–75:311–15; Thür 1985:184.

55. Bammer 1985:124–25.

56. Friesen 1993:72–73.

57. *IvSm* 2,1.635; *IGR* 4.824.

58. Moretti 1953:174–79 #65; and 1954.

59. IvI 1.108.

60. Moretti 1953:181–83 #66.

61. Lammer 1967:3–11; Knibbe 1980:775, 785. For a more detailed examination of these games, see Friesen 1993:114–41, esp. 117–121.

62. IGR 4.336; Stiller 1895; Price 1984b:252 #20. The interpretation of the evidence

is discussed in Raeck 1993 and Schowalter 1998. The temple has been partially restored at the top of the Pergamene akropolis; Nohlen 1997.

63. Bonz 1998:269; Friesen 1995:235–36.

64. Price 1984b:126–32; Friesen 1995:236–39.

4. Municipal Imperial Cults: A Survey

1. *IGR* 4.454 (Pergamon).

2. Robert 1949:209. The inscription also lists representatives of the districts of the province who served as neopoioi. This suggests an intermediate level of organization—district participation—between that of the city and that of the province for which there is little or no evidence beyond this inscription.

3. *IvE* 2.237, 241 (90/91 CE).

4. *IGR* 4.454.

5. E.g., Herz 1992:110–12.

6. *IGR* 4.1756 = *Sardis* 7,1.8.

7. Lines 75, 83–84, 89–90; the agonothesia is mentioned in l. 99–101.

8. G. Julius Pardala: *IGR* 4.1611 and *IvE* 7,2.3825 l. 9–11 (Hypaipa, late Augustan).

9. Included here are the 13 formulaic Ephesian inscriptions discussed in the previous chapter, as well as one inscription commissioned by Philadelphia, which uses a different text. The Philadelphia text may also have been produced for the dedication of the temple because it uses some similar phrases, but it focuses more on the relationship between the two cities.

10. One extant inscription does not name an individual who undertook this responsibility; *IvE* 2.237 (Stratonikeia).

11. I do not accept the identification of Asiarchs and provincial high priests. See Friesen 1999 for the arguments.

12. Habicht 1973:45.

13. *IGR* 4.39 = *OGIS* 456 = *IG* 12.2.58. The inscription can be dated in the period 27–11 BCE. The dissemination of the decree is mentioned in column a, lines 11–14; and b l. 18–23.

14. The inscription is damaged and it is unclear whether a temple was also built.

15. *IvE* 2.241 l. 11–14. The wording is somewhat ambiguous regarding the length of the priesthood. The neokoria was certainly lifelong, but the priesthood may have been for a shorter period. Since the phrase διὰ βίου is so far removed from both titles, it seems more likely that "for life" refers to both offices, just as the name of the institution does.

16. The language of divinization is unusually restrained for a municipal cult, without the use of θεός or ἱερός. This variation from normal municipal cult terminology may be due to the fact that the inscription was destined for display in a provincial temple context, and so provincial cult expectations prevailed.

17. *IvE* 2.232, 232a, 233, 238. In Friesen 1993:137–40, I argued that the reason for these four long erasures (and the erasure in *IvE* 7,1.3005) was that they referred to Ephesian Olympic games in honor of Domitian. These games would have been discontinued and expunged from the public record after his assassination.

18. E.g., *IGR* 4.1581 (Teos); 4.1756 (Sardis).

19. Herrmann 1960:82 #2, and *IGR* 4.977 (Samos).

20. It is possible in this case that Rome was included in the temple but not mentioned in the inscription; Tuchelt 1975:97–98 and n. 33.

21. Herrmann 1960:70–82. The decree is probably datable to the year 6/5 BCE. The reference to the neopoioi of Augustus is probably a reference to the temple of Rome and Augustus rather than to a separate temple of Augustus.

22. Maiuri 1925:237 #680.

23. *BM Phrygia* 229 #11 and pl. 29.4; *CollWadd* 6131.

24. *Mionnet* 4.614–15.

25. *Mionnet* 4.614 portrays the same temple on the obverse but names Agrippina in the inscription: [ΑΓΡΙΠ]ΠΕΙΝΗ.ΣΕΒ[ΑΣΤΗ].

26. Brandis 1896: 479–81; Price 1984b:57–59, 245–48.

27. *BM Phrygia* 307 #181–82; *CollWadd* 6275.

28. *BM Phrygia* 308 #187–88; *CollWadd* 6278–79.

29. *BM Phrygia* 307 #185 and pl. 37.6.

30. The same temple is perhaps portrayed during the Trajanic period; *Mionnet Sup* 7.585 no. 448; *Copenhagen* 573. A hexastyle temple appears on later Laodikeian coins; Imhoof-Blumer 1901–02:273 #49; *CollWadd* 6305, under Caracalla. This could be a representation of the same temple, but there are important differences in the imagery. The imperial statue is togate, not in military garb. Also, the coin indicates that the city is neokorate, and so one would expect a provincial temple on this coin. It is possible that the municipal temple was used as the location for the provincial cult, but it seems more likely that a new temple would have been constructed.

31. *IGR* 4.464 l. 3–6: ἱέρειαν γ[ενομένην] τῆς Νικηφόρου καὶ Πολιάδος ['Αθηνᾶς καὶ 'Ιουλίας συνθρόνου, νέας Νικη[φόρου, Γερμα]νικοῦ Καίσαρος θυγατρὸς.

32. Suet. *Cl* 1.6; 3.2.

33. Tact. *An.* 4.3, 8–10

34. Suet. *Tib* 62.1. Corbier 1995: esp. 182–84, 188, 191.

35. It is possible that sacrifices would have been offered *to* Athena *on behalf of* Livilla; Price 1984b:216–20; Friesen 1993:148–50. In this case, however, such a distinction is unlikely because Livilla was συνθρόνου, "enthroned with," Athena.

36. Oster 1990:1671–73.

37. *IvE* 1,1.10 l. 28–29.

38. For general background, see Merkelbach 1980, Keil 1939, and Oster 1990:1688–91. Knibbe 1981 is a comprehensive analysis of the epigraphic evidence related to the prytaneion and draws out implications for the development of the religious institutions involved. Friesen f.c. provides slides and detailed descriptive text for the complex.

39. *IvE* 4.1058, 1060, 1067, 1070a, 1071. In some cases, other deities were also named in the prayers.

40. *IvE* 2.213. Adapted from Lewis 1974:128 B.

41. Pleket 1965. See chapter 6.

42. *IvE* 5.1595, and commentary; late second century CE. *IvE* 4.1210 (120 CE) comes from a statue base dedicated to Demeter Karpophoros and to the city by her priest Publius Rutilius Bassus. The text indicates that Bassus built Demeter's temple and the forecourt from his own funds. This would be an unusual way to describe the prytaneion, but the possibility cannot be ruled out. This could also be a reference to the sanctuary Before the City, or to a third (otherwise unknown) shrine of Demeter. The relationship of these mysteries to imperial mysteries is discussed in chapter 6.

43. *IvE* 7,2.4337 l. 10–28.

44. Several inscriptions have her sharing an altar with Augustus: *IGR* 4.582–84 (Aizanoi); and 4.555–56 (Ankyra). The provincial cult of Tiberius, Livia, and the Senate at Smyrna was probably established a few years after this decree, showing that a priesthood for Livia was generally considered appropriate.

45. The inscription could be as late as 31 CE when Livilla was condemned to death for poisoning Drusus, but the reference to Drusus is so restrained that it was probably commissioned while he was alive.

46. It is not clear whether these two inscriptions come from the same organization at two different times in the first century CE. My inclination is to conclude that they do come from the same group because they both involve mysteries of Demeter prominent at Ephesos.

47. For the purposes of this study, "group" is defined as a fraction of the population of a city, town, or village who engage in religious rituals that are relatively independent of governmental oversight. See chapter 7.

48. Herodotus *Hist.* 6.16 refers to the observance of the Thesmophoria at Ephesos.

49. These topics are explored in more depth in chapter 6.

50. Koenigs 1993, esp. 395–96.

51. Koenigs 1993:392–94; Schede 1964:49–50. The 15 rooms reach only from the west end to the bouleuterion; the aisles of the stoa extend further east in front of the bouleuterion.

52. Schede 1934:106.

53. ὅπως ἀναγραφῇ τόδε τὸ ψήφισμα τῆς ἀγορᾶς ἐν τῶι ἐπιφανεστάτωι τόπωι. "So then, let this decree be inscribed in the most distinguished place in the agora." *IvPr* 119 l. 24–25; see also 108 l. 378; 117 l. 83.

54. ἡ ἱερὰ στοὰ ἐν τῆι ἀγορᾶι: *IvPr* 113 l. 59; 114 l. 40.

55. The rooms were numbered by excavators from west to east.

56. *IvPr* 106. A larger fragment of a copy of the same text was found in the excavations of the bouleuterion at Miletos; Knackfuss et al. 1908:101–2.

57. *IvPr* 105; discussed in chapter 2.

58. Schede 1964:55.

59. It may be that rooms 2 and 15 were also shrines of some sort, but there is no documentation that provides information as to their functions.

60. Tuchelt 1975:129.

61. Knackfuss et al. 1908:78–79.

62. Herrmann 1994:229–34 considered the older theory as still plausible because the epigraphic evidence might suggest a heroon in this area. He did not take up the architectural or sculptural arguments.

63. Tuchelt 1975:128–31.

64. Tuchelt 1975:126–27.

65. Tuchelt 1975.

66. *Milet* 1,2:84–88 #7.

67. H. Thompson 1952:79–82.

68. Keil 1929:36. The identification of this altar as devoted to the imperial cult was premature and probably wrong. Price (1984b:144 n. 34) pointed out that there was no inscription regarding the altar itself and that the dedication to Antoninus Pius was part of the building dedication, which included also Artemis.

69. Yegül 1982.

70. Yegül 1982:29–31 recognized this but argued that the accumulated indirect evidence was convincing. Price was not persuaded; 1984b:143–44 and n. 34.

71. Radt 1988:138–40; *AvP* 6.38; Tuchelt 1979:31–32.

72. Radt 1988:145.

73. Price 1984b:103–5.

74. *IvE* 4.1104, 1125, 1155, and perhaps 1089.

75. The arguments for the name of the complex and the existence of the games are found in Friesen 1993:114–41. The games were probably on an 4-year cycle and would have been

celebrated only two or three times before the assassination of Domitian, at which time they were abandoned.

76. *IGR* 4.257.
77. *AvP* 8,3:81 36, l. 4–10.
78. Price 1984b:101–32, esp. 101–14.
79. *IGR* 4.68 (Mytilene).
80. *IGR* 4.465 (Pergamon).
81. *IG* 12 Supp. 124.
82. Habicht 1973:83–84.
83. *IGR* 4.72.
84. *IGR* 4.74.
85. *IGR* 4.78.

5. Municipal Imperial Cults: Two Case Studies

1. Reynolds 1980:76.
2. ὁ σεβαστεῖος ναός *CIG* 2839.
3. Tuchelt 1981 argued that there was no set architectural form for a Sebasteion/ Kaisareion, so the intriguing design of this particular precinct is not an argument against the identification.
4. R. Smith 1987:92.
5. Hueber 1987:102 suggested that the orientation of the precincts might be a sign that an older sacred site was renovated for this complex.
6. For summaries, which sometimes vary in the details, see Reynolds 1986:110–11; Hueber 1987:105–6; Outschar 1987:111; R. Smith 1987:90; 1990:88.
7. The propylon uses niches and tabernacles in a manner similar to columnar facades of western Asia Minor. Since the propylon can be dated to the first half of the first century CE, it constitutes the earliest example of such marble niche architecture currently known; Outschar 1987:108.
8. Outschar 1987:108, 111. The transparent effect is reminiscent of the rendering of architecture in wall paintings of the second Pompeiian style.
9. Reynolds 1986:111. Two copies of this dedicatory inscription are preserved from the architrave. The same text was inscribed on both of the tabernacles that separated the three stairways.
10. Ἀφροδίτην, Προμήτορα θεῶν Σεβαστῶν; Reynolds 1986:111.
11. Reynolds 1980:79–82, #11–17.
12. Reynolds 1986:112–13; R. Smith 1987:95. The original locations of the statues are not known with precision. Some may have been displayed in front of the propylon or in the precincts rather than as a part of the gateway. Given the timespan involved, it is possible that the group of statues continued to grow with the proliferation of real and potential heirs to the throne.
13. This was not a new development with the Sebasteion. The Aphrodite/Venus Genetrix tradition goes back at least to the first half of the first century BCE; Reynolds 1996:42–43.
14. The term "portico" is used for convenience. The form might also be called a "pseudo-porticus" because of the unusual interior arrangements and external ornamentation.
15. R. Smith 1987:95. The rooms were not fitted with floors or ceilings. Rooms 1 and 13/14 of the south portico had stairs to the second story, nevertheless.
16. According to Hueber 1987:105, the propylon went up first, but the north portico

was built very close to the same time because some of the pieces in the upper story of the propylon take into account a connection with the north portico.

17. R. Smith 1988:52.

18. The architrave inscriptions are not yet published; the description comes from R. Smith 1987:90.

19. Reynolds 1986:114.

20. Hueber 1987:105.

21. R. Smith 1987:90.

22. Reynolds 1981:317–18 #1. The publication does not make clear where the lacuna restored as Καί]σαρι begins.

23. Reynolds 1981: 318–19 #2. This fragment was at first assumed to come from the north portico because it was found nearby. Later analysis showed that the piece was actually from the architrave of the south portico; R. Smith 1987:90 n. 10; and Outschar 1987:108.

24. The flight of stairs was probably built or extended in the second century CE based on datable fragments found there; Hueber 1987:105. Some similar sort of arrangement would have been needed from the beginning.

25. The capitals of these columns are among the finest preserved architectural pieces from the entire complex; Outschar 1987:111.

26. Hueber 1987:105.

27. Reynolds 1980:79 #10; 1986:110 and n. 12.

28. The two wives—Apphias and Attalis Apphion—may have been relatives.

29. R. Smith 1987:89; Outschar 1987:112.

30. R. Smith 1988:51; 1990:89. For the south portico second story, over 30 complete or nearly complete panels have been identified from the original 45, and large fragments of most of the other panels are known as well. For the north portico second story, pieces of 20–25 of the original 50 have been found. Only about 7 or 8 of the 50 reliefs from the north portico third story have survived. The reason there are so few panels left from the north portico is that its midsection was destroyed by an earthquake in the Byzantine period. The rubble was cleared away and is now lost. The south portico eventually fell into disuse and was never cleared away, with the result that the reliefs were left on the site and excavated centuries later.

31. R. Smith 1987:96.

32. R. Smith 1988:51–53, and pl. 7 #3–4.

33. Polybius 30.25 (31.3; see also Athenaeus 5.195b) records these as part of a procession for Antiochos IV Epiphanes at Daphne in 167 BCE.

34. R. Smith 1987:127–32, and pl. 24–26.

35. So R. Smith 1988:53.

36. There is not enough evidence to establish this as more than a possibility, but the Nero panel is unusual in several ways. It is the single imperial panel in either portico that depicts a specific historical event in a purely historical manner. Most of the reliefs in the north and the south porticoes are abstract or metaphorical, with historical figures portrayed using mythic conventions. The Nero panel, however, presents us with the only clothed emperor in the entire precincts, and none of the other registers has such a stark mixture of historical and allegorical elements. Thus, Nero's accession may have been a later addition that was not a part of the original programme.

37. Nationalities: Egyptians, Andizeti, Arabs, Bessi, Bospori, Dacians, Dardani, Iapodi, Judeans, Callaeci, Piroustae, Rhaeti, and Trumpilini. Islands: Crete, Cyprus, and Sicily. R. Smith 1988:55–57.

38. Reynolds 1981:327.

39. R. Smith 1988:58–59.

40. R. Smith 1988:70–77.

41. R. Smith 1988:75.

42. Smith suggested that the images from the Porticus ad Nationes may have been the ones carried in the procession; 1988:75.

43. *Simulacra gentium*; Servius, *Ad Aen.* 8.721.

44. Dio Cassius 56.34.3; using εἰκών and ἔθνη. Tacitus described the procession as well in *An.* 1.8.4. He did not mention images but wrote that the procession went through the Porta Triumphalis and that the names of all the peoples conquered by Augustus were carried in the front of the procession.

45. R. Smith 1988:75.

46. R. Smith 1988:57.

47. Published in R. Smith 1988:64–66 #3, pl. 3. The details here are based on his discussion.

48. R. Smith 1988:65 argued that this clothing was based on a known Hellenistic model, mediated by a complex process of imperial appropriation and provincial transformation that involved at least three stages, each with its own rationale and function. The first stage was the Hellenistic model, known from a statue of a Muse from the island of Thasos (Thasos Museum, inv. 1472; *Thasos* 133 # 32 fig. 71). The Hellenistic model would have been used by a designer or sculptor at Rome who was engaged to reproduce a Greek ethnic personification for imperial purposes. This appropriation by the imperial center was then copied and recontextualized for municipal purposes in the provinces (i.e., in Aphrodisias) as part of the Sebasteion reliefs. The statue is thus an example of the Greek east reusing its own representations only after these have been reinterpreted for it by the imperial center.

49. R. Smith 1988:62–64 #2, pl. 2.

50. R. Smith 1988:77.

51. For a possible reconstruction of the second and third story reliefs of rooms 1–3 at the east end, see R. Smith 1987:133. The following suggestion is made by R. Smith 1990:98–99 for the myth panels of rooms 1, 2, 13, and 14.

Room 1	left	Aphrodite with baby Eros
	center	Aeneas's flight from Troy
	right	Poseidon
Room 2	left	Three Graces
	center	Sacrifice
	right	Apollo with tripod
Room 13	left	Three heroes with bitch
	center	Seated hero with dog (Meleager and Atalante?)
	right	Meleager and boar
Room 14	left	Herakles and boar
	center	Prometheus freed by Herakles
	right	Child Dionysos with the Nymphs

Other subjects from the second story register include Leda and the swan, Demeter and Triptolemus, Bellerophon and Pegasus, Orestes at Delphi, Centaurs and Lapiths, Achilles and Thetis, Achilles and Penthesilea, Ajax and Cassandra; R. Smith 1987:97.

52. Dionysos appears five times and Herakles six times. Apollo is featured in three panels.

53. R. Smith 1987:97, 132; 1990:97, 100.

54. R. Smith 1990:100.

55. R. Smith 1987: 110–12 #4 and pl. 10–11 (Germanicus); 115–17 #6 and pl. 14–15 (Claudius); 106–110 #3 and pl. 8–9 (Claudius and Agrippina); 117–20 #7 and pl. 16–17 (Nero); 123–25 #9 and pl. 20–21 (two princes).

56. R. Smith 1987:125–27 #10 and pl. 22–23.

57. R. Smith 1987:101–4 #1 and pl. 4–5.

58. The connection of the captive with the bottom of the relief is not finished since it would not have been seen from the courtyard below.

59. R. Smith 1987:104–6 #2 and pl. 6–7.

60. R. Smith 1987:133.

61. R. Smith 1987:134–38. Quoted phrase is from p. 137.

62. Reynolds 1996:41–43; and 1982.

63. See plan of Ephesos, fig. 3.3. All of the Ephesian monuments described in this section have been discussed recently in Scherrer 1995 and Friesen f.c. Those discussions are referenced here only in cases where particular information makes this necessary.

64. Alzinger 1974:1.50.

65. Scherrer 1995:82–84.

66. *IvE* 2.404.

67. In the Latin version: *basili*[*cam . . .*]; in the Greek version: βασιλι[κὴν στοὰν κτλ].

68. Pottery found beneath the floor included pieces somewhat later than this. Either construction continued into the Claudian period, or the later pottery comes from the period of repair after an earthquake damaged the building. Mitsopoulos-Leon 1991:13.

69. *IvE* 2.407 a–b. The inscriptions are bilingual. The honorands are described as the father and the mother of Proclus.

70. Eichler 1966:9–11; 1967:18. The Augustus and Livia statues are about a third larger than lifesize. They are now in the Efes Museum, Selçuk, inv. 1957 (Augustus); 1/10/75 (Livia). Inan and Alföldi-Rosenbaum 1979:57–58 #3 and pl. 2.2 and 4.1; 61 #5 and pl. 4.2 and 5.1–2. Crosses were later carved in the foreheads of the two large heads. This was probably a Christian purification of the statues. The suggestion that the marks constituted a baptism of some sort (Langmann 1985) is unlikely.

71. The date of the destruction of the basilica is not known. Pieces of the structure were reused in the building of the church of St. John.

72. Alzinger 1970:1600–1; Scherrer 1995:80.

73. South gate (at the southeast corner): Alzinger 1970:1600–01; Eichler 1965:98.

74. Alzinger 1974:1.49–50; Scherrer 1995:80–82.

75. The western edge of the upper agora was not occupied by a stoa as one might expect. Rather, there seems to have been a series of monuments and perhaps a wall behind them. The monuments have not been thoroughly excavated with the exception of a fountain from the Domitianic period, which featured a colossal statue of Zeus (executed perhaps in the style of Jupiter Capitolinus). Scherrer 1995:80; Strocka 1989.

76. Merkelbach 1980; *Kl.P.* 4.1206–7.

77. See http://www.missouri.edu/~religsf/officials.edu for a database with information on the Ephesian officials.

78. Knibbe 1981:101–2.

79. Oster 1990:1689–91.

80. Oster 1990:1712–13; Knibbe 1970:286–87.

81. *IvE* 1.10 records some laws regarding the office of prytanis. Inscriptions refer to a variety of deities related in one way or another to the prytaneion. These included Artemis, Hestia, Kore, Clarian Apollo, and the Tyche of the city, as well as the otherwise unknown deities Sopolis and Kinnaios (*IvE* 4.1060; 4.1072).

82. Knibbe 1981 deals with these inscriptions in detail and draws conclusions about the organization and development of the mysteries of Artemis. Strabo *Geog* 14.1.20 refers to these celebrations.

83. Miltner 1958:27–38; 1959: 296–305. Miltner first suggested that the hearth would have been in the main room. Alzinger's objection (1974:1.51–55) is probably correct: other

known prytaneia did not locate the hearth in the main room. In Ephesos, the small room north of the main room is a more likely location for the city's hearth.

84. J. Wood 1877:42–52.

85. Heberdey 1912–13:170–73.

86. Ward-Perkins 1981:262.

87. Alzinger 1970:30.

88. *IvE* 2.460.

89. Alzinger 1970:1630.

90. Descriptions of the complex are found under various titles (der Staatsaltar, der sogenannte Staatsaltar, Temenos (Rhodisches Peristyl), Double Foundation, etc.) in Alzinger 1970:1648–49; Scherrer 1995:86; and Friesen f.c.

91. Miltner 1959:293–94; Eichler 1961:67–68.

92. Alzinger 1970:1648–49; 1974:1.55–57.

93. *Rom Hist* 51.20.6–7. See chapter 2.

94. This conclusion is widely accepted. Price (1984b:254 #27) and Jobst (1980:254–56 and n. 76) considered it possible but not certain.

95. The crepidoma had been pillaged over the centuries but enough of the stereobate blocks remained for an accurate reconstruction. The 15 × 22 m foundations once supported a peripteral temple. The order was either Ionic or Corinthian with 6 columns on the small sides and 10 columns on the north and south. No sign of an altar was found east of the temple; excavators found instead a water basin. The temple was built at the raised agora level; ceramic finds suggested the last half of the first century BCE. Alzinger 1972–75: 283–94; Fossel 1972–75:212–19.

96. This theory was based on several tangential factors: evidence for water at the site (a basin in front and a shaft that may have been a well), a small head of Ammon, a piece of a Harpokrates statuette, an Egyptianizing terracotta figurine, and a bronze bell that might have come from a sistrum. Alzinger 1972–75:283–90.

97. Plutarch *Ant* 56, 58; Alzinger 1972–75:291–94; Knibbe 1980:758. Jobst argued convincingly against this theory; 1980:248–49.

98. Hölbl's theory (1978:27–32) is too speculative to be accepted. He argued that Antony was honored at this temple as Dionysos (Plutarch *Ant* 24.4) and Osiris, and perhaps Cleopatra was honored as Isis. Then after Actium, according to Hölbl, Augustus allowed the temple to continue with dedications to the same deities, but not to Antony or Cleopatra.

99. Since the nineteenth century, scholars had concluded that an Augustus temple was located within the temenos of Artemis outside the city because of two copies of an inscription found there by J. T. Wood. The bilingual inscription from 6/5 BCE recorded in Greek and in Latin that the temple (of Artemis) and the Sebasteion had been walled in with the financial support of the holy revenues of Artemis (*IvE* 5.1552). Wood assumed that the wall in which the copies of the text were found was the peribolos wall for both precincts, but Jobst questioned this on the basis of Wood's own description. It was more likely, according to Jobst, that the wall was late and the inscription had been reused there; Jobst 1980:241–43. We should also note that Wood was under tremendous pressure to produce evidence about the location of the Artemision. He had just received a letter from the Trustees of the British Museum indicating that after six frustrating years they would no longer support his excavation if he could not show dramatic results. So he was probably not disposed to question the connection between the inscription and the wall that allowed him to claim to have found the limits of the Artemision; J. Wood 1877:130–34. In Wood's defense, however, it is quite possible that there would have been a Sebasteion attached to the Artemision and another in the city. Thus, one could support Jobst's argument without denying the possibility of another cult of Augustus outside the walls.

100. *IvE* 3.902 l. 2–4: ὅς καὶ προενοήθη τῆς καθιδρύσεως τοῦ Σεβαστοῦ καὶ τῆς καθιερώσεως τοῦ τεμένους κτλ.

101. *IvE* 2.412 l. 1–6.

102. Jobst 1980:251–54; Scherrer 1989:90.

103. Tuchelt 1981:178–86. The status of the bouleuterion at this period is unknown.

104. This close cultic connection between Artemis and Augustus would be congruent with Wood's "peribolos wall" inscription (*IvE* 5.1552). Also in favor of this alternative is the fact that the double foundation was the closest monument to the findspot of the inscription about the statue and temenos of Augustus (*IvE* 3.902).

105. Scherrer 1989:98–101.

106. To identify the agora temple as that of Rome and Divus Julius requires us to suppose that the most prominent temple in the upper city was one devoted solely to the use of resident Romans; the double cult of the reigning emperor Augustus and of Artemis was built for a larger percentage of the population yet tucked away in an area that was less accessible; and the temple of Julius Caesar was executed in a traditional Hellenistic design while the shrine for Artemis used an Italian design.

107. Reynolds 1996:41–43.

108. Jobst 1980:259.

6. Groups and Individuals

1. By "group" I mean settings that involve a defined number of people in particular activities. Groups normally included a fraction of a percentage of the people in a city or town and are usually funded at least in part by the members of the group.

2. Poland 1909:46–49. For references to hymnodes from a wider geographic area, see Robert 1944:39 and 1959:214.

3. E.g., *IvE* 1,1.27 l. 267; 3.645; 7,1.3247; *IGR* 4.1665 (Tira).

4. *IGR* 4.1587 l. 10–11 (Klaros, involving Laodikeians).

5. *CIG* 2715a (Stratonikeia in Karia).

6. *IvE* 2.275.

7. All three of the texts were inscribed at the same time; Keil 1908:103.

8. *IvE* 7,2.3801 II. The right and left sides of this text are damaged, and most of the reconstructions are not noted in the translation.

9. The last two lines are mostly reconstructed, so the reading is not completely certain.

10. The inscription raises another question. If the hymnodes of all Asia sang at Pergamon on the birthday of Tiberius, who sang at Smyrna where there was a provincial temple for Tiberius? The major annual festival at the temple in Smyrna was probably held on the same day, the birthday of the emperor. We should probably assume that another choir was charged with performing in Smyrna and that other choirs were formed for other provincial temples.

11. *IvE* 7,2.3801 I l. 2–14; minor reconstructions in the text are not noted in this translation.

12. *IvE* 7,2.3801 I l. 19: [τῇ ἱερ]ᾷ ὑμνῳδῶν [συνόδῳ κτλ].

13. *IvE* 7,2.3801 I l. 15–18.

14. A possible explanation for this series of documents is that Asia was seeking—and received—imperial permission to continue the custom of gathering in Pergamon for the birthday of Tiberius; Keil 1908:103–4. It is also possible, though unprovable at this point, that the first gathering for the birthday of Tiberius by the hymnodes took place in 41 at the accession of Claudius. This could have been a way for Asia to affirm its loyalty to Claudius

(Tiberius's nephew) while simultaneously distancing itself from the aborted provincial cult for Gaius at Miletos (between 37 and 41 CE). Such a decision would have been especially appropriate in 41, given the divinization of Tiberius's mother, Livia, in that year.

15. The use of ἁρμάζω ("to fit, to be suited"; in music, "to tune") in this sentence was perhaps intended as a pun.

16. *IvE* 1,1.17 l. 53–63 = 18d l. 4–24. Cf. Dörner 1935.

17. κατὰ τὴν αὐτῶν γνώμην; 17 l. 62 = 18 l. 21–22.

18. *IvE* 1,1.17 l. 63–66.

19. The extant portion of the edict does not mention the provincial cult at Smyrna and so it is not clear if hymnodes also gathered there.

20. *IvE* 4.1145.

21. *IvE* 3.742, 921. Both inscriptions are damaged, but the existing portions support the reconstructions.

22. *IvSm* 2,1.697.

23. *IvSm* 2,1.594 l. 3; 124 CE.

24. *AvP* 8,2:260, 264. The block was not in situ but had been used in a later building project, probably in the Turkish period. The present location of the altar is unknown.

25. [Ἀγαθῆι τύχηι. Αὐτοκρά]τορι Καίσα[ρι Τραιανῶι Ἀδριαν]ῶι Ὀ(λ)υμπίωι, σωτῆρι καὶ [κτί]στηι, ὑμνῳδοὶ θεοῦ Σεβαστοῦ καὶ θεᾶς Ῥώμης κτλ. *AvP* 8,2 374 (= *IGR* 4.353) A.

26. *AvP* 8,2 374 B–D. Another translation of this section is found in Lewis 1974: 125–26.

27. *AvP* 8,2:263, 268.

28. Pleket 1965:340.

29. See table 6.1 for details on imperial birthdays.

30. *AvP* 8,2.268.

31. Robert 1960:340–42. Robert also noted that the use of incense in the funerary rituals was of Roman origin.

32. Keil 1908:107; Mellor 1975:192–93; Halfmann 1990:25.

33. *AvP* 8,2:264.

34. The secondary literature is immense. Metzger 1984 provides a bibliography covering the mid-twentieth century.

35. J. Smith 1990.

36. Gasparro 1985 raised the issue specifically with regard to the cult of Attis and Kybele. Burkert 1987 dealt with a broader range of religious institutions.

37. Pleket 1965:332–34.

38. Pleket 1965:346–47.

39. Price 1984b:190–91. Cf. Herrmann 1996.

40. See Pleket's discussion of Nilsson and Latte; 1965:338–41.

41. Robert 1960:321–23; Pleket 1965:340; Price 1984b:190. Reynolds 1981:321 accepted that this was a provincial office rather than a local one but did not discuss the issue of imperial mysteries.

42. *IGR* 4.1410. The published reconstruction of l. 1–4 is certainly wrong. Buckler's reconstruction (1935:181 a) is better: [. . . γνώμη] Τιβερίου Κλαυδίου Ἡρό[δου τοῦ ἀρχιερέως κ]αὶ σεβαστοφάντου κ[αὶ διὰ βίου ἀγωνοθέτου] θεᾶς Ῥώμης καὶ θεοῦ [Σεβαστοῦ Καίσαρος] Διὸς Πατρῴου.

43. *IGR* 4.1696 (corrected reading of 643, Akmonia; probably late first century according to Reynolds 1981:321 n.17); *IvE* 6. 2037 (partially reconstructed), 2061 II l. 6, 2062 (partially reconstructed), 2063.

44. Trajan is only called "Dacicus" in *IvE* 6.2061 II l. 20, and I l. 8.

45. *IGR* 4.1696. He was honored there as the benefactor of a guild of fullers.

46. *IvE* 6.2063, set up by his freedman Philadelphos.

47. Reynolds 1981:321 #4.

48. An inscription from Doryleion in Phrygia honored a couple who were sebastophants for life and held religious offices for several deities (including some political figures); *IGR* 4.522, probably Hadrianic. He was called σεβαστοφάντης (l. 6), she σεβαστοφάντις (l. 13). A fragment from Sardis probably refers to a sebastophant and mysteries as well, but the damage is too severe to add information on the topic; Sardis 7,1.62. There was a strong connection between the provincial cult of Bithynia and imperial mysteries. Two inscriptions mention the "hierophant of the mysteries of the provincial temple;" *IvPrusa* 17 l. 6–7; 47 l. 12–13. Both men were also listed with the title sebastophant. The inscriptions come from the late second or third centuries, later than the period under consideration here.

49. The altar does not mention a provincial sebastophant; that office tended to be filled by men from other cities who came to serve at a provincial imperial temple. The lacuna at the bottom of side A could have listed a provincial sebastophant, but the character of these inscriptions weighs against this possibility.

50. Sons were also assumed to be present at the banquets given by newly admitted hymnodes; *AvP* 8,2 374 D l. 16–17.

51. The birthday of Augustus involved crowns for the hymnodes and a donation of a mina that could have been used for catering, but no food, beverage, or table settings were recorded as donations for that day.

52. πόπανον καὶ λίβανον καὶ λύχνους τῶι Σεβαστῶι; B l. 19. The wording is imprecise about whether cakes, incense, and lamps were required each day since πάσης ἡμέρας could refer only to garlands and wreaths. The fact that this regulation is placed at this point rather than within the list of requirements for the eukosmos on a single day (B l. 4–12) throws the weight of probability in favor of the former option; that is, that these ritual necessities were needed each day.

53. Pleket 1965:342–45.

54. *IvE* 2.275.

55. His full title was probably "curator of the mysteries," based on the reference to an ἐπιμελητής τῶν μυστηρίων in *IvE* 5.1594 l. 9–11 (probably late second century CE). The editors of the inscription concluded that the same mystery thiasos set up both inscriptions. It is also possible that these were separate groups since the extant part of *IvE* 5.1594 mentions T. Aur. Plutarchos, who was "priest of the Demetriastai Before the City and (priest) of the mystai of Dionysos Phleus" (l. 2–7).

56. *IvE* 5.1600 c, g, and others. These were found in the theater but may have rolled down into the theater from a building further up the slope.

57. Chapter 4.

58. *IvE* 2.213 l. 3–6.

59. *IvE* 5.1600 (Dionysian priests), 1601 (Dionysian mystai).

60. The neglected topic of imperial cults in associations and trade guilds is discussed in Harland 1996.

61. For critiques of such projects, see Price 1984a; 1984b:5–22.

62. *Milet* 1,2 #21–23; 1,9 #290–97, 301, 302. *CIG* 2863, 2866, 2877.

63. *Milet* 1,9:350.

64. Ovid described his household altar while in exile in Tomis in *Pont* 4.9.105–8.

65. Nock 1979b:780–81, 833–34.

66. Pleket 1965:331–32, 346–47; Habicht 1973:42–44; Price 1984a:90–93.

67. Fishwick 1990:125–27.

68. *ILS* 2,2.8787.

69. She was also related to Nero, who was her great-grandson.

70. Chapter 4.

71. Tacitus *An* 6.2.1. The outcome was left unstated by Tacitus. This inscription suggests that the proposals were not passed.

72. Reynolds 1982:182–83 document 54, pl. 32,1. I have adapted the translation of Reynolds. The inscription was first published in Reynolds 1980:73–74 #2.

73. Reynolds 1980:74.

74. Chapter 5.

75. His name indicates that he was a freedman of Livia. The reference to his status as freedman of Caesar might be explained by his manumission under Tiberius; Reynolds 1982:182. The unusual dedication πολείταις might suggest that he had also received Aphrodisian citizenship; Reynolds 1981:74.

76. Reynolds 1996:50.

77. Price 1984a:91–93; Fishwick 1990:121–22.

7. Imperial Cults as Religion

1. *IvPr* 105.

2. *IvE* 2.213.

3. Bickerman 1980:22–33.

4. Bickerman 1980:43–47.

5. For overviews, see Burkert 1985:95–98; Bruit Zaidman and Schmitt Pantel 1992:46–54.

6. For recent contributions that provide entry into the secondary literature, see Bremen 1996; Hawley and Levick 1995; Kraemer 1992; and Pomerory 1991.

7. E.g., Magie 1950:449; Deininger 1965:41; Rossner 1974:102; MacMullen 1980:214. The view has been challenged by Kearsley 1986 and Friesen 1993:81–89.

8. Herz 1992:106–8; Bremen 1996:117–25.

9. *IvE* 2.213.

10. Friesen 1999.

11. According to Speidel 1984:278–79 there was only one cohort in the province at any given time.

12. *IvE* 2.213.

13. *AvP* 8,2 374.

14. Meyer 1987:4–13; Burkert 1987:89–114.

15. *OGIS* 458 l. 5–11 (= *IvPr* 105).

16. Sullivan 1988:672–73.

17. Gasparo 1985; J. Smith 1990.

18. For bibliography on apotheosis and a survey of evidence, mostly from Rome, see Kreitzer 1996:69–98.

19. *IvE* 7,2.3801 l. 2–4 (Hypaipa).

20. *IvE* 2.412 (79–81 CE).

21. Translation adapted from Sheppard 1981:24 #1.

22. Dystopia, a concept based on experiences in the decolonizing world, refers to the disappointing fortunes of some revolutionary movements once they become responsible for building and maintaining newly independent nations; Harlow 1987:154–69.

8. Revelation in Space and Time

1. A history of imperial cults in this province during the entire Roman imperial period would be a worthwhile endeavor, but the scope of this study does not permit such an undertaking.

2. Revelation 6:9; 20:4. A similar idea is expressed in 12:17 (commands of God and testimony of Jesus).

3. Revelation 11:7; 12:11.

4. For a discussion of the legal issues and possibilities, see Yarbro Collins 1984a:102–4.

5. Ramsay 1904:177–96. On Roman roads in the area in general, see French 1980.

6. Moretti 1954:276; Deininger 1965:55 and n. 1.

7. Barr 1998:8.

8. Aune 1997:115.

9. Note the refrain near the end of every message in Revelation 2–3, "Let anyone who has an ear listen to what the Spirit is saying *to the churches*" (emphasis added).

10. Aune 1997:lvii; Barr 1998:21.

11. Sibylline Oracle 5:28–34; translation from Charlesworth 1983:393. The first letter in Nero's name was also the symbol for the number 50 in Greek and in Hebrew.

12. Translation from Charlesworth 1983:387–88. For other references to Nero's return, see SibOr 3:63–74; 5:361–85; and 8:139–59.

13. Tacitus *Hist* 1.2

14. Dio 66.19; Suetonius *Nero* 57.2.

15. If the Greek letters from the name "Neron Caesar" are transliterated into Hebrew, the total of the Hebrew letters equals 666. Some ancient manuscripts of Revelation use the number 616 instead, which would be the total of the Hebrew letters when transliteration is done from the Latin form of "Nero Caesar." For details, see Aune 1998a:769–71.

16. Barr 1998:127–28 objects to this interpretation. He suggests that the wounded head is Julius Caesar: the death of Caesar at first led to fears that the Republic was headed back into chaos, but in the end it did not signal the end of Roman hegemony.

17. Bell 1979:98 argued unconvincingly that speculation about the return of Nero would have been lively only immediately after Nero's death when the facts of Nero's demise were not yet widely known. Both the Sibylline Oracles and the known examples of pretenders disprove his conclusion.

18. "Babylon" first appears in Revelation 14:8, and then again in 16:19; 17:5; 18:2, 10, and 21.

19. E.g., Coogan and Knibb 1979:101–5; Yarbro Collins 1984a:57–58; Murphy 1985: 136–37; Thompson 1990:14.

20. Translation from Reddish 1990.

21. Translation from Reddish 1990.

22. Wilson 1994 emphasized the symbol's theme of domination at the expense of the theme of the destruction of Jerusalem. Exile and domination, however, are predicated on Babylon's destruction of Jerusalem and the temple. Both themes are inherent in the metaphor and cannot be disentangled from each other.

23. For a table of the allusions to Jeremiah 50–51, see Aune 1998b:983; for details see his comments on specific verses in Revelation 18.

24. Jeremiah 50:28; 51:11, 35, 50–51.

25. This critique is elaborated below in chapter 12.

26. Stone 1990:35–36.

27. Revelation 14:9–13; 18:4.

28. Contra Marshall 1997:241–62, who argues for a date precisely during the Roman siege of Jerusalem.

29. For a review of proposals made, see Aune 1998b:945–50.

30. When an enumeration is attempted, the most common position is to follow Tacitus and use Augustus as the starting point. Another model begins with Julius Caesar following Suetonius's *Twelve Caesars*. Others have proposed that Gaius should be the first in the series because of his extravagant claims for divine honors. Still others have suggested Claudius as the starting point because he was probably the first emperor to have to deal with the churches in some way.

31. The main issue here is whether to include the three emperors—Galba, Otho, and Vitellius—who reigned briefly during the year after Nero's death. Wilson 1993:600–2 demonstrated that these should be included in any consecutive list of emperors for that period.

32. Wilson 1993:598–604.

33. Swete 1907:220–21. When source-critical theories are added to this approach, the results can become extremely complex; cf. Charles 1920b:68–70.

34. Roloff 1993:199 notes this problem of multivalent imagery but historicizes the details unnecessarily.

35. Boring 1989:182–83.

36. Coogan and Knibb 1979:240–42. Stone 1990:365 agreed that it is now impossible to list rulers corresponding to all the wings but accepted instead the theory of Schürer and Gunkel that the author had more detailed knowledge than we do. Stone thus concluded that the author of 4 Ezra had a list in mind but that we can no longer reconstruct it.

37. Caird 1966:218–19. Beale 1999:868–72 defends the same principle but does so with parallels from scriptural texts.

38. Sweet 1979:257–58.

39. Wilson 1993:604.

40. Caird 1966:131.

41. Giblin 1984; Bachmann 1994.

42. Caird 1966:132; Wall 1991:142–43.

43. Roloff 1993:129.

44. Morris 1987:141–43; Boring 1989:142–48; Schüssler Fiorenza 1991:76–77. Sweet 1979:182–84 argued, on the other hand, that the temple represented the church in its inward being, sealed and protected by God, while the outer court is the church in its outward being, which is engaged in the mission to the Gentiles.

45. Aune 1998a:575–77, 593–98, and 630–31 surveys the literature and the issues.

46. Barr 1998:91 takes note of the intertextuality; Beale 1999:559–71 goes into more detail.

47. E.g., Yarbro Collins 1984a:55–56; Thompson 1990:15.

48. Irenaeus *Adv. haer.* 5.30.3.

49. In Eusebius *Hist. eccl.* 3.18.3.

50. Wilson 1993:597–98.

51. Tacitus *An* 15.44.

52. Wilson 1993:587–95 dissected the arguments for a Domitianic persecution and showed their weaknesses. For the role played by Eusebius's *Church History* in the Christian traditions about Domitian, see Ulrich 1996.

53. For example, Suetonius *Dom.* 10. But note Thompson's reassessment of the Roman propaganda regarding the evils of Domitian's reign (1990:95–115).

54. For example, "Jezebel," "Balaam," and the Nicolaitans were advocating limited accommodation with Gentile culture, especially in regard to meat sacrificed to idols. John, on the other hand, represented a separatist option.

55. Yarbro Collins 1984a:84–99.

56. Revelation 2:13. While the circumstances of the death of Antipas are not clear, Yarbro Collins argued that it can be connected to the role of Roman government centered in Pergamon.

57. Yarbro Collins 1984a:99–104.

58. Yarbro Collins 1984a:160–61. For a review, see Barr 1988.

59. Schüssler Fiorenza 1991:126–27. For a review, see Thompson 1991.

60. Schüssler Fiorenza 1985:193.

61. Schüssler Fiorenza 1985:194–95; 1991:55–57, 132–36.

62. Schüssler Fiorenza 1985:187–89, 198; 1991:29–31, 119–124.

63. His view is spelled out in Thompson 1990 (esp. pp. 95–167). For a review, see Yarbro Collins 1991:548–50.

64. Thompson 1990:166–67.

65. Thompson 1990:174–76.

66. Thompson 1990:171–97.

67. Schüssler Fiorenza 1991:126–28.

68. One possible exception is Revelation 2:13, where the image of Satan's throne has often been taken as a reference to Pergamon as the alleged center of imperial cults; Schüssler Fiorenza 1985:117; Krodel 1989:115; Klauck 1992:160–61. Part I of this study demonstrated, however, that Asia had no center for imperial cults, and the complete absence of other references to imperial cults in the messages to the seven churches makes this interpretation even more unlikely. The other suggested influence of imperial cults outside Revelation 13–19 is in the imagery of the heavenly court (esp. Rev 4–6); Aune 1983a. The alleged parallels with heavenly worship, however, are too general to demonstrate significant influence.

69. Friesen n.d.

70. Revelation 17:1–18.

71. The older position has not been completely discarded. Roloff, for example, maintained that during the reign of Domitian imperial cults were systematically promoted throughout the empire. He then interpreted the book of Revelation as a reaction to this Roman policy of total confrontation; Roloff 1993:9–10. Schüssler Fiorenza 1985:193 accepted active promotion of imperial cults by the Flavians, but this was not tied so closely to the composition of Revelation. Boring 1989:19–21 maintained that there was an increase in imperial cults under Domitian but suggested that there were pressures both from above and from the populace that led to this development.

72. Suetonius *Dom.* 13.

73. September was to be named Germanicus and October Domitianus. Suetonius does not mention that these followed the months named after Julius Caesar (July) and Augustus.

74. Yarbro Collins 1984a:71–72.

75. Thompson 1990:104–7.

76. See chapter 3 and Friesen 1995.

77. Justin Martyr *Dial.* 80–81; *Apol.* 1.28.

78. Eusebius *Hist. eccl.* 4.26.

79. Eusebius *Hist. eccl.* 3.39.12.

9. Centering Reality: Space and Time in Revelation

1. Sullivan 1988:112.

2. Cf. Barr 1998:16–17.

3. The judgment scene (20:9) further describes God's throne as white.

4. The four creatures are described as being in the midst of the throne and around the throne (καὶ ἐν μέσῳ τοῦ θρόνου καὶ κύκλῳ τοῦ θρόνου κτλ., 4:6b). The description has perplexed commentators. Hall 1994 suggested a literary background in descriptions of the ornamentation of the ark of the covenant. While the connection is plausible, it creates the problem of imagining four creatures who are part of the thone, yet lead the heavenly liturgy and fall down before the throne (5:8); Aune 1997:271–72.

5. Roloff 1993:107 wrote that the seven angels should be identified with the seven spirits before the throne. The identification is unlikely. The seven spirits are an allusion to Zech 4:10 and are associated with the divine omniscience, whereas the archangels usually carry out various aspects of God's activity in the world.

6. The white throne judgment (20:11–15) and the descent of the new Jerusalem (21: 1–4) bring the work of the Messiah to fruition, so the age of sacrifice and temples (21:22) is over. God and the Lamb dwell with humanity.

7. The missing ark took on eschatological significance in Jewish thought during the Second Temple Period. Second Maccabees 2:4–8 records a story that Jeremiah took the ark and sealed it up in a cave on Mt. Sinai, where God would keep it hidden until God's people were reassembled.

8. So Bachmann 1994, extending the argument of Giblin 1984.

9. See Wilson 1993:604–5.

10. Cf. 2 Bar 20:2 for a similar idea.

11. Revelation 10:1–3; 12:1–4.

12. The Messiah is also human in some fashion, but he is in a different category altogether. His human origins are noted (Rev 5:5), but he is more often given cosmic significance. He is portrayed as born of the supernatural Woman (Revelation 12) and depicted as a slaughtered, living Lamb.

13. This division is reflected in Rev 5:13, where "heaven" is used loosely for the sky rather than for the transcendent realm. Rev 14:7 adds fresh water to the list.

14. The phrase appears frequently with minor variations; 3:10; 6:10; 8:13; 11:10; 13:12, 14; 17:2, 8.

15. *ABD* 1.49 "Abyss."

16. Sullivan 1988:628.

17. Sullivan 1988:634.

18. E.g., Schüssler Fiorenza 1985:195; Thompson 1990:121–24.

19. Thompson 1990:54–56.

20. Thompson 1990:53–73; Vanni 1991.

21. Boring 1994:82 and n. 65.

22. Thompson 1990:69–71 noted the community-building and community-defining functions of worship in Revelation. He also concluded that this was an egalitarian community, which I question. The experience of worship in the two realms is distinct, creating longing on earth and fulfillment in heaven. In worship, all creatures are relativized—but not necessarily equalized—in the presence of the Creator.

23. For example, 1:6 and 8 in community worship in Asia, or 4:8 and 10 in heavenly worship.

24. Revelation 1:8; 5:13; 7:12.

26. Sullivan 1988:651–60.

26. Sullivan 1988:388–89. Sullivan dealt mostly with nonliterary cultures, so the masters of tradition in his discussions tend to be ritual specialists. Christian prophets were also involved in ritual (1 Cor 14:26–33; Did 10:7) but their primary claim to authority was ecstatic revelation; Aune 1983b:203–11.

27. Boring 1994:58.

28. Aune 1986:89–90.

29. The identification of the these terms is accepted by a wide variety of commentators; e.g., Swete 1907:133–34; Cerfaux and Cambier 1955:91; Caird 1966:132; Mounce 1977:221; Boring 1989:142, 158.

30. This is comparable to Barr's summary of the Seer's temporal perspective as an effort to locate his audience at the time when they see Jesus coming on the clouds, just before the end of time; 1998:33.

31. It might be better to think of this period as the first part of the resurrection since John did not call the general resurrection (20:12–13) a "second resurrection."

32. Bauckham 1993:107.

33. Stone 1989:131–43; 1990:207–13, 352–53, 368–71.

34. Boring 1994:66–68 described the last scenes of Revelation (19:1–22:5) as independent portraits with few interconnections, rather than as a chronological scenario of the endtimes. While it is true that certain aspects of the last chapters in Revelation cannot be integrated into one consistent picture, Boring goes too far in detaching them. The author of Revelation expects readers to take the scenes together by invoking periods of time and developing narratives with set characters that span several scenes. More can be made of the connections than Boring suggests without violating the multivalent character of the symbolizations.

35. Thompson 1990:78–79.

36. Thompson 1990:81.

37. Thompson 1990:82.

38. Thompson 1990:74–91. Phrase quoted from p. 91.

39. Thompson 1990:187 suggests that there are only boundaries and no centers.

40. Sullivan 1988:130–52.

41. Long 1986:70–71.

42. Thompson 1990:200.

43. John's refusal to describe God and his use of the phrase "One who sits on the throne" are efforts to avoid employing language to signify what is beyond signification.

44. Thompson 1990:81–82.

45. Thompson 1990:82.

46. Thompson 1990:85.

47. *IvE* 2.412; 7,2.3801.

48. Thompson 1990:82 suggested that the Woman was transformed in the wilderness from the godly woman to the prostitute of Revelation 17. Although this might suggest certain homologies between the godly woman and the Dragon, it creates a host of problems as well. Is Rome originally a heavenly woman? Who then are the woman's other children? And why does the Dragon try to attack in Revelation 12 the woman it empowers in Revelation 17?

49. E.g., Thompson 1990:52, 187.

50. Thompson 1990:85.

10. Working with Myth

1. Chapter 5.

2. Chapter 4.

3. E.g., Ruiz 1989 and Beale 1999.

4. Yarbro Collins 1976; Court 1979.

5. Philo, *Peri gig.* 2–4.

6. Goodenough 1958:135–71.

7. Revelation 13; and with a twist 19:17–18.

8. Revelation 2:7 and 22:2, 14; 2:20; 2:14.

9. P. Day 1988; Pagels 1995, esp. 35–62.

10. Richter 1966.

11. Barr 1998:62–63.

12. I am not convinced by the argument that the throne scene of Revelation 4 is influenced by Roman imperial court ceremony (Aune 1983a). The emperor was seldom shown enthroned. Any familiarity with court ritual that might have existed would have perhaps been gained from processions or visits of imperial officials. As John and his communities knew the relevant scriptural texts, this is a more likely source for the description.

13. Note, however, that 2 Baruch and 4 Ezra are even more circumspect than Revelation. In these two texts, there is no attempt to describe the dwelling place or throne of God.

14. R. Smith 1987:132–36.

15. R. Smith 1990:97.

16. Whether the Sebasteion sculptures reflected such a pattern can no longer be determined, but if they were based on a mythic pattern, it was certainly not the one used for Revelation.

17. For a summary of earlier research see Yarbro Collins 1976:207–11.

18. Barr 1998:122.

19. Aune 1998a:670–74.

20. Yarbro Collins 1976:57–85.

21. Yarbro Collins 1976:57–145.

22. Yarbro Collins 1976:23–22, 207–234.

23. Barr 1998:101–22, 147–49.

24. Cf. Aune 1997:xcii–xciii.

25. This would subsume the section of Revelation that Barr calls the "worship scroll."

26. Yarbro Collins 1976:211–17. Her argument was an important extension of Müller 1963.

27. Aune 1998a:667–76.

28. Cross 1973:79–194; J. Day 1985.

29. J. Day 1985.

30. Chapter 2.

31. Georgi 1986.

32. R. Smith 1987:115–17 and pl. 14–15.

33. R. Smith 1987:117–20 and pl. 16–17.

34. Caird 1966:64–65; Roloff 1993:70–72.

35. In Ezekiel, the four beings accompany God's glory as it leaves and then returns to the temple; Ezek 10:1–21; 43:1–12.

36. Boring 1989:107 pointed out that the creatures in Revelation are the premier representatives of categories of animate life, symbolizing the whole of life on earth.

37. J. Day 1985:1–61.

38. In Revelation 13:11–17, the elite of Asia are symbolized as Behemoth. See chapter 12 for details.

39. Aune 1998a:728–29.

40. J. Day 1985:88–140.

41. For examples of divisions of history into periods of 10, 70, etc., see J. Collins 1993:352–53.

42. Chapter 2.

43. Fig. 4.2.

44. *OGIS* 458, from translation in chapter 2.

45. This interpretation of the Beast image is almost universally accepted by commentators.

46. Some have suggested that the saints do engage in the battle against Roman hegemony. They argue that the 144,000 on Mt. Zion (Rev 14:1–5) are the Lamb's army, prepared for the holy war described in 19:11–21 (esp. v. 14); e.g., Caird 1966:178–79. This interpretation need not imply that the saints engage in violence (cf. Bauckham 1993:76–80), but the holy war analogy is wrong anyway on at least two counts: the counting of the 144,000 in 7:1–8 is not a census for war but rather a sealing for protection based on Ezek 9; and holy war requires temporary sexual abstinence and cleansing from nocturnal emissions (Deut 23:9–10; 1 Sam 21:5; 1QM 7), not celibacy (Rev 14:4). Aune rejected the holy war interpretation especially because the Zion scene is set on earth rather than heaven and because the focus of Revelation 14 is on the paradoxical role of Lamb as shepherd and guide, not on a divine warrior figure (1998a:803–4, 812–14, 848).

47. For more on violence in Revelation, see chapters 11 and 12.

48. For example, 4 Ezra 7:28–35; and 2 Baruch 28–30. Each describes this period in a different way.

49. The ethical implications of this stance are examined in the next chapter.

50. Note, however, that in the actual narrative of the destruction of Rome, the imagery reverts back to that of the Beast; 19:17–21. The implications of this imagery for John's audience are discussed in chapter 11.

51. R. Smith 1987:106–10 and pl. 8–9.

52. R. Smith 1987:127–32 and pl. 24–26.

53. The Sebasteion also shared with Revelation the practice of characterizing a city by the image of a virtuous woman, which was a standard iconographic practice in the Greco-Roman world. Rome appeared standing over the reclining female figure Earth in a panel that perhaps came from the third story, room 2; R. Smith 1987:96 n. 30, 132. Rome was also pictured crowning the city of Aphrodisias in a panel that may have come from the third story, room 6; R. Smith 1987:133.

54. Pippin 1992a:103–5.

55. For an examination of archaelogical evidence regarding the evolution of house church architecture, see White 1997. On the social features of housechurches, cf. Osiek and Balch 1997.

56. Thompson 1990:53–63.

57. Barr 1998:171–75.

11. Communities Worshipping Humans

1. Colossians 1:18, 24 (which was also to be sent to Laodikeia; 4:15–16); Eph 5. Ignatius is somewhat more complicated but uses church in a similar way: to the Ephesians 5:1; to the Smyrnaeans 8:2 (ἡ καθολικὴ ἐκκλησία); to Polycarp 5:1 where Ignatius reuses Ephesians 5.

2. The Seer's commission to write down the messages, two references in the vision interpretation (1:20), seven references to the angel of a church, seven calls to hear what the spirit says to the churches, and the statement that all the churches would know that Christ searches heart and mind (2:23).

3. Schüssler Fiorenza 1985:76; 1991:50.

4. Revelation 1:5b–6. A few sentences later John described himself as his audience's "brother and fellow participant in the distress and kingdom and endurance in Jesus" (Rev 1:9).

5. Cf. Revelation 16:10.

6. Schüssler Fiorenza 1972:420; Roloff 1993:26, 81; Beale 1999:193. Support for this view is found, for example, in texts like Revelation 22:3–4.

7. Caird 1966:17, 77; Sweet 1979:66; Boring 1989:78; Beale 1999:193. Cf. Revelation 21:24–26. The role of priest as mediator should be given more consideration in light of its importance in general Greco-Roman concepts of priesthood; Beard and North 1990.

8. Sweet 1979:66, 130. It is surprising that this aspect is mentioned infrequently in light of the importance of proper worship in Revelation.

9. Aune 1998b:1187.

10. Cf. 4 Ezra 10:38–54. Second Baruch 4 preserves a similar idea but it deals with the heavenly temple rather than Jerusalem as a whole.

11. Beale 1999:1070.

12. People of God, however, is not John's primary term for the movement. Revelation 18:4 and 21:3 refer to the redeemed as God's people, but these two references do not have primary conceptual importance in Revelation.

13. Revelation 5:8; 8:3–4; 13:7; 17:6; 20:9.

14. Revelation 11:18; 16:6.

15. Revelation 13:10; 14:12.

16. Revelation 18:20, though the usage here might refer to the angels or, on a variant reading, to the holy apostles.

17. Revelation 18:24.

18. Revelation 19:8.

19. Revelation 1:1 (twice); 10:7; 11:18; 22:6. Revelation 15:3 refers to Moses as the servant of God.

20. Bovon 1972:72. Revelation 11:7, "And when they finished their testimony, the beast that comes up from the abyss made war with them and vanquished them and killed them." The two witnesses finished their testimony and then they were killed.

21. Revelation 1:2, 9; 19:10.

22. For an elaboration of point of view and levels of narration in Revelation, see Barr 1998:26–29.

23. The adultery mentioned here is a metaphor for unfaithfulness in relation to God; e.g., Boring 1989:93.

24. Revelation distinguishes between the twelve apostles who were venerated and contemporary apostles who were not. Paul used a different definition of apostle—one who had seen the Lord and who had a special commission from him (1 Cor 15:3–11)—and included himself in that group.

25. For this reason I have avoided the term in this book.

26. In Revelation 2:19 διακονία ("service") is used as a general description of activities of the holy ones (cf. Eph 2:12) and not in reference to a leadership position (1 Tim 3:8–13). In Revelation the term coheres with the idea that members of the churches are servants of God.

27. Twenty-four elders surround the throne, but this is not relevant to a discussion of the organization of the congregations.

28. The only occurrence of the word comes in Revelation 18:7 where Babylon is said to have gloated in her regal status, which is contrasted to that of a widow. The text is not related to the church practices discussed in 1 Tim 5:3–16.

29. This suggests that the nearly universal practice in modern biblical studies of calling these people "Christians" is a very powerful modern anachronism.

30. The address of "the saints, the apostles, and the prophets" in 18:20 is not directed toward the churches but toward the heavens and so does not help us understand John's view of the churches.

31. Thompson 1990:69–71.

32. The "angels of the churches" in Revelation 2–3 constitute a notorious interpretive problem. I do not consider the references clear enough to be included in this discussion.

33. Pippin 1992b:194–96.

34. Pippin 1992a:57–86, 103–5; 1992b:200–2; 1992c:69, 77–79.

35. Keller 1996:46; author's emphasis. For her overview of the narrative and symbols of Revelation, see pp. 36–83.

36. Aune 1998a:707 mentions Num 16:32–34 and Exod 15:12. The latter is in another mythic context.

37. There are four: the author John, Jesus, Antipas the martyr, and probably "Balaam." Nero could perhaps be included as a fifth male because of probable cryptic allusions to him (Rev 13:18; 17:10). Four or five males is quite a bit more than one woman, but a total of six individuals is a small number for a text this long (compare, for example, the Gospel of Matthew, Acts of the Apostles, or the Letter to the Romans). Apocalyptic styles of writing did not encourage many personal references.

38. Dewey 1992:86–88 does suggest that it is a dangerous text for men as well.

39. J. Day 1985:62–87, Whitney 1992:76.

40. Friesen n.d.

41. Revelation 1:9; 13:10; 14:12.

42. Cf. Pliny *Ep.* 10.96.8; *Acts of Paul and Thecla; The Martyrdom of Perpetua and Felicitas.*

43. Yarbro Collins 1996:198–217.

44. On the idea that the saints are part of the heavenly army, see chapter 10, n. 46.

45. The saints are attacked by the Dragon in 12:17 and 20:8 and by the Beast from the Sea in 13:7. The Beast and the kings of the earth oppose the Messiah in 19:19. The Messiah also engages in battle, but he is a special case among humans. Note also that the Risen Christ threatens to make war on the Pergamene saints who accept the teachings of the Nicolaitans in 2:16.

46. The Beast from the abyss is able to make war on the two witnesses only after their testimony is completed (11:7).

47. See chapter 10.

48. Barr 1998:145–47.

49. Aune 1998b:1057.

50. John's view on the interim state of souls between the first death and the resurrection to judgment is unclear. The souls of martyrs are described as staying under the heavenly altar where they cry out for justice (6:9–11), but the location of other souls is not described.

51. Revelation 3:10; 16:14.

52. Revelation 13:3.

53. Ἄνθρωποι in Rev 9:7, 20; 16:2, 9, 21; 21:3.

54. Revelation 3:10; 6:10; 8:13; 11:10; 13:8, 14. An unusual usage occurs in Rev 17:2 where the same verb κατοικέω is transitive ("those inhabiting earth").

55. Cf. Revelation 5:9; 7:9; 10:11; 11:9; 17:15.

56. Revelation 11:18; 13:16; 19:18; and finally 20:12.

57. Revelation 13:16; only the rich are mentioned in 6:15.

58. Revelation 6:15; 13:16; 19:18.

59. Revelation 6:15; 18:23; 19:18.

60. Revelation 1:5b–6; 5:9–10.

61. Revelation 18:4; 21:3; 22:5. Elliott 1995.

62. Aune 1997:164–65. Kraft 1974:60–61 outlined a minority position. He suggested that the synagogues of Satan were churches that had adopted a Jewish identity in order to avoid hostility against the churches.

63. The use of the plural ἔθνη ("nations, Gentiles") only takes the nuance of "Gentile" in passages where there are intertextual influences from scripture, such as Rev 11:18 and 15:4; or in reference to Israel's temple (11:2).

64. E.g., Revelation 17:8; 21:15.

65. Revelation 13:8; 16:2; 17:8.

66. Revelation 21:8; 22:15. Cf. 21:27. According to 22:19, anyone who removes anything from the scroll of John's prophecy is excluded from the tree of life as well.

67. Revelation 9:21. The reference to those who destroy the earth in 11:18 is a poetic phrase in a liturgical section that does not have much descriptive value.

68. Revelation 2:2.

69. Clement *Strom.* 3.25–26.

70. See Aune 1997:148–49 for a discussion of the issues.

12. Worship and Authority

1. Burkert 1983; and 1985:54–59, 64–66.

2. Detienne, Vernant, et al., 1989; Vernant 1991:290–302.

3. Vernant 1991:301.

4. Peirce 1993:219–260. The quote is from p. 260.

5. Revelation 2:14 (Pergamon); 2:20 (Thyatira).

6. Willis 1985:7–64.

7. For a broader description of mainstream religious life in Roman society, see MacMullen 1981, esp. 1–48.

8. Revelation 9:20–21.

9. Revelation 21:8; 22:15.

10. Revelation 5:8; 8:1–5.

11. In some places, especially in papyri, προσκυνέω was used simply as a verb of greeting (*PLond* 3.1244.4; *POxy* 237 vi 37; *OGIS* 262 line 27). This usage does not occur in Revelation.

12. Herodotus 1.119; 8.118; Aristotle *Historia Animalium* 630b.20.

13. Revelation 9:20–21; 21:8; 22:15.

14. Revelation 14:7; also 4:10; 7:11; 11:16; 19:4.

15. Prostration before God and the Lamb together occurs at Revelation 5:14 and 15:4.

16. Revelation 13:4, 8, 12, 15; 14:9, 11; 16:2; 19:20; 20:4. Cf. Acts 10:25–26, where Cornelius the centurion bows down to Peter. Peter gently urges him to get up because he, as a man, does not deserve such obeisance.

17. Revelation 3:9. This is probably related to the idea that the saints will one day reign with the Lamb, at which time prostration will be appropriate.

18. Revelation 19:10; 22:8–9.

19. See chapter 11.

20. Revelation 22:20.

21. The worshipping characters include the 4 living beings, the 24 elders, innumerable angels and martyrs, all creation, and even the altar of the heavenly temple.

22. Revelation 4:11.

23. Revelation 4:8.

24. Revelation 16:5–7; 19:1–3; and probably 15:3–4.

25. Revelation 19:6–8.

26. Boring 1992:714, 718.

27. I am only attempting to evaluate the symbolization in these vision reports and not to examine the field of New Testament Christology. The interested reader may turn to Dunn 1989 and Hurtado 1988 for an introduction to some of the discussions.

28. For an overview of interpretation of the Lamb image in Revelation, see Aune 1997:367–74.

29. The seven eyes represent the omniscience of God; cf. Zech 4, esp. v. 10b. The seven horns denote power, but there is no clear literary precedent for this particular number.

30. Caird 1966:75; Barr 1998:145–48.

31. Revelation 13:8.

32. E.g., Revelation 21:9, 23.

33. *OGIS* 258. For a translation of the inscription, see chapter 2.

34. Revelation 5:12.

35. Revelation 5:13.

36. Regarding present time, see also chapter 9.

37. For a brief discussion, see Boring 1989:152–53. Swete 1907:147–49 is dated in some ways but includes more detail. Aune 1998a:680–82.

38. Revelation 12:5. John used the same Psalm in Revelation 2:17 and 19:15.

39. This contrasts directly with the theme of the emperor ruling over land and sea, which was a standard part of imperial propaganda. See, for example, fig. 5.11.

40. Revelation 12:14–17.

41. Barr 1998:107.

42. On the interpretation of this passage in Daniel, see J. Collins 1993:274–99.

43. Revelation 13:1–2. Another part of the argument for the identification of the Beast as Roman imperial power comes from the vision report in Revelation 17, where explicit connections are made between a seven-headed, ten-horned beast and the imperial city.

44. Revelation 12:9.

45. Revelation 13:2.

46. Bousset 1906:365–67; Swete 1907:168–69; Charles 1920a:343, 357; Lohse 1960:72.

47. Aune 1988:1313; deSilva 1991:203–5.

48. Caird 1966:171; Bovon 1993:137–38.

49. Weiss 1904:15; Ramsay 1904:96.

50. Kraft 1974:180–81; Cerfaux and Cambier 1955:212–22; Thompson 1990:164.

51. Krodel 1989:146, 254–59; Roloff 1993:161; Prigent 1981:209; Beasley-Murray 1978:216–17.

52. Yarbro Collins 1984b:82.

53. It would probably be wrong to include the Roman proconsul within the symbol of the Beast from the Earth. Aside from the calendar decree honoring Augustus in 9 BCE, the proconsul appears not to have been a prominent player in the array of imperial cult institutions in Asia. Moreover, the proconsul was more involved in imperial administration and so can be included within the symbol of the Beast from the Sea.

54. For more on Revelation 13:11–18, see Friesen n.d.

55. Bowersock 1965, esp. 85–100; Edwards 1996:91–95.

56. Revelation 12:8. Cf. 20:3, 8, and 10.

57. Revelation 13:14. Cf. 19:20.

58. Chapter 5 and especially fig. 5.10.

59. Figure 2.3.

60. Thus, the argument in S. Scherrer 1984 that Revelation 13 can be used as a historical source for imperial cult practices is not convincing.

61. Revelation 4:11; 5:12.

62. Revelation 13:4.

63. Revelation 1:17 (where John falls down as if dead); 4:10; 5:8, 14; 7:11; 11:16; 19:4. In 19:10 and 22:8, John falls down before the glory of an angel but is corrected.

64. Revelation 13:3; 17:6–8.

65. Revelation 19:20.

66. For more on the use of Ezekiel in this section, see Ruiz 1989.

67. This image in prophetic literature probably reflected a topos in international propaganda of the time.

68. Revelation 17:2–3; 18:3.

69. Jeremiah 51:6 and 48 are important here. See also Isaiah 13:21–22; 21:9; 34:11, 14; 48:20; Jeremiah 9:11; Baruch 4:35.

70. Jeremiah 51:59–64.

71. Revelation 18:21.

72. Jeremiah 50:11–13; 51:25–26, 58.

73. Jeremiah 50:28–29; 51:6, 34–37.

74. Jeremiah 50:2–3; 51:15–19.

75. Revelation 18:3; cf. 17:2.

76. This is explicit in the Septuagint.

77. Revelation 18:3.

78. Revelation 18:23.

79. Revelation 18:11–16. The quote is from 18:23. Kraybill 1996 gathered together many literary and archaeological sources regarding commerce in the Roman world.

80. Ezekiel 27:12–25. The long list of their goods in Revelation 18:12–13 reminded educated hearers in the churches of Ezekiel's even longer list of cargoes and ports of call for the Tyrian traders. The list of goods in Revelation focuses especially on luxury items such as precious stones and exotic spices, although there are also references to more common items such as wine, oil, and grain.

81. Revelation 18:3.

82. 2 Kings 19:23 (LXX).

83. This meaning is based especially on certain uses of the related verb στρηνιάω.

84. Lycophron 438.

85. Revelation 18:7, NRSV; emphasis added.

86. Revelation 19:11–16.

87. Revelation 19:17–18.

88. Revelation 19:19–21.

89. Revelation 10:11.

90. Revelation 16:14.

91. Revelation 17:2; 18:3, 9.

92. Revelation 19:19.

93. Revelation 21:24.

94. Schüssler Fiorenza 1991:120.

95. Revelation 1:5.

96. Revelation 17:14; 19:16.

97. In Revelation 15:3 God is praised as the "king of the nations," a title that comes from Jeremiah 10:3.

98. Revelation 1:9.

99. Revelation 5:9–10.

13. Revelation in This World

1. Barr 1998:151–80.

2. Schüssler Fiorenza 1991:6–15 dealt mostly with the second half of the twentieth century. For an overview of earlier interpretation, see Wainwright 1993:11–103. Keller 1996:84–271 treats selected historical episodes.

3. E.g., Boesak 1987; Richard 1995.

4. Schüssler Fiorenza 1991:6–15.

5. Barr 1998:ix-xi, 1–2.

6. Barr 1998:145–47.

7. Keller 1996:2; author's emphasis.

8. Keller 1996:11.

9. For an exploration of this idea from a cultural historian, see Boyer 1992. Wojcik 1997 deals with similar phenomena as a folklorist.

10. Keller 1996:7–15, quote from p. 15.

11. Keller 1996:18.

12. Keller 1996:19–20.

13. Seidman 1996:313–14 made a similar point about the absence of the category "empire" in the discipline of sociology. The same is probably true of biblical studies.

14. Cantwell Smith 1997:65–83.

15. Revelation 19:11–21; cf. Barr 1998:137–38.

BIBLIOGRAPHY

Ahmad, Aijaz
  1992 *In Theory: Classes, Nations, and Literatures.* London: Verso.
  1995 "Postcolonialism: What's in a Name?" In *Late Imperial Culture,* edited by Román de la Campa, E. Ann Kaplan, Michael Sprinker, pp. 11–32. New York: Verso.
Alzinger, Wilhelm
  1970 "Ephesos B: Archäologischer Teil." *PWSup* 12:1588–704.
  1972–75 "Das Regierungsviertel." *JÖAI* 50:229–300 Beiblatt.
  1974 *Augusteische Architektur in Ephesos.* Sonderschriften herausgegeben vom Österreichischen Archäologischen Institut 16. 2 vols. Vienna: Self-published.
Ashcroft, Bill, Gareth Griffiths, and Helen Tiffin
  1989 *The Empire Writes Back: Theory and Practice in Post-Colonial Literature.* New York: Routledge.
Aune, David E.
  1983a "The Influence of Roman Imperial Court Ceremonial on the Apocalypse of John." *BibRes* 18:5–26.
  1983b *Prophecy in Early Christianity and the Ancient Mediterranean World.* Grand Rapids, Mich.: Eerdmans.
  1986 "The Apocalypse of John and the Problem of Genre." *Semeia* 36:65–96.
  1988 "Revelation." In *Harpers Bible Commentary,* edited by James L. Mays, 1300–319. San Francisco: Harper & Row.
  1997 *Revelation 1–5.* Word Biblical Commentary 52A. Dallas: Word.
  1998a *Revelation 6–16.* Word Biblical Commentary 52B. Nashville, Tenn.: Thomas Nelson.

1998b *Revelation 17–22.* Word Biblical Commentary 52C. Nashville, Tenn.: Thomas Nelson.

Bachmann, Michael

1994 "Himmlisch: Der 'Temple Gottes' von Apk 11.1." *NTS* 40:474–80.

Bammer, Anton

1972–75 "Römische und byzantinische Architektur." *JÖAI* 50:386–92 Beiblatt.

1985 *Architektur und Gesellschaft in der Antike.* 2nd ed. Vienna: Hermann Böhlaus.

Barr, David L.

1988 Review of Yarbro Collins 1984a. *RSR* 14:340–44.

1998 *Tales of the End: A Narrative Commentary on the Book of Revelation.* Sonoma, Calif.: Polebridge Press.

Bauckham, Richard

1993 *The Theology of the Book of Revelation.* Cambridge: Cambridge University Press.

Beale, G. K.

1999 *The Book of Revelation: A Commentary on the Greek Text.* Grand Rapids, Mich.: Eerdmans.

Beard, Mary, and John North, eds.

1990 *Pagan Priests: Religion and Power in the Ancient World.* Ithaca, N.Y.: Cornell University Press.

Beasley-Murray, G. R.

1978 *The Book of Revelation.* Rev. ed. New Century Bible. Greenwood, S.C.: Attic Press.

Bell, Albert A.

1979 "The Date of John's Apocalypse: The Evidence of Some Roman Historians Reconsidered." *NTS* 25:93–102.

Bevis, Phil, Michèle Cohen, and Gavin Kendall

1993 "Archaeologizing Genealogy: Michel Foucault and the Economy of Austerity." In *Foucault's New Domains,* edited by Mike Gane and Terry Johnson, pp. 193–215. New York: Routledge.

Bhabha, Homi K.

1990 "Introduction: Narrating the Nation." In *Nation and Narration,* edited by Homi K. Bhabha, pp. 1–7. New York: Routledge.

1994 *The Location of Culture.* London: Routledge.

Bickerman, E. J.

1980 *Chronology of the Ancient World.* 2nd ed. Ithaca, N.Y.: Cornell University Press.

Boesak, Allan A.

1987 *Comfort and Protest: Reflections on the Apocalypse of John of Patmos.* Philadelphia: Westminster.

Bonz, Marianne Palmer

1998 "Beneath the Gaze of the Gods: The Pergamon Evidence for a Developing Theology of Empire." In Koester 1998:251–75.

Boring, M. Eugene

1989 *Revelation.* Interpretation Commentary. Louisville: John Knox.

1992 "Narrative Christology in the Apocalypse." *CBQ* 54:702–23.

1994 "Revelation 19–21: End without Closure." *Princeton Seminary Bulletin* Suppl. 3:57–84.

Bousset, Wilhelm

1906 *Die Offenbarung Johannis.* Kritisch-exegetischer Kommentar über das Neue Testament. 6th ed. Göttingen: Vandenhoeck & Ruprecht.

Bovon, François
1972 "Le Christ de l'Apocalypse." *Revue de Théologie et de Philosophie* 22:65–80.
1993 "Possession ou enchantement. Les Institutions Romaines selon l'Apocalypse de Jean." In *Révélations et écritures: Nouveau Testament et littérature apocryphe chrétienne*, pp. 131–46. Geneva: Labor et Fides.
Bowersock, Glen
1965 *Augustus and the Greek World*. Oxford: Clarendon.
Boyer, Paul
1992 *When Time Shall Be No More: Prophecy Belief in Modern American Culture*. Cambridge, Mass.: Harvard University Press.
Brandis, C. G.
1896 "Ἀρχιερεύς." *PW* 2:471–88.
Bremen, Riet van
1996 *The Limits of Participation: Women and Civic Life in the Greek East in the Hellenistic and Roman Periods*. Gieben: Amsterdam.
Bruit Zaidman, Louise, and Pauline Schmitt Pantel
1992 *Religion in the Ancient Greek City*. Cambridge: Cambridge University Press.
Brunt, P. A.
1961 "Charges of Provincial Maladministration under the Early Pricipate," *Historia* 10:189–227.
Buckler, W. H.
1935 "Auguste, Zeus Patroos." *RPh* 3rd series 9:177–88.
Burkert, Walter
1983 *Homo Necans: The Anthropology of Ancient Greek Sacrificial Ritual and Myth*. Berkeley/Los Angeles: University of California Press.
1985 *Greek Religion*. Cambridge, Mass.: Harvard University Press.
1987 *Ancient Mystery Cults*. Cambridge, Mass.: Harvard University Press.
Caird, George Bradford
1966 *The Revelation of Saint John*. London: A. C. Black. Reprinted by Hendrickson Publishers.
Campanile, Maria Domitilla
1994 *I Sacerdoti del Koinon d'Asia (I sec. a.C.–III sec. d.C.): Contributo allo studio della romanizzazione delle élites provinciali nell'Oriente greco*. Pisa: Giardini.
Capps, Walter H.
1995 *Religious Studies: The Making of a Discipline*. Minneapolis, Minn.: Fortress.
Carrasco, David
1991 "Insight/Signification." Review of Long 1986. *HR* 31:60–68.
Cerfaux, Lucien, and Jules Cambier
1955 *L'Apocalypse de Saint Jean lue aux Chrétiens*. Paris: Cerf.
Charles, R. H.
1920a *A Critical and Exegetical Commentary on the Revelation of St. John*. Vol. 1. Edinburgh: T&T Clark.
1920b *A Critical and Exegetical Commentary on the Revelation of St. John*. Vol. 2. Edinburgh: T&T Clark.
Charlesworth, James H., ed.
1983 *The Old Testament Pseudepigrapha*. Vol. 1: *Apocalyptic Literature and Testaments*. Garden City, N.Y.: Doubleday.
Clifford, James
1988 James Clifford, *The Predicament of Culture: Twentieth-Century Ethnography, Lit-*

erature, and Art, pp. 255–76. Cambridge, Mass.: Harvard University Press [1988]. Reprinted from "Edward Said, *Orientalism.*" *History and Theory* 19:204–23.

Collins, Adela Yarbro

  1976 *The Combat Myth in the Book of Revelation.* Harvard Dissertations in Religion 9. Missoula, Mont.: Scholars Press.

  1984a *Crisis and Catharsis: The Power of the Apocalypse.* Philadelphia, Penn.: Westminster.

  1984b "'What the Spirit Says to the Churches': Preaching the Apocalypse." *Quarterly Review* 4:69–84.

  1991 Review of Thompson 1990. *JBL* 110:748–50.

  1996 *Cosmology and Eschatology in Jewish and Christian Apocalypticism. Journal for the Study of Judaism* Suppl. 50. Leiden: E. J. Brill.

Collins, John J.

  1993 *Daniel.* Hermeneia Commentary. Minneapolis, Minn.: Fortress.

Coogan, R. J., and M. A. Knibb

  1979 *The First and Second Books of Esdras.* Cambridge: Cambridge University Press.

Corbier, Mireille

  1995 "Male Power and Legitimacy through Women: The *domus Augusta* under the Julio-Claudians." In *Women in Antiquity: New Assessments*, edited by Richard Hawley and Barbara Levick, pp. 178–93. New York: Routledge.

Court, John

  1979 *Myth and History in the Book of Revelation.* Atlanta, Ga.: John Knox.

Cross, Frank Moore

  1973 *Canaanite Myth and Hebrew Epic: Essays in the History of the Religion of Israel.* Cambridge, Mass.: Harvard University Press.

Daltrop, Georg, Ulrich Hausmann, and Max Wegner

  1966 *Die Flavier: Vespasian, Titus, Domitian, Nerva, Julia Titi, Domitilla, Domitia.* Berlin: Mann.

Day, John

  1985 *God's Conflict with the Dragon and the Sea: Echoes of a Canaanite Myth in the Old Testament.* New York: Cambridge University Press.

Day, Peggy Lynne

  1988 *An Adversary in Heaven: SATAN in the Hebrew Bible.* Harvard Semitic Monographs 43. Atlanta, Ga.: Scholars Press.

Deininger, Jürgen

  1965 *Die Provinziallandtage der römischen Kaiserzeit von Augustus bis zum Ende des dritten Jahrhunderts n. Chr.* Vestigia 6. Munich: C. H. Beck.

deSilva, David A.

  1991 "The 'Image of the Beast' and the Christians in Asia Minor: Escalation of Sectarian Tension in Revelation 13." *Trinity Journal* NS 12:185–208.

Detienne, Marcel, Jean-Pierre Vernant, et al.

  1989 *The Cuisine of Sacrifice Among the Greeks.* Chicago, Ill.: Chicago University Press.

Dewey, Joanna

  1992 "Response: Fantasy and the New Testament." *Semeia* 60:83–89.

Donaldson, Laura, ed.

  1996 *Postcolonialism and Scriptural Reading. Semeia* 75. Atlanta, Ga.: Scholars Press.

Dörner, Friedrich

  1935 *Der Erlass des Statthalters von Asia Paullus Fabius Persicus.* Greifswald: E. Panzig.

Dunn, James D. G.

  1989 *Christology in the Making: A New Testament Inquiry into the Origins of the Doctrine of the Incarnation.* 2nd ed. Grand Rapids, Mich.: Eerdmans.

Edmunds, Lowell, ed.

1990 *Approaches to Greek Myth*. Baltimore, Md.: Johns Hopkins University Press.

Edwards, Douglas R.

1996 *Religion & Power: Pagans, Jews, and Christians in the Greek East*. New York: Oxford University Press.

Eichler, Fritz

1961 "Die österreichischen Ausgrabungen in Ephesos im Jahre 1960." *AnzWien* 98:65–75.

1965 "Die österreichischen Ausgrabungen in Ephesos im Jahre 1964." *AnzWien* 102:93–109.

1966 "Die österreichischen Ausgrabungen in Ephesos im Jahre 1965." *AnzWien* 103:7–16.

1967 "Die österreichischen Ausgrabungen in Ephesos im Jahre 1966." *AnzWien* 104:15–28.

Eliade, Mircea

1965 *The Myth of the Eternal Return or, Cosmos and History*. Princeton, N.J.: Princeton University Press [1954].

Elliott, Susan M.

1995 "Who Is Addressed in Revelation 18:6–7?" *BibRes* 40:98–113.

Fiorenza, Elisabeth Schüssler

1972 *Priester für Gott: Studien zum Herrschafts-und Priestermotiv in der Apokalypse*. Münster: Aschendorff.

1985 *The Book of Revelation: Justice and Judgment*. Philadelphia, Penn.: Fortress.

1991 *Revelation: Vision of a Just World*. Minneapolis, Minn.: Fortress.

Fishwick, Duncan

1990 "Votive Offerings to the Emperor?" *ZPE* 80:121–30.

Fossel, Elisabeth

1972–75 "Zum Tempel auf dem Staatsmarkt in Ephesos," *JÖAI* 50: 212–19.

Foucault, Michel

1972 *The Archaeology of Knowledge*. New York: Pantheon.

1979 *Discipline and Punish: The Birth of the Prison*. New York: Vintage.

Fränkel, Max, ed.

1895 *Die Inschriften von Pergamon AvP* 8,2. Berlin: Spemann/Reimer.

French, D. H.

1980 "The Roman Road-system of Asia Minor." *ANRW* 2.7.2:698–729.

Friesen, Steven J.

1993 *Twice Neokoros: Ephesos, Asia and the Cult of the Flavian Imperial Family*. Leiden: E. J. Brill.

1995 "The Cult of the Roman Emperors in Ephesos: Temple Wardens, City Titles, and the Interpretation of the Revelation of John." In *Ephesos, Metropolis of Asia: An Interdisciplinary Approach to its Archaeology, Religion, and Culture*, edited by Helmut Koester, pp. 229–50. Valley Forge, Penn.: Trinity.

1996 "The Origins of Lei Day: Festivity and the Construction of Ethnicity in the Territory of Hawaii." *History and Anthropology* 10:1–36.

1999 "Asiarchs." *ZPE* 126:275–90.

f.c. "Ephesos B: The Upper City." In *ARNTS* 3, edited by Helmut Koester and Holland Hendrix. Valley Forge, Penn.: Trinity Press.

n.d. "The Beast from the Earth: Revelation 13:11–18 and Social Setting." Chapter for student reader produced by SBL Seminar "Reading the Apocalypse."

Gallagher, Susan VanZanten

1994 "Introduction: New Conversations on Postcolonial Literature." In *Postcolonial Literature and the Biblical Call for Justice*, edited by Susan VanZanten Gallagher, pp. 3–33. Jackson: University of Mississippi Press.

Gane, Mike, and Terry Johnson

1993 "Introduction: The Project of Michel Foucault." In *Foucault's New Domains*, edited by Mike Gane and Terry Johnson, pp. 1–9. New York: Routledge.

Gasparo, Giulia Sfameni

1985 *Soteriology and Mystic Aspects in the Cult of Cybele and Attis*. EPRO 103. Leiden: E. J. Brill.

Geertz, Clifford

1973 *The Interpretation of Cultures*. New York: Basic Books.

1980 *Negara: The Theatre State in Nineteenth-Century Bali*. Princeton: Princeton University Press.

1983 *Local Knowledge: Further Essays in Interpretive Anthropology*. New York: Basic Books.

Gellner, Ernest

1993 "The Mightier Pen? Edward Said and the Double Standards of Inside-Out Colonialism." Review of *Culture and Imperialism*, by Edward W. Said. *Times Literary Supplement* 4690 (Feb. 19): 3–4.

Georgi, Dieter

1986 "Who is the True Prophet?" In *Christians Among Jews and Gentiles: Essays in Honor of Krister Stendahl on His Sixty-fifth Birthday*, edited by George W. E. Nickelsburg with George W. MacRae, pp. 100–26.

Giblin, Charles H.

1984 "Revelation 11.1–13: Its Form, Function and Contextual Integration." *NTS* 30:433–59.

Goodenough, Erwin R.

1958 *Jewish Symbols in the Greco-Roman Period*. Vol. 7: *Pagan Symbols in Judaism*. New York: Pantheon.

Habicht, Christian

1973 "Die Augusteische Zeit und das erste Jahrhundert nach Christi Geburt." In *Le Culte des Souverains dans l'Empire Romain*, edited by Willem den Boer, pp. 41–99. Entretiens Hardt 19. Geneva: Foundation Hardt.

Hadas, Moses, ed.

1942 *Complete Works of Tacitus*. Alfred John Church and William Jackson Brodribb, translators. New York: Random.

Halfmann, Helmut

1990 "Hymnoden von Asia in Kyzikos." *Mysiche Studien. Asia Minor Studien* 1:21–26.

Hall, Robert G.

1990 "Living Creatures in the Midst of the Throne: Another Look at Revelation 4.6." *NTS* 36:609–13.

Hänlein-Schafer, Heidi

1985 VENERATIO AUGUSTI: *Eine Studie zu den Tempeln der ersten römischen Kaisers*. Archaeologica 39. Rome: Giorgio Bretschneider.

Hardacre, Helen

1989 *Shinto and the State, 1868–1988*. Princeton, N.J.: Princeton University Press.

Harland, Philip

1996 "Honours and Worship: Emperors, Imperial Cults and Associations at Ephesus (First to Third Centuries C.E.)." *Studies in Religion/Sciences Religieuses* 25:319–34.

Harlow, Barbara

1987 *Resistance Literature*. New York: Methuen.

Haussoullier, B.

1902 *Études sur l'histoire de Milet et du Didymeion*. Paris: Émile Bouillon.

Hawley, Richard, and Barbara Levick, eds.
1995 *Women in Antiquity: New Assessments*. New York: Routledge.

Heberdey, R.
1912–13 "IX. Vorläufiger Bericht über die Grabungen in Ephesos, 1907–1911," *JÖAI* 15:157–82 Beiblatt.

Herrmann, Peter
1960 "Die Inschriften römischer Zeit aus dem Heraion von Samos." *AM* 75:68–178.
1989 "Ein Cult für Caligula in Milet?" *IstMitt* 39:191–96.
1994 "Milet unter Augustus: C. Iulius Epikrates und die Anfänge des Kaiserkults." *IstMitt* 44:203–36.
1996 "Mystenvereine in Sardeis." *Chiron* 26 (1996): 315–48.

Herz, Peter
1992 "Asiarchen und Archiereiai: Zum Provinzialkult der Provinz Asia." *Tyche* 7:93–115.

Hölbl, Günter
1978 *Zeugnisse Ägyptischer Religionsvorstellungen für Ephesus*. EPRO 73. Leiden: Brill.

Hueber, Friedmund
1987 "Der Baukomplex einer julisch-claudischen Kaiserkultanlage in Aphrodisias (Ein Zwischenbericht zur theoretischen Rekonstruktion des Baubestandes)." In *Aphrodisias de Carie: Colloque du Centre de recherches archéologiques de l'Université de Lille III*, edited by Juliette de la Genière and Kenan Erim, pp. 107–122. Paris: Recherche sur les Civilisations.

Hurtado, Larry W.
1988 *One God, One Lord: Early Christian Devotion and Ancient Jewish Monotheism*. Philadelphia, Penn.: Fortress.

Imhoof-Blumer, Friedrich
1901–02 *Kleinasiatische Münzen*. 2 vols. Vienna: A. Hölder.

Inan, Jale, and Elisabeth Rosenbaum
1966 *Roman and Early Byzantine Portrait Sculpture in Asia Minor*. London: Oxford University Press.

Inan, Jale, and Elisabeth Alföldi-Rosenbaum
1979 *Römische und Frühbyzantinische Porträtplastik aus der Türkei. Neue Funde*. Mainz: Zabern.

Jobst, Werner
1980 "Zur Lokalisierung des Sebasteion-Augusteum in Ephesos." *IstMitt* 30:241–59.

Johnson, A. C., P. R. Coleman-Norton, and F. C. Bourne
1961 *Ancient Roman Statutes*. Austin: University of Texas Press.

Jones, A. H. M.
1971 *The Cities of the Eastern Roman Provinces*. 2nd ed. [1937]. Oxford: Clarendon.

Kearsley, Rosalinde
1986 "Asiarchs, *Archiereis*, and the *Archiereiai* of Asia." *GRBS* 27:183–92.
1996 "The Asiarchs of Cibrya Again." *Tyche* 11:129–55.

Keil, Josef
1908 "Zur Geschichte der Hymnoden in der Provinz Asia." *JÖAI* 11:101–10.
1919 "Die erste Kaiserneokorie von Ephesos." *Numismatische Zeitschrift* N.F. 12:115–20.
1929 "XIII. Vorläufiger Bericht über die Ausgrabungen in Ephesos." *JÖAI* 24:5–68.
1932 "XVI. Vorläufiger Bericht über die Ausgrabungen in Ephesos." *JÖAI* 27:5–72 Beiblatt.
1939 "Kulte im Prytaneion von Ephesos." In *Anatolian Studies Presented to William Hepburn Buckler*, edited by W. M. Calder and J. Keil, pp. 119–28. Manchester: University of Manchester Press.

Keller, Catherine
  1996 *Apocalypse Now and Then: A Feminist Guide to the End of the World*. Boston: Beacon Press.
Klauck, Hans-Josef
  1992 "Das Sendschreiben nach Pergamon und der Kaiserkult in der Johannesoffenbarung." *Biblica* 73:153–82.
Knackfuss, Hubert et al.
  1908 *Das Rathaus von Milet. Milet* 1.2. Berlin: G. Reimer.
Knibbe, Dieter
  1970 "Ephesos A: Historisch-epigraphischer Teil." *PWSup* 12:248–97.
  1980 "Ephesos vom Beginn der römischen Herrschaft in Kleinasien bis zum Ende der Principatszeit. A. Historischer Teil." *ANRW* 2.7.2:748–810.
  1981 *Der Staatsmarkt: Die Inschriften des Prytaneions. Die Kureteninschriften und sonstige religiöse Texte, FiE* 9.1.1. Vienna: Austrian Archaeological Institute.
Koenigs, Wolf
  1993 "Planung und Ausbau der Agora von Priene: Ein Vorbericht." *IstMitt* 43:381–97.
Koester, Helmut, ed.
  1998 *Pergamon, Citadel of the Gods: Archaeological Record, Literary Description, and Religious Development*. Harrisburg, Penn.: Trinity.
Kraemer, Ross Shepard
  1992 *Her Share of the Blessings: Women's Religions Among Pagans, Jews, and Christians in the Greco-Roman World*. New York: Oxford University Press.
Kraft, Heinrich
  1974 *Die Offenbarung des Johannes*. Handbuch zum neuen Testament 16a. Tübingen: J. C. B. Mohr (Paul Siebeck).
Kraybill, J. Nelson
  1996 *Imperial Cult and Commerce in John's Apocalypse. JSNT* Suppl. 132. Sheffield: Sheffield Academic Press.
Kreitzer, Larry J.
  1996 *Striking New Images: Roman Imperial Coinage and the New Testament World. JSNT* Suppl. 134. Sheffield: Sheffield Academic Press.
Krodel, Gerhard A.
  1989 *Revelation*. Augsburg Commentary on the New Testament. Minneapolis: Augsburg.
Lammer, Manfred
  1967 *Olympien und Hadrianeen im antiken Ephesos*. Ph.D. diss., Cologne.
Langmann, Gerhard
  1985 "Eine Kaisertaufe (?) in Ephesos." *JÖAI* 56:65–69.
Lewis, Naphtali, ed.
  1974 *Greek Historical Documents. The Roman Principate (27 B.C.–285 A.D.)*. Toronto: Hakkert.
Lewis, Naphtali, and Meyer Reinhold, eds.
  1955 *Roman Civilization. Sourcebook II: The Empire*. New York: Harper & Row.
Lohse, Eduard
  1960 *Die Offenbarung des Johannes*. Göttingen: Vandenheck & Ruprecht.
Long, Charles H.
  1986 *Significations: Signs, Symbols, and Images in the Interpretation of Religion*. Philadelphia: Fortress.
MacMullen, Ramsay
  1980 "Woman in Public in the Roman Empire." *Historia* 29:208–18.
  1981 *Paganism in the Roman Empire*. New Haven, Conn.: Yale University Press.

Magie, David
1950 *Roman Rule in Asia Minor to the End of the Third Century After Christ.* 2 vols. Princeton: Princeton University Press.

Maiuri, Amedeo
1925 *Nuova Silloge Epigrafica di Rodi e Cos.* Florence: Felice le Monnier.

Marshall, John W.
1997 "Parables of the War: Reading the Apocalypse Within Judaism and During the Judaean War." Ph.D. diss., Princeton University.

Mattingly, D. J., ed.
1997 *Dialogues in Roman Imperialism: Power, Discourse, and Discrepant Experience in the Roman Empire. Journal of Roman Archaeology* Suppl. 23. Portsmouth, Rhode Island: Journal of Roman Archaeology.

Mellor, Ronald
1975 *ΘΕΑ ΡΩΜΗ: The Worship of the Goddess Roma in the Greek World. Hypomnemata* 42. Göttingen: Vandenhoeck & Ruprecht.

Meriç, Recep
1985 "Rekonstruktionsversuch der Kolossalstatue des Domitian in Ephesos." In *Pro Arte Antiqua: Festschrift für Hedwig Kenner*, edited by Wilhelm Alzinger and Gudrun Christa Neeb, vol. 2, pp. 239–41, pl. XX–XXIII, and fig. 17. Vienna: A. F. Koska.

Merkelbach, R.
1980 "Der Kult der Hestia im Prytaneion der Greichischen Städte." *ZPE* 37:77–92.

Metzger, Bruce M.
1984 "A Classified Bibliography of the Graeco-Roman Mystery Religions 1924–73 with a Supplement 1974–77." *ANRW* 2.17.3:1259–423.

Meyer, Marvin W.
1987 *The Ancient Mysteries: A Sourcebook.* San Francisco, Calif.: Harper & Row.

Miltner, Franz
1958 "XXI. Vorläufiger Bericht über die Ausgrabungen in Ephesos." *JÖAI* 43:1–64 Beiblatt.
1959 "XXII. Vorläufiger Bericht über die Ausgrabungen in Ephesos." *JÖIA* 44:1–64 Beiblatt.

Mitsopoulis-Leon, Veronika
1991 *Die Basilika am Staatsmarkt in Ephesos: Kleinfunde, 1. Teil. FiE* 9.2.2. Vienna: Schindler.

Mohanram, Radhika, and Gita Rajan, eds.
1996 *English Postcoloniality: Literatures from Around the World.* Westport, Conn.: Greenwood.

Moretti, Luigi
1953 *Iscrizioni Agonistiche Greche.* Rome: Angelo Signorelli.
1954 "ΚΟΙΝΑ ΑΣΙΑΣ." *Rivista di Filologia* NS 32:276–89.

Morris, Leon
1987 *The Book of Revelation: An Introduction and Commentary.* Tyndale New Testament Commentaries. 2nd ed. Grand Rapids, Mich.: Eerdmans.

Mounce, Robert H.
1977 *The Book of Revelation.* New International Commentary on the New Testament. Grand Rapids, Mich.: Eerdmans.

Müller, Hans-Peter
1963 "Die himmlische Ratsversammlung. Motivgeschichtliches zu Apc 5:1–5." *ZNTW* 54:254–67.

Münsterberg, Rudolf
1985 [1911–27] *Die Beamtennamen auf den griechischen Münzen geographisch und alphabetisch geordnet.* New York: Georg Olms.

Murphy, Frederick James
   1985 *The Structure and Meaning of Second Baruch. SBL Dissertation Series* 78. Atlanta,
       Ga.: Scholars Press.
Nock, Arthur Darby
   1972a *Essays on Religion and the Ancient World.* Vol. 1. Cambridge, Mass.: Harvard Uni-
       versity Press.
   1972b *Essays on Religion and the Ancient World.* Vol. 2. Cambridge, Mass.: Harvard Uni-
       versity Press.
Nohlen, Klaus
   1997 "Ästhetik der Ruine: Zur Präsentation antiker Baukomplexe am Beispiel des Traian-
       Heiligtums zu Pergamon." *Antike Welt* 28:185–99.
Olupona, Jacob
   1991 *Kingship, Religion, and Rituals in a Nigerian Community: A Phenomenological Study
       of Ondo Yoruba Festivals.* Stockholm Studies in Comparative Religion, 28. Stockholm:
       Almqvist & Wiksell.
Osiek, Carolyn, and David L. Balch
   1997 *Families in the New Testament World: Households and House Churches.* Louisville:
       Westminster John Knox.
Oster, Richard
   1990 "Ephesus as a Religious Center under the Principate, I. Paganism before
       Constantine." *ANRW* 2.18.3:1688–91.
Outschar, Ulrike
   1987 "Betrachtungen zur kunstgeschichtlichen Stellung des Sebasteions in Aphrodisias."
       In *Aphrodisias de Carie: Colloque du Centre de recherches archéologiques de l'Université de
       Lille III,* edited by Juliette de la Genière and Kenan Erim, pp. 107–22. Paris: Recher-
       che sur les Civilisations.
Pagels, Elaine
   1995 *The Origin of Satan.* New York: Random House.
Peirce, Sarah
   1993 "Death, Revelry, and *Thysia.*" *Classical Antiquity* 12:219–60.
Pick, Behrendt
   1929 "Die Neokorie-Tempel von Pergamon und der Asklepios des Phyromachos." In
       Festschrift Walther Judeich zum 70. Geburtstage, pp. 28–44. Weimar: Hermann
       Boehlaus.
Pippin, Tina
   1992a *Death and Desire: The Rhetoric of Gender in the Apocalypse of John.* Louisville:
       Westminster/John Knox.
   1992b "Eros and the End: Reading for Gender in the Apocalypse of John." *Semeia* 59:193–
       210.
   1992c "The Heroine and the Whore: Fantasy and the Female in the Apocalypse of John."
       Semeia 60:67–82.
Pleket, H. W.
   1965 "An Aspect of the Emperor Cult: Imperial Mysteries." *HTR* 58:331–47.
Poland, Franz
   1909 *Geschichte des Griechischen Vereinswesens.* Reprint. Leipzig: Zentral-Antiquariate der
       Deutschen Demokratischen Republik [1967].
Pomeroy, Sarah B., ed.
   1991 *Women's History and Ancient History.* Chapel Hill: University of North Carolina Press.
Prakash, Gyan
   1995 Review of Said 1993. *History and Theory* 34:199–212.

Price, S. R. F.
1984a "Gods and Emperors: The Greek Language of the Roman Imperial Cult." *JHS* 104:79–95.
1984b *Rituals and Power: The Roman Imperial Cult in Asia Minor*. Cambridge: Cambridge University Press.

Prigent, Pierre
1981 *L'Apocalypse de Saint Jean*. Commentaire du Nouveau Testament 14. Lausanne: Delachaux et Niestlé.

Radt, Wolfgang
1988 *Pergamon. Geschichte und Bauten, Funde und Erforschung einer antiken Metropole.* Köln: DuMont.

Raeck, Wulf
1993 "Zeus Philios in Pergamon." *ArchAnz* 381–87.

Ramsay, William M.
1904 *The Letters to the Seven Churches of Asia and Their Place in the Plan of the Apocalypse.* Hodder and Stoughton: London. Reprint. Grand Rapids, Mich.: Baker [1979].

Reddish, Mitchell G., ed.
1990 *Apocalyptic Literature: A Reader*. Nashville, Tenn.: Abingdon. Reprint. Peabody, Mass.: Hendrickson [1995].

Reynolds, J.
1980 "The Origins and Beginning of Imperial Cult at Aphrodisias." *PCPS* 206:70–84.
1981 "New Evidence for the Imperial Cult in Julio-Claudian Aphrodisias." *ZPE* 43:317–27.
1982 *Aphrodisias and Rome. JRS Monographs* 1. London: Society for the Promotion of Roman Studies.
1986 "Further Information on Imperial Cult at Aphrodisias." *StCl* 24:109–17.
1996 "Ruler-cult at Aphrodisias in the Late Republic and Under the Julio-Claudian Emperors." In *Subject and Ruler: The Cult of the Ruling Power in Classical Antiquity, JRA* Supp. 17, edited by Alastair Small, pp. 41–50. Ann Arbor, Mich.: Journal of Roman Archaeology.

Richard, Pablo
1995 *Apocalypse: A People's Commentary on the Book of Revelation*. Maryknoll, N.Y.: Orbis.

Richter, Giesela M. A.
1966 "The Pheidian Zeus at Olympia." *Hesperia* 35:166–70.

Robert, Jeanne, and Louis Robert
1948 "III. Hiérocésarée." *Hellenica* 6:27–55.

Robert, Louis
1944 "Hellenica." *RPh* 18:5–56.
1949 "Le cult de Caligula à Milet et la province d'Asie," *Hellenica* 7:206–238.
1959 "Les Inscriptions grecques de Bulgarie." *RPh* 33:165–236.
1960 "Recherches épigraphique." *REA* 62:276–361. = *Opera Minora Selecta* 2:792–877.

Roloff, Jürgen
1993 *The Revelation of John*. Continental Commentary. Minneapolis, Minn.: Fortress.

Rossner, Margaret
1974 "Asiarchen und Archiereis Asias." *StCl* 16:101–42.

Ruiz, Jean-Pierre
1989 *Ezekiel in the Apocalypse: The Transformation of Prophetic Language in Revelation 16:17–19:10*. European University Studies. New York: Peter Lang.

Said, Edward W.
1978a *Orientalism*. New York: Pantheon.

1978b "The Problem of Textuality: Two Exemplary Positions." *Critical Inquiry* 4,4: 673–714.

1983 *The World, the Text, and the Critic*. Cambridge, Mass.: Harvard University Press.

1993 *Culture and Imperialism*. New York: Knopf.

Schede, Martin

1934 "Heiligtümer in Priene." *JDAI* 49:97–108.

1964 *Die Ruinen von Priene*. 2nd ed. Berlin: de Gruyter.

Scherrer, Peter

1989 "Augustus, die Mission des Vedius Pollio und die Artemis Ephesia." *JÖAI* 59:87–101.

Scherrer, Peter, ed.

1995 *Ephesos: Der Neue Führer*. Vienna: Österreichisches Archäologisches Institut.

Scherrer, Steven J.

1984 "Signs and Wonders in the Imperial Cult." *JBL* 103:599–610.

Schowalter, Daniel N.

1998 "The Zeus Philios and Trajan Temple: A Context for Imperial Honors." In Koester 1998:233–49.

Segal, Robert A.

1987 Review of Long 1986. *JAAR* 55:613–15.

1990 "Misconceptions of the Social Sciences." *Zygon* 25:263–78.

Seidman, Steven

1996 "Empire and Knowledge: More Troubles, New Opportunities for Sociology." Review of *Orientalism* by Edward W. Said. *Contemporary Sociology* 25/3:313–16.

Sheppard, A. R. R.

1981 "Inscriptions from Usak, Denizli and Hisar Köy." *AnSt* 31:24–27.

Smith, Jonathan Z.

1978 *Map Is Not Territory: Studies in the History of Religions*. Studies in Judaism in Late Antiquity 23. Leiden: E. J. Brill.

1990 *Drudgery Divine: On the Comparison of Early Christianities and the Religions of Late Antiquity*. Chicago, Ill.: University of Chicago Press.

Smith, R. R. R.

1987 "The Imperial Reliefs from the Sebasteion at Aphrodisias." *JRS* 77:88–138.

1988 "*Simulacra Gentium*: The *Ethne* from the Sebasteion at Aphrodisias." *JRS* 78:50–77.

1990 "Myth and Allegory in the Sebasteion." In *Aphrodisias Papers: Recent Work on Architecture and Sculpture*, *JRA* Suppl. 1, edited by Charlotte Roueché and Kenan T. Erim, pp. 89–100. Ann Arbor, Mich.: JRA.

Smith, Wilfred Cantwell

1963 *The Meaning and End of Religion*. New York: Macmillan.

1979 *Faith and Belief*. Princeton: Princeton University Press.

1997 *Modern Culture from a Comparative Perspective*, edited by John W. Burbidge. Albany, N.Y.: State University of New York Press.

Spanos, William V.

1996 "Culture and Colonization: The Imperial Imperatives of the Centered Circle." *boundary 2* 23/1:135–75.

Speidel, Michael

1984 *Roman Army Studies*. Vol. 1. Amsterdam: Gieben.

Spivak, Gayatri Chakravorty

1987 *In Other Worlds: Essays in Cultural Politics*. New York: Methuen.

1996 *The Spivak Reader : Selected Works of Gayatri Chakravorty Spivak*. New York: Routledge.

Stiller, Hermann

1895 *Das Traianeum. AvP* 5,2. Berlin: W. Spemann.

Stone, Michael Edward

1989 *Features of the Eschatology of IV Ezra. Harvard Semitic Studies* 35. Atlanta, Ga.: Scholars Press.

1990 *Fourth Ezra: A Commentary on the Book of Fourth Ezra.* Hermeneia Commentary. Minneapolis, Minn.: Fortress.

Strocka, Volker Michael

1989 "Zeus, Marnas und Klaseas." In *Festschrift für Jale Inan: Armağani,* edited by Nezih Başgelen and Mihin Lugal, vol. 1, pp. 77–92. Istanbul: Arkeoloji ve Sanat Yayinlari.

Sullivan, Lawrence E.

1988 *Icanchu's Drum: An Orientation to Meaning in South American Religions.* New York: MacMillan.

Sutherland, C. H. V.

1970 *The Cistophori of Augustus.* London: Royal Numismatic Society.

Sweet, J. P. M.

1979 *Revelation.* Westminster Pelican Commentaries. Philadelphia, Penn.: Westminster.

Swete, Henry Barclay

1907 *The Apocalypse of St. John.* 2nd ed. London: Macmillan.

Thompson, Homer

1952 "The Altar of Pity in the Athenian Agora." *Hesperia* 21:47–82.

Thompson, Leonard L.

1990 *The Book of Revelation: Apocalypse and Empire.* New York: Oxford University Press.

1991 Review of Schüssler Fiorenza 1991. *CBQ* 55:576–78.

Thür, Hilke

1985 "Ephesische Bauhütten in der Zeit der Flavier und der Adoptivkaiser." In *Lebendige Altertumswissenschaft. Festgabe zur Vollendung des 70. Lebensjahres von Hermann Vetters dargebracht von Freunden, Schülern und Kollegen,* pp. 181–87. Vienna: Adolf Holzhausens.

Trell, Bluma

1945 *The Temple of Artemis at Ephesos.* New York: American Numismatic Society.

Tuchelt, Klaus

1975 "Buleuterion und Ara Augusti." *IstMitt* 25:91–140.

1979 *Frühe Denkmäler Roms in Kleinasien: Beiträge zur archäologischen Überlieferung aus der Zeit der Republik und des Augustus.* Tübingen: E. Wasmuth.

1981 "Zum Problem 'Kaisareion-Sebasteion.'" *IstMitt* 31:167–86.

Ulrich, Jörg

1996 "Euseb, *HistEccl* III,14–20 und die Frage nach der Christenverfolgung unter Domitian." *ZNTW* 87:269–89.

Valeri, Valerio

1985 *Kingship and Sacrifice: Ritual and Society in Ancient Hawaii.* Chicago: University of Chicago Press.

Vanni, Ugo

1991 "Liturgical Dialogue as a Literary Form in the Book of Revelation." *NTS* 37:348–72.

Vernant, Jean-Pierre

1991 *Mortals and Immortals: Collected Essays.* Princeton, N.J.: Princeton University Press.

Vetters, Hermann

1972–75 "Domitianterrasse und Domitiangasse." *JÖAI* 50:311–30 Beiblatt.

Wainwright, Arthur W.

1993 *Mysterious Apocalypse: Interpreting the Book of Revelation.* Nashville, Tenn.: Abingdon.

Wall, Robert W.

1991 *Revelation.* New International Biblical Commentary. Peabody, Mass.: Hendrickson.

Ward-Perkins, J. B.

1981 *Roman Imperial Architecture.* 2nd (integrated) ed. New York: Penguin.

Weiss, Johannes

1904 *Die Offenbarung des Johannes: Ein Beitrag zur Literatur- und Religionsgeschichte.* Göttingen: Vandenhoeck & Ruprecht.

White, L. Michael

1997 *The Social Origins of Christian Architecture.* 2 vols. Valley Forge, Penn.: Trinity.

Whitney, Kenneth William, Jr.

1992 "Two Strange Beasts: A Study of Traditions Concerning Leviathan and Behemoth in Second Temple and Early Rabbinic Judaism." Th.D. diss., Harvard University.

Williams, Patrick, and Laura Chrisman, eds.

1993 *Colonial Discourse and Post-Colonial Theory: A Reader.* New York: Wheatsheaf.

Willis, Wendell Lee

1985 *Idol Meat in Corinth: The Pauline Argument in 1 Corinthians 8 and 10.* SBL Dissertation Series 68. Chico, Calif.: Scholars Press.

Wilson, J. Christian

1993 "The Problem of the Domitianic Date of Revelation." *NTS* 39:587–605.

1994 "Babylon as a Cipher for Rome and the Dating of Early Jewish and Early Christian Documents." Paper read at the Annual Meeting of the SBL.

Wojcik, Daniel

1997 *The End of the World as We Know It: Faith, Fatalism, and Apocalypse in America.* New York: New York University Press.

Wood, J. T.

1877 *Discoveries at Ephesus, Including the Site and Remains of the Great Temple of Diana.* London: Longmans, Green, and Co. Reprint. New York: Georg Olms Verlag [1975].

Wood, Michael

1994 "Lost Paradises." Review of Said 1993. *New York Review of Books* 41/5 (March 3):44–47.

Wörrle, Michael

1992 "Inschriftenfunde aus Aizanoi I." *Chiron* 22:337–70.

Yegül, Fikret

1982 "A Study in Architectural Iconography: *Kaisersaal* and the Imperial Cult." *Art Bulletin* 64:7–31.

INDEX OF ANCIENT SOURCES

GENERAL INDEX